NATURALISTS
of the Frontier

Samuel Wood Geiser

NATURAL

of the

ISTS
FRONTIER

Southern Methodist University
1948

PUBLISHED ON

THE SCHOELLKOPF FUND

To The Memory Of

Jacob Boll

Preface to
the Second Edition

This volume deals primarily with the lives of eleven men, sojourners for various periods in the Southwest—especially Texas—during the period 1820-1880.

By way of contrast, and half as an appendix to the other essays, a chapter is included on scientific study in the Old South before 1850, particularly at those times in which the regions dealt with were themselves frontiers. For frontiers of scientific exploration wherever found, if they coincide with an advancing social frontier, show remarkable parallels.

In no study has Socrates' observation that of many things we know nothing, of many other things we know but half the truth, been better illustrated than in the investigations of which this volume is the partial fruit. In the first edition of this work, besides the ten essays dealing with as many men against the social and political backgrounds of their contemporary Texas, thumbnail sketches were included of some 140 more. Two years later, my *Scientific Study and Exploration in Early Texas* (1939) included brief sketches of 343 naturalists, which number, it was believed, "approached the total number for the 1820-1880 period." A year later (after an opportunity had been given for work in libraries in Washington, Baltimore, New York, New Haven, and Cambridge), the number had increased to 755. It has now grown to nearly twelve hundred. This figure does not include some 753 Texas inventors (1846-1885), the physicians of the 1850 and 1860 Censuses (both in manuscript), the 165 horticulturists included in my *Horticulture and Horticulturists in Early Texas* (1945), or the early Texas apiculturists in my corresponding study (now in progress). Provision has been made for the publication at an early date of *Men of Science in Early Texas*. This work will include brief sketches of the majority of early Texan amateurs and professional men in the field of science.

On page 264, I have included partial acknowledgments of assistance received in the preparation of this work. My deepest appreciation should be expressed for the aid given by President Umphrey Lee of this University, who made possible twelve months' work in the great libraries of the eastern United States, and who since that time has evinced a constant and most helpful interest in my continuing studies. My colleague, Herbert Gambrell, has kindly helped with the proofs; and Bessie Teeple Geiser has in numberless ways facilitated the progress from manuscript to finished book. For all of this I am very grateful.

S. W. G.

Southern Methodist University, Dallas
23 November, 1947

Contents

9

Jacob Boll

The Naturalist on the Frontier 1

ON a stifling, sultry July day some years ago I trudged from the exit of the subway in lower New York to a secondhand bookstore on Fourth Avenue. There, I had been told, I could find some books by Kassowitz, Claus, Pallas, Wiedersheim, Oppel, and Steindachner, priced within the reach of the slender purse of a college professor. Fresh from the plains of Texas, far removed from the great libraries of the world, I hoped to gain these for my own. At the foot of my list was a book whose purchase I could hardly justify in view of the state of my purse, Leonard Jenyns' *Observations in Natural History*. Jenyns is not a great figure in the history of science—he lived and died half-obscurely, a priest in the Church of England. But his life and work had always interested me, and I was filled with curiosity concerning the man.

One may expect any adventure to befall in a secondhand bookstore. My books secured, my arms filled with my purchases, already enjoying in anticipation my scientific classics, I turned to go. At that moment my eye fell upon a box of foxed and disordered pamphlets, which seemed to invite inspection. Admonished by the clerk that these were but worthless *rejecta,* still I would examine them, and lo! among them was a pamphlet long desired. It was Cope's brochure, *The Zoological Position of Texas*. I paid the price asked, and with my augmented treasures returned to my hotel. Hours later I emerged, half-famished, for dinner and a turn at exercise. Then I set to work again at the books long denied me, noting with something like affection the browning pages, the loosened stitching, and the breaking covers bound in wretched German leather; wondering, also, what hands, like mine, had thumbed those pages, and to what projects of investigation or research other men had been stimulated by the ideas, now somewhat outmoded, presented in these books.

11

The volume by Jenyns, especially, intrigued me, for I recalled vividly how its author had declined an offer to accompany the *Beagle*, as Naturalist, on its voyage around the world, and thus had opened to Charles Darwin the opportunity to undertake those investigations whose purport has forever changed the face of the scientific world. What would have happened, I could not help asking, had Jenyns made the voyage instead of Darwin? How would he have reacted to the new world of phenomena which Darwin encountered? What, in general, is the effect of exploration—contact with raw frontier life, contact with the riches of unexplored land—on the man of science?

Finally, I came upon Cope's thin pamphlet. As I glanced over its pages, I found numerous references to a Texan collector, Jacob Boll of Dallas, to me entirely unknown. Piqued with curiosity regarding an early naturalist who had collected so widely in north-central Texas, I determined to investigate Boll's antecedents and his life in Texas.

In the course of the following months I amassed a wealth of materials regarding Boll, and my interest was awakened to investigations that have absorbed my time for twenty years and have involved correspondence with scientific investigators in the great museums in Europe and America. After learning that Boll's collections from Texas were distributed from St. Louis to Leningrad, I asked myself if there might not be other pioneer naturalists and collectors who worked in Texas. The answer came slowly, but today I know that several hundred men of science labored in Texas in the pioneer days. Moreover, as I looked into the lives of these men, through their letters, the comments of friends and acquaintances, the records of their work in publications and in great musea and herbaria, I found that the careers and investigations of these pioneer naturalists showed common features. Indeed, when for comparison I came to investigate the lives of explorers and naturalists in other parts of the world, I learned that the phenomena exhibited here were common to scientific explorations and investigations on every frontier. The history of scientific exploration of frontier Texas becomes, in a sense, the history of scientific exploration anywhere on a borderline of cultures.

I have already spoken of the significance of Darwin's voyage on the *Beagle* in the history of the development of science. In many other instances, too, explorations on the frontier have launched men of science upon new tasks, have broken down in their minds old views and old dogmas, have given new discoveries that have broadened our concepts and brought into being new techniques. The

12

results of scientific expeditions have made possible the development of systematic zoölogy and botany. Such journeys have very often been the decisive factor in a scientist's career. Sir Joseph Dalton Hooker, perhaps the world's greatest botanical explorer, first reached full awareness of his calling as a botanist while he was surgeon with the Antarctic Expeditions of the *Erebus* and the *Terror* (1839-43). It was on an exploring voyage to the Torres Straits in 1846-50 that young Thomas Henry Huxley, serving as ship's surgeon of the *Rattlesnake,* made his final decision to desert medicine for natural science. And to mention two other great names, Henry W. Bates, author of *The Naturalist on the River Amazons,* and Alfred Russel Wallace, codiscoverer with Darwin of the principle of natural selection, laid the bases of their great work in the field of natural history when they went out together to the mouths of the Amazon in 1848.

If one cared to examine the history of science (still, alas! largely unwritten) he might easily compile a long list of men distinguished for their labors of exploration. In the first rank of naturalists belong such explorers as François Peron, the expert on mollusks, whose name, bracketed with that of Freycinet, is imperishably associated with Australasian zoölogy; Charles Alexandre Lesueur, naturalist on Nicholas Baudin's voyage around the world, and explorer in the United States from 1815 to 1837; René P. Lesson, the botanist, who accompanied Captain Duperrey on his voyage around the world on the corvette *La Coquille* in 1822-25; L. C. A. de Chamisso, zoölogist with Captain von Kotzebue on the Russian exploring ship *Rurik* during its voyage around the world (1815-18); and James Dwight Dana, naturalist with Captain Charles Wilkes on the United States Exploring Expedition to the South Pacific (1838-42). Among explorers in South America alone one might name such eminent naturalists as Don Felix de Azara, who traveled in the interior of the continent in 1781-1801; Maximilian, Prince Wied-Neu Wied, who explored Brazil in 1815-17 before coming to North America for his work in the Upper Missouri country in 1832-34; Eduard F. Pöppig, explorer in Chile, Peru, and the Amazon country in 1826-32; Johann J. von Tschudi, who worked principally in Peru and Brazil during the years 1838-43 and 1857-59; the Comte de Castelnau; and Sir Robert H. Schomburgk. If one turns to other parts of the world, the list of scientists notable for their explorations is almost endless: it includes, among many others, John Gould, Sir Stamford Raffles, Coenraad J. Temminck, and Caspar G. K. Reinwardt in Australasia; Alfred Grandidier in Madagascar; Dr. Philipp Franz von Siebold in Japan; and Christian Gottfried Ehrenberg and W. P. E. S. Rüppel in Egypt.

13

But the career of the scientific explorer, if it has its glories and its powerful stimulus to intellectual development, has also its dangers, psychological as well as physical. The frontier has broken scientists as well as made them. Isolation from the libraries and museums in the centers of scientific activity, and from both the appreciation and the criticism of fellow naturalists, in many cases has dampened the zeal of explorers who had earlier shown great promise. The case of Aimé Bonpland, the South American explorer with Baron von Humboldt, who ended his miserable days in a small village in Brazil, at once comes to mind. Among naturalists who worked in early Texas, Jean Louis Berlandier and Julien Reverchon might have achieved a great deal more if they could have had a more positive stimulus from their environment. And the same might be said of Gustaf Belfrage.

Indeed, the psychological dangers of the frontier for the naturalist seem to be especially great when, as in Texas, the scientific frontier of exploration coincides with a geographic frontier. In Texas, as in the rest of the United States, the early settlers' suspicion of the scientist was a serious psychological obstacle. Full realization of the attitude current on the frontier is essential to a proper understanding of the men dealt with in the present volume, both in their triumphs and in their failures. Especially did the naturalists who, like Jacob Boll, came out to Texas in the early days to make their homes here, face a task more difficult in many ways than that undertaken by Darwin, say, in his voyage with the *Beagle*. The Naturalists of the Frontier, like Darwin, were representatives of an advanced civilization who undertook to explore an area for the most part unknown to science. But where Darwin was sustained both by the sense of belonging to a definite group of his colleagues, and by the realization that any privations he encountered were but temporary, a man like Boll inevitably had to take upon himself some of the burden of moving the whole of a nonintellectual frontier community along the path toward civilization. It was not merely that Boll had to work alone, or nearly so; he had no London to go back to. His destiny lay in Texas; and only one who appreciates the contrast between the Jena and the Cambridge Boll knew in his youth, on the one hand, and on the other the primitive conditions in North Texas immediately after the Civil War, can realize the courage of Boll's choice. In Darwin's travels with the *Beagle* in the Pacific, he was indeed working on a frontier of scientific exploration. But Boll and the other Texan naturalists were working on a social frontier as well. In fact, two distinct types of frontier are involved in the comparison—the social frontier, described in America by Turner and Paxson, which is a

14

more or less definite boundary phase between an advancing social system and a relatively unoccupied area; and the frontier of scientific exploration, which marks the boundary between the known area of the earth and the areas that have not yet been scientifically explored. The significant fact for our purposes is that in Texas during the period considered in this book, the two types of frontier tended to coincide.

This means that while the naturalists of the Texan frontier are of interest to the historian of science primarily because of their work in extending the bounds of knowledge in various fields of natural science, their careers must be considered always in the light of their social environment. I stress this fact because the historian of scientific exploration in frontier Texas is constantly tempted to deal at length with the social history of the region as well. I have not always resisted this temptation, which seems to spring from the nature of the materials. Social conditions in early Texas offered many obstacles to the naturalists' work; and for any but the narrowest view of the eleven men I have selected for discussion, their failures are of almost as much interest as their successes. While their achievements were due largely to traits of character inherent in the men themselves, their failures were due in almost every case to the environment. This is especially clear in the career of Louis Ervendberg, who, in a work devoted exclusively to the history of science, would surely not deserve as much space as I have devoted to him. As a naturalist he was not important, but he might have been; and the reasons for his failure to accomplish more for science are of great interest to anyone who wishes to understand the conditions under which all the Naturalists of the Frontier worked. Asa Gray's curious indifference to Ervendberg after he had encouraged the collector to work for him was of course a factor in Ervendberg's failure, but other factors inherent in the social conditions of frontier Texas were of equal or greater importance.

The tendency of the frontier of scientific exploration to coincide with the advancing social frontier was a determining factor in the work of pioneer naturalists throughout the United States in the nineteenth century. For as the geographic and social frontier advances it naturally attracts men of science as well as actual settlers. The naturalist who desires to discover new species of plants and animals seeks the frontier of scientific exploration. There, faced with dangers, with sufferings, with privations that a closet naturalist would find intolerable, he advances our knowledge of nature, urged on by an inner drive whose origin he but dimly comprehends. Such men

15

have played a large part in the advancement of science, in America as in other parts of the world.

The list of pioneer naturalists who have explored the advancing frontiers of America is imposing. Readers who are familiar with George Brown Goode's delightful essays on the history of biology in America (published in 1886-88 and, before Smallwood, the only attempt to deal with the whole subject in its proper perspective) will recall his vivid account of the beginnings of natural history in this country, in the labors of such frontier naturalists as the Reverend John Banister of Virginia, and of those other Virginians, John Clayton, Dr. John Mitchell, and Colonel William Byrd. Goode also mentions in the Colonial Period Cadwallader Colden, for many years Lieutenant-Governor of the Colony of New York; Dr. Alexander Garden of Charleston; and Mark Catesby (1679-1749) of Virginia and the Carolinas, America's first extensive scientific explorer, who published in 1731-43 a magnificent work on his travels in Virginia, the Carolinas, and Bermuda, in two folio volumes illustrated with more than two hundred fine colored plates.

The most fruitful period of scientific exploration in this country, however, was the hundred years between the founding of the nation and the passing of the social frontier about 1880. By the close of this period the primary labor of discovery in the natural history of the new continent was nearing its end. The history of scientific exploration in Texas, which is the subject of the present work, belongs to this period, and the Texas naturalists should be thought of as co-laborers with such naturalists and men of science elsewhere on the American frontier as the Audubons, David Douglas the botanical explorer, the herpetologist Holbrook, the Michauxs, father and son, the naturalist Thomas Nuttall, the zoölogist Charles Pickering, the botanist Frederick Pursh, the universal naturalist Constantine Samuel Rafinesque, the entomologist Thomas Say, the mycologist Lewis D. de Schweinitz, and that fine old ornithologist, Alexander Wilson.

Usually the collections of such men were sent back to closet naturalists in Europe and the eastern United States instead of being described and classified by the field workers themselves. Thus but few among the devoted naturalists of the frontier attained immediate fame in their profession, even though their pioneer services are commemorated in names of animals and plants that will always awaken echoes in the minds of men of science: *Rafinesquina, Carlowrightia, Bartramia, Pitchera,* and so on. Despite such tributes from the scientists for whom they worked, the naturalists in the field could expect little reward beyond the joy of the day's work and the consciousness that they had wrought well for science. Too often the scientific explorer has borne the burden of the heat of the day, while the closet naturalist has reaped that whereon he bestowed relatively little labor.

It was natural that the wave of migration from the United States into Texas after 1820 should have been followed by scientific exploration on this new frontier. Texas had of course been a social frontier for three hundred years, subject to desultory efforts at colonization by the Spaniards; but conquistador and missionary seem to have had little inclination to botanize on their *entradas*. Although Alvar Nuñez Cabeza de Vaca explored Texas either shortly before or shortly after 1530, little information that can definitely be taken as referring to Texas is included in his book of travels. None of the later Spanish expeditions into the region seems to have brought back any notes of interest to natural historians. Scientific exploration in Texas seems actually to have begun with the work of Dr. Edwin James, surgeon and naturalist with Major S. H. Long's first expedition to the Rocky Mountains in 1820. In the summer of that year, with Major Long and a part of the military escort, Dr. James came down the Canadian River in what is now the Texas Panhandle and collected numerous plants, which were described for science by Dr. John Torrey. Eight years later a Franco-Swiss botanist sent out by DeCandolle in Geneva, Jean Louis Berlandier, came into Texas with a Mexican Boundary Commission to make collections for his sponsors. In 1833-34 the Scots botanical collector Thomas Drummond worked in Texas; and in 1837, the year after the Republic had won its independence at San Jacinto, John James Audubon visited the new nation in search of materials for his proposed work *The Birds of North America*. Actual settlers in Texas, in these early years absorbed in the struggle to gain the barest necessities of life, had little leisure for scientific interests; but among the many German intellectuals who came into Texas after 1831, many of them with university training in the sciences, were several men who did noteworthy work for science. Associated with the German settlements at New Braunfels and Fredericksburg were Ferdinand Lindheimer, who came to Texas in 1836, Louis Ervendberg, who came in 1839, and later the distinguished explorer Ferdinand Roemer, who spent eighteen months in Texas in 1845-47.

Charles Wright, who had come to Texas in 1837, remained here until 1852; for eight years he collected plants for Asa Gray. After Wright's work there ensued a period of inaction which lasted through the decade of the Civil War. But in the 'seventies there was a marked awakening of interest in natural history in Texas; several naturalists worked in the state whose collections and correspondence made important contributions to knowledge in diverse fields of investigation. This group included the botanist Julien Reverchon of Dallas, in whose honor the genus *Reverchonia* is named; Gustaf W. Belfrage of Clifton, Bosque County, whose magnificent collections of Texan insects made possible Cresson's fine work *Hymenoptera Texana,* and who contributed to several monographs of the well-known naturalist, Professor A. S. Packard; and, last in point of time, the Swiss-American geologist and naturalist, Jacob Boll, of Dallas, a man who by his character and personality as well as by his scientific achievements deserves to stand first among his fellows. In a sense his work includes theirs; he completes the succession of frontier naturalists in Texas; and if he is not the most nearly typical, he is certainly the most versatile and the most admirable naturalist of the group.

In the chapters which follow I shall describe the labors of these men of science and the environment in which they worked. The eleven men selected as subjects of the biographical sketches are of course but a few of the many naturalists who worked in the region during the period under consideration, from 1820 to about 1880; a partial list of over one hundred and fifty of these, with very brief biographical data, is included in an appendix. The sources for each chapter are indicated at the close of the volume.

Jacob Boll 2

AT the end of the Civil War, North Texas was still frontier country. The stirring events of the Texas Revolution, a generation before, had centered in the southern part of the region in the vicinity of San Antonio and Austin's colony, and along the lower reaches of the navigable rivers. Although the black waxy prairies of north-central Texas were destined to become the most populous area of the state, settlement in this region began late, and in the period of the Civil War and Reconstruction population was still relatively sparse. The railroads, building from the south and east, had not yet reached the town of Dallas with their great stimulus to trade and immigration; and to the north and west, the country was even more thinly settled.

Into this region, in the year 1869, came Jacob Boll, one of the most admirable among the naturalists of the Texas frontier. Already an esteemed associate of Louis Agassiz, he was destined to play an important part in the development of the mineral resources of Texas, and to give to the world almost its first glimpse of the fossil animal life of the Texas region. All the other men to be dealt with in this book had preceded him to Texas, some by more than a generation. Berlandier had come and gone years before, as had Drummond, Wright, Ervendberg, and Roemer. More than fifteen years before Boll's arrival, Lindheimer, who had been working in Texas since 1836, had turned from scientific exploration to his highly respected work as editor of the *Neu-Braunfelser Zeitung*. The frontier doctor and naturalist Lincecum, still vigorous at seventy-five, after twenty years of residence in Texas had gone to Mexico in protest against the disturbances of Reconstruction. Reverchon, in whom Boll was to fan a sinking flame of interest in science, had worked a dozen years near Dallas in the very area where Boll chose to make his home. Even Belfrage, the Swedish entomologist, had been in Texas two years before Boll came on his first collecting trip.

Some of these men Boll knew; of others he doubtless never so much as heard the names. But as the last in point of time among the naturalists who worked in Texas during the frontier period, he may well stand first in any account of the group. This place he deserves not only because of his delightfully simple integrity as a man, but also because he worked in all the fields of investigation touched by his predecessors. In particular, he may almost be said to have begun geological investigation in this area. A curious alligator-like fossil skull which Boll discovered during an exploring trip into Archer County in 1876 was the first indication of the presence in the rocks of Texas of a wonderful series of hitherto unknown fossil fishes, reptiles, and amphibians. It was a chance meeting of Boll with Edward Drinker Cope at Dallas in 1877 that led to the first systematic exploration of the rocks of the Wichita region and the unearthing of the extraordinary fossil fauna they contained. And in addition to his work with fossils, Boll collected extensively for various naturalists all kinds of living animals—fishes, reptiles, batrachia, insects, birds, mammals. Altogether, he discovered probably two hundred species of animals new to science.

Jacob Boll was born in the village of Dieticon, Canton Aargau, Switzerland, May 29, 1828, the son of Henry and Magdalena Boll. His father, a man of moderate wealth, was able to send Jacob to a Gymnasium in Switzerland—where, somehow, he seems to have met Professor Louis Agassiz, destined to attain international renown as a scientist for his work at Harvard College, but then teaching in the College of Neuchatel. Later Boll went to the University of Jena, where he spent two years but left without a degree in 1853. Returning to Bremgarten in the Canton Aargau, he married Henriette Humbel and settled down as apothecary in a pharmacy he had bought with his wife's dowry. At Jena he had become very much interested in chemistry and the natural sciences; and during the seventeen years of his residence in Bremgarten he gave free rein to his scientific tastes, to such a degree that the year 1869 saw the publication of a thin duodecimo on the flora of the Bremgarten region—and the bankruptcy of the pharmacy. Troubles now came upon Boll thick and fast. His wife, who had borne him three children, suffered a nervous breakdown, and had to be confined in a sanitarium. Boll's parents and brothers had migrated to Texas before 1858 to join the ill-fated Fourieristic colony at La Réunion, and were now living at Dallas. He decided to follow them to America, hoping there to make a fresh start.

Boll came to the United States in the latter part of 1869, stopping

20

first at Boston and Cambridge. Here he met again his friend Professor Agassiz, who for more than twenty years had held a professorship in zoölogy and geology in Harvard College. Agassiz received Boll with open arms, and introduced him to the circle of young Swiss and American students who had been attracted to Harvard by the radiant, kindly personality of the world's greatest teacher in the natural sciences. Agassiz, who just then had an especial desire to obtain a large and comprehensive collection of the animals of Texas, proposed to Boll that he go to Texas and make such a collection for the famous Museum of Comparative Zoölogy at Harvard.

Boll accepted the proposal, came out to Texas late in 1869, and during the year 1870 gathered an extraordinary collection of specimens of all classes of animals, including many new species, for the Harvard Museum. There were in this collection numerous specimens of bird-skins, crustacea, spiders, and reptiles, as well as numerous invertebrate fossils. The Swiss pharmacist showed himself, in fact, a most gifted collector. Just how admirable Boll's collection was is indicated by Agassiz's comment on it in the *Annual Report* to the Trustees of the Museum of Comparative Zoölogy for 1870, in which he ranks the Boll collection among the "accessions to the Museum during the year of great and surprising importance." Dr. Hermann August Hagen, Curator of the Department of Entomology in the Museum, states that there were among the insects of Boll's collection "1600 species, in 15,000 specimens," and says further:

> The purchase of Mr. J. Boll's collection of Texan insects is in every way an important addition to the Museum. . . . As Mr. J. Boll is a very experienced collector, and a considerable part of his Lepidoptera were raised either from the caterpillar or from the chrysalis, the Museum possesses now a stock of unsurpassed beauty even for the Microlepidoptera. . . . The collection of Mr. Boll is a very important addition, giving beautiful specimens for species before badly represented. Mr. Boll has added some remarks about the plants on which the caterpillars were found, the time of transformation, and similar notes of scientific value. . . . The whole collection of Mr. Boll, made in a certain limited region and in the course of only one year, affords from its unsurpassed beauty of arrangement a very high testimonial to the collector's ability, and furnishes a model of the way in which insects should be handled and arranged for a collection.

During the late winter of 1870-71, Boll returned to Cambridge to be with Agassiz, and there was made a custodian in the Museum as an assistant to Dr. Hagen in the Department of Entomology. Upon Boll's shoulders was placed the responsibility of remounting all insects in the museum that needed attention, eliminating duplicates in the collection, and preparing duplicate specimens for exchange with other museums. In the spring of 1871 he returned to Switzerland in order to look after some matters of personal business, and during the summer experimented with species of American wild silkworms he had taken over as cocoons. In the course of two generations, by feeding the silkworms on food different from that to which they were accustomed in Texas, Boll obtained adults showing marked differences from the parental generation.

In a letter dated May 9, 1871, Agassiz had offered Boll a regular appointment in the Museum, renewable yearly or half-yearly at Boll's option. Accepting this offer, Boll returned to Cambridge toward the end of October, and that winter collected several thousand specimens of the insects of New England for the Museum. In the *Annual Report* for 1871, the following comment is made on Boll's work:

The Texan Lepidoptera purchased from Mr. Boll were carefully revised, . . . and a full set of all species sent to Prof. Zeller of Stettin, for a scientific monograph. All new or doubtful species of the Rhopalocera were sent to Mr. W. A. Edwards. . . . The Hemiptera from Dallas, Texas, have been in the same manner revised, and a full set sent to the well-known American monographer, Mr. P. R. Uhler, of Baltimore. The same work has been done with the greater part of the Texas Coleoptera, and a set sent to Prof. C. A. Dohrn at Stettin.

In the same report, Dr. Hagen states:

The collection of New England insects, I am sorry to say, is one of the weakest parts of the whole, particularly as the specimens are more or less badly set. Professor Agassiz, considering this defect as one of the most important, invited Mr. J. Boll, an experienced collector, to come to Cambridge; during the autumn [of 1871] Mr. Boll collected in and around Cambridge several thousand specimens. . . . It seems beyond doubt that the superior manner in which Mr. Boll arranges the specimens will soon render the Museum of Comparative Zoölogy a pattern for every entomologist. The winter [of 1871] will be employed by Mr. Boll in spreading and setting in a new manner the whole collection of Lepidoptera, which will give it a two-fold value. . . .

This winter was the happiest period of Jacob Boll's life. At Cambridge he was thrown again into association with the brilliant company of young Swiss scientists who had followed Agassiz to Harvard. Although the great teacher was nearing the end of life (he died in 1873), he was still moved by the old enthusiasms and still had the same overflowing kindliness that had won for him scores of friends and disciples. Boll was on terms of intimacy with Agassiz, and was a welcome visitor at his home in Cambridge, where Boll met the charming American wife of the scientist, Elizabeth Cary Agassiz, as well as many of the distinguished guests. A dinner party at Agassiz's might include such professorial colleagues as Felton, the Greek scholar; Henry W. Longfellow; Peirce, the mathematician; Asa Gray, the botanist; and Jeffries Wyman, the anatomist, together with such famous figures from outside the College as Channing, Emerson, Whittier, Ticknor, Motley, and Lowell. Such men as these furnished an enormous stimulus to intellectual life. Nowhere else in America could a man with Boll's scholarly impulses have found more congenial company. Then, too, the rich and growing collections of the Harvard Museum—what a wealth of material was there!

In the Boston Society of Natural History, too, Boll found many kindred spirits. On October 25 and November 22, 1871, he exhibited mounted specimens and collections before this group, by invitation, and on January 3, 1872, he was elected to membership. The manuscript proceedings of the Society record that "Mr. James Boll" exhibited a beautifully prepared winter collection of insects from the neighborhood of Boston and Cambridge before the entomological section on February 28, 1872. It should be added that Boll maintained friendly relations with the members of the Society until his death.

In March of 1872 Boll was recalled to Switzerland by the serious illness of his wife. During the five months of his stay in Cambridge he had been able, according to the *Annual Report* for 1872,

to collect several thousand of insects around Cambridge and Boston, to form a biological set, an entomological herbarium, to spread one-sixth of the butterflies in the collections of the Museum, and to arrange a nursery for raising insects. Besides a lot especially selected and raised in his room in glass jars and boxes, he established in the Museum four closets filled with dry leaves and branches of wood to raise insects contained as larvae on these plants.

Surely a remarkable winter's work! Boll took the greater part of the cocoons to Europe with him and there raised about six hundred specimens. He was beginning to receive enthusiastic recognition for the work done during his stay in Europe the year before, and for his collections, especially of minute butterflies, which were distributed to most of the great museums of the Continent. In March of 1873, approximately a year after his arrival in Europe on this second visit, he was elected to membership in the Academia Cæsarea Leopoldino-Carolina Naturæ Curiosorum of Germany, a great order (founded in 1670) that included all the eminent German students of natural history. Professor Moritz Wagner of the University of Munich praised Boll's scientific achievements both in a cordial personal letter of October 11, 1873, and in papers published in *Kosmos* and the Augsburger *Allgemeine Zeitung*.

During the years 1872-73, Boll was busily engaged in scientific study and publication with a friend of twenty years, Heinrich Frey, professor in the University of Zurich. The two of them studied the collections Boll had brought from America, and published together upon them. Boll spent all of his free time in natural history observations; and Boll and Frey together made a botanical exploration of the Albula Pass in Switzerland—a locality noted for the richness of its flora. Boll also prepared some alcoholic collections of mollusks for the Museum of Comparative Zoölogy, which were acknowledged in the *Annual Report* for 1874. During this period Mrs. Boll was acutely ill: she died in August, 1873. After her death Boll wrote to Agassiz, asking whether he might renew his connection with the Museum. In a characteristic letter dated October 15, 1873, Agassiz, although the hand of death lay upon him, welcomed Boll back to Cambridge. But when Boll arrived in Cambridge early in January of 1874, he learned in detail of the death of his beloved preceptor and friend.

Recalling the happy days in the Museum with Agassiz and Hagen, Crotch and Harger, Boll knew that the past was gone forever. Here in Cambridge were still appreciative friends who knew worth and appreciated scholarship. Europe ended with the Allegheny Mountains; there in Texas were ignorant people to whom the "little old Swiss naturalist," with his feathered *Alpenhut,* yellow linen duster, tin collecting case, and forked reptile-stick was an object of mistrust, if not of derision. Yet with Agassiz gone, Cambridge hardly seemed like home. Feeling himself drawn back to Texas by family ties, Boll returned to Dallas. Again his letters, which he so carefully marked "J. Boll, Naturalist, Box 71, Dallas, Texas, U.S.A.," began to bridge the gap between frontier Texas and the intellectual world.

For seven years, from 1874 until the time of his death in 1880, Boll investigated the mineral resources of Texas and studied its natural history. By his work he gained the confidence and esteem of governors and legislators, and at the time of his death a movement was on foot to establish a geological survey of Texas, with Boll at its head. In this same period he was appointed Special Assistant, in charge of the Texas area, with the United States Entomological Commission for the study of the Rocky Mountain locust—headed by the distinguished entomologist Dr. C. V. Riley, with whom Boll had previously corresponded. Boll's report to the Commission, twenty pages in length, was printed in 1878 as an appendix to the *First Report* of the investigators.

In these years Boll had ranged far and wide in his studies of the natural history of Texas. In a covered wagon he had gone out in 1876 into the wilds of Northwest Texas, and on another trip had collected some curious heads of fossil animals from the rocks in Archer

24

BOLL IN TEXAS
1869-1880

INTENSIVELY EXPLORED AREA

County. He gathered other remains of vertebrate animals on Onion Creek, a small tributary of the Little Wichita River, a few miles east of present Archer City. These he brought back to Dallas, along with other collections. In 1877 Edward Drinker Cope, a brilliant young paleontologist who during the preceding six years had been investigating the fossil vertebrates of the western United States, came to Texas, and in the course of a field trip encountered Boll at Dallas. When Boll showed him some of the fossils he had collected in Archer County, Cope saw at once that here was something absolutely new, a world of primitive reptiles and amphibians whose very existence had been hitherto unsuspected. Cope spoke enthusiastically of Boll's specimens in a letter to his wife written in San Antonio in 1877:

At Fort Worth I collected fossils and living reptiles and fishes. At Dallas I met a German naturalist named Boll, from whom I am procuring some very fine objects of the same kind. In fact, I learned of wonderful things from him, which I will use in future.

25

What the "wonderful things" were is hinted at in a sentence from a letter written by Cope in Houston the same month, and reproduced by Persifor Frazer in his biography of Cope in the *American Geologist*: "I obtained a nearly complete skull at Dallas, and a wonderful saurian."

The two specimens which Cope carried back to Houston from Dallas were the type-specimens of two species of fossil batrachia common in the Permian rocks of Texas, and known to paleontologists as *Eryops megalocephala* and *Trimerorhachis insignis*. Cope might very well have been pleased with his experience at Dallas. The upshot of the matter was that Boll received an appointment from Cope to collect for him in the Wichita country of Texas, and for three seasons, from 1878 to the day of his death in 1880, he was Cope's paid collector.

Not that Cope ever mentioned him as such during Boll's lifetime. One may search in vain for any reference to Boll in the series of papers in which Cope described the fossil vertebrates from the Permian rocks of Texas. Those were strenuous days in vertebrate paleontology, and Cope was engaged in a titanic contest with Professor Othniel C. Marsh of Yale College to see who should describe first the fossil vertebrates of the West. Charles H. Sternberg in his *Life of a Fossil Hunter* has told amusingly of the secrecy with which the moves of collectors for these two men were made. Thus Cope thought it advisable to conceal even the name of the collector who had unearthed the strange and wonderful fossil fauna of the Texas Permian. But when Boll had passed from scenes of warring paleontologists, Cope wrote in an obituary published in a journal he edited:

> For two years previous to his death [Boll] was engaged in explorations for Professor Cope in the Permian region of Texas. He discovered numerous remarkable extinct vertebrates, which formed the subject of various papers. These number thirty-two species, and they have thrown great light on the nature of vertebrate life at that early period.

This includes practically all the new species described by Cope in his first two contributions to the history of the vertebrates of the Permian formation of Texas (published in the *Proceedings of the American Philosophical Society* in 1878 and 1880). Years after Boll's death, the fellow who succeeded him as collector for Cope, in a paper published in the sixteenth volume of the *Journal of Geology,* said with characteristic modesty: "The vertebrate fossils from the Permian formation in Texas described by Professor E. D. Cope were collected by myself and others. . . ." An examination of Cope's papers, however, will reveal that thirty-two out of the fifty-seven new species and genera of Permian vertebrates described by him from Texas were discovered to science by the labors of Jacob Boll. Boll also, in a paper published in the *American Naturalist* in September, 1880, first intelligibly identified the Permian rocks of Texas. And Boll was one of the first men to discover and report the occurrence of various mineral deposits in northern and western Texas.

The work of a fossil collector calls for physical bravery, unswerving devotion to science, and the highest degree of resourcefulness in the field. As Henry Fairfield Osborn has said:

> The fossil hunter must first of all be a scientific enthusiast. He must be willing to endure all kinds of hardships, to suffer cold in the early spring and the late autumn and early winter months, to suffer intense heat and the glare of the sun in summer months, and he must be prepared to drink alkali water, and in some regions to fight off the attacks of the mosquito and other pests. He must be something of an engineer in order to be able to handle large masses of stone and to transport them over roadless wastes of desert to the nearest shipping point; he must have a delicate and skillful touch to preserve the least fragment of bone when fractured; he must be content with very plain living . . . he must find his chief reward and stimulus in the sense of discovery and in the dispatching of specimens to museums which he has never seen for the benefit of a public which has little knowledge or appreciation of the self-sacrifices which the fossil hunter has made.

In order to evaluate Boll's achievement, one must keep in mind the conditions under which he worked—and must remember that, in addition to the hardships described by Professor Osborn, he had to endure the unsympathetic attitude of a frontier society that had little understanding of the aims of science.

In Boll's first trip out into the Wichita country for Cope, in 1878, he reached the field January 10: the last entry of collection in the memorandum sent in to Cope, which reached him April 1, 1878, bears the date of March 18. It would be useless to list in detail all the finds that made this trip fruitful. Yet it may not be pedantic to point out that in one month, February, Boll and his companion, J. C. Isaac (an old collector who had worked for Cope in Wyoming), found stegocephalian amphibians, ancestrally allied to the reptiles, and cotylosaurian and theromorph reptiles. These discoveries were of extraordinary value. The animals were all land forms which had died and had been buried in what evidently were delta-formations along Texas rivers in Permian times. At the American Museum of Natural History in New York may be seen many of these early specimens unearthed by Boll—some of them skeletons of a high degree of completeness, and beautifully collected.

Boll's original collection lists sent to Professor Cope have a peculiar interest. Their titles are often quaintly spelled: "List of fossils sendt

May 24 from Seymour in 3 boxes, by J. Boll" (containing, incidentally, bones of *Eryops, Dimetrodon obtusidens, Naosaurus cruciger*—"Sceleton of a Reptile in clay with very long spines—Beaver Creek"—and *Dimetrodon gigas*). And sometimes the English of the collector in the field failed him altogether, so that lists which had bravely started out in quaint English ended in still quainter German. Mr. Nathaniel A. Taylor, in an obituary notice published in the Galveston *Daily News* of October 10, 1880, speaks of Boll's linguistic handicap as a deterrent to publication, saying:

Prof. Boll did not write much. There were two reasons for this. He was naturally very modest and unobtrusive, as all men of great merit are. . . . Although a fine writer in his own language, he was distrustful of himself in English. He wrote in English with remarkable clearness, but in a singularly idiomatic way, so much so that his manuscript required revision by a good writer for publication. This was a great stumbling block to him.

As a sample of what could happen when manuscripts slipped past the reviser, the following passage from Boll's report on the Rocky Mountain locust in Texas in 1877 may serve:

After my own minute observation, the unwinged locusts moved from southwest to northeast; fences, creeks, etc., changed somewhat in that direction. The very young ones assembled already in very thick masses. After they consumed the scarcely developed leaves of the lower plants, I saw them eat also dry leaves on the bottom; then they climbed the dry stalks and consumed the old leaves. They migrate nearly always after each transformation, and the more they grow, the more they travel. . . .

When Boll was filled with enthusiasm in the field, writing to Cope of his discoveries, he forgot in the light of his divine fire even the conventions of his mother tongue. The sheerest, purest genius! Witness the following passage, from a report sent to Cope on August 25, 1880, only a month before his death:

Ein Box enthält 4 Jars mit Thieren in Alcohol. . . . Das eine ist von dem grossen gelben catfish & das andere von einer Percoider Art, dieser Fish wird hier Proms genant, & hat drayerlay Zähne im Munde & in der Höhle des Gehirns finden sich zway freie, abgeflachte runde Knochen. . . . Vom Volke werden diese zwey Knochen "Diamonds" genant. Ist Ihnen dieser Fish bekant? und wie heisst er?. . . Es sind zway verschiedene Arten & sind auffaland fast rothgelb, während dieselben Arten hier im Trinity ganz grünlichgrau sind.

This was the gentle-spirited, soft-spoken Swiss naturalist who by the sheer force of his integrity and the purity of his devotion to science had won the affectionate regard of Louis Agassiz, Moritz Wagner,

Philip R. Uhler, Heinrich Frey, August Weismann, Philipp C. Zeller, and H. A. Hagen, and also had merited election to the Leopoldina! Of his singular modesty and lovableness there is universal testimony. Cope has spoken of it in print, saying that "Mr. Boll was a most amiable man, and his death is a serious loss to Science," and this statement is borne out in the words of humble acquaintances of sixty years ago, still resident in Dallas. "I can remember him so plainly riding upon his little yellow pony 'Gypsy' to his home at the corner of Swiss and Germania avenues," said one. "We thought him peculiar because he caught butterflies and snakes. And yet he was very good to us." "He was so kind to us little children," said a white-haired woman, "and used to let us feed his silkworms, and look at the Mastodon skeleton when we had found insects for him. I never knew him to speak unkindly of anyone. His one passion was music, which affected him deeply."

After a summary of Boll's work in the Permian beds of Texas, any account of the splendid collections made for Cope of living Texas reptiles, amphibians, and fishes would be in the nature of an anti-climax. Even the early collecting done by Boll for the Harvard Museum, admirable as it was, cannot be compared with his last work, his fossil collecting. *Finis coronavit opus.* When one considers the all but insuperable difficulties under which Boll worked, the wildness of the country, the roads—hardly passable even at the most favorable times of the year—and his distance from his base, one realizes the stuff of which the man was made.

Death came to the explorer in the dugout hut of a collecting camp on the Pease River near its confluence with the Red River, on September 29, 1880. Here, surrounded by the fossils he had gathered in the last few days of his work, and attended only by his teamster—a mere boy terrified by the sufferings of the naturalist—Boll succumbed to peritonitis after an illness of ten days.

Without the applause of the crowd, his merit unknown to many workers even in his own field, lacking the academic recognition that would have been dear to his soul, with only the memories of Zurich and Jena and the unforgettable days at Cambridge, he died alone in the wilderness. And yet who of us would not have his reckoning for the advancement of science?

In Defense of
Jean Louis Berlandier 3

M ANKIND must have its heroes. It must exalt the successful man—recount his talents and his virtues, weave legends about him, and build up a tradition of veneration, sometimes to the point of worship. Thus does human nature proclaim the worth of its own poor humanity. And mankind must also have its scapegoats, upon whose shoulders can be loaded the censure for its own sins. Scientific men and historians of science are no exceptions. We recount with something like exaltation the glorious, independent career of a Vesalius: immediately afterward, with hardly less zest, we descant upon the villainy and plagiarism of his renegade student, Realdus Columbus. Again, at the same time that we celebrate the productive life of Marcello Malpighi, who by his inspired work laid the foundations for much of modern biology, we dip our pen into corrosive ink in order to describe Borelli's ingratitude to him. And thus we at once glorify our humanity and compensate for our own lapses from the mores of our tribe.

Jean Louis Berlandier is a scapegoat in the history of botanical exploration in the Southwest. No less a man than Auguste-Pyrame DeCandolle,* the famous Genevese author of the gigantic *Prodromus* of the botany of the world, in his memoirs stigmatized Berlandier as a malcontent and an ingrate; and Asa Gray, in his obituary of Dr. Charles W. Short, has lent the weight of his great name to the defamation of Berlandier's character. What appears to be almost a conspiracy of silence entered into by later botanists has prevented any adequate account of Berlandier's work from getting into the history of scientific exploration in America. Then, too, the disper-

*The orthography of this name varies in the sources; I have for convenience normalized the spelling even in quoted passages.

sion among several libraries of the materials dealing with his life and work, making it difficult to study and evaluate them, has further obscured the facts of his career. In connection with Berlandier, students of American botany have a confused notion of a Swiss botanical explorer sent to Mexico by the elder DeCandolle at the beginning of the second quarter of the nineteenth century, who is supposed to have ill requited the favors which (according to DeCandolle's account) were showered upon him. Berlandier's subsequent career is usually dismissed with a brief statement to the effect that he set up as a physician and pharmacist in Matamoros and died near there in 1851.

There is, however, something to be said in Berlandier's defense, and a few facts can be added to what is generally known of his career. The collections he sent to DeCandolle, for instance, contain several thousand species of plants, many of them represented by several specimens; and an understanding of the conditions under which Berlandier worked suggests some qualification of the harsh judgments that have been passed on his achievement. It is my purpose to present here, as fully as the still fragmentary state of the materials will allow, an account of the inner life and the outer works of Jean Louis Berlandier.

The city of Geneva, which was for long the center of French Protestant culture, has occupied a unique position in the history of the learned world. The famous Academy was founded there as early as 1559; in the next year was established the public library, which later grew to great proportions, and at one time had as its librarian the distinguished naturalist, Abraham Trembley. The nineteenth century saw the founding of the Museum of Natural History (1811), the Botanical Garden (1817), and the Conservatory (1824). The old Academy, which through the centuries had maintained unbroken the tradition of sound scholarship, took on new life, and in 1873 assumed the rank of a university.

The great alpine scholar, W. A. B. Coolidge, perhaps the leading authority on Switzerland in the last half of the nineteenth century, never wearied of speaking of the unique status of Geneva among the cities of the world.

Considering the small size of Geneva, till recently [he wrote], it is surprising how many celebrated persons have been connected with it as natives or as residents. . . . In the sixteenth century, besides Calvin and Bonivard, we have Isaac Casaubon, the scholar; Robert and Henri Estienne, the printers; and, from 1572 to 1574, Joseph Scaliger himself, though but for a short time. J. J. Rousseau is, of course, the great Genevese of the eighteenth century. At that period, and in the nineteenth century, Geneva was a center of light, especially in the case of various of the physical sciences. Among the scientific celebrities were de Saussure, the most many-sided of all; DeCandolle and Boissier, the botanists; Alphonse Favre and Necker, the geologists; Marignac, the chemist; DeLuc, the physicist, and Plantamour, the astronomer. Charles Bonnet was both a scientific man and a philosopher, while Amiel belonged to the latter class only. . . .

Amid this distinguished group of Genevese scientists of the nineteenth century, the outstanding naturalist was Auguste-Pyrame DeCandolle. Nordenskiöld, the Swedish historian of biology, in writing of the progress of botany after Linnæus, calls DeCandolle "one of the foremost pioneers" in that science, and says of him:

He was born in 1778 at Geneva, where his family had for generations enjoyed a great reputation. At an early age he began to study the natural sciences, which at that time—the age of Bonnet and Saussure—stood in high favour in his native town. After preliminary studies there, he betook himself to Paris in order to continue his education as a botanist. In the company of Lamarck, Cuvier, and Geoffroy he spent ten years there, during which his reputation increased year by year and public commissions were entrusted to him; amongst other things he was sent, with the financial assistance of the State, on scientific expeditions in different parts of France; Lamarck handed over to him the editing of his French flora and he was finally elected professor at Montpellier. In 1816, however, he returned to Geneva, which during the Revolution had become incorporated with France, but after the fall of Napoleon was again united to Switzerland. He then lived in his native town as professor of botany and member of the high council, honoured and respected, until his death, in 1841. DeCandolle mastered the whole field of botany better than anyone else in his time; he was at once systematist, morphologist, and physiologist. He started a gigantic work, *Prodromus systematis naturalis regni vegetabilis,* which was to describe all known plants, but which for obvious reasons was never completed in his lifetime; his son and many others worked at it after his death. The principles on which he classified the vegetable kingdom he laid down in a work published in 1813 entitled *Théorie élémentaire de la botanique,* which he revised several times and which is without doubt his finest work, worthy to be associated with, and at the same time representing a great advance on Linnæus's *Philosophia botanica,* which doubtless gave him the idea.

In such an age as this, and only a few miles from the home of such a master, Berlandier was born. Regarding his early life little is known. Even the time of his birth is uncertain, although it was probably before 1805. Berlandier is known to have been born in France near Fort de l'Ecluse, a now-abandoned boundary-fortress only a short distance from Geneva. DeCandolle, who was in a position to know all the facts, states that Berlandier came of impoverished parents (*"d'une famille fort pauvre"*), and that as a youth he went to Geneva to make his way in the world, apprenticing himself to a pharmaceutical house. Young, active, and eager, Berlandier set himself to learn Latin and Greek in his spare time by his own efforts. On coming into contact with the boy, DeCandolle was touched by his energy and ambition. He admitted the young apprentice to his classes, and as Berlandier made progress in botanical knowledge, opened up the herbarium of the Academy to the youth and took him with him on his field trips.

In many other ways did DeCandolle show his good will to the young student, and Berlandier reacted well to responsibility. For instance, when a living ostrich was presented to the newly-founded Museum of Natural History, DeCandolle caused Berlandier to be sent to Marseilles to receive the bird and transport it to Geneva, a commission which he executed successfully. Berlandier spent two or three years at Geneva in most profitable obscurity under DeCandolle's patronage, presumably at the same time serving his apprenticeship at the druggist's trade.

Under this admirable master of botany, comparable with Agassiz as a productive teacher, and in surroundings remarkably stimulating, Berlandier prepared himself for a career as a botanist. The whole atmosphere of Geneva was favorable to scholarly activity. In Mrs. Humphrey Ward's introduction to Amiel's *Journal* is presented a vivid picture of the city at the time when Berlandier was in his *Lehrjahre* as a botanist:

. . . the prosperity of Geneva was at its height, the little state was administered by men of European reputation, and Genevese society had power to attract distinguished visitors and admirers from all parts. The veteran Bonstetten, who had been the friend of Gray and the associate of Voltaire, was still talking and enjoying life in his *appartement* overlooking the woods of *La Bâtie.* Rossi and Sismondi were busy lecturing to the Genevese youth, or taking part in Genevese legislation; an active scientific group, headed by the Pictets, De la Rive, and the botanist Auguste Pyrame DeCandolle, kept the country abreast of European thought and speculation, while the mixed nationality of the place—the blending in it of French keenness with Protestant enthusiasms and Protestant solidity—was beginning to receive inimitable and characteristic expression in the stories of Töpffer. The country was governed by an aristocracy, which was not so much an aristocracy of birth as one of merit and intellect, and the moderate constitutional ideas which represented the liberalism of the post-Waterloo period were nowhere more warmly embraced or more intelligently carried out than in Geneva.

At the Academy, Berlandier had frequent association with DeCandolle's students, a polyglot group, among whom were Philippe Dunant, Jacques Denys Choisy, François Marcet, and the younger DeCandolle, Alphonse: all of them destined to become productive botanists. When Berlandier was studying with DeCandolle, the master was in his prime—his middle forties—and was just beginning the publication of his magisterial *Prodromus*. Upon this great work, of which seven volumes appeared during the author's lifetime, Berlandier collaborated in a slight way by contributing a monograph on the gooseberries, or *Grossularieæ*. "This work," said DeCandolle, "without being distinguished, still for a beginner was not without merit"—an obvious understatement. The work on the gooseberries was first published in the *Mémoires* of the Society of Natural History of Geneva in 1824, and was revised for publication in the *Prodromus* two years later. In DeCandolle's laboratory Berlandier also learned the sketching, drawing, and painting of natural-history objects from Jean-Christophe Heyland, botanical artist and illustrator for DeCandolle. This ability was to be of use to him later.

The impression the young student had made upon his superiors may be gauged by the fact that when DeCandolle, together with Étienne Moricand, Philippe Dunant, and Philippe Mercier, conceived the idea of sending a botanical collector to Mexico (then largely *terra incognita* with respect to its botany and zoölogy), Berlandier was chosen for the task. He was so responsible, so vigorous, so eager, and so intelligent! Arrangements for sending him to Mexico were made, some time in 1824 or 1825, with Lucas Alamán, the Minister of Foreign Affairs of the newly established Republic of Mexico, who was a former student of DeCandolle. Alamán had decided to send a Boundary Commission to survey and establish the boundary between the Mexican Republic and the United States, and he agreed to attach Berlandier to this Commission in the capacity of botanist. Late in 1826, accordingly, Berlandier left Europe for Mexico. Before his departure from Geneva an unpleasantness occurred which, according to DeCandolle, completely altered Berlandier's attitude toward the four Genevese botanists who were sending him to Mexico. Some teasing on the part of those charged with the details of the voyage irritated Berlandier, says DeCandolle, and as his disposition, "greedy of applause, unstable, foolishly ambitious and independent," could not accommodate itself to the circumstances, he "departed maldisposed." Thus closed the European chapter in the life of Berlandier. He was but little more than twenty years old.

Berlandier's manuscript account of his journey to Mexico indicates that he left Le Havre on the American brig *Hannah Elizabeth,* Captain Reling, on October 14, 1826, and on December 15 landed at Panuco, near Tampico, on the Mexican coast. Here Berlandier lived and collected for a short time, and then proceeded along the road from Huasteca to Pachuca, Tacubaya, and Chapultepec. After collecting in the valley of Toluca and Cuernavaca, he arrived in the City of Mexico.

The scientific expedition into Texas which Berlandier was to accompany was the outgrowth of a long series of events. In 1819 the United States, in spite of the clamor of a group in Congress who demanded a line farther west, had made a treaty with Spain establishing the western boundary of Louisiana at the Sabine River. The imperialists in Congress could base a vague claim to some territory west of the Sabine on the fact that LaSalle, the explorer of Louisiana, had in 1685 landed with his men at Matagorda Bay and had established the French fort and village of St. Louis near the mouth of the Lavaca. In taking over French rights in the region, argued the expansionists, the United States had acquired a right to the territory at least as far west as the Lavaca. They strenuously objected to the treaty of 1819 which established the Sabine as the boundary, declaring that "alienation of national territory" was beyond the power of Congress. Fortunately for the expansionists, before ratifications could be exchanged the Mexicans had secured their independence of Spain, and it became necessary to reopen the question of the western boundary, this time with the new government of Mexico.

The United States had given early recognition to Mexican independence, and in 1825 Joel R. Poinsett of South Carolina had been appointed first Minister of the United States to Mexico. His task, as set forth in his instructions, was to seek from the Mexican Government a revision of the terms of the Treaty of 1819 that would fix the boundary of Louisiana at a point west of the Sabine.

Before Poinsett's arrival in Mexico in 1825, Alamán, who had become Mexican Minister of Foreign Affairs after the fall of the "Emperor" Iturbide, had instructed Torrens, Mexican chargé at Washington, to inform the American Government that Mexico desired to fix the western limits of Louisiana in accordance with the provisions of the Treaty of 1819. Poinsett arrived in Mexico in midsummer of 1825, six months after the arrival of the British chargé, H. G. Ward. British jealousy of American interests in Spanish America, especially strong after the enunciation of the Monroe Doctrine toward the end of 1823, had found an efficient tool in Ward. During his six months in Mexico before Poinsett's arrival he had succeeded in sowing the seeds of distrust of America in the minds of Mexican statesmen, and had persuaded Alamán, LaLlave, and other officials of the danger of American aggression, particularly in the Mexican province of Texas. Ward assured Mexico of the steadfast desire of Britain that Mexican independence be maintained, and tactfully suggested to Alamán, ripe for such an idea, that Mexico establish a monarchy.

When Poinsett arrived in Mexico he at once took up the boundary question with Alamán, but soon reached an impasse. As a compromise, on August 7, 1825, Alamán proposed a treaty of commerce between the United States and Mexico, and suggested that commissioners be appointed by both countries to examine "the country within a given latitude, from one sea to the other," in order to secure "exact information upon which limits might be established."

Ward thereupon suggested to the Mexican president, Guadalupe Victoria, that he appoint as the Mexican commissioner a young artillery officer who was head of the Artillery School in the City of Mexico, General Manuel de Mier y Terán. Terán was unquestionably the best officer of the army for such an appointment, with excellent training in military and topographic science, but Ward favored him for the post primarily because he was known to be deeply distrustful of American influence in Texas. The appointment was made in July, 1826, and General Terán planned to leave Mexico that autumn on the work of delimitation.

But the departure of the Commission was repeatedly postponed. A shortage of funds in the national treasury made provision for the expedition extremely difficult. In 1823, under Alamán's management, the Mexican Government had borrowed sixteen million dollars from a Quaker banking house in London, the Barclays. As a sequel to the British banking disaster of September, 1825, the Barclays had failed, and by their failure deprived the Mexican Government of a balance of two and a quarter million dollars still in their hands. Thus even after the Mexican Congress, early in the autumn of 1827, had appropriated the sum of fifteen thousand dollars for the expenses of the Commission, the departure of the expedition was still delayed because of an actual lack of money in the national treasury.

Poinsett had in the meantime remonstrated with Alamán and Terán against sending a Commission to eastern Texas to examine the question of delimitation while the problem of the boundary was still, as far as the United States was concerned, unsettled.* But the money appropriated by the Mexican Congress having at last been made available, the Boundary Commission left the City of Mexico on November 10, 1827. As the Commission was constituted, it consisted of General Mier y Terán, the head; two Commissioners, Lieutenant-Colonel José Batres and Lieutenant-Colonel Constantino Tarnava, both medical officers; Rafael Chovell, mineralogist; Second-Lieutenant José María Sánchez, cartographer; and Berlandier, who had been waiting in Mexico for almost a year. Colonel José María

---

*In the following January, when the Commission was already on its journey, Poinsett signed a treaty with Mexico which recognized the Sabine as the boundary.

Díaz Noriega accompanied the expedition as secretary to Terán. The expedition was furnished with a small military escort, and took along in a special instrument wagon the indispensable books and instruments. Following the familiar road of the early days from Mexico to Texas—passing through Querétaro, San Miguel, Guanajuato, Saltillo, Monterrey, and Carrizal—the expedition reached Laredo exactly thirteen weeks after its departure from the capital.

At Laredo, then "one of the most desolate presidios in the Mexican eastern states," the Commission remained from the second to the nineteenth of February, 1828, and Berlandier made botanical collections. The route from Laredo to Bexar followed the Old Bexar Road (not the Presidio Road, which crossed the Rio Grande farther up), through present Webb, McMullen, Atascosa, and Bexar counties. At the Medina the party were met by Lieutenant-Colonel Antonio Elosua, commander of the presidio of Bexar; they reached the presidio on the first of March and spent all of March and the first half

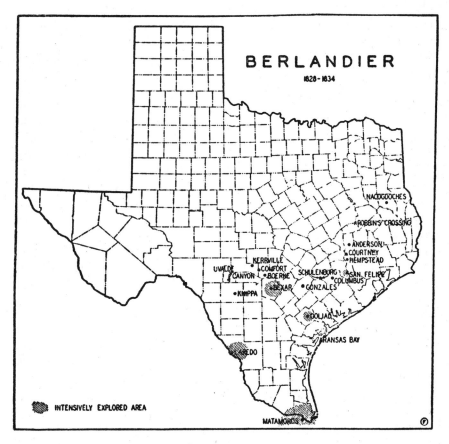

of April there. This prolonged stay accounts for the rich collection of plants Berlandier made in the environs of San Antonio. On the twelfth of April, accompanied by a military escort furnished them by Elosua, Terán and the Commission left Bexar for the capital of Austin's Colony, San Felipe on the Brazos. The route followed the so-called Middle Road, which led from present San Antonio to Gonzales, then a newly-organized settlement still in the painful process of being born as the capital of Green DeWitt's Colony on the Guadalupe. To the eastward of Gonzales the road, after crossing the La-Bahía road, continued to the Colorado River. Here it joined the Atascosito road leading to San Felipe. The Commission reached San Felipe on April 27. Because of recent very heavy rains, the Brazos was so high that an enforced stay was made in San Felipe until the ninth of May. On that day the river receded enough to permit the Commission to cross, and on May 11 the expedition started up the east-of-the-Brazos road toward Jared Groce's plantation, "Bernardo," near present Hempstead in Waller County; enjoyed Groce's equivocal hospitality; and made camp on the night of May 13 not far from present Hempstead. At this place the road they had been following joined the Magdalena road and led them approximately up the route of the present Hempstead-Navasota highway.

Incessant rains made going all but impossible through the swampy places, and the wooded hills offered obstructions almost as serious. Added to these difficulties were the incredibly great hordes of mosquitoes encountered after the Commission left San Felipe. On the night of May 14 they encamped not far from Groce's "Second House," near present Courtney. On May 16, after two days of very difficult going through heavy, boggy ground, they reached Holland's Place, near present Anderson. Here, on May 17, Berlandier fell ill with malarial fever, and on the next day General Terán came down with the same disease. Berlandier continued seriously ill until the party reached the Sertuche Crossing, where the road from Bexar to Nacogdoches (the old *Camino Real* or Upper Road) crossed the Trinity. At this place, between the twenty-fifth and the twenty-eighth of May, more of the men fell sick. The illness of the men, the scarcity of provisions, and the exhaustion of animals and men alike persuaded Terán to send Berlandier and the other members of the Commission back to Bexar by the Upper Road. As they left, Terán directed the scientific staff of the Commission to meet him at Matamoros at the end of the summer; he also sent back to Bexar the troops assigned to him by Elosua, and, retaining only Sánchez and seven soldiers, pressed on toward Nacogdoches, which he reached on June 3.

In the meantime, the scientific staff set out down the Upper Road to Bexar. They left the Trinity River on May 30, with Berlandier still a sick man; camped during incessant rains on the Brazos, June 3-6; passed the Colorado on the twelfth, narrowly escaping drowning in a sudden rise of water after a cloudburst in that region; crossed the San Marcos River on the fifteenth, and reached Bexar on the eighteenth of June. Here they remained about a month, delayed in their departure for Matamoros, as Berlandier said, "by much and continued rain." On the fourteenth day of July, however, the staff finally left Bexar for Laredo; passed the Medina on the sixteenth; and camped the night of the twentieth on the Frío. They reached the Nueces on the twenty-fourth. Four days later, after riding through a country possessing some very beautiful vegetation, they entered Laredo.

The party remained in Laredo from July 28 to August 11 in order to repair the General's coach, which had been broken at the crossing of the Frío. All things having been duly set in order, they crossed to the right bank of the Rio Grande, and proceeding by way of Mier, Camargo, and Reinosa, reached Matamoros on August 20, 1828.

Here the staff waited in constant expectation of the arrival of General Terán, who (as it turned out) had been forced to change his plans and remain in East Texas waiting for the appointment of Dr. John Sibley of Natchitoches as Boundary Commissioner for the United States. Terán took advantage of the enforced delay to consider military dispositions for the protection of the boundary against possible American aggression.

After some weeks spent in Matamoros, Berlandier returned to Bexar, presumably with General Anastasio Bustamente, Comandante-General of the Eastern Mexican States.

In August the Comanche captain Barbaquista, accompanied by many of his braves, had come to Bexar to ratify and renew a treaty made with Bustamente at Bexar in the early summer of 1827. In the absence of Bustamente the Comanches had been cordially received by the authorities, both civil and military, and had been given many proofs of friendship. As some of the Bejareños desired to see the nature of the country to the northwest of San Antonio and to investigate the reported silver mines on the San Saba, an excursion was arranged. Lieutenant-Colonel Francisco Ruiz, the popular "Pancho" Ruiz who had been in command at Tenoxtitlan before the presidial companies were recalled from Texas, planned to ride with a number of Comanches at least as far as the head of the Guadalupe River to hunt bear and buffalo. Some sixty or eighty Comanches were left at Bexar under orders of their captains, Reyuna (Queyunes) and El

Ronco. Berlandier, who had by this time arrived at Bexar, accompanied Ruiz and the Indians on the expedition.

The party left Bexar on November 19, escorted by thirty dragoons, and returned on December 18. Their route led up the course of present Helotes Creek, and included Leon Creek, Comanche Springs, and Balcones Creek, south of present Boerne, where they passed the night of November 21. From this point they proceeded to the banks of the Guadalupe, near present Comfort, and on the night of the twenty-third camped somewhere between present Comfort and Kerrville. The next morning the Mexicans parted from the Comanches and turned westward into present Kerr County, where buffalo and bear were to be found in the oak woods.

The next few days were for the most part cloudy and stormy; the party, after several exploratory side-trips, decided to remain in camp until they had got bear and bison, of which there was an abundance of sign. On the morning of November 28, Berlandier, in company with Ruiz and the others, set out in a northeasterly direction from their camp near an unidentified arroyo on the east bank of the Guadalupe. They finally reached some rocky hillocks, generally known to the Mexicans as the "Pedernales," and struck an arroyo of permanent water which can with certainty be identified as Town Creek, at present Kerrville. Here Ruiz shot a buffalo.

On December 2, the party resumed its march to the headwaters of the Guadalupe, up a stream which the hunters called the "Arroyo de Terán," but which can be identified as the Bear Creek of the north fork of the Guadalupe. In this general neighborhood they stayed five days. On December 6 the party broke camp and, directing their course to the southwest, set out for the head of the Cañon de Don Juan de Ugalde. The country was beautiful. By midday of December 7 they had reached the throat of Ugalde Canyon, and entered the canyon by a steep and very difficult descent. Its immense meadows, of a brilliant green even in December, served as pasturage for numerous deer, while extensive oak woods in the canyon concealed many black bear, once common in all the woods of Texas.

The party spent eight days in traversing the canyon, and left it on December 14 at a point near present Knippa, in Uvalde County. They then turned eastward, crossing the Seco and Hondo on December 15 and the Medina on the seventeenth; and on the eighteenth, after crossing Hondo Creek and the Leon and San Antonio rivers, returned to the presidio from which they had set out a month before.

On this trip Berlandier seems to have made few or no botanical collections, and but few botanical observations.

During the winter of 1828-29 Berlandier apparently remained for some time in the vicinity of Bexar. He struck up a firm friendship with both Ruiz and Elosua. On February 3, 1829, he went with Elosua from Bexar to Goliad, to quell a popular uprising against the Comandante at the presidio there. Berlandier's delightful account of the trip (filling some twenty pages of manuscript) gives a good view of the country. They seem to have returned to Bexar about February 14. On the twenty-fifth of the same month, Berlandier left Bexar for Aransas Bay with a party of Mexicans. They camped that night about ten miles south of Bexar; during the night, their horses were stolen, and they had to return to Bexar on foot. On the twenty-eighth, remounted, they set out again. The time appears to have been one of Indian activity, for Berlandier in his journal speaks also of an attack made upon Goliad by the Indians.

Arriving at Goliad after five days on the road, Berlandier met there the captain of the galette *Pomona,* and decided to accompany him to New Orleans. On March 7 they set out for the port of Aransas Bay, about five leagues south-southeast of Goliad. On March 12 they embarked, but calms retarded their progress, contrary winds drove them back, and it was not until the twenty-third of the month that they sailed past the port of Barataria. The twenty-fifth to the twenty-seventh of March were also hard days, with head winds and contrary currents. They arrived at the Belize on April 1.

The notes describing Berlandier's stay in New Orleans are missing. The manuscripts contain only his meteorological observations made on board the *Pomona* in the port of New Orleans, April 25-May 5. It is evident, however, that Berlandier loved the French people of Louisiana, and parted from them with profound regret. "Fatigued by the monotony of a semi-savage life, of prejudices cultivated and spread by ignorance and superstition," he wrote in his journal, "I found among the descendants of our ancestors the urbanity, the *soins prévenances,* the benevolence, the freedom, and the gayety which will always be the permanent characteristics of this unhappy nation, by all men considered the most civilized on our planet."

The naturalist left New Orleans for Texas on the eighth of May. He noted in his journal the numerous steamboats on the Mississippi, and made some acute observations concerning New Orleans and the causes of its prosperity. The ship remained two entire days on the bar at the mouth of the river. About the eleventh of May it finally managed to sail into the open Gulf; Berlandier reached Texas on the thirteenth, and the next day was safe in Aransas Bay. On the seventeenth he reached Goliad, which, after his visit in New Orleans, impressed him very unfavorably—"a miserable presidio," he called it, "without industry and without resources, today being pompously called 'Goliad' to the end of still further involving the geographic nomenclature." In less than three days he rejoined his companions on the Commission in Bexar.

The group, it will be recalled, had been ordered to meet Terán at Matamoros, but constant rains prevented their departure. We accordingly have among Berlandier's papers weather records made at Bexar for the interval of June 6-July 4, 1829. Leaving Bexar at last on July 14, the party stopped the first night at the mission San José, about six or eight miles to the south; on the twentieth of July they reached the Río Frío, where they were forced to camp until the twenty-third, waiting for the swollen waters to recede; on the twenty-fifth they passed the Nueces, and finally reached the presidio of Laredo on the twenty-eighth. When they arrived at Matamoros, some time before the thirtieth of August, Berlandier's work with the Commission was virtually over; the Commission itself seems to have been dissolved in November. For reasons which will be explained later, Berlandier determined at this time to take up residence at Matamoros, and he was to live there until his death in 1851.

Although in later years Berlandier made other excursions for botanical collecting, notably a journey to Goliad and Bexar in the spring of 1834, his place among the Naturalists of the Frontier depends primarily upon the fact that his work with the Boundary Commission was the first extensive collecting done in Texas, antedating by five or six years Drummond's important work in the vicinity of San Felipe and Gonzales. For this reason, some particular account of Berlandier's scientific activities seems desirable, in extension of the brief narrative already presented. Fuller discussion may be of value also in determining whether DeCandolle's criticism of the naturalist's work with the expedition was justified.

Berlandier's experience with Texas botany began when the Commission, on February 2, 1828, crossed the Rio Grande at Laredo and set foot on Texas soil. As far as his activities as a member of the Commission are concerned, it practically closed at Robbins' Crossing of the Trinity River on May 28 of that year.

The time spent at Laredo (February 2-20, 1828) was so much time lost, for, as Berlandier says in his journal, the vicinity was "a very desert place." At this time events of the first importance were occurring in Texas. On the third and fourth of February the first elections were being held in all the seven old alcalde districts of Austin's Colony. In those weeks, too, Stephen F. Austin was struggling with the Political Chief at Bexar, Ramón Músquiz, and with Representatives José Antonio Navarro and Miguel Arciniega for a stabilizing law with respect to slavery in Texas. Austin was also campaigning for open ports and for legislation facilitating domestic and foreign trade in the Colony. But no news of these events reached the members of the Commission at the deadly-dull presidial town on the Rio Grande, the character of whose life and morals Lieutenant Sánchez of the Commission portrayed in lurid colors.

The Commission left Laredo, it will be recalled, on the twentieth of February. Two days later, on a small stream called La Parida, Berlandier first began to collect Texan plants; and here, for the first time, he heard the cry of the bullfrog—a circumstance which so impressed the members of the Commission that three of them mentioned it in their reports. The crossing of the Nueces offered some difficulty, as it was necessary to carry over all the instruments, baggage, and supplies by hand, and to swim the horses. The waters of the stream had an abundance of catfish, and the woods bordering it were full of turkeys. These were easily hunted with success at night, and were a welcome addition to the fare of the soldiers. Berlandier saw many deer, mustangs, and bison in the region. As the Commission proceeded from point to point, Terán made nightly observations of the satellites of Jupiter to determine the party's position; and in this work Berlandier helped as far as possible.

The vegetation became more abundant as the Commission approached Cañada Verde (Green Branch, in present McMullen County), and by the time they had reached the Río Frío (February 25), it showed the richness and variety that make Texas the wild-flower garden of the world. From this point until they reached Bexar (March 1) the members of the party traversed a succession of flower-strewn plains and rolling hills sprinkled with live oaks and walnuts.

The six weeks (March 1-April 13) that the Commission spent at Bexar were full of interest for all members of the scientific staff. Berlandier was impressed with the beautiful surroundings of the old capital of Texas (its cathedral was at that time nearly a hundred years old), and bewailed the fact that the Spanish and Mexican governments had so inadequately protected the citizens against Indian attacks in the past. Lieutenant Sánchez sought on every hand information concerning the Indians of Texas, especially the Comanches, thus extending the knowledge he had gained at Saltillo from Juan Antonio de Padilla. Terán conferred regarding confidential matters with Músquiz; with Erasmo Seguín, who had met Stephen F. Austin upon his arrival in Texas in 1821, and who deserved well at the hands of the Texans; with Bustamente, a warm personal and political friend; and with Elosua. Berlandier made rich collections to be sent to DeCandolle, and the writings of the Genevese botanist show many Texas species originally collected in the neighborhood of Bexar.

Leaving Bexar on April 16, the Commission (diminished, apparently, by the loss of Colonels Tarnava and Noriega, whose names from this point cease to appear in the records) reached Gonzales on the Guadalupe after a leisurely march of four days "along verdant hills covered with spring flowers" and "rolling hills, woods, and small valleys bedecked with beautiful flowers, where numerous butterflies flitted about making the solitary regions all the more charming." Berlandier found the Guadalupe country near Gonzales attractive botanically, although the town was insignificant, consisting of but six log cabins. The Commission camped at Gonzales on the sixteenth of April and left next day; and although Berlandier had but a short stay (from two o'clock of one afternoon to ten o'clock of the next morning) he made excellent use of his time. Six years later, in June of 1834, Thomas Drummond was to explore extensively in the region of Gonzales.

The route now taken by the Commission carried them over Peach Creek and through the high country of the Lavaca, where, near present Schulenburg at the Loma Grande, they enjoyed the magnificent prospect that was the culminating experience of every early traveler from San Felipe to Bexar. Thence they passed on to the site of present Columbus on the Colorado River. Here, at Beeson's Ferry, the cavalcade halted to mend one of the wagons, and received a most cordial welcome which included good lodgings and excellent food. At this prosperous settlement Judge Cummins could show them with pride his young peach orchard, well set to ripen peaches for the first time that year. A grist mill, a saw mill, and a blacksmith shop gave an almost metropolitan air to the place, which was graced by the presence of the two daughters of Judge Cummins and the two Beeson girls. The Alley brothers, Missourians, also had very prosperous farms in the vicinity.

Heavy rains at Beeson's and in the upper Colorado basin on the eighteenth and twenty-second of April caused the river to rise, and delayed the advance of the expedition. On Saturday, the twenty-sixth, however, the river had subsided to such an extent that the Commission could set out for the San Bernard and Austin's capital. The road led through very dense woods and over wet and muddy hills. About twelve miles from San Felipe the party was met by Samuel May Williams, Austin's confidential secretary, who, in the temporary absence of Austin from San Felipe, did the honors to the

Commission and lodged the staff in "a house prepared for the purpose," which was probably the hall of the newly-established *ayuntamiento*. When Austin returned, Terán presented to him formal letters of introduction from Músquiz and from Seguín, who begged Austin to be especially cordial to his old friend. The members of the Commission were detained in the village to make extensive repairs on the wagons. Since the Brazos was rising, "seeking," as Austin remarked, "to emulate the Mississippi," the party was forced to remain at San Felipe for two weeks (April 27-May 9, 1828).

The members of the staff amused themselves variously. Colonel Batres became intimate with Williams and visited him at Austin's house on the bank of the *Arroyo Dulce,* in the "West End" of San Felipe. Here he saw Austin's extensive library, and noted with something like amazement Rees's Encyclopædia in forty-seven volumes, containing admirably illustrated articles on natural history by several eminent American naturalists, such as Alexander Wilson, Thomas Say, and George Ord. The articles on botany and Say's epoch-making articles on entomology and conchology profoundly impressed Batres. Yet that such a work of learning could be found far from the borders of civilization, in Texas, was only a seeming incongruity on the frontier, as will become evident in the course of later chapters. It was precisely what should have been expected.

The soldiers who had been assigned to Terán as a bodyguard enjoyed themselves in Vicente Padilla's faro game in Cheeves's saloon. Berlandier employed his time in making botanical collections. This locality was later to be very carefully explored for plants by Thomas Drummond (1833-4) and Ferdinand Lindheimer (1839 and 1844). Of the collections made here on this journey in 1828 by Berlandier, relatively few, apparently, ever reached DeCandolle and the other Genevese botanists. Most of the species that were collected by Drummond and Lindheimer were described as new by the British botanist, Sir William Hooker, and by Asa Gray. The loss of the specimens destined for DeCandolle is doubtless to be ascribed to the conditions under which the Commission worked, to Berlandier's serious illness, and to the inclement weather that prevailed at the time, which must have jeopardized very seriously the collections he had made. But more of that later.

Terán, a reticent though polite man, with his own reservations in respect of Americans, made friends with Austin, and apparently was sincere in his friendship, though not always ingenuous. Gaspar Flores, the Mexican land commissioner at San Felipe, a friend of both, cemented the relation.

Sánchez, the cartographer of the expedition, left an account of the town of San Felipe which throws interesting sidelights on the social life of early Texas, viewed through critical Mexican eyes.

This village [he wrote] has been settled by Mr. Stephen Austin, a native of the United States of the North. It consists, at present, of forty or fifty wooden houses on the western bank of the large river known as Río de los Brazos de Dios, but the houses are not arranged systematically so as to form streets; but on the contrary, lie in an irregular and desultory manner. Its population is nearly two hundred persons, of which only ten are Mexicans, for the balance are all Americans from the North with an occasional European. Two wretched little stores supply the inhabitants of the colony: one sells only whiskey, rum, sugar, and coffee; the other, rice, flour, lard, and cheap cloth. It may seem that these items are too few for the needs of the inhabitants, but they are not, because the Americans from the North, at least the greater part of those I have seen, eat only salted meat, bread made by themselves out of corn meal, coffee, and home-made cheese. To these the greater part of those who live in the village add strong liquor, for they are in general, in my opinion, lazy people of vicious character. Some of them cultivate their small farms by planting corn; but this task they usually entrust to their Negro slaves, whom they treat with considerable harshness. Beyond the village in an immense stretch of land formed by rolling hills are scattered the families brought by Stephen Austin, which today number more than two thousand persons. The diplomatic policy of this empresario, evident in all his actions, has, as one may say, lulled the authorities into a sense of security, while he works diligently for his own ends. In my judgment, the spark that will start the conflagration that will deprive us of Texas, will start from this colony. All because the government does not take vigorous measures to prevent it. Perhaps it does not realize the value of what it is about to lose.

More informative concerning San Felipe, and certainly more objective in its graphic description of this mother-town of American settlements in Texas, is Smithwick's account:

The town was still in its swaddling clothes when the writer made his advent therein in 1827. Twenty-five or perhaps thirty log cabins strung along the west bank of the Brazos River was all there was of it, while the whole human population... could not have exceeded 200. Men were largely in the majority, coming from every state in the Union, and every walk of life. . . . The buildings all being of unhewn logs with clapboard roofs, presented few distinguishing features. Stephen F. Austin had established his headquarters something like half a mile back from the river on the west bank of a little creek . . . that ran into the Brazos just above the main village. . . . Austin's house was a double log cabin with a wide "passage" through the center, a porch with dirt floor on the front with windows opening upon it, and chimney at each end of the building. . . .
Going down to the town proper . . . the first house on the left was my bachelor abode, and near it, on the same side, stood the "village smithy" over which I presided. Then came the Peyton tavern, operated by Johnthan [sic] C. Peyton and wife; the house was the regulation double log cabin. The saloon

and billiard hall of Cooper and Chieves [Cheeves], the only frame building in the place, was next below the Peyton's. The first house on the right as you entered the town from above was Dinsmore's store, and next to it the store of Walter C. White. The office of the "Cotton Plant," the first newspaper in the colonies, and near it the residence of the genial proprietor, Godwin B. Cotton, filled the space between White's store and the Whiteside Hotel, which differed from its companion buildings only in point of elevation, it being only a story and a half in height; through the center ran the regulation "passage," and at either end rose a huge stick and mud chimney.

It must not be understood that these rows of buildings presented an unbroken or even regular line of front; every fellow built to suit himself, only taking care to give himself plenty of room, so that the town was strung along on either side of the road something like half a mile. . . . Professional men, as a rule, did not affect offices.

The alcalde's office was in a large double log house standing back some distance from the main thoroughfare almost immediately in the rear of the Whiteside Hotel, which building it much resembled. By whom it was built, or for what purpose, I do not now remember, but my impression is that it was designed for a hotel. The walls of hewn logs were roofed in and abandoned at that stage. It was here the ayuntamiento held its sittings, and this window-less, floorless pen, through the unchinked cracks of which the wild winds wandered and whistled at will, was presumably the Faneuil Hall of Texas.

As the second week of their stay in San Felipe drew to an end, the members of the Commission, with their food supply daily becoming more and more depleted, planned to set out for Nacogdoches and the Sabine country. At least three routes were possible. Terán chose to cross the Brazos at the Atascosito Crossing at San Felipe, to continue on this road for two or three miles to Donahue's where it crossed the road leading from Groce's to Harrisburg, and then to continue up this road until he reached the Magdalena road at present Hempstead. This he planned to follow until it joined the LaBahía road, and so on to Nacogdoches. Ample food supplies could be got on the way at Colonel Jared Groce's plantation of "Bernardo," for a round price, of course.

And so, with some misgivings, the party prepared to cross a much-swollen Brazos; on May 9 the mules and carriages, with the horses, were taken over to await the arrival of the scientific staff of the Commission next day. The expedition was now in the last lap of its journey. Berlandier's opportunities for botanical collecting would soon be past; the success of his mission depended on securing a large number of specimens to be sent to his patrons in Geneva. How well he performed his duties has been made a matter of controversy. It is therefore of interest to examine the conditions under which the young naturalist had to work.

DeCandolle, in his broadcast censure of Berlandier, has the follow-

47

ing to say as the gravamen of his complaint. Speaking of the interest of a coterie of Genevese botanists in Middle-American botany, even after the poor success of Wydler, one of their collectors, in Puerto Rico, he remarks:

We had thought of Mexico because of its natural riches, then but little known, and because I had made an arrangement with M. Alamán, Minister of the Interior, who promised protection for my employee. He did not fail to fulfill every promise; and, among other favors, he attached him to a great government expedition for the delimitation of the northern frontier. But Berlandier profited little from these advantages. He sent some dried plants in small number, badly chosen, and badly prepared; he neglected completely the sending of animals and seeds, and the communication of notes on the country. At the end of some time he neglected even to write, so that for a long interval we did not know whether he was living or dead. We then found that we had spent some sixteen thousand francs for some dried plants that were not worth a quarter of that amount. This result, together with [the experience with Wydler], completely disgusted us with expeditions of this sort. . . .

And Asa Gray, in his obituary note on Dr. Charles Short (who, after Berlandier's death, came into possession of his herbarium), speaks with scorn of Berlandier, who "through apparent dishonesty, had failed to make any adequate return to the Swiss botanists who had sent him to Mexico."

But there is something else to be said in the matter. Dr. John Briquet, DeCandolle's successor in the directorship of the Botanical Garden at Geneva, wrote these just and wise words in comment on DeCandolle's complaint:

Without wishing to excuse Berlandier for his negligence and the shortcomings which his work presented as far as it concerned animals, seeds, and manuscript notes, one ought nevertheless to observe that botanical explorations in Mexico were carried on at that time under *very* difficult material conditions, which it was hard to conceive of in Europe. Then again . . . it should be remembered that the collections of Berlandier aggregated several thousands of species, many of which are represented by a considerable number of specimens. . . . The collections of Berlandier have furnished . . . materials for the description of a great number of new species; it is by no means rash to affirm that the importance of the herborizations of this naturalist has gradually increased in the course of the last eighty years, and that the outlay of the little coterie of botanists at Geneva was not made in vain.

Early explorers have described with quiet eloquence the hazards of collecting in Texas: the swift "northers" which effect a drop of thirty degrees of temperature in as many minutes; the torrential rains which seem like an opening up of the windows of heaven; the torments of droves of gadflies by day, and incredible swarms of mosquitoes by night. Let the botanist, with unflagging diligence, gather hundreds of specimens by a hard day's work: at night there might come a rainstorm that despite every precaution would completely wet not only the specimens in the driers, but all the botanical drying paper as well. Or floods might carry away the drying paper and leave the naturalist stranded a thousand miles from any source of supply, as once happened to August Fendler on an expedition from St. Louis to Santa Fe. Elsewhere in this book (pp. 191-92) is reprinted a letter of Charles Wright showing how the fruits of the labors of weeks might be swept away by storms. The field-naturalist in Texas has ample reason to know that Sánchez' description of a storm encountered at San Felipe was not mere Latin exuberance:

At about five in the afternoon the sky was covered by black clouds, and a little after it seemed as if all the winds blew furiously at the same time, impelled by the pressure of the clouds. By about six the most terrible storm I have ever seen was raging. The rain was so heavy that it seemed as if the entire sky, converted to rain, was falling on our heads. The woods were afire with the vivid flashes of lightning, and nothing but a continuous rumbling of thunder was heard, louder or softer as the distance where the numberless thunderbolts from the heavy clouds fell was [less or greater]. The shock of the shrill howling winds was horrible and it continued until eight o'clock next morning, when only the northwest wind that had triumphed in the struggle was blowing and a slight rain remained. I gave thanks to the Almighty for having come out unharmed from such a furious storm.

I doubt whether DeCandolle ever experienced such difficulties in his botanical travels.

In what way do these facts affect Berlandier's responsibility for nonperformance of his duties to his Genevese patrons? The answer lies in several considerations. First of all, collections faithfully made were ruined by conditions of weather for which Berlandier could hardly be held responsible. Here is an example: At Gonzales, at two o'clock on the morning of April 18, 1828, the expedition encountered a "furious" thunderstorm. The afternoon before, Berlandier had spent several hours in extensive collection of plants. The storm was a tropical thunderstorm lasting until four o'clock, followed by a light rain that did not cease until eight o'clock. Berlandier's plants were wet through, and this necessitated shifting them into new driers, an operation that delayed the departure until ten o'clock. Tents were no protection against such deluges; even in the General's tent, protection was to be had only by covering the bed with buffalo robes. Subsequently, the weather was hot and moist, proper drying was impossible, and spoiling was imminent. Thus may be explained in part the poor preservation of the Gonzales specimens.

Again, when Terán's train was halted by a broken wheel on Scull Creek, west of the Colorado (April 22), and Berlandier again had time to collect intensively, his efforts were brought to naught by rains that fell during a considerable part of the afternoon. In addition, the difficulties of transportation and shipping to the seacoast were an obstacle that materially reduced the effectiveness of the botanical explorer.

But the hardships encountered west of the Brazos were as nothing compared to those met with between San Felipe and the Trinity. Sánchez, no special pleader for Berlandier, can present the case without comment of our own:

May 10 [leaving San Felipe de Austin].—It must have been three in the afternoon when all the baggage was placed in the ferry boat, and, boarding it, we started down the river in search of a landing agreed upon because it was thought, and rightly, that on the opposite side of the village the landing would be very difficult. . . . We traveled this way for about two leagues, and then we entered, still on the same boat, through the midst of the flooded woods until we reached the road we were to follow afterward. We landed after the sun had disappeared completely, and we were trying to decide what to do, being ignorant of the whereabouts of the carriages [which had been sent on the day before], when we heard someone calling from the opposite bank of the bayou where we were. We at once made our way to the spot where the voice was heard. We found a soldier of our escort who told us that the carriages had not been able to pull out of the mudholes, and that they would not arrive until next morning. . . . Having heard this, . . . the General [Terán] ordered his cot to be placed in the woods, and Mr. Berlandier and I remained in the boat lying on the cargo. To the unbearable heat were added the continuous croaking of frogs . . . and a numberless legion of mosquitoes that bit us everywhere, all of which kept us from sleeping a wink. When the longed-for dawn broke we saw the terrible onslaught that these cursed insects had made upon us, leaving us full of swollen spots, especially on the face of the General, which was so raw that it seemed as if it had been flayed. . . .

May 14 [Between present Hempstead and Courtney].—We continued our march along hills covered chiefly with live-oak and walnuts, and some only with grass. The ground was so full of water, and there were so many mudholes, that it was necessary for the soldiers and the drivers to pull out the carriages, and even the mules at times by hand. For this reason we were barely able to travel more than four leagues during the entire morning and part of the afternoon. . . .

May 15 [Near present Navasota].—The road continued along hilly and wooded country with low marshes and such serious mudholes that it was necessary to pull out the carriages and horses by hand almost at every step because they sank so deep in the mud. With terrible fatigue we traveled about three leagues, and then the axle of one of the baggage wagons broke and we were obliged to halt at twelve o'clock in the midst of a very heavy thicket. There a soldier was almost [sunstricken] as the result of having lain down in the sun for about ten minutes. . . . In the afternoon, a furious rain came down that lasted until midnight, after which it continued to drizzle all the rest of the night, the ground being turned into a lake on account of its location, while we were in the most pitiable condition imaginable.

May 16 [Navasota to William Burney's].—In spite of the rain we continued our painful march through the flooded woods and after seven hours of fatigue, during which we advanced but one league because of mudholes, we camped near the house of [William Burney]. . . .

Holland's Place, May 17.—In the morning Mr. Berlandier and John, the cook, were sick with fever . . . in the afternoon we advanced about a quarter of a league in order to reach the house of [Francis Holland]. We carried the sick men in the [General's] carriage, and at the house we were provided with milk and chickens to feed them.

May 18.—Near the aforesaid house there was a great mudhole, and, in order to cross it, it was necessary to unload the baggage and take it across on mules, a task that lasted until midday. . . . As we were crossing a small creek, the shaft of the instrument wagon was broken [three times previously, since crossing the Rio Grande, the cavalcade had been halted by the breaking down of the instrument wagon, and it would be halted twice again before the party reached Robbins' Ferry on the Trinity] and it became imperative to remain on the spot. . . . Our patients continued to grow worse. . . . It was decided to make a bed in the carriage for Mr. Berlandier. . . . Mr. Chovell took charge of the sick, and Mr. Batres and I took charge of the kitchen, about which neither he nor I understood a thing. . . . In the afternoon the General fell ill with the same fever as the others, and he would have been as bad off as Mr. Berlandier had not an accident saved him. At midnight the sky became overcast with heavy clouds and a furious storm broke out which lasted until dawn. As the water that fell in torrents came through the tents, the General ordered that a buffalo skin be thrown over his bed to protect him, and with this weight over him, he perspired so freely that the following day he had no fever.

May 19 and 20.—We remained in the same place and the sick men became worse, their condition being serious. . . .

May 21.—. . . By persistent efforts on the part of the troops and drivers we succeeded in crossing [a swollen creek] after losing three hours in this task, during which time we suffered considerably because of the mosquitoes that attacked us without pity. Hardly had we overcome this obstacle when we came across others of the same nature, for these thick woods have numerous creeks and marshes that make traveling through them very difficult. Finally, the instrument wagon broke down [for the fifth time], and we had to halt, much to our displeasure.

May 22.—. . . food is scarce, even now. The patients have become better.

May 23.—Although we traveled for eight hours in the morning and afternoon on the 23rd, we hardly covered more than three or four leagues because we had to cross five creeks . . . covered by thick clouds of mosquitoes that bothered us considerably.

May 24.—The following day we had to cross many creeks like the previous ones, and we were obliged to halt at about three because the instrument wagon broke again [for the sixth time]. The patients were better in the morning, although still very weak. There was no other food but rice, half spoiled, all that remained of our provisions.

By the time they had reached the Trinity, the malaria had so weakened Berlandier that he could collect hardly any plants on the return trip to Bexar over the Upper Road; and the great botanical expedition that DeCandolle had set so much store by was over, with results that, to the sponsors back in Geneva at least, were to seem entirely inadequate. Disasters at the Brazos and the Colorado on the way back still further damaged such specimens as Berlandier had preserved.

DeCandolle, as we have seen, expressed the opinion that Berlandier had failed in the mission assigned. Our judgment in the matter must take into account the difficulties under which the collector labored, and these were clearly so great as to make it impossible for Berlandier to do all that was expected of him. But another question concerns the actual number and value of the specimens that finally reached DeCandolle and his associates in Geneva. Here, too, some qualification should be made of DeCandolle's estimate. Among the archives in the library of the United States National Museum is a little volume in Berlandier's handwriting labeled "Expédition." It is a list of shipments of plants, seeds, and animals sent to DeCandolle and to Moricand in Geneva. The list gives a full invoice of all items included; and from it I learn that between April 25, 1827, and November 15, 1830 (the approximate date when the Commission was dissolved), Berlandier sent in all 188 packets of dried plants totaling some 55,077 specimens; 198 packets of plant seeds; 935 insects; 72 birds; 55 jars and bottles of material in alcohol; and more than seven hundred specimens of land and fresh-water mollusks, mostly from Texas. These are but the chief collections sent.

It may be thought that for some reason DeCandolle did not receive all the items dispatched to him. I know only that Berlandier's manuscript lists 2320 "numbers"; and in a catalogue sent by Alphonse DeCandolle to Asa Gray, giving the names of plants collected by Berlandier, received by his sponsors in Geneva, and by them distributed, there are 2351 numbers. The manuscript catalogue in the Gray Herbarium library and the covering letter from Alphonse DeCandolle, dated April 24, 1855, are all the evidence needed to show that the shipments entered by Berlandier in his private book, for his eye only, reached their destination.

Berlandier went out specifically to collect for the Geneva group during the life of the Boundary Commission. He fulfilled, or nearly fulfilled, his task. If it seems odd that he apparently made no effort to defend himself against DeCandolle's criticism, we must try to understand the mental processes of the collector, remembering that men are often impelled by behavior complexes to do that which is inwardly repugnant to them. Berlandier soon became aware of De-Candolle's outspoken dissatisfaction with his work in Texas. He alone

knew at what cost of health and spirit he had made those fragmentary and imperfect, but nevertheless respectable collections. Had he
felt equal to a presentation of his case before DeCandolle such as
Charles Wright made in the face of Asa Gray's petulance (to Gray's
lasting good), he might have vindicated himself and continued with
his explorations. But he was a mere boy, while DeCandolle was a
mature man with a continental and more than continental reputation. Berlandier had known him at Geneva, and had observed how
the whole world came to DeCandolle. What defense could this
twenty-two-year-old youth make that would be satisfying to the great
European scientist? There was only one thing Berlandier could do:
run away from the undeserved censure and build up within himself
a compensating sense of injury and of his own rectitude. Had he
been able to talk over matters with Terán, whom he ardently ad-
mired, things might have been well. But Terán was a busy man,
called to the highest responsibilities of state. And six years after Berlandier's arrival in Mexico, Terán died, under tragic circumstances,
at Padilla.

So Berlandier remained in America even after the conclusion of
the labors of the Commission. He settled in Matamoros, married a
Mexican woman, engaged in the pharmaceutical business, and continued to indulge his interests in natural history. Between 1830 and
1851 he made frequent botanical explorations in various parts of
Mexico; and in the spring and early summer of 1834, with his old
friend Chovell, who had been mineralogist with the Boundary Commission and was then living at Goliad, Berlandier made a collecting
trip as far as Bexar. He set himself up as a physician to the Mata-
moreños, upon his own recognizance; and, by the admission of the
younger DeCandolle, practiced medicine "in a manner equally honorable and disinterested." Lieutenant (later General) D. N. Couch, who
visited Matamoros and bought Berlandier's collection, wrote to Professor Spencer F. Baird in the 'fifties that "Berlandier . . . was uni-
versally beloved for his kind, amiable manners, and regard for the
sick poor of that city; being always ready to give advice and medicine
to such without pay." He became a man of influence in Matamoros,
and when General Zachary Taylor, at the outbreak of the Mexican
War, marched from Corpus Christi to the Rio Grande, Berlandier
was the bearer of a message from General Arista, at Matamoros, to
General Taylor demanding that the Americans refrain from crossing
the Arroyo Colorado. He was in charge of the hospitals at Matamoros during the early part of the war. And at the Worth-Vega
conference in that city, Berlandier served as interpreter for the Mexican general.

Berlandier met death by drowning in an attempt to cross the San Fernando River, south of Matamoros, in 1851. In 1853 his extensive collections of Mexican animals, his ample herbarium, his books, papers, publications, unpublished drawings, and political pamphlets dealing with events of the time in Mexico—all were purchased by Lieutenant D. N. Couch, and have been dispersed. In the portions of Berlandier's collections preserved in various libraries there are manuscripts on the topography of Texas and Mexico, and on the Indians of Texas; Terán's notes on Texas; and a host of other materials. But of the man himself, very little is known. Neither Kew, Geneva, nor Stockholm (although the *Iconothèque* at the Botanical Garden in Stockholm is one of the finest in the world), nor the Gray Herbarium at Cambridge, possesses a portrait of Berlandier. The man's work, however, is memorialized in scores and scores of scientific names of botanical species named in his honor. In Mexico, and also in Texas, the epitaph of Sir Christopher Wren is most appropriate for Berlandier: *"Si monumentum requiris, circumspice."*

Berlandier was born of a very poor family. He acquired for himself a sort of classical education: Latin, Greek, surveying, drawing. He did monumental work for botany in early Texas and in Mexico. Before he died he had become a person of substance in his adopted city in Mexico, a man genuinely respected in a day when such men were conspicuously rare. Had he not been handicapped by the psychological effects of struggle and privation in his youth and by a sense of poverty, had he had in his later years the stimulation of his Genevese home and his early associates, he might have become one of the lights of botanical science in his day. *¿Quién sabe?*

Thomas Drummond 4

TO set the stage for the entrance of Thomas Drummond into the Texas of the eighteen-thirties, one must paint a backdrop of pestilence, flood, and social disorganization in that remote province, which was then a barely planted colony.

The plague had begun far away—in India. Early in 1826, cholera, always endemic there, was on the increase throughout lower Bengal. In the spring it reached Benares, and the next year Nahin, in the Himalayas. It broke out in Teheran, near the Caspian Sea, in 1829, and reached Moscow the next year. In April of 1831 the plague reached Warsaw, and in the autumn Hamburg. A ship carried it to Sunderland, near Newcastle, in October. On June 3, 1832, the brig *Carricks,* of Dublin, arrived at Grosse Isle in the St. Lawrence with a passenger list of 145 immigrants, of whom forty-two had died of cholera. On June 24, the first case of cholera appeared in New York City, with the first death two days later. Thence the plague spread to Erie, Pennsylvania, on June 26; Cleveland, July 22; and St. Louis, September 10. At the end of October it had reached New Orleans, where it wrought terrible havoc. Thus by the routes of trade did the dread disease spread itself throughout the world. Europe and North and Central America bore the brunt of a progressive epidemic that carried to death hundreds of thousands of victims.

Austin's struggling colony in Texas did not escape. At this time it had been ten years in the making. In December, 1822, Stephen F. Austin, with his band of twenty families, had arrived on the banks of the Brazos, "in the center of the wilderness, surrounded by hostile Indians, and far remote from all resources." In the intervening years the twenty families had grown to many thousands; a score of thriving towns had sprung up and a rudimentary culture was beginning to be evident. Austin had laid the foundations of his enterprise with foresight. His ideal, as he outlined it in a letter, was to "take from my native land and from every other country the best that they contain and plant it in my adopted land—that is to say, their best inhabitants, their industry and their enlightenment." In spite of the difficulties that surrounded the colony, in spite of weather conditions that year after year brought bad crops ("this year has been bad—unusually wet, and filled with trouble, but next year will be better," Austin wrote to his sister at the close of 1832), the Empresario saw his dreams for Texas slowly being realized. Then came the cholera.

It is difficult to learn how the plague reached Texas. Between the first and the twelfth of April, 1833, the disease suddenly broke out in the village of Velasco at the mouth of the Brazos River; as Austin stated in a report to the Political Chief at Bexar, about a dozen of the American settlers there were attacked by the disease, and several died. Later the epidemic spread to the town of Brazoria, thirty miles distant, where it carried off a number of victims, the disease being generally fatal. The history of Texas might have been very different had not this epidemic deprived the colony of that military genius, Captain John Austin of Brazoria. At Guadalupe Victoria the cholera took off Don Martín de Leon, the empresario, and at Bexar it raged in a highly fatal form. Later the cholera spread to Mexico; in the capital more than ten thousand persons died of the disease. Stephen F. Austin himself, in the City of Mexico, was attacked by the cholera, but recovered.

Following the epidemic, which took its toll of the best in Texas, came the Great Overflow of 1833. The whole season was an abnormal one. At San Felipe, on the Brazos River, the last part of January had been unusually cold. In March, throughout a considerable part of Texas there had been heavy rains and extremely high water. The Brazos rose out of its banks, so that boats arriving at Velasco were compelled to wait a week before coming up the river to Brazoria, then the most important shipping point in Texas. Fields of cotton and corn, planted usually at Brazoria between the first and fifteenth of March, were completely inundated; in fact, all crops subject to overflow were lost. Not until late June did the water recede enough to permit the replanting of cotton. Corn, which was the chief staple of food, was not raised this year in sufficient quantities to feed the people; sometimes families went for days without meal. Even as late as May 9, Austin, then at Bexar, speaks of the country as flooded by excessive rains. To cap it all, an early frost, occurring at Brazoria on the twenty-first of October, injured much of the cotton, then just opening, which had been planted during the last week of June.

After a very wet spring and summer, from the middle of September on the weather had been very dry. It was in general a "year of misfortune," as Mrs. Holley said, "which threw the colony back some say seven years."

Added to all this were difficulties of a civil and political nature. The original settlers brought in by Austin, "The Three Hundred," were remarkably law-abiding citizens. Austin wrote in December, 1824, to Baron de Bastrop that during the preceding eighteen months there had been only one theft. In the ensuing decade, however, great changes had taken place in the composition of the population of Texas. The frequent revolutions in Mexico and the resulting administrative changes in Texas induced a condition of anarchy which gave to all good men grave concern. Administration of justice almost ceased. Overflow and cholera had wrought their havoc, but here was a canker at the heart of the body politic. The situation is forcefully described by Jonas Harrison, a cultivated citizen of Tenaha district (in present Shelby County), in a letter to Stephen F. Austin:

Look at our situation under the present constitution and the state's laws as organized among us. To say nothing of assaults and battery, Slander, Libels, Larcenies in every sense of the word, and there have been about twelve men killed among us in a few years and not a person judicially punished for any of these offenses.

Austin himself, in the Address of the Central Committee to the Convention of April 1, 1833, at San Felipe, said:

A total interregnum in the administration of justice in criminal cases may be said to exist. A total disregard of the laws has become so prevalent, both amongst the officers of justice, and the people at large, that reverence for laws or for those who administer them has almost intirely [sic] disappeared and contempt is fast assuming its place, so that the protection of our property our persons and lives is circumscribed almost exclusively to the moral honesty or virtue of our Neighbor.

And in a report to the Mexican Minister of Relations Austin wrote:

Texas is today exposed to being the sport of ambitious men, of speculators and reckless money changers, of seditious and wicked men, of wandering Indians who are devastating the country, of adventurers, of revolution, of the lack of administration of justice and of confidence and moral strength in the government. In short, for the want of government that country is already at the verge of anarchy. . . . If crime is punished, it has to be done extra-judicially. . .

Thomas Drummond, the Scottish naturalist, came into this distracted country in the spring of 1833, from New Orleans, where he had been collecting specimens of plants and birds. His stay in Texas was to extend over but a short period of time—from March, 1833, to the middle of December, 1834—but during this interval he was able to make remarkable collections of plants and thus stimulate the later studies of such botanical collectors as Lindheimer and Wright. Drummond himself had become interested in the plant and animal life of Texas while visiting in Missouri in 1831 and 1832. There he had learned of the collections Berlandier had made in Texas, and as a result had resolved that at the earliest opportunity he would himself collect in that area.

He was enabled to make the trip under the patronage of Sir William Jackson Hooker, who was then Regius Professor of Botany in the University of Glasgow, and was later to become Keeper of the Royal Botanical Gardens at Kew. Working for Hooker, Drummond made extensive collections of plants and birds in Texas—embracing seven hundred and fifty species of plants, and about a hundred and fifty specimens of birds. His explorations coincided with the time of the cholera epidemic and the Great Overflow, the growing unrest over the encroachments of the Mexican Government in Texan affairs, and the increasing social strain. In spite of difficulties, however, Drummond's collections were the first made in Texas that were extensively distributed among the museums and scientific institutions of the world.

This pioneer botanical collector's experiences in Texas are best described in his letters to his patron, Professor Hooker. These are five in number: a sixth, written in October, 1834, apparently never reached Hooker. The first letter, written from Velasco about two months after Drummond arrived in Texas, is reproduced below (technical botanical matters being omitted):

Town of Velasco, mouth of the Rio Brazos, Texas,
[May 14, 1833.]

. . . We had a favourable passage from New Orleans to this place, and on our arrival [about March 14?] found the river so high that it occasioned a delay of a week before we could reach the town of Brazoria, which is only about twenty miles up the river. The country, in general, is low and swampy, and ever since we came here, it has been flooded by the river: it consists almost entirely of prairies, except that the watercourses are bordered by woods, consisting chiefly of Live Oak and Poplar, with an undergrowth of Carolina Cherry. I remained a few days at Brazoria, and having an opportunity of sending by vessel to New Orleans, I dispatched the specimens which I collected without delay. Never having seen any part of the sea-coast in this neighborhood, I determined on returning to the mouth of the Rio Brazos, and commencing my operations there. I accordingly came back [about April 2] to this place, which nearly proved fatal to me, for when I had been here about ten days, and completed a collection of the few plants then in flower, and made arrangements for going to Galveston Bay in the same vessel that brought me hither, I was suddenly seized with cholera. Though ignorant of the nature of the disease and the proper remedies, I fortunately took what was proper for me, and in a few hours the violent cramps in my legs gave way to the opium with which I dosed myself. In the course of the same day the Captain [of the boat on which Drummond had come to Velasco some days before] and his sister were taken ill and died, and seven other persons died in two or three days—a large number for this small place, where there are only four houses, one of which was unvisited by the disease. All the cases terminated fatally, except mine, and always in ten or twelve hours, save one person, who lingered a few days. The weather was particularly cold and disagreeable for more than a week before the cholera appeared; indeed the air here is constantly saturated with moisture, so as to render the proper preservation of specimens a work of absolute impossibility. I am almost afraid that the accompanying collections, which I have taken the utmost pains to dry sufficiently, may not reach you in good order. My recovery from cholera was very slow. When my appetite returned, I was nearly starved for lack of food, the few individuals who remained alive being too much exhausted with anxiety and fatigue to offer to

procure me anything. I am now, thank God, nearly well again, though my face and legs continue much swollen, a symptom which was very violent when I first began to recover, and is gradually wearing off. As far as possible, I am endeavoring to replace the specimens which were spoiled during my illness, and have just packed up the whole, consisting of about a hundred species of plants, and as many specimens of birds, consisting of about sixty species, some snakes, and several land-shells. . . . Among the plants are several which I would particularly recommend as deserving of notice for their beauty: two are species of *Coreopsis,* one . . . extremely handsome. There is also . . . [a beautiful variety of *Gaillardia*]—the blossoms are copper-coloured, and the whole rises to about a foot high, and covers a diameter of three or four feet; I may safely say that I have seen more than a hundred flowers open on it at the same time. . . . I trust that my collection of bird-skins from Louisiana has reached you safely. . . . The want of my tent and the chief part of my ammunition, which I was obliged to leave at St. Louis, proves a serious inconvenience to me. To-morrow I intend making an attempt to reach Brazoria again, but the greater part of the journey is waist-deep in mud and water; thence I shall go to San Felipe, whither my baggage is already sent, sixty miles beyond Brazoria. Above the latter place, the river is not navigable for boats so that my luggage must go in waggons. I feel anxious about my collections, which I leave here, to await a vessel going to New Orleans; but there is no help for it, and from the interior of the country it is still more difficult to obtain conveyances, the charge for freight being so enormous as to exceed the value of the collections. The cost from Brazoria to New Orleans is forty cents per [cubic] foot, and the amount of my passage and luggage hither was fifty dollars. Boarding averages six dollars a-week, and that of the roughest kind. It is, however, so long since my hope of being able to realize any thing more than will cover my expenses has been dispelled, that I am not disappointed, and my only desire is to remunerate those who have contributed to my outfit, and by the collections of Natural History specimens which I shall send home, to give a good general idea of the productions of this part of the world. . . . I could ask a thousand questions about my plants, for I am shut out from all information; though Pursh's American Flora is among my luggage, I hardly get a sight of it. You may form an idea of the difficulties I have to encounter in this miserable country (more miserable, however, as to its inhabitants than in any other respect) when I tell you that all the bird-skins I sent you were removed with a common old penknife, not worth two cents, and that even this shabby article I could not have kept had the natives seen anything to covet in it; and that I am obliged to leave behind my blanket and the few clothes that I have brought, because of the difficulty of carrying them, though I feel pretty sure that I shall never see them again. These trifles I only mention to give you some idea of my present situation; they do not affect me much, except as preventing me from pursuing the objects of my journey with the success that I could wish. I have not yet positively fixed my future plans, but I wish to go westward from San Felipe. . . .

Velasco, at the time of Drummond's arrival, was but a small village, having been laid out the year before. In the spring of 1833, according to Major George B. Erath in his *Memoirs,* Velasco had about fifty inhabitants. This figure is probably an overstatement, for Stephen

F. Austin places the population at about twenty. The houses were mere shanties, with one unfinished building of two storeys and a small salt works maintained by the Porter brothers near the beach. A keel-boat ran from Velasco to Columbia, but here travel by water ended, and the remainder of the journey to San Felipe, the "town of Austin," had to be made by ox team. Brazoria was fifteen miles distant by land from Velasco, and thirty miles if one followed the meanders of the Brazos. Its citizens had made more progress than had those of Velasco, although the town was surrounded by the Brazos bottom and subject to overflow. In 1833 more than a score of houses had been completed there, and it was the most important shipping point in Texas. It had two streets paralleling the river, with intersecting cross streets. San Felipe, the capital of Austin's colony, had been laid out in 1824 by Austin and the Baron de Bastrop at a distance from Velasco of eighty miles by land or one hundred and eighty miles by the Brazos River. In 1832 it was a settlement of about thirty families, with several stores and two taverns where travelers, such as Drummond, might stay as guests, living on the very simple fare to which Texans were accustomed.

Other travelers have left descriptions of the hardships that the way-farer in early Texas had to endure. Olmsted, who visited the country twenty years later, complained of the cornbread-and-bacon diet that was still the constant fare, and Dr. Martin Ruter, the Methodist missionary in Texas, described living conditions in 1838 as follows:

The accommodations, of course, are often poor. Many of the houses are cabins, without glass windows, and with but little furniture. The chief food is corn bread, sweet potatoes, and meat. Butter, cheese, and milk are scarce [where he was, at Egypt in Wharton county].

Too, the Overflow of 1833 was unprecedentedly high: Erath, in his memoirs, states that Indians at San Felipe who were a hundred years old declared they had never seen the Brazos as high as it was in early May.

During the summer of 1833, nevertheless, as occasion offered, Drummond continued his botanical explorations in the Austin Colony. His activities are described in two letters written to Hooker during the summer and autumn of that year:

San Felipe de Austin, Aug. 3, 1833.

. . . Early in May last, I put up a box of specimens for you, while I was staying at Velasco, at the mouth of the Rio Brazos; and I then stated my intention of going to Brazoria, and proceeding higher up in the country. This plan I accomplished, though in an unexpected manner, for the river had risen to a height so unprecedented, that a boat brought me across the prairies, which were flooded to a depth of from nine to fifteen feet! On arriving at Brazoria, I found the whole town overflowed, and the boarding-house floor was covered with water a foot deep. I determined, therefore, that my stay should be as short as possible, and took the first opportunity of a boat to Bells [Landing], where I was so happy as to see some dry land; a commencement of the prairie country, which extends uninterruptedly to the West. I had been very uneasy about my luggage, which preceded me, and I feared it had been deposited in the stowage, where the water stood six or eight feet deep, and much property had been consequently destroyed: but all was safe, and after remaining a few days at Bells, to recruit my strength for the journey, I commenced my walk to this place, collecting what plants I could find by the way. As it would be impossible to give you a detailed account of my adventures in this letter, I will endeavor rather to convey to you some idea of the botanical produce of the country. The collection which I left at the mouth of the river, amounted to one hundred species, and my list now contains three hundred and twenty, which are packed in excellent order: also, seeds, roots, and bulbs, with some bottles of reptiles. I hope these may reach Europe safely; but I am not without fears on that score, as the cholera is raging in this neighborhood and has nearly depopulated Brazoria. My health continues to be good, since I recovered from that disease, although I am necessarily much exposed from the nature of my pursuits; the weather, too, is extremely hot, probably near 100° of Farenheit [sic]. From this place, I intend to proceed immediately to a distance of about forty miles, near the source of the Brazos, when I shall be nearly half way to the Colorado river; but I have no prospect of carrying the requisite stock of botanical drying paper myself, together with a change or two of linen, which this warm climate renders absolutely necessary. . . .

About one-third of the plants collected on my route, were destroyed by the overflowing of the river. Vegetation is now recommencing, but I never witnessed such devastation; it has extended even two hundred miles [farther] up the river than this place. You will perceive that it is impossible for me to collect anything like a given number of species in a certain time, even during the winter, in this climate. . . .

During the summer Drummond collected plants west of the Brazos, as the following letter shows:

San Felipe de Austin, Oct. 28, 1833.

. . . I have this day forwarded a box of specimens, together with some growing plants, and several bottles, containing the fruit of a shrub, and some curious lizards and snakes. Amongst . . . the packets of seeds, are several very choice plants, not excelled in beauty by any species now in cultivation. The intention of pursuing my way westwardly, which I mentioned in my last, was carried into effect, and I returned here [from present Austin and Colorado counties] about ten days ago. The journey has produced about one hundred and fifty species of plants, bringing up my list to nearly five hundred; and I have sent numerous samples of nearly every kind. This collection may give you some idea of what might be expected, if I could reach the mountains; my prospect of effecting this would be, however, very precarious, even if ample means were within my reach, as the Indians have been very troublesome on the frontiers, and have killed several Americans on the Colorado river this autumn. During the approaching winter, I think of visiting the sea-coast; probably Harrisburg, near Galveston Bay, whence I may forward such things as I can collect, to New Orleans. I do not expect to make a very great addition to my number of plants, but rather anticipate that they will be of a different class. . . . After spending next summer in Texas, I should wish before returning to Scotland, to visit the extreme western parts of Florida. . . . Since commencing this letter, two or three nights of frost have destroyed every vestige of vegetation. . . .

According to his plan, Drummond spent the winter and spring months of 1834 on Galveston Island and the shores of the bay, hoping there to collect for the museum of the Zoölogical Society of London and for Hooker as complete a set as possible of the birds and mammals of that region. His efforts, however, met with comparatively slight success, as for some unknown reason scarcely any migratory birds visited the bay during the winter. In April he returned to San Felipe intending to explore the Brazos in its upper reaches and to make a journey to the Colorado, and to the hills of the Edwards Plateau. He describes his difficulties vividly:

. . . It is my desire this summer to advance as far into the interior as possible; but several difficulties lie in the way. The Indians are becoming very dangerous, and news has just arrived of the murder of a surveying party, consisting of Captain [Francis W.] Johnston and nine men, at one hundred and fifty miles above this place. [The report was incorrect.] This is another instance of the mercy of Providence in sparing my life, as I had designed to join this very party, if I could have arrived from the coast in time. The necessity of having all *the luggage carried,* is another great hindrance to my movements; I may state that I had to navigate an old canoe from Galveston Bay to Harrisburg, a distance of from eighty to one hundred miles, all by myself, and with hardly any provisions; for, owing to the failure of last year's crops, famine is threatening the inhabitants of this district: and when [I] arrived there, I was obliged to hire a cart and oxen to come to this place, for which I paid sixteen dollars. But amidst all these difficulties, there is one blessing, for which I cannot be too thankful— I enjoy excellent health; and, I can assure you, that it has been tried with such fatigue that would have broken down thousands. I have added a few plants, lately, to my stores, some of them very handsome. . . . This is the worst country for insects that I ever saw; the custom of burning the prairies probably accounts for it. I have procured many specimens of a curious Lizard [perhaps *Sceloporus spinosus*] found about Galveston, but I detain them to go with the others from New Orleans. . . .

Some months later, after returning to San Felipe from collecting journeys to Tenoxtitlan and Gonzales, Drummond writes to his patron as follows:

San Felipe de Austin, Sept. 26, 1834.
. . . You are, doubtless, anxious to hear from me, no opportunity of forwarding any letters to you having offered since April last, when I stated my intention of proceeding to the Upper Colony [of Austin], as soon as possible. This

I did, and had reached the Garrison [or Tenoxtitlan], one hundred miles above this place; and made arrangements for joining a band of friendly Indians, who were going to hunt near the sources of Little River [in present Bell County], one of the tributaries of the Rio Brazos, when the news that a packet of letters was here, which might contain instructions for my movements, reached me, and I returned hither to take them up, and, consequently, lost the chance of accompanying the Indians. . . . I am sorry to say that I have found no insects, as they are very scarce in these and all prairie countries, owing to the frequent burning [over] of these lands. The whole country, from the Rio Colorado to the Guadaloup [sic], a distance of eighty or ninety miles, is as destitute of verdure as the streets of Glasgow, except some small patches along the creeks. After returning to San Felipe [from Tenoxtitlan], for my letters, as I before stated, I joined a waggon which was bound for Gonzales, in Guadaloup, one hundred miles distant; but having exposed myself to the burning sun, in the middle of several days, I was seized with bilious fever, which was nigh proving fatal, and has been followed by violent boils and a disease, here called Felon [paronychia] in my thumb. The latter rendered my hand useless for about two months, and I caused the place to be opened, and several bits of bone to be removed; and some other pieces have since worked out, so that I have been threatened with the loss of my thumb; but I hope to escape this disaster. Were it possible for me to reach the mountains, I could easily double the seven hundred species, which is the number of what I have collected in Texas. . . .

Evidently a letter written in October, 1834, miscarried, for although Drummond refers to it in his next letter to Hooker, it is not to be found among the letters published in Hooker's account of Drummond's journeys in the Southwest.

Drummond left Texas about the fifteenth of December, 1834, and arrived in New Orleans the nineteenth of that month. His last weeks in Texas had not been pleasant. "My last opportunity of writing you was from San Felipe, in October," Drummond wrote to Hooker the day after his arrival in New Orleans.

I am sorry to say [he continued] that I have had a violent attack of diarrhoea, accompanied by such a breaking out of ulcers, that I am almost like Job, smitten with boils from head to foot, and have been unable to lie down for seven nights: but as I am a little better, I hope to be well in a short time.

Altogether, during his explorations in Texas Drummond had conceived a highly unfavorable view of the country and its inhabitants. His sojourn, what with the Overflow, and the cholera, and the shortage of food, undoubtedly entitled him to entertain such an opinion. Yet in his next letter to Hooker we find Drummond making plans to bring his family to Texas, where, as he said, "a few years would soon make me more independent than I can ever hope to be in Britain." This letter, which he wrote on Christmas Day, 1834, from

64

New Orleans, outlined plans to Professor Hooker that if carried out would have been of the greatest importance in the scientific exploration of Texas:

> The question naturally arises as to what I shall do at home, and as I do not think it would be advisable for me to remain there, I have determined, if sufficient funds can be obtained, to return with my family to Texas, where I can buy a league of land for one hundred and fifty dollars, and if I can add the purchase of a dozen cows and calves, which cost ten dollars each (that is, the cow and calf) [my fortune is made.] . . . I should then have an opportunity of exploring the country from Texas to the city of Mexico, and west to the Pacific, which would occupy me seven years at least. I am perfectly satisfied of the novelty which such a plan would afford. I have been given to understand that the Mexican Government wishes particularly to have the Natural History of its territories examined, and would liberally reward the person who did it. Now I am not vain enough to expect much remuneration for what I could do, still, with your assistance, I think I might, in the course of two or three years, publish a tolerably complete catalogue of the plants of that country, and, were proper application made, a grant of land would certainly be given me. . . . I find it would be absolutely necessary for me to return to Britain, in order to purchase a stock of necessaries, clothing, instruments for collecting insects, &c. Upon such articles as knives and forceps a person who could afford to lay out two or three hundred dollars would make cent. per cent. here, and a thousand per cent. on many things, so that the journey would cost nothing.

But Drummond was not destined to carry out this exciting plan for the exploration of the botanical resources of Texas. From New Orleans he went to Apalachicola, Florida, and from there, on February 9, 1835, he sailed for Havana, whence he intended to make a short collecting tour of the island of Cuba. It was his intention then to go to Charleston, where he would take passage for Britain. The particulars of Drummond's last days are not completely known, but in June, 1835, Professor Hooker received a communication from the British Consul at Havana enclosing a certificate of Drummond's death in that city early in March. Thus, far from home and kindred, after surviving a thousand perils in his career as a botanical collector, including the dread cholera in Texas, he met death, alone. If we would seek an epitaph, let it be that of Albrecht Dürer, *Emigravit.*

Thus much regarding the work of Thomas Drummond in Texas. I must confess that the record of his life here is all too meager. One follows with a feeling akin to dismay an account that proceeds from discouragement to the promise of more ambitious achievements and then—the finality of death. This proposal of Drummond's to make a complete botanical survey of Texas—was it merely the grandiose scheme of a visionary? If he had lived, should we have had any tangible results from his proposed survey, or would his work have fallen short of his anticipations? How might his further labors have affected the development of science in Texas? Useless thoughts, these, the balancing of might-have-beens!

As Drummond is revealed in the letters to Hooker, he does not wear the habiliments of heroism. We demand a hero with the strength of a Hercules, the will of a Loyola, and the impetuousness and zeal of a Vesalius. In the Texas episode Drummond seems almost entirely lacking in these qualities. His bitter complaints against country and people left as ill an opinion of him in Texas as he had formed of his surroundings. His letters, published after being edited by Hooker, evoked from Mary Austin Holley a rejoinder which, as the only contemporary record of Drummond in Texas, I quote in its entirety:

Mr. Thomas Drummond of Glasgow has done more than any other man toward exploring the botany of Texas. He sent home many plants and seeds which have been successfully cultivated there, and drawings of them have been given in late numbers of Curtis's Botanical Magazine. He had made arrangements to settle his family in Texas, where he could have devoted himself with ardor to his favorite science, and where *with his land* and *his cows,* to use his own language, he could *have been more independent in a few years than he could ever have hoped to be in Great Britain.* Unfortunately for science, as for himself, Mr. Drummond took the year of the flood and cholera, 1833, to make his first, and only visit, to his adopted land; and in common with every body else, suffered much inconvenience and consequent sickness. Hence his views of the country are partial and drawn from present personal experience. He saw through jaundiced eyes—and not with the eyes of a philosopher. Notwithstanding he liked nothing, and nobody, he sent home seven hundred new specimens [species] of plants; and a hundred and fifty preparations of birds, obtained in a very few excursions; and resolved there to live and die; no poor compliment, surely, to any place, however we may, for the time being, abuse it.

However he may have fared in Texas, Drummond was a gifted naturalist having a distinguished record as an explorer and collector in Canada with Sir John Franklin's Second Overland Expedition (1825-27). Too, his sets of mounted mosses of Scotland (*Musci Scotici*) and of Canada (*Musci Americani*), issued in the late 'twenties, had been well received by botanists; and in 1830 he had been elected an Associate of the Linnæan Society of London. Both during his lifetime and after his death, new species of plants were named in his honor by such substantial botanists as Arnott, Bentham, David Don, Douglas, Asa Gray, Greville, Hooker, Lindley, Meyer, Nees, Richardson, Torrey, and Trinius. One does not receive such recognition unmerited. Yet so short a thing is fame that botanists of the present day have almost completely forgotten Drummond. His own contemporaries knew nothing of his parentage, birth, early life, or education; and with the passing of the years his botanical explorations in Canada—a truly heroic work—have been to a large extent forgotten. I shall endeavor to do partial justice to the personality and career of this great but almost forgotten naturalist.

Of Thomas Drummond's parentage, and the place and date of his birth, we can say nothing certain. He was born probably in the county of Perth, Scotland, about the year 1790. His family was a most distinguished one, having lived from time immemorial in Perthshire; the earls of Perth had been members of the family from the creation of the earldom. The family takes its name from the village of Drymen in Perthshire, and is descended from a Hungarian immigrant who came there in 1068.

It is not known where Thomas Drummond studied botany; perhaps he was encouraged in his scientific interests by his older brother James, Director of the Botanical Garden at Cork, who in 1810, when Thomas was about twenty years old, was elected an Associate of the Linnæan Society of London. Dr. Perley Spaulding states that Thomas Drummond in his youth worked in the nursery-garden of George Don the elder at Dog Hillock, near Forfar in the county adjoining Perthshire. This would have been a valuable experience, for Don was a botanist of parts who had retired to the management of the nursery-garden at Dog Hillock after service as Director of the Botanical Garden at Edinburgh. George Don, it might be remarked parenthetically, was the father of fifteen children, two among whom later did distinguished work in botany: Professor David Don (1800-41), of King's College, London; and George Don the younger (1799-1856), who served as a botanical collector.

Drummond's first opportunity for important collecting in the field came in 1825 with his appointment as Assistant Naturalist with Sir John Franklin's Second Overland Expedition, on the recommendation of Sir William Jackson Hooker, the eminent botanist. Hooker, who was, as Charles Darwin once said, "of a remarkably cordial, courteous, and frank bearing," had been since 1820 Regius Professor of Botany at the University of Glasgow, and during Drummond's early years had probably had a hand in the development of his botanical interests.

It was a great honor to be chosen a member of the second expedition that Sir John Franklin was leading to Arctic America; and when the chance of an appointment came to Drummond, he seized upon it eagerly. Sir John was known not only as a remarkably gifted Arctic explorer, who combined to a rare degree all the qualities requisite to investigation in the high latitudes, but also as a most humane man, one for whom his helpers, even the humblest, felt a warm personal affection. It was an incalculable privilege to work with such a leader. Then, too, very little had been done on the botany of western Canada. David Douglas, a former assistant in the Botanical Garden of the University of Glasgow (of which Drummond's patron, Professor Hooker, was Director), in 1824 had visited Oregon and California as a botanical collector for the Horticultural Society of London. Douglas was a Perthshire man, and it is certain that he and Drummond had early become acquainted. No doubt his accounts of the botanical riches awaiting the collector in the northern part of North America increased Drummond's eagerness to go with Franklin.

The personnel of the Second Overland Expedition was largely that of the First, of 1819-22. There was, of course, Franklin himself, no longer Captain Franklin, but Sir John, F.R.S., knighted and made a member of the Royal Society for his gallantry and his scientific achievements on the First Expedition. At this time he was thirty-nine years old. He was seconded by Dr. John Richardson, surgeon and naturalist to the expedition, the author in later years of the splendid volumes of the *Fauna Boreali Americana* covering the zoölogical findings of the two expeditions. Gruff though he was, and brusque to the point of insolence, Richardson was yet extremely kind to his men. Thomas H. Huxley's letters give several glimpses of this extraordinary man in later life. Huxley once said, for instance, that he "owed what he had to show in the way of scientific work or repute to the start in life given him by Richardson." In the 'forties he had been a pupil of Richardson at the Royal Naval Hospital at Haslar, and the teacher, seeing that Huxley's real interest was not in medicine but in natural history, had secured his appointment to H.M.S. *Rattlesnake,* then off to the explorations in Torres Strait. Huxley speaks of "Old John" in one of his letters as "an old hero . . . not a feather of him is altered, and he is as gray, as really kind, and as seemingly abrupt and grim, as ever he was. Such a fine old polar bear!" In another place he reiterates, "I always look upon him as the founder of my fortunes." At the time of the Second Overland Expedition, Richardson was thirty-eight years old, and had already proved his abilities in Arctic exploration with Franklin.

Another member of the party was Lieutenant (later Sir) George Back, who was then just twenty-nine. He had been with the earlier expedition and had shown dauntless determination. By incredible exertions and sufferings during the passage through the "Barren Grounds" of the Northwest Territory he had once saved Franklin from starvation. Later he was to become an admiral in the British navy, for "in bravery, intelligence, and love of adventure he was the very model of an English sailor." No danger or hardship on the two expeditions with Franklin was too great for Back. As another writer has declared, "It may be safely said that few sailors survived more terrible perils and hardships than Back did in the two expeditions under Franklin, and the two which he commanded himself."

These three were the chief members of the expedition; Drummond, appointed assistant to Richardson, made the fourth. They all were cast in heroic mold.

To Drummond was assigned the task of making a botanical exploration of the mountains of western Canada, while the rest of the expedition, under Franklin, Richardson, and Back, explored the Mackenzie and Coppermine rivers, and surveyed the coast of the Arctic Sea. The expedition set sail from Liverpool, February 16, 1825, on the American packet boat *Columbia,* and landed at New York on the fifteenth of March. The members of the party spent eight days in New York, where they were feted by officials of city and state. On March 23 they proceeded to Albany by boat, and thence by coach to Lewiston, through Utica, Rochester, and Geneva. They crossed the Niagara River, entered Canada, and viewed the Niagara Falls. Their itinerary took them finally to Penetanguishene on Lake Huron, whence in two large canoes they set out for the Northwest on April 23. On May 10 they reached Fort William on Lake Superior, and thence, by river, lake, and portage, they proceeded to Cumberland House on the Saskatchewan, fifteen hundred miles away as the crow flies. Their route led them up the Rainy River and Lake, Lake of the Woods, Lake Winnipeg, and the Saskatchewan River. They arrived at Cumberland House on June 15, and on the following day Drummond parted from other members of the expedition to botanize in the Rocky Mountains. From Cumberland House, Franklin led the rest of the party to Fort Chipewyan, the Great Slave Lake, and the Mackenzie River, and after a fruitful period of exploration in the far north, brought them back again to Cumberland House in the spring of 1827.

Drummond spent the summer of 1825 (June 28 to August 20) botanizing near Cumberland House and on the plains bordering the Saskatchewan River. On the twentieth of August, the boats of the Hudson's Bay Company arrived at Cumberland House. These were part of a "brigade" that was going from York Factory on Hudson's Bay to the Columbia River country in Washington and Oregon, in search of furs. Every spring such parties set out for all parts of Canada, and either returned that summer to their bases, or wintered in the wilderness, returning the following year. With the brigades traveled armed men. The journeys were made in long canoes, the use of which was made possible by the numerous streams and lakes of the Canadian northwest, and the shortness of the portages between them. Joining the brigade which was headed for the Columbia River country, Drummond set forth in one of the canoes, and arrived at Carlton House on the Saskatchewan the first of September.

It had been a part of Drummond's plan to stay here for some time, making collections in the neighborhood; but as the Indians at that time were menacing, he continued with the brigade to Edmonton House, also on the Saskatchewan. It was an unusual trip for Drummond, heretofore accustomed only to the hilly country of Perth, Stirling, and Forfarshire. It was, at the same time, work that called for the best in a man—for industry, persistence, and devotion to science. In the account of his Canadian explorations, Drummond describes his method of work during the trip up the Saskatchewan and other rivers to the Rocky Mountains, in present Saskatchewan and Alberta:

> The plan I pursued for collecting was as follows. When the boats stopped for breakfast, I immediately went on shore with my vasculum, proceeding along the banks of the river, and making short excursions into the interior, taking care, however, to join the boats, if possible, at their encampment for the night. After supper, I commenced laying down the plants gathered in the day's excursion, changed and dried the papers of those collected previously; which occupation generally occupied me until daybreak, when the boats started. I then went on board and slept till the breakfast hour, when I landed and proceeded as before. Thus I continued daily until we reached Edmonton House, a distance of about 400 miles, the vegetation having preserved much the same character all the way.

On this journey Drummond made many observations concerning the birds and mammals of the prairie, some of them extended, and all of them evidencing powers of accurate and discriminating judgment. At Edmonton House the brigade left the river for a portage of a hundred miles—which they made in six days—to the Athabaska River. Because of the lack of proper facilities for carrying luggage, Drummond was obliged to leave most of his equipment at Edmonton, for later forwarding. The brigade reached Fort Assiniboine on the Athabaska, where they spent three days preparing the canoes— this time smaller ones, as the river in places was shallower than the Saskatchewan had been—for the ascent of the Athabaska to the mountains, a distance estimated at two hundred miles. They quitted the Fort on the first or second of October, 1825, some of the party, because of the heavy loading of the canoes, being obliged to travel by land. Drummond, as he says in one of the rare bursts of enthusiasm in his narrative, "gladly agreed" to be one of these. I quote from his account of the trip:

We quitted the Fort accordingly . . . and started in high spirits for a journey on horseback [the horses being furnished from the Hudson's Bay post at the Fort]. A heavy fall of snow, however, which took place on the 4th, put a final period to collecting for this season; it also rendered our progress through these trackless woods very unpleasant, our horses becoming soon jaded, when the only alternative was to walk, and drive these before us. To add to these misfortunes, the poor animals were continually sinking in the swamps, from which we found it no easy task to extricate them. . . . The weather during this part of our journey, proved very unfavorable; snow and a thick fog prevented my making much observation on the vegetation, which, however, appeared to bear the same character until we approached the mountains.

They reached Jasper House, in present Jasper National Park of western Alberta, on the eleventh day (October 12 or 13, 1825) and the canoes arrived the following day. Henry House, where the portage began, was some fifty miles farther up the Athabaska River, and the traveling distance of the portage was about fifty-four miles. They stopped a day or two at Henry House to unload the canoes and pack the horses for the portage. The brigade departed on October 18, and Drummond was left alone with the Indians. "Everything was so new to me," he wrote, "and I had such agreeable anticipations as to the results of my next summer's occupations, that I scarcely felt the solitariness of my situation." An Iroquois Indian hunter named Baptiste had been assigned to Drummond by MacMillen, one of the Hudson's Bay officials; and in late October Drummond, Baptiste, Baptiste's sister, and her husband set out down the Athabaska for the Little Smoky, one of the eastern tributaries of the Peace, where Baptiste had proposed they should spend the winter. They never reached their destination. It appears that Baptiste's sister was on their journey taken in labor; that according to the customs of the Iroquois, she had to quit their tent until labor was over; and that, "owing to the extreme severity of the weather, the ground being covered with snow, and the mercury indicating 38 degrees below zero, both the mother and her infant perished." The surviving brother and husband were paralyzed by grief, and became so despondent that it was ten or fifteen days before they could be induced to quit the spot. They then went eastward to the Berland River, which they reached on January 1, 1826. In this locality Drummond remained until April.

Drummond has left an account of his first winter in the Canadian northwest, a narrative which is of value in showing the stuff of which the man was made. In his record of his travels, he says:

As we were now likely to remain stationary for a short time, I set about building myself a brushwood tent, formed of the boughs of the *White Spruce,* and soon completed it. . . . A slight shower of rain fell about the 10th of January, which is a very rare phenomenon at this time of the year; and it caused us great inconvenience . . . it became almost impossible to get near any animal [desired for food], owing to the noise made in walking, by the breaking of the [snow] crust. At this time, . . . the snow was about two feet deep, and it gradually increased till the 27th of March, its greatest average depth being from five to six feet. . . . The animals of all kinds were becoming more and more scarce, so that my hunter resolved upon leaving this spot, and accordingly removed 80 or 100 miles farther down the river, but I preferred remaining where I was, though my situation became very lonely, being deprived of books or any source of amusement. When the weather permitted, I generally took a walk, to habituate myself to the use of snow shoes, but I added very little to my collections. The hunter returned about the beginning of March, bringing with him some venison.

On April 1 Drummond set out for Jasper House, more than a hundred and fifty miles away as the crow flies. Here he hoped to receive letters from Sir John Franklin, who with all his company had been passing the winter at Fort Franklin on Great Bear Lake. Drummond hoped also to have word from home; and he was eager to collect specimens of the many migrant birds that stopped on the lakes near Jasper House—Brulé, Jasper, Maligne, and smaller lakes along the Athabaska. He made the trip, "the greatest journey [he] had ever yet performed in snow shoes," in six days, arriving at Jasper House on April 7, 1826. Two days later an official of the Hudson's Bay Company arrived from Edmonton House with Drummond's luggage, and more paper for pressing plants. From April 9 to May 6 Drummond collected birds on a small lake fifty miles away near Henry House, subsisting largely on whitefish, which he found abundant in the lake. The fur brigade returning from the Columbia River country came over the portage the sixth of May, and found Drummond at Henry House. He yielded to their importunities to accompany them as far as Jasper House. On the way he had an adventure which threatened to end his botanical career then and there. I quote from his account:

I went on before [the brigade] for a few miles, to procure specimens of a [moss], which I had previously observed in a small rivulet on our track. On this occasion I had a narrow escape from the jaws of a grisly [*sic*] bear; for, while passing through a small open glade, intent upon discovering the moss of which I was in search, I was surprised by hearing a sudden rush and then a harsh growl, just behind me; and on looking round, I beheld a large bear approaching towards me, and two young ones making off in a contrary direction as fast as possible. . . . This was the first I had met with. She halted within two or three yards of me, growling and rearing herself on her hind feet, then suddenly wheeled about, and went off in the direction the young ones had taken, probably to ascertain whether they were safe. During this momentary absence,

I drew from my gun the small shot with which I had been firing at ducks during the morning, and which, I was well aware, would avail me nothing against so large and powerful a creature, and replaced it with ball. The bear, meanwhile, had advanced and retreated two or three times, apparently more furious than ever; halting at each interval within a shorter and shorter distance from me, always raising herself on her hind legs, and growling a horrible defiance, and at length approaching to within the length of my gun from me. Now was my time to fire: but judge of my alarm and mortification, when I found that my gun would not go off! The morning had been wet, and the damp had been communicated to the powder. My only resource was to plant myself firm and stationary, in the hope of disabling the bear by a blow on her head with the butt end of my gun, when she should throw herself on me to seize me. She had gone and returned a dozen times, her rage apparently increasing with her additional confidence, and I momentarily expected to find myself in her gripe, when the dogs belonging to the brigade made their appearance, but on beholding the bear they fled with all possible speed. The horsemen were just behind, but such was the surprise and alarm of the whole party, that though there were several hunters and at least half-a-dozen guns among them, the bear made her escape unhurt. . . . For the future, I took care to keep my gun in better order, but I found, by future experience, that the best mode of getting rid of the bears when attacked by them, was to rattle my vasculum, or specimen box, when they immediately decamp. . . . My adventure with the bear did not, however, prevent my accomplishing the collecting of the *Jungermannia* [moss].

The summer and autumn of 1826 were filled with incessant travel and collecting, in spite of the plagues of mosquitoes caused by unusually heavy rains in the spring. After remaining at Jasper House from May 17 to June 15 collecting plants, Drummond spent the last half of June and nearly all of July near Lac-la-Pierre in the mountains to the north, returning to Jasper House before the end of July. In early August he again set out for Lac-la-Pierre, and later continued his journey to Providence on the Smoky River. This trip (August 4-24) was rather unproductive. In late September Drummond was still on the Smoky making pemmican from buffalo flesh in preparation for a return to the Columbia Portage. The return journey to the portage, which he reached October 17, was made by way of Edmonton House on the Saskatchewan. Joining a party of fur-traders that were making the portage, he went to its west end, the Boat Encampment of the Columbia. On the way he fell in with Finan Mc-Donald, a man of twenty years' service with the Northwest Company in western Canada. McDonald, who was quitting the country which he had long made his home, was setting out for the east, accompanied by his wife and family. The party reached Jasper House on October 30, and taking a boat to carry their belongings, started on November 12 to descend the Athabaska River to Fort Assiniboine. When they were about halfway to their destination, the stage of the water being very low and the weather being cold, with heavy snow, they stuck fast in the ice, and had to continue their trip by land. To quote Drummond:

As Mr. M'Donald's family were incapable of travelling, he agreed to encamp and remain with the luggage, . . . [while Drummond went on foot to Fort Assiniboine] whence we were to send horses to his assistance. We had calculated on reaching this place in three days, but it was the fifth evening before we arrived, having, however, met with no other hindrance than the unavoidable hardships of such a journey. . . . We received much kindness, on our arrival, from . . . the gentleman who has charge of the Fort, who also sent horses . . . to the relief of Mr. M'Donald who had suffered great anxiety . . . and whose provisions were nearly exhausted. He reached us, happily, about the 1st of December, bringing with him the whole of the luggage in good order.

On December 15, 1826, Drummond reached Edmonton House, and he remained there until mid-March preparing his specimens for shipment to England in the spring. Edmonton, which had been founded as a post of the Northwest Company about 1778, was now a small settlement of employees of the united Hudson's Bay and Northwest Company. It was the northwest center for the Company, and offered a convenient wintering-place for the naturalist. In early February, Drummond received a letter from Richardson telling him of the success of the northern expeditions, and asking Drummond to meet him at Carlton House, two hundred miles up the Saskatchewan, as soon as was convenient. On March 15, 1827, accompanied by an Indian guide, Drummond set out for his destination, but fearing hostile Indians, they took a course that led them greatly out of their way. Snow-blindness retarded their progress and made it impossible for them to shoot game. As a result, their provisions gave out, and they were driven to the ultimate necessity of devouring the dried skins of animals which Drummond had taken for the Zoölogical Society of London. "Our dogs became [excessively] fatigued," Drummond relates, "and so we were under the necessity of cutting up our sledge and carrying our luggage ourselves." Furthermore:

The provisions were wholly spent, and I was compelled to destroy a fine specimen of the *Jumping Deer*, . . . although it was the only one that we had been able to procure, and I had carried it all the way from the Columbia River, where I had procured it. As I had not been very particular in divesting this skin of the flesh, it proved the more valuable on that account. . . . Within about a day's journey of the Fort, . . . we had the good fortune to kill a *Skunk*, . . . which afforded us a comfortable meal. This creature, when hunted, discharges an intolerably fetid liquor upon its pursuers, and few dogs will afterward attempt to destroy it. The one we killed on the evening before we reached the Fort, proved tolerable eating, though it had a strong flavour of this obnoxious liquid.

At Carlton House they found that Richardson had become anxious about them. From April 5 until July 14 Drummond remained in the neighborhood of Carlton House, or engaged in explorations on the South Branch of the Saskatchewan River, probably getting as far south as present Saskatoon. He joined the rest of the party at Cumberland House on July 19, and with them went down the Saskatchewan and Nelson rivers, by portages, to York Factory on Hudson's Bay, whence they set sail for England. On October 15, 1827, two years and eight months from the time of their departure from Liverpool, they arrived in London.

The rest of the story is soon told. In 1828-29 Drummond was curator of the Botanical Garden at Belfast. In the years immediately following his return to Britain, he issued exsiccati of American mosses under the title *Musci Americani* in two quarto volumes, which included specimens collected chiefly on his journey with the Franklin Expedition. "The number of distinct species, thus procured," says Professor Hooker, "exceeds two hundred and forty, which, with the well-marked varieties, amount to two hundred and eighty-six kinds . . . the whole of the continent of North America has not been known to possess so many Mosses as Mr. Drummond has detected in this single journey." It was notable work. Many new species of flowering plants were also added to the known flora of America, some of which are so rare as to have escaped the ken of naturalists since Drummond's day.

In 1830-31 Drummond made another journey to America to collect plants in the western and southern parts of the United States. From New York he went successively to Philadelphia, Baltimore, and Washington, and then on foot followed the pike to Wheeling, collecting by the way. He planned to reach St. Louis in time to accompany Kenneth MacKenzie, a fellow-Scot of distinguished family who was in charge of the Upper Missouri Outfit of the American Fur Company, on his journey up into the Blackfoot and Assiniboine country of the upper Missouri valley, in present Montana. But as Drummond arrived too late to join MacKenzie, he remained at St. Louis until winter, making large collections of plants for Hooker in the vicinity. In Hooker's papers on Drummond's collections he lists numerous species collected in the Alleghenies, in Ohio, and at St. Louis, Jacksonville, Covington, and New Orleans. Drummond's best collecting during the years 1831-32 appears to have been done in the vicinity of New Orleans. In the spring of 1833 he left for Texas, on the journey which has already been described.

And now we come back to the central questions of Thomas Drummond's life. What was his essential character, and what would have been his influence on the development of botany in Texas had he lived and carried into effect the plans sketched for Hooker in his letter of Christmas Day, 1834? I confess to a sense of inadequacy in forming a judgment concerning a man of Drummond's cast of mind. Racial characteristics are so marked that only a Scot can judge a Scot. An admirable people, indeed, of brusque tenderness and grim kindness!

Yet the personality of the man emerges from his writings, however he may avoid the personal note. He was innately modest, but still he had a wholesome self-respect and a habit of self-appraisal of his work. The experiences recorded in the account of the Canadian explorations are narrated objectively. There is neither strutting nor mock heroics. Running through the whole is an undercurrent of conviction that the tasks were all in the day's work, duties that must be done without praise and without clamor. The descriptions of hardship, privation, severe exertion, and even of mortal danger merge into a tale of quiet brevity that runs along without break, highlight, or straining for dramatic effect. In Drummond's description of the country he explored in the vicinity of the Portage, he shows the greatest moderation. Few who have been in the territory he explored, and have gazed at Mount Robson, or Lake Maligne, or the Athabaska as it winds through the mountains to the east of the Great Divide between walls of snow-capped mountains, have been so restrained. An alpine region of incredible beauty—the finest on the continent, and among the finest in the world—prompted Drummond to only brief comment. One is almost reminded of Herbert Spencer, who gazed on Niagara (was it from the American side?) and remarked: "Much what I expected!"

As a rule men easily bear exceptional hardships and dangers, only to sink under common and long-continued burdens. Every traveler in the Arctic regions, even Sir John Franklin, has mentioned as chief among the burdens to be borne, the incredible clouds of mosquitoes that make life in high latitudes a misery. Such pests Drummond dismisses with a shrug—"the mosquitoes are much more plentiful here than I saw them anywhere else"—until one gets almost the sense of profanity when later he ejaculates, "The mosquitoes are also dreadfully numerous!"

There are a few touches of beauty in Drummond's account which reveal the hidden poet: descriptions of the fragrance of a flower, or the courtship or song of a bird—but these matters, also, are treated with restraint. Of a range of mountains whose beauty could hardly be suggested by a rainbow of words, he said, "They gratified me extremely." A few pages later, describing another sierra, he wrote with true Spartan frugality, "a fine range of mountains." This is the highland Scot, feeling dimly and massively the beauty and grandeur of nature, yet burying the current of his emotion deep beneath the surface.

The privations that Drummond underwent in the mountains of Canada far surpassed those he suffered in Texas. Yet in the one account we find a quiet Scottish song of jubilation; in the other, a succession of jeremiads. It must be recalled, however, that during his sojourn in Texas Drummond was suffering the cumulative effect of past privations and exposures. During a good share of the time that he had spent at St. Louis in 1831, he had been ill. Seven years had passed since he had done his best work in the Canadian Rockies. For two years and more he had been separated from his family, without the bracing stimulation of association, in spirit at least, with the heroic men of the Franklin Expedition. Too, he was working in a territory which might have been called American, instead of British, and that made a vast difference. And finally, not to speak of the personal afflictions that beset him, it must have been hard for the scientist from Glasgow to endure the social conditions of frontier Texas. Accustomed to a civilization where intellectual pursuits were respected for their own sake, where that fine aphorism of John Knox had worked itself into the inner consciousness of the people—"Every scholar is so much added to the riches of the Commonwealth"—Drummond must have found it disheartening to see how little attention was paid to education and intellectual pursuits generally in the Texas of the early 'thirties. Reared as he had been with an ingrained respect for law and order, Drummond must also have viewed with sharp distaste the looseness of administration of justice in early Texas. One does not need to share the attitude, but one can comprehend it. When all is said, the fact remains that law and order, as we conceive them, were in the Texas of Drummond's day ideals to be sought after rather than possessions to be enjoyed.

Yet Drummond saw potentialities in Texas. For him Texas was indeed the opportunity of a lifetime. Had he made his permanent home here, the botanical history of Texas would have been written very differently. There would have been no Lindheimer, no Wright, no Reverchon, no S. B. Buckley, no Lincecum, collecting plants for Asa Gray and Elias Durand and George Engelmann. Before their day the flora of Texas would have been described by Hooker, Bentham, Lindley, David Don, and other British botanists. By the time that Charles Wright and John James Audubon came to Texas, the botany of all that part of Texas which had been wrested from the Indians would have been open to the world. And the work in Mexico, begun by Berlandier, would have been greatly advanced. For where Berlandier was weak, there Drummond was strong.

A man of tremendous physical energy, of persistence, of unsuspected idealism, of complete devotion to science: forgetful of self, pursuing his unreasoning love for botany without any recking or calculating of the end—such was Thomas Drummond. It seems an unnecessarily cruel fate that kept him from bringing to completion his work in Texas.

Audubon in Texas 5

IN HER pioneer period America has produced her full quota of naturalists: picturesque and ardent, luxuriant and genuine. There was that incomparable original, Constantine Samuel Rafinesque of Old Transylvania, whose career will intrigue the interest of curious-minded students of the history of science as long as men shall study natural history; Robert Kennicott, the intrepid collector of animals in the Canadian wilds of the middle of the last century; Gerard Troost, of the University of Nashville, geologist before the Civil War; James Hall, the paleontologist of the New York Geological Survey; and others. But surpassing all the rest "in his enthusiasm, his impressibility, his unworldliness, his simplicity, his love of nature, his good faith . . . ," was John James Audubon, the ornithologist. "He suggests and is allied to some of the finest characters in history." His great work on the birds of North America was the first earnest of the repayment of the debt owed by the New World to the Old, for past inspiration and leadership in science. His published work, hailed by Baron Cuvier as the "most magnificent monument that art has ever erected to science," constituted a service to the science of ornithology surpassing perhaps that of any other man that ever lived, and renders him one of the most striking figures of our history.

The life of Audubon has been the object of devoted attention from fellow-naturalists and biographers. Among biographies of him, perhaps the most unfortunately conceived was the first, issued in 1868 by Sampson Low, Son & Marston, of London, under the unenlightened editorship of Robert Buchanan. The manuscript which had been furnished to the publishers by the widow of Audubon was by Buchanan pared down to a fifth of its original length. In this compression but little of what Audubon had to say about birds was retained; and the narrative, while it still enjoys popularity as one of the numbers in "Everyman's Library," is distinctly disappointing to the naturalist. For Audubon kept in the most careful manner daily journals of detailed observations, from which he later extracted long comments for his volumes of descriptive works on the birds of America; and these detailed entries would be of value to workers in the field of natural history. There are also apparent in the Buchanan *Life* numerous errors in dates and names. With the hope of correcting many of these omissions and errors, his widow, in 1869, and his granddaughter, in 1898, issued new biographies of the naturalist. What may be considered the definitive biography of Audubon, however, is perhaps the admirable recent work of Professor F. H. Herrick, published in 1917. In this work is given a discriminating and informing account of this most interesting of American naturalists.

The concern of one interested in naturalists of the Southwestern frontier, however, is the fact that in the course of his wanderings over the face of his world, Audubon made a journey to Texas. It was in the spring of 1837, the year which looms so importantly in the history of Texas. In this year the United States of America recognized the independence which the Texans had won the year before on the field of San Jacinto. The recognition of Texan independence by the sister republic of the north was but preliminary to similar recognition

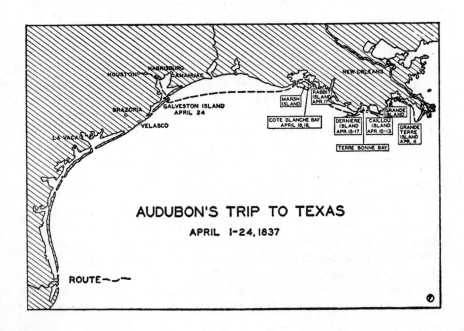

AUDUBON'S TRIP TO TEXAS

APRIL 1-24, 1837

ROUTE —·—

on the part of France, Belgium, and Great Britain. Audubon's visit to Texas, lasting from April 24, 1837, to May 18 of that year, was contemporaneous with the visit to Texas of the first consular representative sent by the British Foreign Office. All in all, Audubon's journey to Texas coincided with a number of events of the greatest significance to our country.

The voyage of Audubon hitherward was also of great importance in the history of American science. In a letter to a correspondent, written after his return from Texas, Audubon stated that his visit to Texas had been unusually fruitful, for although he had collected no new species of birds on the journey, nevertheless "the mass of observations that we gathered connected with the ornithology of our country has, I think, never been surpassed. I feel myself now tolerably competent to give an essay on the geographical distribution of the . . . [birds of America]." The ornithological results were incorporated into Audubon's *Birds of America;* but the original journals have long since perished.

In the present chapter, by a careful reading and collation of the descriptive parts of the *Birds of America,* I have attempted to reconstruct the lost journal of Audubon's journey to Texas. This collation, with the use of such extant contemporary letters as Audubon wrote to correspondents, has made it possible in a slight measure to visualize the travels and experiences of the naturalist on this trip to Texas. The voyage, which began April 1, 1837, at New Orleans, and ended May 25, lasted fifty-four days. In Buchanan's *Life,* for these fifty-four days we have but twenty dated entries—these practically devoid of anything of interest to the naturalist. There is an especial cause for disappointment in Buchanan's book in the fact that the first three weeks are left practically blank: weeks in which Audubon was cruising in and out of the bays and bayous of southern Louisiana—a paradise of birds. It was here that Audubon found some of the finest collecting and observation in all his journey. Galveston Island also was full of interest to the naturalist, since here he found nesting of birds; but the earlier part of his trip, from April 1 to April 21, was the time in which the birds were making their great migrations. In the reconstruction, when the interests of the connected narrative seemed to demand it, I have taken the liberty of changing in places the wording of the original records, without changing the sense.

Audubon spent the winter of 1836 with his friend, the Reverend Dr. John Bachman, of old St. John's Lutheran Church, at Charleston, South Carolina. In the early spring of 1837 he set out overland for New Orleans to meet the ship for Texas. The previous year he had received from the government at Washington the promise of a revenue cutter in which to explore the coasts of West Florida, of Louisiana, and of the Mexican Gulf as far as Galveston. On this cruise he proposed to take with him an intimate friend, Edward Harris, and his son, John Woodhouse Audubon. He was delighted to learn that the captain of the revenue cutter selected for his trip, the *Campbell* (of 55 tons burden and carrying a crew of 21 men), was Napoléon Coste, the old pilot of the *Marion,* in which, in the spring of 1832, Audubon had explored the eastern coast of Florida as far south as Key West. The Audubon party had planned to leave in the *Campbell* from Charleston, but the Seminole War, then raging, somewhat disarranged their plans. To quote from Herrick's account of events of this period:

As spring approached and the long awaited *Campbell* had not arrived, Audubon, with Harris and John, started overland for New Orleans. After several days of hard travelling by coaches they reached Montgomery, and descended the Alabama River by steamboat to Mobile. When that district had been ransacked for birds, they went on to Pensacola, where they learned that the government cutter would soon be at their service at New Orleans; accordingly they retraced their steps to Mobile, passed through the lakes, and entered . . . [New Orleans].

Finally, on the first of April we see them on the *Campbell* sailing down the Southwest Pass into the Gulf of Mexico. On the fourth of April, they reached Grande Terre Island and Barataria Bay; on the ninth, Caillou Island and Terre-bonne Bay; they reached Côte Blanche Bay on the seventeenth; and Galveston Bay on the twenty-fourth. From the twenty-fourth of April to the eighth of May, they explored Galveston Island and the lower bay; on the eighth of May, they left Galveston for Houston, the new capital of the republic. Here they visited President Houston, witnessed the results of the Indian "Big Talk" with Sam Houston, and met Crawford, the British special agent sent on consular business. On the sixteenth, they began the return to Galveston, and departed for New Orleans two days later. On the evening of the twenty-fifth of May they reached the point from which they had first set out. The journal, reconstructed as far as reconstruction is possible from the fragments that are left, follows.

II

Saturday, April 1, 1837.—With my son John and my good, generous friend, Mr. Edward Harris, I came down from New Orleans, this day, in the U. S. Revenue Cutter *Campbell,* Captain Napoléon Coste, to the Southwest Pass. We are provisioned for two months and are bound westwardly from the mouth of the Mississippi to Galveston Bay, in Texas, intending to explore the harbor, keys, and bayous along the coast, to examine the habits of the birds of this region, and to search for new species, which may furnish materials for the completion of the fourth volume of the *Birds of America*. During the day I observed the Black-and-Yellow Wood Warbler in considerable numbers on its way to the United States. The Blue Winged Teal we found very abundant, in flocks of various sizes, and in full plumage. Large flocks, also, of the Red Breasted Snipe, still in winter plumage, were observed on their way eastward.

Sunday, April 2.—Arrived at the Southwest Pass of the Mississippi, and stopped for some time to shoot birds on the marshy flats. Here we saw a Marsh Hawk seize a bird (perhaps a Marsh Wren) on its nest, and carry it off in its talons with the nest! A pair of Marsh Hawks was hovering over the marsh during the whole of our stay, and probably had a nest thereabout.

Monday, April 3.—We were joined this day by Captain W. B. Taylor, of the Revenue service, with the schooner *Crusader,* twelve tons burden, two guns, and four men completely equipped for our expedition with a supply of seines, cast-nets, and other fishing tackle. Great numbers of birds are observed entering the United States from Mexico. Among these is the Coerulean Warbler, in perfect summer plumage, the Black and Yellow Warbler, migrating in considerable numbers, and also the Yellow Winged Bunting. [The weather was threatening, and unseasonably cold. This day they entered Barataria Bay and commenced operations.]

Tuesday, April 4.—Landed at Grande Terre Island, in Barataria Bay (a bay much infested twenty-five years before with pirates). Great numbers of migrating birds are to be seen. Some of these, such as the Red Breasted Snipe, begin to show a change to summer plumage (several specimens of this species showing reddish feathers scattered over their lower parts). Great numbers of Laughing Gulls attended on porpoises which were fishing, and also on the Brown Pelicans, tormenting the latter. This morning, while I was seated among the driftwood accumulated on the southern shore of Grande Terre Island, I noted a flock of about thirty Long-Legged Sandpipers, and for three-quarters of an hour observed with much pleasure their feeding habits. My son, John, also obtained some of these birds today on the margin of a freshwater pond.

The American Coot here congregates in such vast numbers that one of the crew of the *Campbell* killed eighty of them at a single shot. From my lookout on the pile of driftwood I observed a number of White Pelicans swimming and fishing. They swam against wind and current, with their wings partially extended and the neck stretched out, the upper mandible alone appearing above the surface. The lower mandible must have been used as a scoop net, as I saw it raised from time to time, and brought to meet the upper, when the whole bill immediately fell to perpendicular position; the water was allowed to run out, and the bill being again raised upwards, the fish was swallowed. After thus swimming for about a hundred yards in an extended line, and parallel to each other, they would rise on wing, wheel about, and realight at the place where their fishing had commenced. Then they would repeat the same actions. I continued watching them for more than an hour, concealed among a large quantity of logs, until their fishing was finished; when they all flew off to the lee of another island, no doubt to spend the night there, for these birds are altogether diurnal. When gorged, they retire to the shores, to small islands in bays and rivers, or sit on logs floating in shallow water, at a good distance from the beach; in all which situations they are prone to lie down, or stand closely together. Being anxious to procure several specimens of these birds for anatomical study of the soft parts, I set out with a select party—Edward Harris, my son, John, and myself—toward a small island in Barataria Bay, leeward of Grande Terre Island. After a while we saw large flocks of these birds on some grounded logs, but found it no easy matter to get near them, on account of the shallowness of the bay, the water being scarcely two feet in depth for upwards of a half-mile from us. Quietly, and with all possible care, we neared a flock of some hundreds of grave and sedate White Pelicans, huddled together on a heap of logs stranded on a small bank of raccoon oysters. They were lying on their breasts; but as we neared them they all rose deliberately to their full height. Some, gently sliding from the logs, swam off toward the nearest flock, as unapprehensive of danger as if they had been a mile distant. A volley of buckshot netted us three dead birds in the water; and another shot from a different gun brought another down from on wing. About a quarter of a mile farther on we killed two more; so that we returned with a full cargo of dead and wounded birds. The pelicans appeared tame, if not stupid, and at one place, where there were about sixty on an immense log, could we have gone twenty yards nearer, we might have killed eight or ten at a single discharge. But we already had a full cargo.

Wednesday, Thursday, April 5, 6.—[There are no entries for these days, which other records indicate were probably cold. It is probable that on these two days Audubon noted the arrival in the United States of great crowds of Ruby Throated Hummingbirds, advancing eastward along the Gulf shore.] The weather having become very cold one morning, many hummingbirds were picked up dead along the beaches, and those which bore up were so benumbed as almost to suffer the members of my party to take them with the hand. The Scarlet Tanagers also appeared to be very abundant on some of these islands, but were restrained from proceeding eastward by the unseasonably cold weather. Many of the Tanagers were obtained in their full summer dress, and a few in the garb of the females. These plain-colored individuals turned out to be males, which confirms my opinion (for this and other species) *that the males precede the females by about a fortnight* in their spring migrations.

Friday, April 7.—A severe gale from the northwest. Today I saw a flock of about thirty Brown Pelicans flying only a few feet above the water and against the gale. Having proceeded a few yards, they plunged into the water, generally to leeward, and threw their bodies round as soon as their bills were immersed, giving a very curious appearance to the wings, which seemed as if locked. On seizing a fish, they drained the mouth as did the White Pelican [*v.* April 4 entry]. In this way the whole flock kept dashing and plunging pell-mell, like Gannets, over a space of about a hundred yards; fishing at times in the very surf, and where the water could not be more than a very few feet deep. Each of them must have caught upwards of a score of fishes. As soon as they were satisfied, they flew in a line across the channel, and landed on low banks under the lee of the island, opposite our harbor. During all the time of their fishing they were attended by a number of Black-Headed Gulls, which followed all their movements, alighting on their heads, and feeding as I have already described.

Saturday, April 8, 1837.—[Left the vicinity of Grande Terre Island and Barataria Bay, and after leisurely cruising past the mouth of Bayou Lafouche, probably arrived April 9 at Caillou Island, an island-bar across the mouth of Terre-bonne Bay.]

Monday, April 10.—Caillou Island. At midday, great flocks of Blue and Green Herons were seen arriving from the westward. They flew at a considerable height, and came down suddenly, like so many hawks, to alight on the low bushes growing around the sequestered ponds. They remained until sunset, when they all flew away.

Tuesday, April 11.—Caillou Island. Migration of birds in full swing. No Herons today, but large and dense flocks of Blue-Winged Teal flying to the eastward.

Thursday, April 13.—Caillou Island. A heavy gale from the west. My generous friend, Mr. Edward Harris, saw a flock of about twenty Least Bitterns arriving from the westward. They were driven before a heavy wind, and on their arrival at the island plunged, as it were, into the marshes, and hid themselves so closely (from fatigue or otherwise) that neither he nor the dog could raise one of them. The Red-Breasted Snipe [*v.* entries for April 1; 4] begins to show considerable change of color, in the transition to summer plumage. The change is greater in the older birds, while the younger are still quite gray above and white beneath. [Audubon probably spent this day and the next in general investigations in Terre-bonne Bay and its immediate vicinity; then transferred the seat of operations to Derniere Island, five miles from Caillou Island. Derniere Island caps the southernmost coast of present Parish Terrebonne, Louisiana.]

Saturday, April 15, 1837.—Derniere Island. Birds are still in full migration. The Blue-Winged Teal very plentiful and gentle. Red-Breasted Snipe and all other water fowl in abundance, and migrating. We met with a flock of Oyster Catchers, fourteen or fifteen in number, flying compactly, and uttering their usual cry of *weep, weep.* Two of them were shot down into the water, but one of them which had only been winged dived so effectually as to escape from us, in spite of the most strenuous exertions of the sailors to recover it.

Sunday, April 16.—Derniere Island. Captain Coste shot three specimens of the American Avocet (on an immense sand-bar, intersected by pools, about twelve miles from Derniere Island) and brought them to me, in perfect order. They are larger, and perhaps handsomer, than any I have seen; and were killed while feeding, out of a flock of five. Several other flocks of Avocets were feeding in the vicinity. Of the Red-Breasted Snipes that I killed on this island, practically all, even of the younger birds, showed change from summer to winter plumage. The species is extremely abundant locally.

Monday, April 17.—[En route to Côte Blanche Bay. Sailing past Atchafalaya Bay, and stopping briefly at Rabbit Island, a small spot of land at the mouth of East Côte Blanche Bay.] Blue-Winged Teal especially abundant on Rabbit Island. [Reached Côte Blanche Bay today.]

Tuesday, April 18.—Côte Blanche Bay. Innumerable land and water birds, caught in the spring migrations: Snipes, Blackbirds, Gallinules, Curlews, Herons, etc. The shores of the bay are high—twenty to thirty feet—and the waters of the bay are so shallow as to make navigation difficult. This bay for a number of years was infested with pirates, in consequence of which, a few years ago, a United States revenue cutter was sent to protect the coast. Our black-painted revenue schooner *Crusader,* of twelve tons burden, although she flies the stars and stripes, has been suspected by the fearful planters of being a pirate ship!

Thursday, April 20.—Côte Blanche Bay. Yesterday afternoon about four o'clock Mr. Edward Harris killed a Yellow-Crowned Night Heron on an island in the bay. This morning when we opened it we found an inch-and-a-half terrapin which it had swallowed. The terrapin was still alive, and greatly surprised my companions as well as myself in crawling about when liberated.

Friday, April 21.—[Probably back to Atchafalaya Bay, for the last lap in the journey to Texas.]

Monday, April 24.—Galveston Bay. Arrived in Galveston Bay this afternoon, having had a fine run from Atchafalaya Bay. We were soon boarded by officers from the Texan vessels in the harbor, who informed us that two days before the U. S. sloop of war *Natchez* fell in with the Mexican squadron off the harbor of Velasco, captured the brig *Urrea,* and ran two other vessels ashore; another report says they sunk another ship and went in pursuit of the squadron. These vessels were taken as pirates—the fleet, having sailed from Vera Cruz without provisioning, had been plundering American vessels on the coast. There is also a rumor that the Texan schooner *Independence* has been captured by a Mexican cruiser. The American schooner *Flash* was driven ashore a few days since by a Mexican cruiser, and now lies on the beach at the lower end of the island. The bird-fauna represented on Galveston Island is about what it has been on the whole trip to Texas. The Blue-Winged Teal, Snowy and Blue Heron, various species of Sandpipers, and Black-Necked Stilts are abundant. I was amused today to see how the Purple Heron, although larger than the Snowy Heron, is considerably inferior to it in courage. A Snowy Heron in my view lighted near a Purple Heron, attacked it, and pursued it out of sight.

Tuesday, April 25.—A heavy gale blew all night, and this morning the thermometer in the cabin is 63°. Thousands of birds, arrested by the storm in their migration northward, are seen hovering around our vessels and hiding in the grass, and some are struggling in the water, completely exhausted. We had a visit this morning from the secretary of the Texan navy, Mr. S. Rhoads Fisher, who breakfasted with us. He appeared to be a well-informed man, and talked a great deal about the infant republic. Then he left us for the seat of government at Houston, seventy miles distant, on the steamer *Yellow Stone,* accompanied by Captains Coste and Taylor, taking the *Crusader* in tow. [Fisher, who seems to have been something of a sportsman, also gave Audubon information regarding the nesting habits of many of the game-fowl of the region.]

Wednesday, April 26.—Went ashore at Galveston. The only objects we saw of interest were the Mexican prisoners; they are used as slaves; made to carry wood and water, and cut grass for the horses, and such work; it is said that some are made to draw the plow. They all appear to be of delicate frame and constitution, but are not dejected in appearance. Among the many birds observed today may be mentioned: The Blue-Winged Teal, which I found on all the ponds and salt bayous or inlets of Galveston Island, as well as in the interior, where I am assured they breed in great numbers; the Black-Necked Stilt, which occurs in small flocks on the brackish ponds of the bay, where they were so shy that it was difficult for us to procure specimens. When breeding, they are much less shy than at other times. Black-Headed or Laughing Gulls, now paired, and very noisy, were not infrequently seen hovering over the inner ponds of the island, as if in search of food.

Thursday, April 27.—We were off at an early hour for the island, two miles distant; we waded nearly all the distance, so very shallow and filled with sandbanks is this famous bay. The men made a large fire to keep off the mosquitoes, which were annoying enough for even me. Besides many interesting birds, we found a new species of rattlesnake, with a double row of fangs, on each side of its jaws.

Friday, April 28.—We went on a deer hunt on Galveston Island, where these animals are abundant; we saw about twenty-five, and killed four. Edward Harris, my son, John, and some others of our party shot the deer. These the sailors brought to our little camp near the shore. Feeling myself rather fatigued, I did not return to the bushes with the rest, who went in search of more venison for our numerous crew, but proposed, with the assistance of one of the sailors, to skin the deer. While doing this, and washing the meat afterward, I was delighted to observe the behavior of four Turnstones, busily engaged in ingeniously searching for food along the seashore.

Saturday, April 29, 1837.—John took a view of the rough village of Galveston with the Camera Lucida. We found much company on board on our return to the vessel, among whom was a contractor for beef for the army; he was from Connecticut, and has a family residing near the famous battle-ground of San Jacinto. He promised me some skulls of Mexicans, and some plants, for he is bumped with botanical bumps somewhere. Hundreds of pairs of the Least Tern are breeding on the islands of Galveston Bay. Also, on one of these islands I found eight or ten nests of the Roseate Spoonbill, placed in low cactuses, amid some hundreds of nests belonging to Herons of different species. Snakes are abundant on the island, and live on the eggs of nesting birds, whence the old name for Galveston Island of "Snake Island." The Common Tern is strangely rare just now: only a few are arriving from the west. The Gadwell Duck is quite abundant on all the inland ponds and streams, as well as on the brackish pools and inlets of the islands and shores of Galveston Bay. Many of them have paired and separated from the other ducks; and I was assured by Mr. S. Rhoads Fisher, the Texan Secretary of the Navy, that this species breeds here, as does also the Dusky Duck, the Mallard, the Blue-Winged Teal, the Widgeon, and the Shoveller Duck; and he says the young of all these species are plentiful in the end of June and beginning of July.

Monday, May 1.—Galveston Bay. I was much fatigued this morning, and the muscles of my legs were swelled until they were purple, so that I could not go on shore. The muskrat is the only small quadruped found here, and the common house-rat has not reached this part of the world.

Tuesday, May 2.—Went ashore on Galveston Island, and landed on a point where the Texan garrison is quartered. We passed through the troops, and observed the miserable condition of the whole concern; huts made of grass and a few sticks, or sods cut into square pieces, composed the buildings of the poor Mexican prisoners, which, half clad and half naked, strolled about in a state of apparent inactivity. We passed two sentinels under arms, very unlike soldiers in appearance. The whole population seemed both indolent and reckless. We saw a few fowls, one pig, and a dog, which appeared to be all the domestic animals in the encampment. We saw only three women, who were Mexican prisoners. The soldiers' huts are placed in irregular rows, and at unequal distances; a dirty blanket or coarse rag hangs over the entrance in place of a door. No windows were seen, except in one or two cabins occupied by Texan officers and soldiers. A dozen or more long guns lay about on the sand, and one of about the same caliber was mounted. There was a lookout house fronting and commanding the entrance to the harbor, and at the point where the three channels meet there were four guns mounted of smaller caliber. We readily observed that not much nicety prevailed among the Mexican prisoners, and we learned that their habits were as filthy as their persons. We also found a few beautiful flowers, and among them one which Harris and I at once nicknamed the Texan daisy; and we gathered a number of their seeds, hoping to make them flourish elsewhere. On the top of one of the huts we saw a badly-stuffed skin of a grey or black wolf, of the same species as I have seen on the Missouri. . . . We walked down to the shore bordering a shallow bayou, for the purpose of fishing for prawns (which here grow to a very large size and are extremely abundant) and of catching fish. Our fishing over, we were on the point of returning, when we saw three spoonbills alight on a sandbar, and almost immediately proceed to the water in search of food. John, by wading over some muddy shallows, succeeded in getting near enough to kill the finest of the three. Almost at the same instant the back fins of a large fish resembling those of a shark appeared meandering above the surface of the shallow waters. We called to John, and he, wishing to kill the monster, which moved but slowly, rammed home a couple of bullets, and lodged them in the body of the fish. Thereupon it floundered about apparently in great agony. One of our boats immediately pushed toward the spot and took John aboard, while the animal used its best efforts to get into deeper water. Sailors and all joined in the chase. The gun was again charged with balls; my son waded once more toward the fish; and lodged the missiles in its body, while from the bow of the boat it received several blows from oars and gaffhook. The tars all leaped into the water, and the bleeding fish was closely beset. The boatswain at a single lucky stroke cut off its tail, and having fastened the hook in one of its eyes, we dragged it to the beach. About a hundred Mexican prisoners, Texan soldiers, and officers were there; but instead of our prize turning out a shark, it proved to be a sawfish, measuring rather more than twelve feet in length. . . . From her body we recovered ten small sawfish, all of them alive and wriggling about as soon as they were thrown on the sand. The young were about thirty inches in length, and minute sharp teeth were already formed.

Wednesday, Thursday, May 3, 4.—[No definite records. From context of records of succeeding days, it is probable that there was on these days a severe gale from the east.]

Friday, May 5.—Hunted birds over the interior of Galveston Island today. While I was watching some Marsh Hawks that were breeding in the neighborhood, I was much surprised to find a large flock of Skimmers alighted, and apparently asleep, on a dry grassy part of the interior of the island. These birds usually rest much nearer to the shore. On returning thither, however, I found that the tide was much higher than usual, in consequence of the recent severe gale, and had covered all the sand banks on which at other times I had observed them resting by day. In spite of the coldness of the season I found broods of the Spotted Sandpiper, or Tattler, already well grown.

Monday, May 8.—Today we hoisted anchor, bound for Houston; after grounding a few times, we reached Red Fish Bar, distant twelve miles, where we found several American schooners and one brig. It blew hard all night, and we were uncomfortable.

Tuesday, May 9.—We left Red Fish Bar with the *Crusader* and the gig, and with a fair wind proceeded rapidly. Soon we came up to the new-born town of New Washington, owned mostly by Swartwout, the collector of customs of New York. We passed several plantations;

and the general appearance of the country was more pleasing than otherwise. About noon, we entered Buffalo Bayou, at the mouth of the San Jacinto River, and opposite the famous battle-ground of the same name. Proceeding smoothly up the bayou, we saw abundance of game, and after traveling some twenty miles stopped at the house of a Mr. Batterson. This bayou is usually sluggish, deep, and bordered on both sides with a strip of woods not exceeding a mile in depth. . . . It was here today that I found the Ivory-Billed Woodpecker in abundance, and secured several specimens. . . . It rained and lightened, and we passed the night at Mr. Batterson's.

Wednesday, May 10.—It rained again today, but we pushed on in the gig toward Houston. The rain had, however, so swollen the water of the bayou and increased the current that we were eight hours rowing twelve miles.

Monday, May 15.—We landed at Houston, the capital of Texas, drenched to the skin, and were kindly received on board the steamer *Yellow Stone,* Captain West, who gave us his stateroom to change our clothes in, and furnished us refreshments and dinner. The Buffalo Bayou had risen about six feet, and the neighboring prairies were partly covered with water; there was a wild and desolate look cast on the surrounding scenery. We had already passed two little girls encamped on the bank of the bayou under the cover of a few class-boards [clapboards?], cooking a scanty meal; shanties, cargoes of hogs-heads, barrels, etc., were spread about the landing; and Indians drunk and hallooing were stumbling about in the mud in every direction. These poor beings had come here to enter into a treaty proposed by the whites; many of them were young and well-looking, and with far less decorations than I have seen before on such occasions. The chief of the tribe is an old and corpulent man.

We walked towards the President's house, accompanied by the Secretary of the Navy, and as soon as we rose above the bank, we saw before us a level of far-extending prairie, destitute of timber, and with rather poor soil. Houses half-finished, and most of them without roofs, tents, and a liberty pole, with the capitol, were all exhibited to our view at once. We approached the President's mansion, however, wading through water above our ankles. This abode of President Houston is a small log house, consisting of two rooms and a passage through, after the Southern fashion. The moment we stepped over the threshold, on the right hand of the passage we found ourselves ushered into what in other countries would be called the antechamber; the ground floor, however, was muddy and filthy, a large fire was burning, a small table covered with paper and writing materials was in the center, camp-beds, trunks, and different materials were strewn around the room. We were at once presented to several members of the cabinet, some of whom bore the stamp of men of intellectual ability, simple, though bold, in their general appearance. Here we were presented to Mr. Joseph T. Crawford, British Vice-Consul at Tampico, an agent of the British Minister to Mexico, who has come here on some secret mission.

The president was engaged in the opposite room on national business, and we could not see him for some time. Meanwhile we amused ourselves by walking to the capitol, which was yet without a roof, and the floors, benches, and tables of both houses of Congress were as well saturated with water as our clothes had been in the morning. Being invited by one of the great men of the place to enter a booth to take a drink of grog with him, we did so; but I was rather surprised that he offered his name, instead of the cash, to the bar-keeper.

We first caught sight of President Houston as he walked from one of the grog-shops, where he had been to prevent the further sale of ardent spirits to the Indians. He was on his way to his house, and wore a large, gray, coarse hat; and the bulk of his figure reminded me of the appearance of General Hopkins, the Indian fighter, of Virginia, for like him he is upwards of six feet high, and strong in proportion. But I observed a scowl in the expression of his eyes that was forbidding and disagreeable. We reached his abode before him, but he soon came, and we were presented to his excellency. He was dressed in a fancy velvet coat, and trousers trimmed with broad gold lace; around his neck was tied a cravat somewhat in the style of seventy-six. He received us kindly, was desirous of retaining us for a while, and offered us every facility within his power. We were severally introduced by him to the different members of his cabinet and staff, and at once asked to drink grog with him, which we did, wishing success to his new republic. Our talk was short; but the impression which was made on my mind at the time by himself, his officers, and his place of abode, can never be forgotten.

We returned to our boat through a mêlée of Indians and blackguards of all sorts. In giving a last glance back we once more noticed a number of horses rambling about the grounds, or tied beneath the few trees that have been spared by the axe. We also saw a liberty pole, erected on the anniversary of the battle of San Jacinto, on the twenty-first of last April, and were informed that a brave tar who rigged the Texan flag on that occasion had been personally rewarded by President Houston with a town lot, a doubloon, and the privilege of keeping a ferry across the Buffalo Bayou at the town, where the bayou forks diverge in opposite directions.

Tuesday, May 16.—Departed for New Washington, where we received kind attentions from Col. James Morgan; crossed San Jacinto Bay to the *Campbell,* and the next day dropped down to Galveston. On the way down the bayou, I noticed with great surprise how well adapted the Texas prairies were to the habits of the Black-Throated Bunting. These birds were extremely numerous in every open piece of ground covered by tufts of tall grass. Before we left the country I made particular note that the American Widgeons were all paired. I had been informed by the Honorable S. Rhoads Fisher that a good number of these breed in the maritime districts, along with several other ducks, and that he annually received many of the young birds.

Thursday, May 18.—Left the bar at Galveston, having on board Mr. Joseph T. Crawford, British Vice-Consul at Tampico, and a Mr. Allen of New Orleans.

Wednesday, May 24.—Arrived at the Southwest Pass, and proceeded to the Belize, and thence to New Orleans, where we arrived in three days.

III

The Audubon party tarried a few days in New Orleans, which was very hot and nearly deserted. On May 28, Audubon and his friends breakfasted with former Governor A. B. Roman, and on the last day of the month they separated, Audubon and his son John proceeding by steamer, mail-cart, coach, and railroad to Charleston, while Edward Harris took boat up the river for further exploration before rejoining the party at Charleston. The extensive collections, including a very large number of birds' eggs packed in a large box, were left to be sent north by Audubon's friend, Governor Roman. For some unexplained reason, a large portion of the collections made in Texas never came to hand. Especially regrettable to Audubon was the loss of the large box of eggs, which contained specimens belonging to most of the species encountered on the expedition to Texas. Farewells were said to the crews of the *Campbell* and the *Crusader,* and the Texas trip was over. "We crossed to Mobile in the steamer *Swan*," said Audubon in his journal, "paying fare twelve dollars each, and making the trip of one hundred and fifty miles in twenty-one hours. If New Orleans appeared prostrated, Mobile seemed quite dead. We left in the afternoon for Stockton, Alabama, forty-five miles distant, where we were placed in a cart, and tumbled and tossed for one hundred and sixty-five miles to Montgomery; fare twenty-three dollars each, miserable road, and rascally fare. At Montgomery we took the mail coach, and were much relieved; fare to Columbus twenty-six dollars each. Our travelling companions were without interest, the weather was suffocating, and the roads dirty and very rough; we made but three miles an hour for the whole journey, walking up the hills, and galloping down them to Augusta, and paying a fare of thirteen dollars and fifty cents each, and thence by rail to Charleston for six dollars and seventy-five cents each, distance one hundred and thirty-six miles, and making eight and a half days from New Orleans."

Louis Cachand Ervendberg 6

ONE GOES to the little town of New Braunfels in South Texas with a recurrent sense of renewal in spirit—that is, if he is of German descent, and if his heart responds to the old German song, German literature, German *Sittlichkeit,* German *Mässigkeit.* There one hears the German tongue still spoken with remarkable purity and finds old German customs still observed, so that now, as in the closing days of the Republic of Texas, a visit to New Braunfels is like entering into the life of a little German city. The landscape is beautiful, with the *Missionsberg* to the north, forest-crowned; the Guadalupe and the Comal rivers, clear, swift, with rapids in their courses; and the magnificent cypresses along the Guadalupe. In the town itself stand old houses with an enduring charm. To be sure, many of the landmarks mentioned by early Texas travelers are gone. The ferry across the Guadalupe, at the point where the Comal flows into it, has not been in use since the iron bridge was built across the river near the old San Antonio Road in the 'eighties. Torrey's Mill was torn down three-quarters of a century ago. Seele's *Sängerhalle* is also gone. The old *Sophienburg,* long in ruins, has been replaced by a fine modern museum devoted to the history of the town. But there are still many precious reminders of the past. The old *Camino Real,* in "Nacogdoches Street," can yet be traced going down to the ford of the Guadalupe where the millpond of the textile mill is now; and the Comal Springs, "Las Fontanas" of Mexican days, retain the beauty that evoked comment a century ago. The old *Waisenhaus,* or orphan's home, still stands also, a grim reminder of the terrible days of 1846, and on the high ground on Zink Street, near the Comal Creek, can be seen the place where the immigrants of 1845 camped until huts and houses could be built. The forest on the east bank of the Guadalupe at the ferry-site holds memories of the ghastly sufferings of the later immigrants in the summer of 1846. But to me, at any rate, the most interesting spot in New Braunfels is the bit of ground under an oak tree—the only one remaining of three that formerly marked the place—where Louis Ervendberg, the Protestant pastor of the German settlers, held the first religious services in New Braunfels, and where Hermann Seele held the first school.

Ervendberg was one of the most enigmatic and tragic characters that ever lived in New Braunfels. The town, for that matter, could claim its full quota of remarkable inhabitants—men like Carl Jonas Love Almquist, the Swedish man of letters, who worked on the *Neu-Braunfelser Zeitung* with Lindheimer for a couple of months in the summer of 1853; or the Polish Franciscan, Father Moczygeba, pastor of the Catholic church in Almquist's day; like barefooted Otto Friedrich, a lepidopterist and entomologist of no mean ability, who in ante-bellum days was sending insects to H. A. Hagen before Agassiz called Hagen to the Museum of Comparative Zoölogy at Cambridge; or like Ottomar von Behr, an old friend of Alexander von Humboldt and Bettina von Arnim, and Dr. Julius Froebel, who in the late 'fifties was publishing in the *Reports* of the Smithsonian Institution notable articles on the physiography of America while he engaged in trade between Texas and Chihuahua.

But even in such a company, Ervendberg is a notable character. His own descendants freely acknowledge that the name Ervendberg is assumed. Although he claimed to have studied at Heidelberg, no German university records him as a student; the Central Bureau for personal genealogy knows nothing of Ervendberg's family; even the parish church of Rhoden in the old Principality of Waldeck, where he said he was born, has no record of him or his family.* Out of obscurity he came, and into obscurity he went. And a tragic destiny seemed to pursue him. He deserved enduring honor among all that bear the German name in Texas for his labors as first German pastor in Texas, as the progressive and liberal leader in the formation of "The Christian Church of the Germans in Texas" in 1841, as the first teacher in the German communities of Colorado and Austin counties in the early 'forties, and as the heroic pastor of his flock in 1846, the terrible second year of the German migration, as well as during the

---

*As these pages first went to the printer, in 1937, my three-year search for the true name and antecedents of Ervendberg (unknown even to his own descendants) was in part rewarded, and I hoped to be able, in a later publication, to clear up the mystery surrounding this tragic figure. I instituted a check of the records at German universities in an effort to confirm the newly discovered facts, and to obtain additional light on the life of Ervendberg before he left Germany. The events of recent years will probably preclude a completely satisfactory solution.

96

cholera epidemic of 1849. But whatever Ervendberg may have deserved, his sun went down in clouds of shame in New Braunfels, where he had carried on the best labors of his life; and in the memorials set up in honor of German pioneers in Southwest Texas, his name is absent.

Perhaps it may seem a disservice to Ervendberg to bring out into the light of day the facts of his life, now that three-quarters of a century have passed since his murder in a little Mexican town. Yet his life was bound up with movements of great import in Texas, and the history of those movements cannot be written without taking Ervendberg into account. Moreover, his life vividly illustrates the play of forces involved in human behavior; it is a familiar if pitiful tale, with moments of heroism as well as of sordidness. Though Ervendberg was not highly trained in science when he came to Texas, and, as we shall see presently, was seriously handicapped in his efforts to acquire a fuller knowledge of botany, still he deserves an honorable place in the company of the Naturalists of the Frontier. Furthermore, he was a leader in the movement toward scientific and experimental agriculture among the Germans of Southwest Texas; and, perhaps most important of all, his life throws much light on the conditions under which all the Naturalists of the Frontier worked.

If the record in the Church Book of the First Protestant Church at New Braunfels is indeed true, Ervendberg was born on the third day of May, 1809, at the village of Rhoden in the former Principality of Waldeck in west-central Germany. It is a town of some five hundred inhabitants, for the most part belonging to the Evangelical confession, situated some twenty-five miles southwest of Paderborn. There are no records of Ervendberg's childhood or of his education, but he almost certainly received some formal theological training—probably at an Evangelical seminary, of which Germany has a number, some of great distinction. As a young man Ervendberg seems to have held an ecclesiastical post at Anklam in Pomerania, where he made friends with Baron Ottfried Hans von Meusebach (who later became Commissioner General of the Mainzer Adelsverein at New Braunfels), and Georg Klappenbach, Burgomaster of Anklam and later Mayor of New Braunfels. Subsequently Ervendberg lived for a time at Herford, a considerable town at the junction of the Werre and the Aa in the county of Ravensburg in Prussia. Herford had been a member of the Hanseatic League, and was rich in historical associations dating back to the ninth century; in Ervendberg's day, the Gymnasium of the town was nearly three hundred years old. The fine old Romanesque cathedral and a Gothic church of the Virgin date back to the thirteenth and fourteenth centuries. To the south and west of Herford lies the

Teutoberg forest, where the Germans under Hermann defeated the Roman legions under Varus in 9 A.D. In addition to its well-established textile industry, Herford was notable in Ervendberg's day for its agricultural school and for two Orphans' Homes established on the plan of the famous institution of August Hermann Francke at Halle. I have not been able to unearth any particulars of Ervendberg's life at Herford and Anklam, but apparently he was highly regarded. That Ervendberg stood well in Germany before his departure for America is indicated by the fact that when Georg Klappenbach was sent out by the Adelsverein in July of 1846 to be Mayor of New Braunfels, he was introduced, according to Viktor Bracht, as "a friend of Mr. Meusebach and of Reverend Ervendberg."

I have mentioned the great uncertainty concerning Ervendberg's name. One of Ervendberg's grandsons by his first wife tells of overhearing a conversation between his mother (a daughter of Ervendberg) and another person, in which it was stated that the name was assumed, and that the father came to Germany originally as a French refugee. The children of the second wife of Ervendberg spontaneously reported to me the same tradition. But the matter is at best obscure. Ervendberg himself wrote his name variously. In early portions of the Church Books of the First Protestant Church at New Braunfels he hyphenated it, "Cachand-Ervendberg," but this was soon changed to Louis Cachand Ervendberg, the name under which he went while he was pastor at Houston and in Colorado and Austin counties. Pastor Schuchard of New Braunfels, in completing the parish church-record for the Ervendberg family, wrote the name in full as "Christian Friedrich Ludwig Cachand Ervendberg." Captain Friedrich Wilhelm von Wrede, in his *Lebensbilder* (1844), spells Ervendberg's name "Ervensberg," and Pastor Gustav Eisenlohr, in letters to his father in Germany, consistently spells it "Erwendberg." These are no doubt minutiae, but some scholar more fortunate than I may find them clues to the man's real name. I should add that directories of American cities having a large German population—metropolitan New York, Milwaukee, Cincinnati, Chicago, St. Louis—list no persons of the name Ervendberg. Moreover, the archives of the library of the University of Berlin and, as stated above, the Central Bureau at Leipzig can give no help in the matter. On the whole, it seems justifiable to conclude that family tradition is correct in stating that "Ervendberg" is an assumed name.

The question of where Ervendberg studied theology is equally difficult. The period was one of much strife among the sects of German Protestantism, dating back to the time of Luther's death, which had helped to increase the disaster wrought by the Thirty Years' War, and which was finally "healed" only by the interposition of the civil authorities in the period 1817-27. Ervendberg belonged to the Evangelical or Philippist group of German Protestants—the group that founded in 1820 the General Synod of the Evangelical Church of the United States.

From a study of the traits of mind shown by Ervendberg, I suspect that he either studied theology at the Francke Foundation in Halle, or in some other way came deeply under the influence of the Francke tradition. He was essentially Pietistic, but showed also, as did Francke, a strongly humanitarian tendency. As will be seen later, in his work at New Braunfels Ervendberg tried unsuccessfully to imitate several of Francke's institutions that came to such glorious fruition at Halle. But however it was obtained, Ervendberg's theological training seems to have been substantial, as was that of every German Protestant clergyman of that day—Hermann Seele, who was in a position to know, speaks of Ervendberg's "theological and philological training gained at German universities." This would imply mastery of the Greek New Testament and the Hebrew Old Testament, as well as the usual classical and scientific training of the German Gymnasium. A thesis of some hundred and forty-six pages on *"Die Erklärung des Evangelii Johannis nach dem Verbungen [?] des Presbyter Matthäus,"* written in the best exegetical style of the time, is in the Sophienburg Museum at New Braunfels: it is ascribed to Ervendberg, but I have my doubts. It is, of course, replete with parallel readings in Greek from the gospel of Matthew. Whether the document is an original study by Ervendberg, or a copied thesis in which he was interested (as I suspect), makes little difference, for in any case it evidences the interest and competence of the man in the substantial scholarship demanded of German clergymen of his day.

One familiar with the thought of Ervendberg's time can easily visualize the scanty library the young minister probably collected. Besides the Bible, it would contain August Hermann Francke's *Segensvolle Fusstapfen,* with an account of the famous orphan-house at Halle; Spener's two volumes of *Theologische Bedenken;* Johann Arndt's *Sechs Bücher vom wahren Christenthum,* edited by G. A. Franck, and published at Halle in 1830; Count von Zinzendorf's *Herrenhuts Gesangbuch;* Schleiermacher's *Der Christliche Glaube;* von Mosheim's works on ecclesiastical and Christian history, some in Latin and some in German; Thomas von Kempen's *Vier Bücher von der Nachfolge Christi;* and Krummacher's and Hofacker's sermons. Of these books, Johann Arndt's *True Christianity* was doubtless Ervendberg's most constant and unfailing companion in the early days.

Ervendberg seems to have come to America in the early part of 1837, or a short time before; for in that year we find him an Evangelical pastor among the Germans in northern Illinois. According to a somewhat garbled (and, it is to be feared, embellished) account of himself that Ervendberg gave Frederick Law Olmsted in 1854, he had landed in New York, and had come to the West by the common route of all immigrants: up the Hudson River by steamboat, and then across New York State by way of the Erie Canal. It must have been a wonderful experience for the young German clergyman to view this new canal, more than three hundred and fifty miles long, with its eighty-four locks and its feeder canals entering the main channel at Troy, Utica, and other points along the route. The aqueducts carrying the canal across rivers, the turning-basins and docks—here was cause for admiration! The New York State canals were then in the heyday of their prosperity; in 1837 the combined Erie and Champlain Canals netted a round million dollars over all expenses.

Ervendberg probably traveled by one of the "line boats," which made three miles an hour, and paid for his passage at the rate of a cent a mile, with the privilege of buying and cooking his food aboard the boat. Arriving at Buffalo, he no doubt took deck-passage on a lake steamer to Detroit, paying three dollars for the trip, and from Detroit traveled across Michigan to the raw town of Chicago at the foot of Lake Michigan.

Chicago, of course, was still in its infancy. In the year before Ervendberg's arrival, the first schoolhouse had been built. In March of 1837, the town, then boasting some four thousand inhabitants, had been incorporated. The Illinois & Michigan Canal, designed to connect Lake Michigan with the Desplaines River, was under construction; the Rush Medical College had just been incorporated; and the continued prosperity of Chicago seemed assured. In 1837, however, came the Panic, which for two years stopped all increase in the town's population, and caused a cessation of work on the Illinois & Michigan Canal. The price of flour went up to twenty-eight dollars a barrel; the financial situation in Illinois became desperate, and was to grow worse after the passage of the Internal Improvement Act. By 1839 the debt of Illinois had mounted to fourteen million dollars, with an annual interest charge of $800,000. Repudiation of the debt followed —the beginning of an inglorious chapter in the history of state finance in the United States.

Upon his arrival in Chicago in these distressed times, Ervendberg seems to have entered at once upon his pastoral functions. Working among the German settlers who were just then beginning their migration into the Middle West, he established Protestant Evangelical congregations in Chicago, in the German settlement of Teuto on Salt Creek in DuPage County, at East Prairie on the Desplaines River, and at Schwemm's Grove. Altogether, he seems to have had a total of fifty-six church members and 221 associates in his combined charges. But his aggregate income was fantastically small—probably not more than a hundred and fifty dollars a year.

Among the younger members of his congregation at Teuto, Ervendberg found an attractive Hanoverian lass, fair-haired and blue-eyed, named Maria Sophie Dorothea Muench. She lived with her uncle. With him she had left her home at Landesburg, near Nienburg; upon their arrival in America in 1836, they had settled in Chicago, but in 1837 had removed fifteen miles west to Teuto in order to escape the malarial marshes along the lake shore. On the tenth of September, 1838, Ervendberg and Maria were married in Chicago by Ervendberg's friend, the Reverend John Blatchford, a Presbyterian minister.

Although Ervendberg was in a sense isolated at his home parish on Salt Creek, still he had many pleasant associations. In the congregations he served were many compatriots of his wife, some of whom had even been close neighbors in the old home, so that life, in spite of financial stringencies, had its pleasant side. Their first-born, a son, came to the couple in Teuto in July of 1839. The child's death on the twelfth of the following September plunged the family into deep grief. Ervendberg, disconsolate and harassed by economic difficulties, began to consider migrating to the Republic of Texas, the goal of so many persons in the United States who had been ruined by the financial crash of 1837.

It was not an easy thing to leave home and friends. Besides his parishioners in Cook and DuPage counties, Ervendberg had many congenial acquaintances in Chicago. Three of his ministerial colleagues, in particular, were close friends. Dr. John Blatchford, fifteen years Ervendberg's senior, a graduate of Union College and Princeton Theological Seminary and pastor of the Presbyterian Church of Chicago, stood in the place of mentor and confidant, and of course the two men shared similar theological views. Another friend was the Methodist minister, the Reverend Peter Ruble Borein, of an age with Ervendberg—one of the most beloved pastors in Chicago. Most amiable as a man, and an eloquent preacher, he read his Hebrew Bible easily in a day when scholarship was rare on the raw frontier. The Methodist presiding elder, the Reverend John Clark, later to become prominent in the church in Texas, was a third member of the trio of colleagues whom Ervendberg found congenial.

Many years later, Hermann Seele, in an extended obituary notice of Mrs. Ervendberg (published in the *Neu-Braunfelser Zeitung* on January 12, 1888), leaves the impression that a certain worldly love of ease and gain sent Ervendberg to Texas. This suggestion is far from the truth. Understanding of Ervendberg's decision to migrate must begin with a realization of his intense financial distress in Illinois. Church dues had dwindled to almost nothing, and prices of food and other necessities were soaring. Moreover, the prospect of an increasing family naturally turned Ervendberg's attention to the wider opportunities of Texas, which were an interesting topic of discussion among his friends. John Clark, for instance, was also planning to go to Texas, and did so a year later.

In the autumn of 1839 the Ervendbergs, having laid away their first-born son in the German graveyard at Teuto, packed up the possessions of a humble and impecunious German pastor and took boat down the Illinois and Mississippi rivers, bound for New Orleans and Houston. When they arrived in Houston, probably in December of 1839, the settlement was but two years old. It had been "founded" in 1836, but had taken shape only in 1837, when it became capital of the new republic.* In 1839 Houston was still a town of shanties, with a population of less than two thousand. The town served as a port of entry for immigrants, and here numerous Germans on their way to the interior stopped for counsel with their compatriots. Ervendberg, securing a small plot of ground just outside the town, engaged in market gardening while he looked about for an opportunity to resume his ministerial labors. It is quite possible that at this time he made the acquaintance of two other Naturalists of the Frontier, Lindheimer and Fendler, who were also working as market gardeners near Houston.

These German gardeners were recognized as an asset in early Texas. The British consul William Kennedy wrote in 1844 in a diplomatic dispatch to the Earl of Aberdeen:

Among the European settlers, the Germans have the reputation of being the most successful. They are generally laborious, persevering, and eager to accumulate—orderly for the most part—and they keep well together. They have formed thriving Communities at different points of the interior, and they constitute a considerable proportion of the trading and working population of the towns adjacent to the Coast. In common with the French, they become Market-gardeners. And they divide with the Irish the profits of drayage and cartage, which are pretty large during the business season.

Ervendberg lost no time in beginning work as a pastor; on December 22, 1839, he preached to a congregation of German immigrants

---

*In 1839 the seat of the government was moved to the newly laid out town of Austin.

in Houston. Two weeks later, announcement was made in the newspaper of regular preaching at the home of a Mr. Thiel. Thus began German preaching in Texas. For the better part of a year Ervendberg ministered to his congregation in Houston, which came to comprise "thirty members and fifty-eight souls."

From all accounts, Houston in that day was a chaotic frontier community not noted for its piety. Yet many religious denominations were attempting to get a foothold in Texas, and Houston was key to the interior. The Reverend William Y. Allen, a Presbyterian minister from Tennessee, had preached in Houston at the end of 1838, in the face of great discouragement; Abel Stevens, later a famous historian of Methodism, during the first six months of 1839 had held Methodist meetings in the capital, and was followed by Edward Fontaine. In 1840 the Protestant Episcopal Church sent Dr. Leonidas Polk, Bishop of Louisiana, on a missionary tour of the country between the Brazos and the Colorado, and a parish was established in Houston with the Reverend Henry B. Goodwin as rector. But to judge from the experience of Ervendberg's ministerial colaborers in Houston, it was a thoroughly discouraging field. It is not surprising that after a scant year's sojourn at Houston, Ervendberg sought the higher, more healthful hill-country of Colorado County, where in the fertile valley of Cummins Creek an extensive German settlement, Blumenthal, had already been formed by the Yordts, Zimmerscheidts, Frelses, Biegels, Brodbecks, Ullrichs, and von Wredes. From fragmentary sources I surmise that the elder Yordt, a native of Holstein and a soldier in the Texas Revolution, had known Ervendberg in Germany, and may have been instrumental in bringing him to the settlement of Blumenthal.

Ervendberg left Houston at the beginning of December, 1840. His route was the familiar path of most immigrants to Texas—overland from Houston by way of San Felipe, Austin's former capital. Most travelers stopped in the beautiful little hamlet of Industry at the "hotel" kept by the Oldenburger Friedrich Ernst, who had come to Texas in 1831—an "oasis," as Prince Solms once said, for the German traveler in Texas.

From Industry Ervendberg proceeded about fifteen miles west to the German community of Blumenthal, or Cummins Creek, as it came to be called; and here, on December 10, 1840, he entered with zeal upon his ministerial work. Although a certain Reverend Mr. Fiebiger had previously established an independent Evangelical Church at Frelsburg, not far away, he had died soon after the congregation was organized, and when Ervendberg arrived there was almost no formal ecclesiastical organization in the community. Soon,

ERVENDBERG
1839 - 1855

INTENSIVELY EXPLORED AREA

however, in addition to his home congregation at Blumenthal, Ervendberg had formed small congregations at Industry and Cat Spring in Austin County, at Biegel and Lagrange in Fayette County, and at Columbus on the Colorado. Among his parishioners and acquaintances were the Amslers, Stoeltges, Von Roeders, Klebergs, and Dannkers, of Cat Spring; Henry Amthor and his neighbors on the western border of Austin County; and Friedrich Ernst and J. G. Sieper at Industry. Within a short time Josef Anton Fischer, a domineering Württemberger (some say Bavarian) with Swiss theological training, who was destined to play a turbulent part in the history of the German Protestant Evangelical Church in the United States, joined Ervendberg. Between the two, they seem, for short periods at least, to have conducted schools in the German settlements of Austin and Colorado counties.

Fischer, six years older than Ervendberg, was of an overbearing and contentious disposition, while Ervendberg was mild and gentle, with a broadly tolerant spirit. But the two men were somehow able to work together in establishing the first Synod of German Christian Churches in Texas, neither Reformed nor narrowly Lutheran, but founded upon the broad basis of the two confessions. When one remembers how prone German Protestants of that period were to break up into sects because of trivial metaphysical and dogmatic differences, Ervendberg's part in founding the united synod stands out as a signal achievement.

Dr. Fischer seems to have left Texas some time in the early 'forties (probably before September, 1842), for he did not sign the petition requesting a charter for Ervendberg's great hope, the Hermann's University in Texas, and in 1844 he helped to organize at Cincinnati the German United Evangelical Synod of North America. In 1842 he went to Chicago as pastor of the St. Paul's Congregation, Ervendberg's former mission congregation and the oldest Evangelical parish in the city.

Ervendberg, on the other hand, was fully decided upon Texas as his permanent home. In May of 1842 he had bought a tract of thirty-five acres, part of Peter Pieper's headright league about ten miles north of Columbus on Pieper's Creek; and when Fischer's departure left him alone as religious and educational leader of the German settlements, he pushed resolutely forward with his cherished plan to found a German institution of learning in Central Texas. Realizing the real need among his people, and encouraged by the Education Acts passed by the Texan Congress in 1839 and 1840, in the latter part of 1842 Ervendberg circulated among his compatriots in Austin and Colorado counties a petition calling for the establishment of a university which should offer instruction in both German and English. The Congress of the Republic had appropriated four leagues of land for Rutersville College, founded in 1840, and Ervendberg was eager to secure similar aid from the Government for his projected school. As a result of his efforts, the Texan Congress passed an act chartering the Hermann's University, to be located near Industry or Blumenthal, with Ervendberg as president. Certain provisions of the act, written in by Ervendberg, are significant of the scope of his dream and the breadth of his tolerant spirit:

Sec. 6. Be it further enacted, That the . . . President and Trustees shall establish the necessary preparatory schools, and shall have the right to establish four faculties, one Theological, one Judicial, one Medical, and one Philosophical . . . and they are hereby empowered to grant such degrees as are usually granted by similar institutions in the United States and Germany . . .

Sec. 8. Be it further enacted, That no religious qualification, or test of any kind whatever, shall be requisite, in order to become a Trustee, Professor, Instructor or Student in said University, and the Theological faculty shall never be styled by the name of any singular religious confession, but Protestant Faculty . . .

The Congress of the Republic authorized the grant of a league of land to the new University, and provision was made for selling fifty-dollar "shares" in the University to "subscribers." But as Tiling says in his *History of the German Element in Texas, from 1820-1850* (1913):

. . . when the trustees tried to sell the "university shares," they met with insurmountable obstacles. The shares at the par value of $50 could only be sold for land in exchange; nobody paid in cash, money being too scarce. But it was ready cash that the trustees needed and not land, of which the university had plenty. The attempt to raise the necessary funds proved a failure, and in January, 1846, the franchise was annulled, but was renewed on April 11, 1846 . . . To make the shares more attractive, the subscription price was reduced from $50 to $15. The trustees succeeded in obtaining enough money to build a large, two-story stone building [it was in actuality a frame building, which burned in 1935], but that was all. This building was later used for the public school of Frelsburg, and thus fulfilled its mission in some way, even if it did not bear the proud name of "university."

Perhaps the general conditions in Texas during the years 1840 to 1844 may help to explain the failure of Ervendberg's projected University to materialize. Not one of the educational enterprises started in Texas during those years prospered—Rutersville College, Wesleyan College at San Augustine, the University of San Augustine, all went under after a few years of precarious existence. Ervendberg had left troublous conditions in Illinois only to find fully as much distress in Texas. The finances of the Republic were in a deplorable state, and the furloughed soldiers, out of employment, were dispirited and desperate. During the spring and summer of 1839 occurred the Cherokee War in East Texas; in 1840 there were Comanche troubles, beginning with the Council House Fight at San Antonio in February, and by no means ending with the Comanche capture of Victoria in early August and the sacking and burning of Linnville. During Mirabeau Lamar's presidency (1838-41), the national debt of Texas was trebled, and the Government's paper fell in value to twelve cents on the dollar. In June, 1841, the ill-fated Santa Fe Expedition set out from Austin, and later was captured in New Mexico. Greatly exasperated, the Mexicans next year invaded Texas, capturing Goliad, Refugio, San Antonio and Victoria. San Antonio was again taken by Woll in September of 1842, at the same time that Dawson's men were exterminated at the Salado. Indeed, the summer and autumn of 1842 was the gloomiest period Texas had known since the Runaway Scrape of 1836, and the year closed with the incredibly foolish and disastrous Mier Expedition. During the years 1842-44, the Regulator and Moderator feuds of East Texas made life and property unsafe in that region, and the Texan navy was engaged in all sorts of ill-advised escapades in the western part of the Gulf of Mexico. After the preposterous Snively Expedition to capture the Santa Fe trade in the spring and summer of 1843, both the Texas and American congresses began to consider more seriously than ever the annexation of Texas.

During these years Ervendberg encountered many difficulties in his pastoral work. There was always fear of the Indians—Rutersville, for instance, suffered severely from Indian raids in the early 'forties. The acute financial distress of the country resulted in the almost complete withdrawal of money from circulation, and probably Ervendberg did not receive a total of two hundred dollars during his four years at Blumenthal. Many of the German people among whom he traveled and to whom he preached were unconcerned and indifferent in religious matters. Nevertheless, he was among friends, and gradually, by thrift and industry and self-denial, he was able to build up a small but well-arranged homestead at Blumenthal. It was not much that he possessed—he sold all his holdings for a hundred dollars when he left the locality—but perhaps no other German pastor in Texas could lay claim to success as great as Ervendberg's in his ministerial work. During this time, too, Ervendberg formed a friendship with the naturalist Ferdinand Lindheimer which, in spite of Lindheimer's outspoken criticisms of clergymen and churches, was to endure through the years as a source of great pleasure to both.

In July of 1844, Prince Carl von Solms, first Commissioner General of the Adelsverein, came to Blumenthal in the course of his travels in Texas in the interests of the Verein's plans for colonization. I suspect that "Father" Ernst of the hamlet of Industry had sent him there. At any rate, from some of the German settlers at Industry and Cat Spring, Solms had heard of the earnest, popular, and effective young Evangelical pastor at Blumenthal. After interviewing Ervendberg, Solms, upon whom rested the responsibility of making all arrangements for the prospective colony, invited him to serve as Protestant minister for the German immigrants who were expected in a few months. Ervendberg could hardly ignore such a call to larger work and greater responsibility; with few misgivings, he gave up his work at Blumenthal. It was hard to say goodbye to the old friends, and to leave the grave of a little daughter, Anna. But the die was cast; and late in 1844 Ervendberg and Lindheimer set out for Port Lavaca to meet the immigrants.

The first settlers sent out by the Adelsverein reached Port Lavaca during the first week of December, and Lindheimer and Ervendberg were there to meet them. It had been planned that the march on to the interior, to the Fisher & Miller Grant owned by the Verein, should begin at once. But Henry Francis Fisher's failure to secure wagons and other means of transport greatly delayed the departure of the colonists, and at Christmas they were still waiting at Indianola. Prince von Solms, in his Sixth Report to the Administration of the Verein, says that Ervendberg held the first Protestant service for the group on December 23; "it induced a very earnest and tender feeling in the congregation, and many shed tears of heartfelt emotion." On Christmas Eve Solms provided a large oak tree decorated with many lights and hung with gifts for the children—a bit of thoughtfulness that endeared him to parents and children alike; and on Christmas Day Ervendberg officiated at Communion.

On December 29 the last of the immigrants arrived at Indianola from Galveston. By January 5, 1845, Solms had established his camp at Chocolate Creek, twelve miles from Indianola, where Ervendberg again held divine service. Commanded by wagonmaster George Ullrich, and guided by Nicholas Zink, engineer of the Verein, who had built roads in Greece during the War of Liberation, and by Jean J. von Coll, a former lieutenant in the service of the Duke of Nassau, the caravan slowly passed up the Guadalupe, delayed by rains and heavy roads. The immigrants reached New Braunfels on Good Friday, March 21, 1845, and entered into possession of the new colony.

Mrs. Ervendberg was waiting for the caravan when it arrived at New Braunfels. She had been compelled to remain behind at Blumenthal with her young daughter Augusta, awaiting the birth of a son, Ludwig Carl, on the eighth of January, 1845. When she was sufficiently recovered she had set out for New Braunfels with her daughter and the baby in a covered wagon, bringing the family cows and the meager household equipment, and had reached the east bank of the Guadalupe before Ervendberg arrived with the immigrants from Indianola.

The new settlers made camp on the high bank of Comal Creek near the intersection of present West Zink and North Castell streets. Here they waited while the town was laid out and the lots apportioned. Each head of a family was to receive a half-acre town lot and a ten-acre farm. To the Protestant church were assigned two lots at the corner of present Seguin Avenue and West Coll Street, and the adjoining lot was given to Ervendberg as his own. The immigrants at once began to erect their cabins and houses, which were of the most miscellaneous construction. Ervendberg's house seems to have been the first erected.   On October 5, 1845, the German Protestant congregation of New Braunfels was founded, with Mrs. Ervendberg as the first member.   Presbyters were elected, and the building of a church was begun.   Dr. Ferdinand Roemer, the geologist sent out by the Verein, on his arrival at New Braunfels in February of 1846, speaks of the church as being completed except for the windows; it was finally dedicated on March 22.

In his history of the German settlements Biesele describes the church services that were held in these early months of the colony:

When the weather permitted, Rev. L. C. Ervendberg conducted services regularly every Sunday under a beautiful group of oak trees at the foot of the Vereinsberg [on West Coll Street, near Castell]. A rustic table covered with a white cloth, on which was embroidered a black cross, served the combined purposes of an altar and a pulpit. The Society's officials sat on a long bench made of a thick board; the rest of the people stood.

Seele, in his obituary of Mrs. Ervendberg, tells how she decorated the altar under the trees with flowers, and how, when the weather was inclement, she cleared the little living room of the Ervendberg cottage so that divine service might be held there.

At the end of August the Ervendbergs suffered the loss of the little son who had been born the previous January at Blumenthal.   But they could not allow private sorrow to turn them aside from their many responsibilities to their people.   The new settlers, unaccustomed to life on the frontier, needed advice about adjusting themselves to the primitive conditions and the strange climate.   To the children and the sick of the colony, Mrs. Ervendberg furnished milk freely; for the many visitors she had always a friendly word of welcome, and often a place at her table.   A woman of unflagging industry, strong and capable, conscious of her duty as wife and mother and her position as leading woman of the parish, she won the cordial respect and friendship of the colonists.

And then came the terrible second year of the settlement at New Braunfels—the fateful summer of 1846.   At his own request, Prince Solms had been replaced as Commissioner General of the Verein by Baron von Meusebach in May of 1845.   Only through Meusebach's resourcefulness had the colony been kept solvent during the ensuing year.   In Germany, agents of the Verein had created a great interest in Texas, and some thousands of persons had offered themselves as emigrants.   But even though shiploads of colonists were coming out to Texas, the Commissioner was given almost no funds to provide for them on their arrival.   He often found himself at his wit's end to make ends meet and keep up the credit of the Verein.   Toward the end of 1845, the management of the Verein sent word to Meusebach that they were dispatching 4,304 immigrants to Texas, and that a credit of $24,000 was being established with the agents in New Orleans. But the debts of the colony already exceeded that amount. Moreover, when the second contingent of immigrants landed at Indianola in the late winter of 1846, excessive rains had left the roads almost bottomless. As a climax to the colonists' difficulties, John F. Torrey, who had made an agreement with the Verein to move the colonists from Indianola to New Braunfels, broke his contract because all means of transportation were needed to carry supplies for the troops that were advancing toward the Rio Grande just before the outbreak of the Mexican War. In his history of the first German Evangelical-Lutheran synod in Texas, Mgebroff summarizes the sufferings and difficulties that beset the colonists at Indianola:

The little town at that time consisted of a single house. They built several barracks of lumber, in which as many as possible found shelter. The others lived in tents. Rain and northers penetrated boards and tents, and wet the occupants through and through. There was also a shortage of wood and water. But although there was a lack of drinking water, water stood in marshy pools all about them, breeding mosquitoes and malignant fevers. In the meantime, spring came, and with it the heat of a half-tropical climate. The long inaction of the people and the uncertainty of the future brought about a terrible demoralization of the colonists. All conditions fostered climatic diseases. The mortality increased in terrifying fashion, but it became more difficult to leave the place. The war with Mexico had broken out, and all available agencies of transport were commandeered for forwarding food and materials of war to the soldiers. Besides, the unusually long-continued rains made the roads impassable.

Then came the summer, and many families set out for New Braunfels. Their sole means of travel was by ox-wagons, and the trip was a matter of weeks. Dysentery and other diseases made fearful inroads. Along the road lay human bones, together with beds, tools, chests, and trunks. As Mgebroff continues:

One found whole camps of Germans suffering from fever and half-dead, lying lamenting about a dead fire, with no fresh water for their parched tongues, while around them extended the comfortless prairie, glowing with the heat of the sun. Numerous graves marked the route. By day buzzards followed the wagons, and at night, rest was disturbed by the howl of the wolf and the shrill yell of the savage Comanche.

One man set his sick wife out of his wagon, in order to get rid of the trouble of caring for her. Man and wagon went on their way; the wife was left to her misery, to which she ultimately succumbed, and then became the prey of the wild animals! Soon the man fell ill; his companions meted out in punishment the same inhumanity he had shown to his wife—he was put out of the wagon just as she was! Misery loosed all bonds of decency, writes one authority on

110

that terrible journey, and the prairie became the witness of crimes at which human feeling stands aghast, and which have soiled the German name in the strange land.

Slowly the colonists advanced up the Guadalupe, so slowly that one witness of the journey called it a *Leichenzug*—a funeral procession. Benjamin published a vivid description of the trip in the seventh volume of *German-American Annals* (1909); and a score of narratives by survivors of the movement have been published—the most readily accessible, perhaps, being that contained in the *Deutsch-Texanische Monatshefte* for 1902. But the most impressive account of all is that written by Hermann Seele, long a leading citizen of New Braunfels, who had come to the colony in May, 1845, had acquired a little farm on the west bank of the Guadalupe (where the International & Great Northern Railway crosses the river now), and was the schoolteacher of the town.

On the fourteenth of July, 1846, Seele relates, he went with A. Benner, one of the officers of the Verein, down to the landing-place of the ferry over the Guadalupe at the mouth of the Comal near New Braunfels. The immigrants who had made the terrible journey up from the coast had reached their destination, only to be forced by high water to wait across the river from the town. The few who had been able to get across the flooded river were in almost equal distress, for the officials of the Verein were without means to make adequate provision for them. It was unbearably hot along the river, relates Seele, and "a foul stinking vapor that oppressed our breathing arose from the low-lying Comal bottom, which had been overflowed, as well as from the river itself, still high and muddy."

The opposite bank [he goes on], low and hemmed in by thick cypresses, sycamores, and other trees of the primeval forest, rose in terraces to the prairie, and was almost completely covered with thick woods and bushes. In the neighborhood of the stream the ground was covered with mud and driftwood, among which herbs and vines grew luxuriantly. Farther up were the camps of the immigrants, who had been obliged to remain there several weeks because of the high water. Here and there a tent showed through the foliage, and between the trees shimmered protecting shelters fashioned of sheets and tablecloths. Everywhere lay chests and household utensils brought by the immigrants from the homeland, in the places where they had been unloaded . . . Washed clothing was hung to dry on bushes and grapevines. Fires burned, and in the shadow of the trees men, women, and children were walking, standing, or sitting . . .

Seele crossed the flooded river on the ferry with Benner. They were greeted by frantic pleas from a group of the new colonists for aid in dealing with an American teamster who was threatening to carry their

111

belongings away with him unless he was paid at once for his services. Seele followed Benner up the sloping bank to the prairie beyond. There they found an appalling scene:

An almost overloaded wagon, to which a constantly-cursing American had hitched his oxen in readiness to drive away, stood at the edge of the bushes. A number of gesticulating immigrants stood helplessly looking on, unable to utter a word of English. On a feather-bed near the wagon lay an old farmer in a high fever. Not far from him, under a bush, the body of a woman lay wrapped in a bedspread. She had died on the journey up from Seguin an hour before. Little children sat huddled close together on the ground and wept bitterly for the dear, dead mother, while their older sister attempted in vain to quiet them and to suppress her own sobs.

The father, strong and well-knit in body, cast anxious and perplexed glances at his possessions and sought in vain to understand what Benner was saying in English to the wagoner. . . . Casting one last look on the sorrowing group of children, I stepped back into the forest, deeply moved, only to be shocked by another picture of misery and woe. At the foot of a tall sycamore tree I saw a man sitting, upon whose head (from which his hat had fallen) the sun, now beginning to sink in the west, cast its burning rays. I called to the sleeping man to put on his hat, since otherwise he might suffer a sunstroke. He did not hear me. In order to awaken him from his deep sleep, I stepped up to him and shook him, giving a loud halloo. When I lifted up his head, sunken upon his breast, his wide-open eyes gazed upon me, fixed and unearthly. I drew back terrified—*he was dead*.

Benner arranged for the burial of the two corpses on the edge of the prairie.

Their graves [continues Seele] were the markers for the last travel-station before the cemetery of the colony of New Braunfels, soon to contain more than three hundred new graves. Every camp site from the coast at Indianola to New Braunfels—and there were many, since weather, roads, and the use of oxen to draw the wagons had made the trip last several weeks—was marked by such graves: horrible mileposts on the road which German colonization in West Texas had to travel.

Returning to the river, Seele heard a cry of anguish from within one of the tents, and went over to it. "We are all sick with dysentery and fever, yet no one brings us a drop of water," called a weak voice from within. Seele brought a bucket of muddy water from the river, which the unfortunates in the tent drank eagerly.

That evening, as Seele sat looking at the river from the high bank on his farm, the children of an immigrant who was camping on Seele's land brought word that their father wished to see him.

I went with the children [Seele relates]. The sick man joyously stretched his emaciated hand out to me; his cheeks burned with a dull red; his eyes glittered with uncommon brightness. He wanted to let me know that he had no more pain—that he now felt better, and soon would be in a position to return with his wife and children to his beloved homeland. Full of hope and joy, the wife and children listened to the father's words. But, taught by recent dark experiences at the bed of death, I saw his end approaching. Concealing my thoughts, however, I spoke a few comforting words of sympathy. On arriving at my house, I said, "We must get up early in the morning and be ready to dig another grave." And when the sun rose next morning, the sick man had calmly gone to rest. We dug his grave in the field, laid him gently down, and prayed a silent *Vater unser* for him and his family.

Years passed away; the dead man rested in the grave with others whom we buried there. The green grass had long covered it when the railroad came to New Braunfels. There the railroad workers came upon a few bones preserved in the sandy clay soil, and scraped them in again. Now the train rolls over the place in haste, with its snorting and stamping and puffing.

If any man deserves the remembrance and gratitude of his people, that man is Louis C. Ervendberg. It is an injustice that when some years ago the citizens of New Braunfels placed a bronze tablet on the site of Hermann Seele's first school, they did not mention in the inscription the German pastor who on that same spot, at an earlier date, had held the first religious services in the colony. Moreover, Ervendberg had been instrumental in establishing Seele's school under the trees. Alas! that a man must be remembered for his worst moments: that Ervendberg's lapses from the mores of the tribe, rather than his years of devoted and sacrificial living, should have determined his place in the minds of his people.

While the newly arrived colonists, smitten with disease, crowded the east bank of the Guadalupe, Ervendberg, with his wife and von Meusebach, manfully set about doing the things humanity called for. Unshaken by the moral disintegration about them, these three took matters into their own hands. For the sick who came to New Braunfels during that dreadful summer (the church records of that year show three hundred and four deaths within the parish), they erected a pavilion of cedar posts covered with branches and thatched with long grass. The orphans—some sixty in number—were gathered together and brought to a great tent near the church and Ervendberg's cottage, where the pastor and his wife sought to care for them. Soon a competent woman caretaker was secured for the orphans, and later a better, roomier home was erected.

Slowly matters came to a better pass. The survivors among the new settlers took up homesteads and fell to work. From the terrible experience a new spirit arose in the colony, and German industry and German tenacity saved the day. Within two years the settlement at New Braunfels was on a firm basis, and other settlements were being laid out to the north and west.

113

Ervendberg continued faithful to the responsibilities he had assumed in caring for the orphan children of the colony. In March of 1848, together with Hermann Spiess and Ludwig Bene, he secured from the legislature of Texas an act to incorporate the Western Texas Orphan Asylum, to be located in Comal County. Ervendberg was president of the corporation. In the spring of 1849 an orphans' home (or, as it has been called for many years, the *Waisenhaus*) was completed on a tract of land which eventually came to include some two hundred acres on the west bank of the Guadalupe about three and a half miles from New Braunfels. Well in advance of the epidemic of cholera that ravaged the town about the middle of April, Ervendberg moved the orphans under his care, now numbering about twenty, to this location; and here with the faithful help of his wife, he continued to labor unremittingly for the welfare of his helpless charges. During his first two years at the *Waisenfarm,* Ervendberg continued to hold his pastorates at New Braunfels and at the church of near-by Comalstadt. His removal from the town, however, alienated a portion of the congregations, who felt that he was running away from the cholera in the face of his manifest duty—quite oblivious of the fact that the orphans' home had been incorporated the year previously, and the further fact that the *Waisenhaus* had been built before the outbreak of the cholera. Those who criticized Ervendberg also overlooked the fact that the welfare of the orphans was necessarily a primary consideration, and that the plainest duty would have dictated their removal from New Braunfels.

Nevertheless, Ervendberg later had occasion to regret deeply his departure from the town. Having lived through their sufferings, his people quickly forgot the great services he had performed for them. Too, Ervendberg's occasional absence from service when rain made the roads difficult or cold rendered any journey a hardship bred dissatisfaction in his flock. Many of the first settlers of New Braunfels who might have remembered Ervendberg's services had moved on to the new German settlements to the northwest. But the principal cause of Ervendberg's loss of his people's sympathy seems to have been a controversy over church support.

After 1847, the Verein ceased helping immigrants, and a short time later it withdrew support from a number of agencies in the colony that it had pledged itself to maintain. The church, the school, and the orphans' home were the first institutions which it ceased to support, although the orphans' home was provided for in the organic law of the Adelsverein. When the question of Ervendberg's salary arose in 1851, he asked for a stated allowance rather than a free-will offering; and when this proposal was rejected by the congregation,

he resigned, feeling sure that by such a protest he would bring them
to their senses. But as ill luck would have it, at the precise moment
when Ervendberg's resignation was before the congregation, the brilliant young Reverend Gustav Eisenlohr, a revolutionary refugee from
Baden, offered himself for the place. Ervendberg, dismayed that a
gesture he had intended as chastisement of an unruly congregation
was about to result in his dismissal, attempted to withdraw his resignation, and when that proved impossible, offered himself again as a
candidate. But when it came to the election, the brilliant and roman-
tic young minister from Baden (he seemed young, although there
was a difference of but two years in their ages) received a decisive
majority. Ervendberg, grieved almost beyond endurance by this re-
pudiation, retired to the farm at the *Waisenhaus,* which he now named
"New Wied." A good deal of light is thrown on the whole episode
in a letter, naturally prejudiced, written shortly afterward by Eisenlohr to his father, Pastor Jakob Friedrich Eisenlohr of Freiburg.
Gustav Eisenlohr first suggests that Ervendberg had been somewhat
grasping in his relations with the Adelsverein:

. . . the Adelsverein [he writes] had promised to establish and support church
and school, and had apportioned two town lots for the church and a third for
the parsonage. Ervendberg, who seems always to have been on the lookout
for his own welfare rather than the common good, saw to it that this third lot
was apportioned to him as private property by the Verein, and put up a house
on it at his own expense. I didn't care to live in it, anyway, because of its
smallness and its lack of comfort.

With regard to the vacancy in the church, Eisenlohr states that in
his opinion Ervendberg resigned "just for show," "to make [the con-
gregation] feel how indispensable he was, in order to obtain a better
living." In the election, however, "of ninety-eight votes, he received
only twenty-seven and I seventy." Furthermore, although when he
resigned Ervendberg had promised to take care of the church until
a new pastor should be installed, "when the vote went against him,
he never entered the door of the church again." "When I came here,"
continues Eisenlohr, "he sought to make the Comalstadt church independent of the New Braunfels church, in order to found a new parish
there; but in this he was unsuccessful." And Eisenlohr accuses Ervendberg of other unwarranted actions:

Also he delayed handing over the church-books until we got a court order.
In the beginning [of my pastorate] he continued all sorts of spiritual functions,
confirmed several of the orphan children, etc. Now, however, he has stopped
it entirely, since he would like to enter the political field and since [in this
state] no minister can be elected as a representative . . . At first I visited him

115

several times, but as I became aware of his intrigues, I did not repeat my visits, and have now no personal relations with him . . .

Against this interpretation of Ervendberg's character must be weighed the opinions formed by others who knew him, and who perhaps had less reason to emphasize Ervendberg's faults. There is no reason, for instance, to think that Ferdinand Roemer's remarks concerning Ervendberg, whom he knew in New Braunfels in 1846, are inaccurate. Roemer wrote:

> It filled me with a downright respect for the man to see how he set an example to his flock through his industry in all matters and through his cheerful endurance of the privations and difficulties that are inseparable from a first settlement in the wilderness; and especially how he also, in that tragic time, when virulent climatic diseases decimated the population, exercised himself without ceasing to give comfort and support, in true understanding of his calling.

And Frederick Law Olmsted, who made a journey on horseback through Texas in 1854, left a similarly glowing account of Ervendberg and his labors.

It was characteristic of Ervendberg that even in his great bitterness over the election of Eisenlohr he retained buoyant hopes for the future. His was a sunny, sociable nature, radiating friendliness and earnestness of purpose, which almost nothing could permanently crush. He saw that he was repudiated by his people as a spiritual leader: very well, he would work for them as a teacher, as an educational leader. Lindheimer, his good friend and botanical mentor, was establishing the *Neu-Braunfelser Zeitung,* and other cultural movements were beginning to be in evidence. What though Hermann's University had come to naught? Here in German Texas he would establish a school like the one Francke had established at Halle: he would add a training school to teach scientific agriculture. Father Ernst over at Industry had taught him how to raise tobacco and make cigars: he would raise tobacco here, and he would teach the boys of the *Waisenhaus* the trade of cigar-makers. Ottomar von Behr was experimenting with the improvement of wool at Sisterdale; he would help von Behr. In the 'thirties and 'forties Ernst had filled Austin County with fruit trees and other valuable plants brought from elsewhere: Ervendberg could introduce new plants and trees also. The German farmers wanted wheat bread, yet varieties of wheat that thrived well in Ohio and Illinois did poorly in this climate—well, he would experiment with wheat from semiarid countries where conditions of climate and soil were like those of Texas. He would write to Asa Gray for seeds of plants having pharmaceutical value: his Texas German compatriots should learn to raise these. On the *Waisenfarm* Ervendberg

116

set out experimental beds of economic plants, selected the produce from these varieties, and looked forward to the final breeding of sorts adapted to the soils and climate of Texas. In February of 1850 he had Lindheimer write to Asa Gray for silkworm eggs, so that he might experiment with these; and he mastered the technique of raising silk (*Texas State Gazette,* July 20, 1850). Plans, plans, plans! Meanwhile, Ervendberg had embarked on another venture in higher education. In 1850 he had secured the passage of an act by the legislature of Texas incorporating the Western Texas University, and reading in part as follows:

Section 1. Be it enacted by the legislature of the State of Texas, That the Directors of the Western Texas Orphan Asylum shall be, and they are hereby authorized to establish, in addition to said Asylum, an Agricultural School and such other institutions of learning, in any branch of the arts and sciences, as they may deem proper; and they shall have power in their corporate capacity, to control and govern the same, in the same manner and to the same extent, as they are now permitted to control and govern said institution. *Section 2.* Be it further enacted, That said directors shall have power upon the establishment of any such institution, to appoint a President and such other officers as may be necessary for conducting such institution; to appoint such Professors as they may deem proper, and regulate and prescribe their duties; and in conjunction with the faculty, and professors of such institution, may grant and confer such degrees, in arts and sciences, as are usually granted by Colleges and Universities. *Section 3.* Be it further enacted, That no religious qualification, or test whatever, shall be necessary to become a Professor or student of any institution established by said Directors; nor shall any student be excluded from the benefits of the same, in consequence of his religious faith . . .

It is a noteworthy document, both in the catholic conception of education it exhibits and in the breadth of spirit shown by the prohibition of religious qualifications or tests. In this respect, the charter of what came to be known as the "West Texas University" is similar to the charter of the old Hermann's University, and both reflect accurately the spirit of Ervendberg himself. His broad tolerance, both on this occasion and in his earlier work in founding the united synod, is the more remarkable in view of his theological training and his service as a pastor in an age notable for doctrinal controversies.

His interest in the welfare of the community continued unabated. In May, 1852, he was a leading force in the organization of the *Land- und Gartenbau Verein* of Comal County, and became its first president. He was very proud of this distinction, and mentions it in one of his letters to Gray. In August, 1853, Ervendberg was instrumental in the organization of a social and political club at New Braunfels, and was elected its first president also—a club, by the way, which under

117

the name of *Der Gesellige Verein* continues as an important institution in New Braunfels to this day. A similar club at Sisterdale, *Der Freie Verein,* was headed by those two grand old scholars, Dr. Ernst Kapp and August Siemering. This indicates the esteem in which Ervendberg was held by an influential portion of his fellow townsmen, even after he left the pastorate.

Nor did Ervendberg show himself lacking in civic courage. Many of the Germans in the United States were outspoken in their aversion to slavery during the 'fifties; the question was of course coming more and more to the front as a national issue. In 1854 it was proposed to hold a national convention of German-Americans in St. Louis to discuss the question of slavery; and Ervendberg was made one of a committee of three members to raise the funds necessary to send delegates to the convention from the New Braunfels region.

In this same year, as has been noted above, Frederick Law Olmsted, the landscape architect, who later was to plan Central Park in New York City, and the grounds of the Columbian Exposition in Chicago, came through Texas and visited the *Waisenfarm.*

In his *A Journey Through Texas,* Olmsted has left the following account of his visit:

> The Orphan Asylum, as we approached it, had the appearance of being a small American farm-house, with a German rear erection of brick laid up in a timber frame-work. A large live-oak sheltered the stoop, but the whole establishment was very rough, with a common rail fence about it, and not the least indication of fashionable philanthropy. As we entered a large, dark, unpainted hall, a man came forward from an inner room, who, from his dress, might have been taken for a day-laborer. It was the gentleman [Ervendberg], however, whom we wished to see—a courteous and cultivated professor.
>
> It was a holiday, and he had been engaged in preparing some botanical specimens, but immediately left them to ferry us over the Guadalupe, which ran through his grounds [so that Olmsted might call on Otto Friedrich, of whom he was in search] . . .
>
> Leaving the house, we passed through a garden in the rear, where he showed us little plots of wheat from Egypt, Algiers, Arabia, and St. Helena, which he was growing to ascertain which was the best adapted to the climate. Wheat-growing of any sort, is a novelty here, but the Germans are not satisfied with corn, nor are they willing to pay for the transportation of flour from Ohio, like the Anglo-Americans. There has been, therefore, considerable wheat grown among them, and that with satisfactory success.

Ervendberg then showed Olmsted his open-air theater among the trees, which in the summer was used for informal concerts and even for classes or lectures. Failing to find Friedrich, Olmsted passed "a delightful day" with Ervendberg, who related to the traveler a highly interesting if not entirely reliable account of his life:

He had come to this country in 1839. In the steerage of his ship there were about forty Norwegians with their families. They suffered much hardship, and he assisted and comforted them as much as was in his power. They were very grateful, and before reaching New York they unanimously requested him to continue with them as their pastor, and assist them in forming their settlement at the West. While the ship was detained at Quarantine, he went to the city with the captain to make arrangements for their necessary stay in the city. Returning to Staten Island, he found the ship had gone up, and the ferry-boat had discontinued running for the night. It was not until late the next day that he succeeded in finding the ship at her wharf in New York, and then all the Norwegians had departed.

As Ervendberg learned later, he said, the Norwegians had fallen into the hands of unscrupulous persons who had pretended to sell them land in Wisconsin—the deeds turning out to be forgeries. Ervendberg, according to his own account, went on to Wisconsin, and thence

he had come to Texas, and joining the first company of the settlers who had established Neu-Braunfels, became their pastor. The following year several thousand [immigrants] were landed upon the coast; and, unprovided with food or shelter, perished like sheep. Slowly, droves of them found their way into Neu-Braunfels, haggard and almost dying, having lost all family affection or fellow-feeling in intense despairing personal suffering. Many children came whose parents had died, and he found them starving upon the river bank. He could not bear the sight, but collected sixty of them, and went to work upon this farm with them. He had no means of his own, but took what he could find belonging to the children, and has since sustained them. Working with his wife and children in the field he has managed to raise corn and keep them alive, until now, in better times, they are mostly distributed as helps in various homes. Eighteen are with him still, all calling him papa. He had obtained from the Legislature an incorporation for a University at Braunfels, and himself, as yet, sole Professor, had given a classical education to a few pay scholars.

The whole narrative [continued Olmsted] was exceedingly interesting, as we heard it at our simple farm-house dinner—the Professor, with his horny hands, and with his much-patched coat, telling us of his own noble conduct in the simplest manner, but sometimes glowing and flushing with a superb home eloquence.

After this beautiful and touching story, so full of truth in many of its details, I regret to say that the most careful investigation, in which I have had the unstinted aid of many students of early Norwegian immigration into the United States, has yielded no jot of confirmation for the early part of Ervendberg's tale. Why must human nature succumb to the temptation to dramatize itself?

On the other hand, there can be no question as to the gracious task that Ervendberg and his wife steadfastly performed at the *Waisenfarm*. According to Ervendberg's daughter, he was always gentle and soft-spoken to the children under his charge, and they all seem to have been devoted to him. Hermann Seele has left among his writings an attractive picture of the normal, happy life at the farm, based on a visit to the establishment on New Year's Eve of 1849. As Seele approached the comfortable building amid its grove of live oaks, he relates, the orphan boys raced out to open the gate for him, while the girls waited smiling on the porch—all of them very pleasant-looking in their neat clothing and their new Christmas caps. Ervendberg and his wife received the visitor cordially and took him at once to the schoolroom in a wing of the house, where stood

a table covered with a snowy cloth, with Christmas presents for each of the children. On the right, the Christmas tree—a beautiful young cedar. In the little garden around it, several . . . stones . . . represented the mountain upon which . . . the shepherds of Bethlehem pastured their flocks. On one of these pieces of rock stood the hut that sheltered the Christ-child slumbering in his manger. Across the room, between the windows, shone from the bookshelves the latest volumes of Smithsonian publications, and over the blackboards hung silkworm cocoons strung upon threads, whitish, reddish, and nankeen-colored. These, with the insect collection over the table and the stuffed and mounted birds, gave the walls an interesting decoration . . .

After a good supper prepared by the girls, whom Mrs. Ervendberg was training to be meticulous German housewives, the party returned to the schoolroom for coffee, and the men smoked cigars—good cigars, according to Seele—made at the farm from tobacco raised on the place.

There was much to tell about the making of the Christmas presents, and how everything had been kept secret. For eight weeks the girls had all sewed on the clothes for the boys, and knitted socks, and still they had to work up to the last night. "And just think, on the very night before Christmas, Minna [Koether] sat with Caroline [Schuessler] in her room; and Franzeska [Langer] with Lisette [Schmidt] in hers, and crocheted and sewed presents for each other without knowing that they were theirs." . . .

Then, in the children's room, the quilts were viewed, all filled and stuffed by the girls with cotton raised on the farm. Oh, the quilting days! How beautiful they had been! Everyone whose quilt was ready for quilting had had to play hostess on one day to the others who helped; and each had tried to surpass the others in baking. How happily they jested, and laughed and sang in innocent, joyous, youthful pleasure!

After a walk about the grounds, everyone had tea by the fireside, "and many a merry game was played with the children, and many a happy song was sung, and many a verbal nut was cracked along with the pecans." Truly a pleasant picture! Ervendberg was very fond of children, and one is justified in regarding Seele's description of life at the *Waisenfarm* as accurate.

I have not been able to determine the exact date when Ervendberg

120

began to correspond with Asa Gray; probably it was after 1851, when he resigned his pastorate and became more deeply interested in scientific farming because of his work at New Wied. The earliest extant letter from Ervendberg to Gray, indicating the German's reawakening interest in botany, dates from the autumn of 1854, after Olmsted's visit. The ineptness of his quaint English is somewhat surprising in a man who had been living in America for seventeen years.

> New Wied, Texas—Comal Co
> October the 8th, 1854.

Dear Sir,

Having received your favor of the 10th Aug. I send You herein some Styrax platanifolium. This plant was here at my doors nearly, at first discovered by me; Mr. Lindheimer had not scen [sic] it before, I could not know if it was new or not, and am now very glad to have the name of it, at the same place grows an Ephedra, if the species is known or not, I could also not ascertain, as Lindheimer, had also not seen it. I make me the pleasure to send You within a Register of all the plants, which I collected on the territory of New Wied, three miles and ½ above New Braunfels on the Guadalupe, the flora is so rich and new to me here, that I look up my former beloved studium of botany, but being not acquainted with the American flora and without books and means here in finibus litterarum, I find many difficulties to get through, and I am therefore very happy that You will do me the favor to help me, where I can not further. I began this year to collect the Gramineae [grasses], can I send them? to name these is certain [sic] not possible without a good Instrument [magnifying glass]. Plants by me collected I will be very happy to send You any time You desire.

Some plants within send [sent], please give me the names from according to number.
I am
Yours
very truly
L. C. Ervendberg.

The register of plants accompanying the letter is still preserved in the archives of the Gray Herbarium at Cambridge.

Ervendberg's next letter was written in reply to a courteous note from Gray asking if he could help Ervendberg with books and papers, and naming the plants.

> New Wied . . . November the 8th 1854

Many years already I tried to become [obtain] different seeds for making the experiment to introduce them here, but I never could get them. But being to [o] much interested to introduce among my industrious german neighbors these plants first as president of the "Western Texas University" and also as a member of the Land and Gartenbau-Verein of Comal County, I have the liberty to address You for the seeds: It is: Rheum Emadi Wall. (Australe Don.) or other species [of rhubarb], and Cassia senna and marylandica, and if possible Thea viridis [tea]. In the case that You should not find these seeds in Your Botanical Garden, I am friendly for the address of some place, where they can be had. Every time happy to do You any service I am able to do . . .

This letter crossed another one of Gray's, sent under date of November 7, 1854, to which Ervendberg replied as follows:

New Wied Dec 10th 1854
. . . My best thanks for your letter of November the 7th. Books I only have Plantae Wrightianae pars I et II and will be glad to receive from You what You can send me, the best way I think will be by Mail.
I send again some plants wherefrom I wish You would give me the names. No. 11 of the last I could not make out. No. 18 Eupatorium serotinum as You give me the name I send again under No. 47, and thereto what I until now took for Eupatorium serotinum under No. 40. What is the right name of both plants? Of Desmanthus reticulatus I possess only one specimen. I will collect it for You next year and send it. A letter from me, wherein I did ask for a little seed, if possible, of Rheum Emadi, and Cassia sennae or Marylandica I hope You have received and will be happy for a successful answer . . .

Gray answered this letter, probably during the Christmas holidays, and Ervendberg pursued his quest for seed yet further:

New Wied . . . January the 8th 1855
. . . In your letter wherein You had the favour to write that the seeds I did ask for are not to be had in this country, You ask: what other kinds of Rheum do you want? or what other species of Rheum are wanted? Is Rheum palmatum, undualatum [sic] or any other to be had? please send me a few seeds! Do you know any place in the States; where Cassia Sen. or Maryl. is raised? Is there any seed of medical plants to be had, which might be raised here with profit? . . .

Ervendberg, of course, hoped to introduce among the German settlers of New Braunfels the cultivation of such simple pharmaceutical herbs as Turkey rhubarb, quassia, Virginia snake root, gentian, chamomile, boneset, dandelion, and so on. But little seems to have come of his efforts in this direction. The pot-herbs of European kitchen gardens, in fact, seem to be singularly absent from the sites of early German settlements in Texas.

Other things, also, were not going as well as they should at the *Waisenhaus*. Of course the routine of life, simple, contented, happy, went on in its wonted course; but the West Texas University, from which Ervendberg had hoped so much—that was quite another matter! All during the spring of 1853 he had made especial efforts to increase the number of pay-pupils from the outside by inserting an advertisement (in German) in the *Neu-Braunfelser Zeitung*:

West Texas University, New Wied, Comal Co., Texas. Pupils are taken at any time for the three divisions of this educational institution: (1) Elementary

School; (2) Latin School; (3) High School [*Oberschule*]. Further information will be given by L. C. Ervendberg, President of the University.

But this and other efforts to attract students met with small success. It was not a question of Ervendberg's lacking the personal respect of his townsmen, as I have pointed out above. During that spring he had been appointed a member of the Democratic Assembly of Comal County, along with Doctors Koester and Remer, Ottomar von Behr, and six other leading citizens; and in April, in spite of the fact that he lived outside the town, he had been chosen by the town council as a member of the board which was charged with organizing a public school. Ervendberg took his place as a member of the board on May 9, 1853; and a set of regulations for the conduct of the school which he drew up was subsequently adopted by a unanimous vote.

This was a real distinction—but an ironic one; for the establishment of the free public school at New Braunfels marked the end of Ervendberg's hopes for the success of his school at the *Waisenfarm.* It was only natural that he should now pause to cast up his accounts and go over the events of his life. He was not an old man—only forty-five —but the last ten years had taken heavy toll of his youth. And now the venture which he had entered upon with so much enthusiasm when he left the pastorate was likewise at an end. It was hard to face the future.

Ervendberg was a man who was supported in time of adversity by the consciousness of his leadership, the sense of his importance among his fellows. It was natural for him to think of himself as the pastor of his flock. With his congregation about him, looking to him, feeling with him, he was unconquerable. And he derived much strength from his awareness of the continuity of religious tradition. The songs they sang in church—grand old hymns of the sixteenth and seventeenth centuries: ah! here was nothing trivial or evanescent, but, as he thought, a taking hold upon the very hem of eternal truth. These earnest, humble people about him on the Texas frontier, far from the thousand-year-old culture of their homeland, forgot their separation from home and kindred in Martin Luther's grand old battle hymn *"Ein' feste Burg ist unser Gott,"* in Count Zinzendorf's *"Jesu geh voran auf der Lebensbahn,"* or in Gerhardt's *"Ich singe Dir mit Herz und Mund"* and *"O Haupt voll Blut und Wunden."* In days of festival and rejoicing, there had been the noble *"Nun danket alle Gott"* and *"Lobe den Herren den mächtigen König der Ehren";* while in days of sorrow and bereavement, *"Jesus meine Zuversicht"* had brought comfort and surcease of grief. But now, that was all past. No longer was Ervendberg the pastor of his flock; his flock

123

had repudiated him. New men were coming in who knew not Joseph; his educational hopes and plans, long cherished—it was almost fifteen years since he had first planned to found the Hermann's University—were falling into dust. Moreover, he was getting old; that could not be escaped.

He had tried to do many things, and he had failed. University, pastorate, agricultural school, all of them had fallen through. Why? He began to search out sources of failure in his past: furtively, secretly. As he probed within himself, he must have grown somewhat desperate in his eagerness to lay fresh hold upon a life that seemed slipping from his grasp. And before the busy world realized it, before his own close neighbors dreamed of any domestic conflict, Ervendberg's name was coupled in shame with that of one of his orphan girls, and he was a fugitive from Texas.

Such an uproar resulted as can arise only in formally religious small towns, where one can know every external act of one's neighbors without in the least comprehending the underlying motives. As a result, the name of Ervendberg has ever since been conspicuous for its absence in accounts of the heroes of German colonization in Southwest Texas. From the vantage point of the present, however, one can realize that the responsibility for Ervendberg's irregular conduct was not entirely his. The society in which husband and wife had been reared had failed to prepare them for the most important work of life; it had taught them much of everything but the fundamental realities of marriage. And through the years, buried but unforgotten resentments had accumulated between them which came to the fore in the face of other distresses.

It is easy to recount the bare facts of Ervendberg's departure. During the summer of 1855, Mrs. Ervendberg became aware of her husband's increasing interest in one of the orphan girls entrusted to his care, whom he had seen growing into young womanhood. She was the daughter of a Bavarian artist who had died at sea on the way to America with the first immigration, which reached Texas in December of 1844. She had been confirmed in 1850 by Ervendberg. Now, at seventeen, she was the innocent cause of the downfall of her pastor, protector, and teacher.

Mrs. Ervendberg confronted her husband with what she had discovered; he acknowledged the facts. Together they planned for better days. They would go back to Chicago, where her people lived; they would leave Texas, where all their great hopes and plans had come to naught. They planned to depart for the North in September. Mrs. Ervendberg was to take the three daughters with her, and Ervendberg, after winding up the business affairs of the *Waisenhaus*, would come

124

on later with the two boys. In this understanding, she departed. Ervendberg, with his sons, stood on the west bank of the Guadalupe at New Braunfels watching the wagon pass through the ford and up the opposite bank. He waved his hand in farewell as long as the wagon was in sight.

On the first of October, 1855, he left New Braunfels with the two boys—and the orphan girl. When we next hear of him, he is in Mexico City, having come there by way of Galveston, perhaps New Orleans, and Vera Cruz. Later he went to a new German settlement north of Vera Cruz called "Wartenberg," not far from Pastoría on the Río Calabozo. He lived at Wartenberg for some time (at least from the beginning of 1857 to the end of 1860) collecting plants for Asa Gray, as we shall see later. He subsequently returned to Mexico City, and then removed finally to Pachuca, northeast of the capital, where he established a sort of experiment station on a small scale, like that at New Wied. Here on a night in February, 1863, when all the servants and laborers had gone to celebrate a Saint's Day at a neighboring village, several bandits forced their way into the house, shot Ervendberg down in cold blood, and made good their escape with a considerable sum of money that was in the house against the next day, which was payday.

There remains but to describe Ervendberg's botanical explorations in Mexico. The materials on which such an account must be based are unfortunately somewhat meager. In tracing the steps of other naturalist-explorers who worked in the Southwest I have been impressed with the remarkably abundant traces left by most of them in the public records, in the newspapers, and in the specimens they sent to scientific institutions. In some instances (as in the case of Audubon) it is possible to reconstruct a naturalist's itinerary in considerable detail by studying dated locality-labels on museum specimens. But concerning Ervendberg's extensive travels in Mexico, we have only six letters he wrote to Gray. Even the colony of Wartenberg seems to have left no trace in the memory of living man. One can learn its location from a map Ervendberg sent to Asa Gray, but that is all. The German Ambassador to Mexico, after a most careful search generously undertaken at my request, found no trace of the colony; and a charmingly obliging eighty-five-year-old German botanist of the State of Vera Cruz, Dr. C. A. Purpus, was unable to find out anything at all concerning Ervendberg's work in Mexico. Ervendberg undoubtedly spent the last eight years of his life in that country, but he left no enduring memory there.

Ervendberg's letters to Gray are thus of considerable biographical importance; and to me they are of great interest as showing a tendency, occasionally exhibited by Gray, to leave his collectors in the lurch. In the Gray Herbarium, for instance, is an early letter of Augustus Fendler to Gray, in which he chides him for neglecting to send the most necessary and indispensable helps for collecting—a reproof so telling that Gray was not again guilty of such neglect toward Fendler. As is apparent in the Ervendberg letters, to the very end Gray was remiss in rewarding Ervendberg's labors, although there is no indication that he was dissatisfied with the collector's work.

The first letter is dated at Mexico City, March 4, 1856. After describing his journey up from Vera Cruz, with much botanical detail about the country he has passed through, Ervendberg touches upon general conditions in the capital:

. . . The people seems to be good harted but bigott; sciences are more than hundred years back. They have a Museum here, where You see birds all pêle mêle, no order in it nothing named and without catalogue. I collected some plants but I could not do much on account of the revolution; but however the collection of plants is all the time difficult on account of robbers and thiefs in the country it is necessary to take all the time some man along for a safeguarde and therefore not to be done without great expenses. Here was one man collecting for English botanists for a yearly salary of thousand dollars, but under the condition not to give one plant away. This man died, I could perhaps get this engagement, when I applied for it, but I do not like to be bound under such condition, I wish to collect for America, where is my home. If You find someway, that I could collect Plants, Coleoptera etc. for American Institutions or societies, I am willing to do it. South of the valley are two snow mountains, there must be a great variety of plants I[t] would be interesting for You to have these Epidendrons, Bromeliaceæ, filices arboreæ (I saw one 15′ long 4″ diameter) etc. in Your botanical Garden, I could deliver them all as living plants. If You favor me with an answer, please send Your correspondence through the hands of the American Legislation [Legation], General Gadsden, the only sure way, where I am acquainted with . . .

Apparently Gray did not reply to this letter. Ten months later Ervendberg addressed Gray from Wartenberg, again offering to make botanical collections for him.

I made now another journey to the tierra caliente [wrote the collector] and live at present about 30 leguas N. W. from Tuxpan in a very beautiful contry, full of new plants of all classes. I made also here already great collections and would like to send them to your disposition, wherefor I request [?] your answer. They are to be send by way of Tampico. I will S[t]ay here for some years, and it appears that my botanical harvest will be very great . . .

In a reply dated March 4, 1857, which Ervendberg received at the end of August, Gray told him to go ahead and collect plants, and promised to sell ten or twelve sets of any specimens he collected. Gray also advised Ervendberg to collect mosses for Dr. Sullivant, the bryologist, of Cincinnati—these latter to be shipped in care of Gray. He promised to send plenty of botanical drying paper. An answer which Ervendberg wrote on September 2 from Wartenberg apparently never reached Gray; and on January 10, 1858, Ervendberg repeated his previous letter, which described his journey from Mexico City to Wartenberg. Passing through a rugged and mountainous country with much interesting vegetation, some of it resembling the flora of Texas, Ervendberg had descended some four thousand feet to the bed of the Río Calabozo, where he found scattered Indian settlements. Crossing and recrossing the river continually in his passage through the canyon, the naturalist had lost his horse with his saddlebags containing all his money and papers, and barely escaped with his life. The colony of Wartenberg stood on a beautiful plateau, perhaps three thousand feet above sea level, that opened out beyond the canyon.

Many plants which I saw in Texas I have seen also here [Ervendberg continued] . . . I collected already a good deal but for want of paper and money I am bound to stop very soon.

The people here are Indians without culture like brutes but Christians by name; few families of better education, the land owners, and some Indians which live in little villages and speak spanish call themselves hombres de razon (man of reason). Agriculture is in the deepest state of infancy, a kind of great knife (matcheta) is the only tool to cut trees, to build houses (which they make very good from bambus covered with palma without any kind of nail only binding them with a kind of liane). So [they] make fence and [illegible] their fruits. Mais, frijol, beans; a little sugar tobacco and cotton; they live on tortillas, cakes made from the mais prepared on a stone for a mill, beans and Chille (Capsicum) They are all lazy and stupid.

On account of my losses in the Cañada I am somewhat in a bad position, having rented a tract of land for making my living and being without [a] horse, etc: You could do me therefore a great favour if possible to send me $150. in advance on account of plants; You find perhaps a friend, if You are not able who can borrow it. It would be only to buy a horse and to procure the necessary boxes from Tuxpan or Tampico for to pack up the plants; here is no foot of a board to make a box, all that makes much expenses and I would hardly be able to send on plants without that favour . . . You might send me paper as much as possible by Boston with a schooner or by New Orleans from where every time run schooners.

After repeating the contents of his earlier letter, Ervendberg adds fresh pleas for help from Gray:

I have been hunting all around for News papers, but this people, and that is in these little towns, Tantoyuca, Chicontepec, Huantla, read no papers no[t] one dozen was found. I have all full of plants. Do me the favour for to send paper, paper, paper, as soon as possible by Tampico, no way by Vera Cruz where from I could not get it here. Send me that money. I have already thousands of plants or all will be lost here, what would be a great damage . . .

There was no answer to this repeated letter and no paper was sent, although Gray had promised some months before to send Ervendberg an ample supply of paper. After nine months Ervendberg ventured again to address Gray regarding the promised supplies:

Wartenberg . . . October 14, 1858

Your letter [of March 4, 1857] wherein you give me orders for sending plants I had received, and send since that time two letters particularly for paper for drying plants, in it, but I never received an answer and no paper and nothing. For the difficulty to get paper and boxes I could send no plant[s] until now. This paper I get very dear from New Orleans. I have more plants, but not more boxes; and I am collecting but with difficulty and trouble with that little paper I have in hand.

The plants I send, 226 of all kinds, on[e] package with fern[s] and one package with mos[s]es for Dr. Sullivan[t], are mostly 12 of every species and certainly of all species one specimen for You. Some could not be well pressed for want of paper but I have made it as good as the circumstances will allow.

Fruits I had collected a good many also, but for a long time, they were lying about, many are destroyed by insects, and only the few left I send this time. What You do want of seeds and fruits, You may write me, and I will collect. Should anyone wish the different kinds of pieces of the ligna [woods], I am willing to collect.

. . . You will consider about the payment, that the difficulties are greater, than any where else and that I not could get very far on account of the revolutions which where [sic] around me.

All plants are collected in the neighborhood of the German colony Wartenberg and I will go further of[f] when I possess means to hold a man to go with me and to buy a horse.

The plants which are safed from my journey from Mexico [City] until here are in my hands, I could not pack up from want of means, and will be send as soon as I can get up a box . . .

But Gray did not answer this letter either, although he received the box to which Ervendberg refers, in February of 1859. Five months later, Ervendberg, still refusing to feel rebuffed, asked Gray again for the help promised him two years before:

Wartenberg . . . March the 11th 1859

. . . In the month of October of last year I did send to you a large box with plants, but having received no answer until now, I would ask with this, if the one [was] lost and never received by You. Two letters I send before that were not answered but I thought, that by reason of the revolutions here they came not in Your hands; but as the box makes a great volumen I can not declare her lost. I did send box with on[e] Mr. Herman Schultz of Tampico, who will also receive your answer. Said box contained. [sic]

        19 species of fern
        226 species of other plants and a collection
          of mos[s]es of this neighborhood.

Of all species where I could send them I send 13 specimens, as You had the friendship to write me that You could [sell] ten—twelve. For want of a box or boxes all seeds I had were destroyed by insects and I could therefore send only few, but I am collecting them now for the next time.

I had to pack up that box very much in [dark?] therefor[e] I forgot to remember that the mos[s]es as all were collected on the mesa of this colony Wartenberg between November [1857] and February [1858]. At present I am requesting your friendly answer and if possible some paper, as all things are very high here, I had to pay for that paper, (and other better paper is not here) $7.50 without fr[e]ight. I would like to explore more this part of the country but You [must] consider that the difficulties are very great, no road, no taverns; all the time camping and in middle of a revolutionary people; hardly is to be found a little plank for pressing the plants. All the plants and ferns which I collected from Mexico [City] until here are ready to be send to You as soon as I received your answer and also another large collection made here. I am now more acquainted with all things here and would go further of[f] from this part of the country as soon as I receive some money from You, so that I can have a man go out with me. You might send the best [drying paper] to a person in New Orleans who must give it to the schooner who runs weekly between New Orleans and Tampico. To get things here by way of Vera Cruz is very difficult.

In response to this letter, as in response to his earlier ones, Ervendberg received, to adapt a phrase of his, "no answer and no paper and nothing." But in spite of Gray's silence Ervendberg prepared and sent still another box of plants, and the following letter:

Colony Wartenberg . . . April 12, 1860
. . . With this letter I send You the second box with plants from No. 227-385, a packet with mosses for Mr. Sullivan[t] some Fern and seeds: Also You find within some specimens of Agave Americana? wherefrom they make nearly in the whole Republic of Mexico a vegetable beer, named Pulque and some of a plant of the genus Bromelia, named here Pita and I think botanical [illegible] for your botanical garden; the last grows in this neighborhood in the thickest woods on very remote places; I was not able until now to see not the flower and not the fruit. It contains, shaving of the epidermis a fibre fine as Linum and as strong as cannabis, here they use the thread of it to all kinds of sewing works by shoemakers, saddlers etc., some of the Germans commence to cultivate it. I send a little with the plant, it grows 4-6 foot.

This is my sixt[h] letter I write *without having received any answer*. My first box I send of[f] in the month of October 1858 and have answer of the merchant, that said first box arrived in good order on the 5th January [Jan. 29] 1859 at New York. I am very anxious to hear of You, if the said first box arrived in Cambridge or not and if in good order or not. Fr[e]ight I paid from here to Tampico with $5, and for this second box with $2.50. Letters from here to Tampico must be paid with 25 Cents, but further they do not take payment. Paper is very high and not good, therefor[e] I ask Your goodness as You wrote and promised in your first letter to send me some papers. I had with my family a great part of the time we are here very bad fevers on account of the hot clima, therefore I think to go a little higher up in a more cold and healthy part for my northern constitution, but all things are dear here on account of the revolutions and the want of industry in the land. Therefore I am very short in means and would ask your favour to send me as soon as possible some money, when [if] my plants arrived, when not, to give anyhow some answer, that I can hunt for the box, if not arrived. I had a great deal more of Cacti collected and seeds, and I think I have now more than three hundred species here, but having no answer from You, I could not send them of [f] and a great part are spoiled by insects. This box I send for having a good opportunity through a friend, who goes direct from Wartenberg to the U. St. You might consider here, that to make collections here in this tropical clima is very difficult; at first to find good specimens for insects and birds, the most fruits are eaten before ripe; and now from October until June it is nearly impossible to go on 5 steps from the house, by brushing a single bush thousands of ixodes [ticks] kreep on You, that a person can hardly live for pain; not counting snakes and aunts [sic]. Some plants are eaten, when drying in the paper, so I had for some of the ferns (there are 5 species here) more than twenty specimens of every one species drying, but I could not save one for ants. I think they must be send in alcohol. . . .

Please send me Your answer etc. and money and paper.

This letter Gray has endorsed, "Ansd June 26th." I do not know the details of his answer, but it evidently set a price on the plants sent in the first box, and terminated any arrangement existing between him and Ervendberg. On October 24th, 1860, Ervendberg made a sight draft on Professor Gray for ninety dollars—somewhat meager pay for several years' work. The draft was duly paid.

In the *Proceedings* of the American Academy of Arts and Sciences (Volume v, 1862) Professor Gray prefaces a twenty-five-page account of Ervendberg's collection (which contained nine new species and three new varieties of higher plants) with the following introduction:

This collection, being made by a person of limited botanical knowledge, contains a number of plants which are common weeds in most warm regions, but also a fair number of new or little-known species,—enough to show that this district of country, in which Mr. Ervendberg resides, would well reward a proper botanical exploration, which it is the object of this notice to encourage him to undertake. This Mr. Ervendberg is fully disposed to do, if the possessors of herbaria could be sufficiently interested in this regard, by subscribing for his collections at the usual rates, to defray the necessary expenses. Supplied with proper appliances and facilities, Mr. Ervendberg would make a good, as he is a zealous collector . . .

Surely no enemy could have more effectively damned Ervendberg with faint praise than Gray did in this notice. Thus did the great botanist assist in the advancement of science in the ancient Mexican province of Huasteca.

I have alluded elsewhere to the danger the pioneer naturalist ran of being overcome by the intellectual mediocrity of the frontier, and of being forced to give up scientific pursuits by the stern necessity of making a living in an uncivilized environment. Ervendberg's career in Mexico clearly illustrates these difficulties—as well as some others.

Ervendberg cannot in any sense be said to have had adequate fundamental training for scientific exploration. Rather was he of a type, common enough among graduates of German Gymnasia and universities, who had received more or less formal instruction, with field-excursions, in "natural science"; and then, coming to a newly settled country rich in strange and impressive productions of nature, he had been reawakened to the beauty of the physical universe. Berlandier, Lindheimer, Fendler, Wright, had all had excellent instruction in botany, or had seriously cultivated botanical interests over a term of years, before they set up as collectors. Moreover, these men all found in their scientific work those social and spiritual values that most people find in human relations. They were adapted to the collector's mode of life, isolated from humankind for months at a time. Ervendberg, on the other hand, could not devote himself intensively to scientific work. He was interested primarily in the application of science to the betterment of human conditions. He gained most of his satisfactions through his social contacts, as pastor, as director of the orphans' home, as leading member of various organizations, as would-be educator. To the extent that he tried to fill the role of botanical collector in the New Braunfels region, in a territory already classically explored by Lindheimer, he was miscast. And he always retained a certain didactic and pastoral quality of mind—at least until he went to Mexico.

I think it probable that if he had received from Professor Gray even the minimum of advice and counsel that simple humanity would seem to have dictated, he would have developed into a good and useful collector. To me the fiasco of Ervendberg's career in Mexico rests not on his shoulders, but squarely upon those of Gray. No one who reads Ervendberg's letters to Gray can fail to be deeply touched by the pathos, even the tragedy of his situation as it is revealed in them.

In the end, despite the cloud that rests upon his name, the life of Ervendberg is to me one of rare attractiveness, because he was so human. Capable of unremitting labor and self-sacrifice, full of tenderness for his people and quick to respond to their needs and their sufferings, he still was unable to avoid the most egregious blunders in handling his own affairs. He deserves credit and honor, not for the clearness of his head, but for the greatness of his heart; not for what he accomplished and saw to fruition, but for what he dreamed.

131

Ferdinand Jakob Lindheimer 7

I T was the year of Waterloo. The Arch-Egotist had gone down to final defeat. At Vienna the Powers were sitting, Metternich in their midst, to effect the political reconstruction of Europe. In Prussia, King Frederick William III was promising a liberal constitution for that loyal people which to a man had risen in the *Befreiungskrieg* against Napoleon. In the university town of Jena was being created the *Burschenschaft* system, dedicated to the spiritual emancipation of German youth through the noble ideal of the *Turnverein.* Led by "Turnvater Jahn," the movement took on an earnest, almost religious character. It was spreading to all German universities of whatever land—to Strassburg in France and Dorpat in Russia; to Leyden in Holland and Vienna in Austria, and to Kiel in Denmark. A new Germany for the Germans, bound together by the German tongue! How that *Burschenschaft* manifesto rings across the years! Even though the *Burschenschaft* movement was crushed, at least temporarily, after the student protests at the Wartburg Festival in 1817 and the murder of the supposedly reactionary Kotzebue two years later, says Poultney Bigelow, "ever afterwards German universities felt so strongly its past influence that never again did undergraduate life revive the licentiousness and brutality which was but too common under the old regime."

It was this stirring time, when the liberals of Germany were struggling violently against reactionary Austria and Russia of the Holy Alliance, that shaped the personality of Ferdinand Jakob Lindheimer, who was to become a pioneer Texan botanist and naturalist. During his school years, the German universities and Gymnasia had become, according to the *Cambridge Modern History,*

the center of political agitation; professorial chairs were turned into platforms, lectures into harangues, and classes into public meetings. . . . The intellectual

132

atmosphere of Germany was indeed charged with electricity; but it was the repressive conduct of Governments which gave a political direction to the storm.

In 1827 the *Burschenschaft,* which "gave nightmares to Metternich," was revived at Erlangen and spread to other universities, among them Jena and Heidelberg; and in May of 1832 Siebenpfeiffer delivered his violently democratic speech before the tens of thousands of students gathered at Hambach. Then followed repressive measures in the Diet at Frankfort, in July of 1832, and as a consequence the Frankfort Riot of April 3, 1833.

The words of Turnvater Jahn may stand as the slogan of all young Germany of the time: "The German people cry out, 'We want no longer to be merely Bavarians and Saxons, no longer merely Prussians, but Germans above all!' Hence comes the general cry for a constitution, which the inner freedom of the great German people, in spite of conflicting voices of the governments, manifestly authenticates!"

It was with phrases such as these ringing in his ears that Lindheimer grew to manhood. He had been born at Frankfort-on-the-Main on May 21, 1801, the youngest son of Johann Hartmann Lindheimer, a well-connected merchant in affluent circumstances. Deprived of his father in early life, Ferdinand Lindheimer was given a good education by his mother, probably in the Gymnasium at Frankfort. He was thoroughly schooled in mathematics and the classical languages. His lifelong love for mathematics is evidenced by his fondness for teaching higher mathematics, without charge, to pupils in the town of New Braunfels in his old age; his classical tastes and abilities are everywhere manifest in his writings. From Lindheimer's youth, the glorious past of Greece and Rome lived again for him so vividly that when he entered the University of Bonn on November 7, 1825, he matriculated as a student of classical philology. After an abbreviated career in the university (he left Bonn at the Easter holidays, 1827, without a degree), Lindheimer took a position as teacher in the preparatory school of Georg Bunsen at Frankfort. Although his formal education was largely in the field of classical philology, Lindheimer had gained in his German schools an ardent interest in botany. He had also made the acquaintance of Georg Engelmann, a fellow Frankfurter destined to play a great part in the development of American botany.

The Bunsen School seems at this time to have been itself a hotbed of political discussion—to such an extent that it was under constant surveillance by the police. Lindheimer entered upon his work at the School in the autumn of 1827: in the seven years that elapsed between 1826 and the spring of 1833, when the Government closed the School after the Frankfort Riot of April 3, six of its teachers had been sentenced for sedition.

Lindheimer, it seems, took no active part in the Frankfort Riot; in later years he told his son Eugene that he had not been a participant. Nevertheless, he was seriously compromised by his long association with Georg Bunsen and his School, and probably also by active participation in the student discussions which had brought about the revival of the *Burschenschaften* in the German universities in 1827, the year he left Bonn.

Lindheimer's political activities seem to have evoked severe reproof and condemnation from other members of his family. As a result he cut himself completely off from them, rejecting all financial aid and apparently even refusing to accept his share in the partition of his mother's estate. Lindheimer's son Eugene, in an unpublished letter, alludes to these family difficulties, and adds that Lindheimer spoke very little of his early life unless specifically questioned.

Whatever may have been the immediate cause of Lindheimer's break with his family, he showed himself throughout his life bitterly hostile to compromise of any sort. There can be no doubt in the mind of one conversant with the facts that Lindheimer's intense devotion to the cause of universal human liberty, as well as his implacable hatred of organized and dogmatic religion (a hatred that, like a fixed idea, colors all his writings), was a violent emotional reaction brought about by the parental repression and severely formal religious atmosphere of his early life. How much his dependent position in the family as a younger son and his early loss of his father may also have contributed to his attitude, one can only guess.

In the face of family disapproval and official suspicion at home, what course remained for Lindheimer but to escape to that political haven, America? Governmental reaction and oppression in Germany at that time were encouraging a large-scale exodus to America of political refugees, who were dotting the Mississippi Valley with German "Latin Farmer communities" such as those at Belleville, Illinois; in Warren County, Missouri; and at other places in Ohio and Indiana. Here congregated former Gymnasium and university men, frequently of great ability—*émigrés* who had left the homeland solely because every movement for a constitutional government in Germany was being thwarted by the arbitrary and incompetent autocrats who were in power. Lindheimer directed his steps to Belleville, drawn by the presence there of his old colleagues in Frankfort, Bunsen and Berchtelmann. When he reached Belleville in the early months of 1834, he found in the community not only his Frankfort friends, but such other eminent Germans as the great Bavarian jurist, Dr. Theodor E. Hilgard, with his three sons, all of whom were destined to attain eminence in the field of science; Gustav Körner, later Lieutenant-Governor of Illinois; Dr. Georg Engelmann, the botanist, and his brothers Theodor and Adolf; and a number of other persons of only slightly less eminence. Bruncken must have had in mind such a settlement as Belleville when he wrote in his *German Political Refugees*:

These Latin Settlements have played a part in bringing about a higher standard of civilization in the states of the Mississippi Valley, which will be appreciated at its true worth when the history of the cultural development of that section comes to be written. . . . The Latin settlements were centers of light, from which higher ideals of life than were customary among the ordinary settlers spread among wide portions of the country. Especially in educational matters, these men set the standard, not only for their German countrymen, but for their American neighbors.

But in spite of the congenial company Lindheimer found at Belleville, he remained there only a few months. In late September of 1834 he set out with five companions by boat down the Mississippi to New Orleans, on a proposed journey to Mexico by way of Texas. When they arrived at New Orleans, however, Lindheimer's party heard reports of Indian depredations in Texas (false reports, as it turned out); and there were no guidebooks to Texas, or even maps, to be had in the bookstores of the city. Discouraged, three of the travelers turned back to the North. Lindheimer and his two remaining companions, after several weeks of indecision and waiting in New Orleans, set sail in a Yankee schooner for Vera Cruz. The account of Lindheimer's voyage and his adventures in Mexico, although it is highly interesting, must here be omitted. Suffice it to say that he remained in Mexico for sixteen months, in the upland region near Jalapa, west of Vera Cruz, and at the German colony of Sartorius and Stein in Mirador, where at different times he managed a distillery on the plantation of Sartorius & Lavater and served as overseer of a banana and pineapple plantation. It is significant that while he was in Mexico, Lindheimer joined with Otto Friedrich in making extensive collections of insects and plants. From his first activity as a collector his talents for the work were evident. The minute and extended descriptions of the plant and animal life of Mexico published many years later in Lindheimer's *Aufsätze und Abhandlungen* show remarkable native powers of observation and analysis, which were developed by practice and experience to a high degree of acuteness.

The botanist's decision to come to Texas in 1836 sprang from mingled motives. His son Eugene ascribes Lindheimer's departure from Mexico to the anarchy and unsettled conditions which he found there. Lindheimer himself states in his *Aufsätze* that he decided to go to Texas to fight for Texan independence because of his hatred of all political oppression, and anyone who knows the man will feel this was undoubtedly an important consideration. But let us allow Lindheimer to tell his own story. He is writing of conditions in Mexico during the last months of 1835:

Often one could see very clearly, from articles in the papers, that an important party in Mexico had the greatest sympathy for the Texans. . . . In the *Diario del Gobierno,* side by side with bombastic articles describing "how the invincible Mexican army with the holy picture of the Virgin of Guadalupe would cross the Río Grande to chastise and put to flight the heretics who had been taken up like snakes into their bosoms," appeared other articles which clearly had been written by friends of the Texas uprising. . . . The Mexican newspapers often fawningly called Santa Anna "the Napoleon of the West" and (in a fashion that seemed ironic if indeed it was not due to the stupidity of the editorial writer) drew parallels between the "glorious northern expedition" [that was to be made into Texas] and the Russian expedition of Napoleon. I recognized this was the moment to carry out my original plan of going to Texas, before the decisive battle—perhaps even before Santa Anna's army had met the Texans. . . . My decision to go to Texas was already made.

Lindheimer reached Texas in roundabout fashion by way of Mobile, joining a company of volunteers commanded by Captain Jerome B. Robertson who were going to fight for Texan freedom. "My company was composed mostly of Irishmen," Lindheimer told his son many years later. "With other troops we were stationed in Galveston Island as a kind of coast defense in case Mexico should undertake to land troops at that point. Before the battle of San Jacinto we had orders from General Houston to join his army as soon as possible. Houston, however, gave battle to the Mexican army sooner than he had expected, and for that reason we reached Houston's command one day after the battle of San Jacinto."

Little is known of Lindheimer's life during the three years following the battle of San Jacinto. This was the period when Audubon, accompanied by his son, made his visit to Galveston and Houston, and called upon General Sam Houston at the capital; when Charles Wright, the young schoolmaster and surveyor from Connecticut, was beginning the work in Texas that was to link his name inseparably with Texan botany. After the war for freedom, Lindheimer seems to have been completely submerged in the flux of incoming settlers. His compatriots and contemporaries have left no record of

him. There were many German settlers in Texas before the Adelsverein immigration of the years following 1844, particularly in the
Baron de Bastrop's and Austin's colonies, and Lindheimer may well
have lost himself among these. But there is no scrap of evidence
concerning his activities.

During this period Lindheimer no doubt was collecting plants and
corresponding on things botanical with his intimate friend Engelmann, who was in St. Louis. But the first definite information we
have concerning him after the war is found in specimens collected
for Engelmann at San Felipe in March of 1839, as Lindheimer was on
his way to New Orleans and St. Louis. From this time on, the record
is ample.

Lindheimer spent the winter of 1839-40 in St. Louis with Engelmann. Upon his return to Texas in 1840, he took up truck farming
on some land near Houston, and followed this occupation for more
than two years. But the work was completely unsuited to him, and
in 1842 he wrote Engelmann to ask whether he might not make his
lifelong interest in botany a source of livelihood. Engelmann wrote
to Professor Asa Gray of Harvard College, asking him to suggest a
way in which Lindheimer might at the same time feed soul and
pocket. Engelmann called to Gray's attention the beautiful collection
that Lindheimer had sent him, and pointed out that the Texan flora
appeared to represent a transition from that of Mexico to that of the
United States. He also reminded Gray of the collections Drummond
had made ten years before for Hooker, with their hundreds of new
species of plants found in Texas. This touched a tender spot in Gray,
who was already burning to be the first botanist of America. The
correspondence resulted in an arrangement among Engelmann, Gray,
and Lindheimer, whereby the latter was to make extensive collections
of Texan plants in sets; these were to be named and mounted by the
botanists, and new species described by them; and the sets were to be
sold for the benefit of the collector at the rate of eight dollars per
hundred plants. Fortified with this arrangement, Lindheimer, who
had gone back to St. Louis in the autumn of 1842 to carry on negoti-
ations, left for Texas early in March of 1843. He was never to venture
north again, having discovered in himself a constitutional weakness
of the lungs that made northern winters inadvisable for him.

Lindheimer's travels through Texas to investigate the botanical
treasures of the region are of absorbing interest to botanist and lay-
man alike. After leaving Engelmann in St. Louis, he arrived in Galveston by the end of March; the herbarium of the Missouri Botanical
Garden has specimens of dried plants labeled by Lindheimer at Galveston during that month. Ferdinand Roemer, who became a close

friend of Lindheimer's during Roemer's stay in New Braunfels three years later, has left a vivid account of how the naturalist made his collections:

He bought a two-wheeled covered cart with a horse, loaded it with a pack of pressing-paper and a supply of the most indispensable provisions, namely flour, coffee, and salt, and then set forth into the wilderness, armed with his rifle and with no other companion than his two hunting dogs, while he occupied himself with collecting and pressing plants. He depended for his subsistence mainly upon his hunting, often passing whole months at a time without seeing a human being.

Until the first of June, 1843, Lindheimer was occupied in making extensive collections around Houston. Early in that month he left Houston for the Brazos bottom in present Waller and Austin counties, and collected in the bottoms during the major part of June and July. In early August Lindheimer crossed the Brazos, and for a few days

collected west of the river, probably near the present towns of Sealy and Bellville. After returning to Houston in the middle of August, at the end of the month he made a collecting trip to Chocolate Bayou, fifty miles to the south, and collected there in late September and early October. He returned to Houston by way of Galveston: his return was slow, for we find plant records reading "Galveston Island, Oct., Nov., 1843" on his herbarium labels.

In 1844 Lindheimer spent the whole season west of San Felipe, between the Brazos and the Colorado. He left San Felipe in February, and probably did not go beyond the confines of present Austin and Colorado counties. During this trip Lindheimer lived for a time with Robert and Rosa Kleberg at Cat Spring in Austin County. "On his little Mexican cart he would sally forth on excursions into the wilds of the Brazos bottom, returning with a wealth of new and strange forms of plants and animals," says Rosa Kleberg in her reminiscences of early days in Texas. "He was a fine gentleman and a splendid scholar." Lindheimer's collections also show that he spent three months of this season at Industry, in Austin County, but do not give any evidence of his having collected in the Colorado bottoms, as Engelmann and Gray state in one of their papers. Perhaps the data on which the statement was based were contained in the collections of Lindheimer, mentioned by Engelmann, which were lost in transmission to St. Louis during this year.

The reader will recall that at Industry and the near-by community of Cat Spring Lindheimer had struck up a friendship with Louis Ervendberg, whom Prince Solms had invited to become pastor for the Adelsverein colony. It is probable that Lindheimer and Ervendberg went together to Port Lavaca in December of 1844 to meet the first group of immigrants. In any event, they were both at the port when the colonists arrived, and accompanied the party on the slow journey up the Guadalupe to the site that had been selected for the town of New Braunfels. Lindheimer's collections on this trip show specimens from Matagorda Bay and the Guadalupe bottom in Victoria County. When New Braunfels was laid out, Lindheimer secured rights as a colonist, built himself a house, and during the year gathered plants in the locality. He also explored the wild, mountainous region to the northwest, a country still occupied by Indians.

Lindheimer's way of life at this period is vividly described by Ferdinand Roemer, who met him in New Braunfels early in 1846.

At the end of the town [wrote Roemer in his *Texas*] and at some distance from the last houses, right upon the bank of the Comal River, stood a hut or small house partly concealed by a group of elms and oaks. With its enclosed garden and its arrangement and position, it furnished an idyllic picture. As

I neared this simple and homely dwelling for the first time I espied before the door of the hut a man busily engaged in splitting wood. Apparently he was accustomed to this labor. A thick black beard covered his entire face; he might have been in his early forties. He wore a blue jacket open in front, yellow buckskin trousers, and coarse shoes, such as are worn by farmers in this vicinity. Near him lay two beautiful brown-spotted bird dogs, and a dark-colored pony was tied to a near-by tree.

According to the description, the man could be none other than he whom I sought. The answer he gave to my question corroborated my assumption. He used the speech of a cultivated man, with a soft, hesitant voice that contrasted with his rough external appearance. It was the botanist, Mr. Ferdinand Lindheimer, of Frankfort-on-the-Main. He has done a lasting service in his many years of assiduous collecting of the plants and study of the botany of Texas. . . . Here he built the hut described above, and with greater leisure and convenience than he had ever before enjoyed in Texas, began to collect systematically the rich and largely unknown flora of the region. . . .

In spite of the hardships and misfortunes that marked the terrible year of 1846, Lindheimer kept on with his collecting in the New Braunfels region, sometimes in company with Roemer, and also engaged in work for the colony. The following year he traveled up the Guadalupe to the new town of Fredericksburg, near the Pedernales River. After some time spent in this locality he joined the Darmstadt group who were on their way to establish their colony, Bettina, between the Llano and San Saba rivers. It appears that he remained at this colony through the winter of 1847-48, returning to New Braunfels the following February. From February to June, 1848, he collected at New Braunfels; and his plant labels indicate that in July and August he returned to the Pedernales and the Llano. No later records for this year are to be found among Lindheimer's collected plants. It was a poor collecting season, that summer of 1848, for the burning sun had almost destroyed the vegetation of the granitic soil that had gone for months without a rain.

From Lindheimer's plant-labels it appears that he spent the whole of the collecting season of 1849 in the neighborhood of Comanche Spring (later known as "Meusebach's Farm"), a camping place about twenty miles north of San Antonio on the Fredericksburg road. He collected there from February to November, and then, after a short trip up the Cibolo, returned to New Braunfels. His last two years of collecting for Engelmann and Gray, 1850 and 1851, were spent at New Braunfels, and his collecting arrangement with them terminated that year. With Lindheimer's assumption of the editorship of the newly-founded *Neu-Braunfelser Zeitung* late in 1852, his active career as a botanical collector was brought to a close; but botany remained his avocation to the end of his life.

Buried in forgotten accounts of the hardships encountered by the Adelsverein immigrants who landed at Indianola in 1844, the name of Lindheimer appears as that of a humble but resolute leader. In the preceding chapter I have described the difficulties of the first colonists, and the terrible sufferings of the second group who landed at Indianola in the spring of 1845. Life in New Braunfels in the early years was indeed precarious. An account written by Alvin H. Sörgel only two years after the events he describes will suffice to recall the conditions under which Lindheimer worked in 1846 and 1847:

The hostility of the Indians had kept the settlers near together and prevented their spreading out into neighboring territory. Harvests had not been plentiful, and many of the inhabitants . . . had grown indolent and thriftless. Many would work for a few dollars in the service of those who still had a little money. Some in their desperate plight, surrounded by disease and ruin, sought to enjoy after their own fashion the brief span of life still left them. Resorting to a wooden booth where there was dancing every night, the hale and sick together raved in a dizzy reel of enjoyment to the shrill music of a clarionetist, an individual who was also the professional grave-digger of the place. This midnight dance of death was the dreadful culmination of the sights the travelers had witnessed on their way to New Braunfels,—human bones, cast-off pieces of clothing, beds, tools, chests strewn along the desert path between Indian Point and New Braunfels. . . . The next summer, in 1847, New Braunfels received additions to its population and gained in stability. . . . Disease became less frequent and the harvesting of crops placed a premium on work. As soon as the colonists were made to stand on their feet, the sturdy class prospered and the idlers fell away like frost-bitten leaves in autumn.

One acquainted with Lindheimer only in his later years, when his deep blue eyes had lost their fire, his thick black beard had grown snow-white, and his compact, well-knit frame had become the trembling body of an old man, would never have guessed the heroic life he had lived. In exploring the country around New Braunfels he had a number of encounters with the Indians. He seems to have had little fear of them, and they molested him not at all. Doubtless when they saw him gathering his plants they considered him a great Medicine Man gathering herbs for his magic brews. In Lindheimer's book there is a long chapter on his experiences with the Indians, only a few of which may be mentioned. Chief Satanta, or Santa Anna, of the Comanches, was very friendly to Lindheimer and visited him several times in New Braunfels. On one of these occasions he gazed with approval on Lindheimer's little son Eugene, a bright-eyed lad of two years who was running around without clothes like a Mexican child. The old chief said nothing, but on his next trip to New Braunfels he brought with him two handsome mules and a little Mexican girl, saying, "You take mules and Mexican, I take boy!" and could hardly understand why the exchange could not be made.

Another incident related by Lindheimer in the *Aufsätze* well illustrates his quick intelligence in dealing with the Indians.

At the beginning of our New Braunfels settlement [he writes], as the locality here was almost without roads, and uncertain, curiosity impelled me to see the territory which lay on the other side of the rocky slope . . . to the north of New Braunfels. . . . I suddenly found myself in the neighborhood of a band of Indians. They were astounded that I had climbed the rocks with my horse, and said that I had a good horse; I instantly cocked both hammers of my double-barreled gun, and they asked me the reason for it. I answered them [in Spanish], "It's well to be careful!" and they laughingly agreed.

Lindheimer's friendliness toward the Indians, and theirs toward him, made it possible for him to accompany them on several journeys—not without grumbling on their part, to be sure, for they felt his great collections of plants and his bundles of drying paper were useless impediments.

Out of the many episodes of Lindheimer's life it will be possible to select here only a few that have a direct bearing on his work or on his environment. Among the most significant experiences of Lindheimer's middle life were his exploration of the country northwest of New Braunfels toward Fredericksburg and the Llano-San Saba purchase, in 1847 and 1848, and his part in the founding of the Darmstadt Colony.

By 1847 the hardest times were over in New Braunfels. Meusebach, successor to Prince Solms, aided by the sturdy German pluck and persistence of the colonists themselves, had saved the day. And new settlers of outstanding ability were on the way. The time was ripe in Germany for another political upheaval and abortive revolution, that of 1848. In the German Gymnasia and universities, agents of the Texan colonization project had been giving lectures to students, representing to them the great advantages of emigration. Prince Solms himself had addressed the students of the Technical School and the Gymnasium at Darmstadt. As a result forty young men, chiefly from Darmstadt, with great care and skilful planning formed a colony to come to Texas. Among them were two graduate physicians, seven lawyers, five foresters, two mechanics, two carpenters, a ship's carpenter, a butcher, a miller, a blacksmith, a hotel-keeper, a maker of musical instruments, a farmer, and a brewer, as well as a young student of theology and a fifteen-year-old boy, Louis Reinhardt, sent out to botanize for the Technical School at Darmstadt. The guiding spirits of the enterprise were Dr. Herff, who became in later years a prominent physician of San Antonio, and the engineer, Gustav Schleicher, a graduate of Giessen, who later represented Texas in the Congress of the United States.

At this time Texas was beginning to attract the choicest spirits from many German advanced schools and universities. For some years the same forces that had brought about the formation of Latin Farmer communities in the Mississippi Valley had been causing that influx of cultivated Europeans to Texas which Olmsted mistakenly supposed was entirely a result of the revolutionary disturbances of 1848 in Europe. He says:

> After the events of 1848 . . . came numbers of cultivated and high-minded men, some distinctly refugees, others simply compromised, in various degrees, by their democratic tendencies. . . . I have described how wonderfully some of them are still able to sustain their intellectual life and retain their refined taste, and, more than all, with their antecedents, to be seemingly contented and happy, while under the necessity of supporting life in the most frugal manner by hard manual labor. There is something extremely striking in the temporary incongruities and bizarre contrasts of the backwoods life of these settlers. You are welcomed by a figure in a blue flannel shirt and pendent beard, quoting Tacitus, having in one hand a long pipe, in the other a butcher's knife; Madonnas upon log walls; coffee in tin cups upon Dresden saucers; barrels for seats, to hear a Beethoven symphony upon the grand piano; . . . a fowling-piece that cost $300 and a saddle that cost $5; a book case half filled with classics, half with sweet potatoes. . . . [Their most prominent faults] are a free-thinking and a devotion to reason, carried, in their turn, to the verge of bigotry, and expanded to a certain rude license of manners and habits, consonant with their wild prairies, but hardly with the fitness of things.

But to return to the forty young Darmstädters, intent on forming a colony in Texas. They reached Texas early in 1847, and weighed down with all conceivable tools and equipment they might need for a colony (they carried with them all the necessary equipment for a flour mill, and even a cannon), began the march to New Braunfels and Fredericksburg. They reached the latter town probably in July, and remained there a few days before setting out for the tract, lying between the Llano and San Saba rivers, which had but recently been purchased from the Indians as a site for their colony. As has been indicated above, Lindheimer, who had been collecting for some time in the vicinity of Fredericksburg, made ready to go with them to the new purchase.

The colony, which was of the Icarian type proposed by Étienne Cabet, was called "Bettina," after Bettina von Arnim. Louis Reinhardt, the young botanist who accompanied the group, has given an informative account of the life of the colony:

Having spent several days in Fredericksburg [he says], we set out for our tract, [Baron von] Kriewitz again being our guide. Of course we had to move very slowly; and when we arrived at the Llano, we hunted a ford for three days. The best one finally proved to be but a few yards from our camp, where we had to lift the wagons four feet upon a rock in the bottom of the river by the aid of windlasses, and this work took us from morning to night. The Llano was then a beautiful stream, as clear as crystal, and known in our party as the "silvery Llano." One could see the bottom at the deepest places. The whole country was covered with mesquite grass as high as the knee, and abounded in buffalo and deer.

The colonists arrived at the grant early in September of 1847; and in November a party of Indians arrived for a visit, making camp a short distance from the settlement.

During the night a number of our utensils were stolen by the squaws; but the next day the men returned them. For everything we gave them we were paid back three-fold. As they stayed some time, we became well acquainted. Whenever we came into their camp, they would spread out their deer skins, bring out *morrals* full of the biggest pecans I ever saw, and tell us to help ourselves. They even tried to learn German from us, in spite of the great difficulty they found in pronouncing some of the words. The word *Pferd* they could not say at all; *Ross* was easier; but best of all they liked *Gaul,* which seemed to afford them great amusement. Other tribes visited us, but none caused us the least annoyance. There were Lipans, Delawares, Kickapoos, Wacos, Choctaws, Shawnees, and Comanches, making seven different tribes. After January, 1848, no more Indians came.*

Lindheimer, it will be remembered, returned to New Braunfels in February. The colony of Bettina proved to be short-lived; in the summer of 1848, in Reinhardt's words, it "went to pieces like a bubble";

. . . it was a communistic society [he adds] and accordingly had no real government. Since everybody was to work if he pleased and when he pleased, the result was that less and less work was done as time progressed. Most of the professional men wanted to do the directing and ordering, while the mechanics and laborers were to carry out their plans. Of course, the latter failed to see the justice of this ruling.

Lindheimer is known in the history of the German element in the United States not only as a naturalist, but also as a gifted editor who for nearly twenty years managed the *Neu-Braunfelser Zeitung.* This paper, founded in 1852, partly by popular subscription, became one of the leading journals in the German language in the United States.

---

*This account apparently disproves the oft-repeated statement that Indian troubles brought about the dissolution of the colony.

144

The paper reached a high journalistic plane which seems fantastic in this day of the yellow press. With its long, scholarly articles, well larded with classical quotations and allusions, it still makes good reading, if one can get over the Latinity. An example or two from the *Aufsätze* (which consists of essays reprinted from the *Zeitung* and the *Neu-Yorker Staats-Zeitung*) will suggest Lindheimer's editorial manner. In speaking of the cattle industry in Texas, he says: "The Indians . . . from their own point of view, consider their robbing expeditions great deeds and themselves heroes, like Odysseus and Diomede, who stole the horses of King Rhesus; or Hercules, who robbed the children of Geryon." And in another place, dealing with his favorite controversial topic, the conflict between theology and science, he writes: "Everyone . . . can appreciate the importance of this conflict . . . and if we cannot be banner-bearers or field generals in this *Kulturkampf,* we can at least fight faithfully in the front ranks, so that in our deaths we may join in the Spartan battle-song of Tyrtæus: 'Beautiful it is to die, fighting in the front rank!' "

In an editorial concluding his service with the newspaper, Lindheimer reviews frankly the unpleasant features accompanying the founding of the *Zeitung,* describes the sinister forces he had warred against, and then proceeds to his own apologia:

As far as I know, I myself have never made use of the columns of this paper for personal defense, because I considered the newspaper an auditorium for public opinion and the property of the public, and not a [illegible] for private parties. . . . I have never spoken against my conviction. . . . My political opponents have nevertheless honored me with the title *"Lügenheimer,"* but have never made use of my offer to publish proof of their accusation in the *Neu-Braunfelser Zeitung,* though they have frequently been invited to do so. . . . Perhaps never did a Roman say with more conviction *"Beatus ille qui procul negotiis,"* than I who say good-bye to the newspaper business.

It was Lindheimer's manner seldom to speak of his past or of his achievements. He was always a quiet man, never losing his temper or expressing himself strongly—unless he was paying his respects to the clergy, when *"geistliche Raubritter," "Lohnpriester," "Leviten,"* or perhaps on mild days, *"Pfaffen,"* was the order of the hour. He lived a long and useful life, one filled with great content in the doing of his work, in communing with nature, and in his contemplation of that great philosophy of life which he has beautifully summarized in his essay in the *Aufsätze* entitled *"Optimismus."*

His motivation in life was a pursuit of the good life for its own sake. "Do right and justice for the sake of right and justice, not for the reward!" he says in his essay *"Ueber Schulunterricht."* "The heroes, martyrs, and saviors of mankind have by their lives tried to demonstrate that the individual man has no special or peculiar interest for himself, and that he cannot with happiness to himself seek his own aims independently of the interest of humanity." Lindheimer's hatred of religious bigotry rises to a high pitch again and again in his essays. Most of them bear the impress of the intense bitterness bred of the reactionary oppression which curbed his youthful enthusiasms in Germany, and do not give a true impression of Lindheimer's naturally sweet temper under any less provocation. During his life, it is said, he counted many ministers and priests among his personal friends; we have seen how harmonious was his friendship with Pastor Ervendberg. In all his diatribes he drew the distinction between religion and what he called *"Priester-Christenthum."* And while he could declare in an essay on education, "I really need no God for my ethics . . . no special World-God, no Demiurge," still he could continue by saying, "I will deny neither the necessity of such a God for the pious, childlike *Weltanschauung* of the people, nor the actual existence of such a God. I am neither atheist nor deist." Yet toward the last, when he celebrated his seventy-fifth birthday (he had but three years more to live), he could write in his "Birthday-Thoughts of a Man of Seventy-Five":

In the United States of North America, where the terrorism of the orthodox rabble often reaches almost the ferocity of the sordid Anachoretes of Egypt, who in Alexandria stripped Hypatia naked and tore her to pieces, because she gave lectures before an educated public on the highest questions of humanity: here in our republic, where the religious zealots love to obscure the light of Truth by their industrious stirring up of [verbal dust] . . .

Surely here is no trembling, or weakening of the antagonism he felt toward organized religion! The sown wind of childhood repression had reaped the whirlwind: it is for us to attempt to understand, knowing that to comprehend is to pardon.

Lindheimer met death bravely on December 2, 1879. A contemporary estimate of his life and character, especially in relation to his newspaper, is to be found in an unidentified clipping, probably from the *Neu-Braunfelser Zeitung,* of December 9, 1879:

Lindheimer has led as happy a life as is possible for a man entirely devoted to his science. He was sufficient unto himself. His demands on life were slight and thus he never battled with want in the true sense, though his eventful life may have known many days of struggle for existence. . . . [His editorship of the *Neu-Braunfelser Zeitung*] yielded him little pleasure, but rather many annoyances and irritations in abundance. But as in other things, here too the work itself was enough enjoyment for him. The contents of the paper were frequently beyond the comprehension of the majority of the readers; he did not write to please the masses but to uplift them, and thus the first eighteen volumes of the *Neu-Braunfelser Zeitung* offer to the educated man even today a rich treasure of instructive reading.

In the field of botany, Lindheimer is honored by having a round score of species of plants named in his honor by scientific specialists. His name, along with that of Charles Wright, whose friend he was, is indissolubly connected with the botany of Texas, to which in his collections for Engelmann and Gray he made contributions of outstanding value. In his essay on optimism, in which he sums up the philosophy of his whole life, he utters a sentence that deserves to be his epitaph: "Yes: he in whose mind humanity has been realized as a single, indivisible whole, whose personal efforts are but the individual manifestations of the aim of this whole, himself lives the eternal life of humanity." Even so: and Lindheimer's name lives forever in the very nomenclature of the science he loved.

Ferdinand Roemer, and His Travels in Texas 8

PRINCE SOLMS, the first Commissioner-General of the Adelsverein, seems from the very beginning to have been interested in the mineral resources of the colony. In his fourth report to the directors of the Verein he stated that he had secured from an old Mexican a promise to guide him to the nearest of the fabulously rich silver mines on the San Saba River reputed to have been worked by the Spaniards; and in a later report he referred again to the matter in discussing the need for fifty miners in the colony. When, in the spring of 1845, he relinquished the Commissioner-Generalship, he engineered the appointment as his successor of an accomplished student of the natural sciences, Baron Ottfried Hans von Meusebach, hoping that under von Meusebach's direction the mineral resources of the lands of the Colony would receive proper investigation and development. Solms also wrote to the Berlin Academy of Sciences (of which Baron Alexander von Humboldt, Leopold von Buch, Heinrich Ernst Beyrich, M. H. Lichtenstein, Johannes Müller, and Christian Gottfried Ehrenberg were leading members) requesting the aid of the Academy in securing the services of some competent young geologist to make a careful survey of Texas, especially of the area included within the Adelsverein grant. After much deliberation, the members of the Academy chose Dr. Ferdinand Roemer of Hildesheim, a member of a prominent family of that city. With the financial assistance of the Berlin Academy and personal aid from Humboldt and von Buch, Roemer came to Texas late in 1845. For eighteen months he worked so effectively that as competent a geologist as Professor Frederick W. Simonds, in his excellent biographical sketch of Roemer, justly calls him the "Father of the Geology of Texas." Roemer also did excellent work here in other fields of natural history, and hence merits inclusion among those naturalists who have identified themselves with the Southwestern frontier.

148

When Ferdinand Roemer came to Texas he was a young man, in his twenty-eighth year. He had been born in Hildesheim, in Hanover, on January 5, 1818, of an excellent family, several members of which were actively interested in natural science. In this ancient city filled with medieval art and with many interesting old buildings, including the earliest dated timbered house in Germany, Roemer had come to adolescence. His father was a counsellor to the High Court of Justice in Hildesheim; and the boy, intended for the law and the government service, was prepared for the university at the Gymnasium Andreanum in his native city. During his Gymnasium days, an obscure teacher of mathematics stimulated an interest in nature that later, strengthened by the influence of Roemer's elder brother and some of his friends, confirmed a boy's interest into an absorbing avocation. After passing his *Abiturienten-examen* from the Gymnasium, Ferdinand Roemer, at the age of eighteen, matriculated at the University of Göttingen as a student of jurisprudence. The next three years he spent in preparation for his father's profession. But because of some obscure political complications, for which young Roemer was apparently not responsible, he was excluded from the state examination required of all those who entered the government service in the law.

During his years at Göttingen Roemer had indulged his early love of science by attending some lectures on geology, and in the summer semester of 1838 he had studied natural history at Heidelberg. Here he had made the acquaintance of the renowned Professor Heinrich Georg Bronn, who was just then crowning his first years of work as a professor at Heidelberg by the publication of the last volume of his magnum opus, his *Lethæa Geognostica.* So deep an impression did the young student make upon the master, then and later, that fourteen years afterward Bronn invited Roemer to collaborate with him on the third edition of the work, which appeared in six octavo volumes in the years 1852-56.

Finding a legal career closed to him, Ferdinand Roemer, acting on his brother's advice, decided to become a geologist. In furtherance of his aim he matriculated at Berlin, and there attended the lectures of a number of eminent scholars. During his stay in Berlin, young Roemer made many warm friends among men of science, including Julius Ewald, the paleontologist, Dr. Leopold von Buch, Professor von Dechen, and the youthful Heinrich Ernst Beyrich, later professor of geology at Berlin. On the tenth of May, 1842, Roemer defended his thesis before the university faculty at Berlin and received his doctoral degree.

Armed with a doctor's diploma, but not spoiled by it, Roemer then set out actively to study the geology of Germany. He tramped over and studied the mountainous country along the Rhine in Westphalia. Two years later, in 1844, he published a memoir on the geology of this region, dedicated to the venerable von Buch, which is still a classic. Subsequently Roemer published other contributions (chiefly in the *Neues Jahrbuch für Mineralogie,* 1845) dealing with his researches into the mountain structure of Rhenish Westphalia, especially in the Teutoberg Forest region. As a result, when Roemer set out for the Adelsverein colony in Texas he bore an open letter of introduction from Baron von Humboldt commending the young geologist to American men of science and declaring that "Dr. Roemer, like a book, needs but to be opened to yield good answers to all questions." Thus the years moved toward the greatest single event in Roemer's life: in the autumn of 1845, armed with his letters and credentials from the Berlin Academy of Sciences, he arrived in America.

The eighteen months that Roemer spent in Texas were so packed with adventure and with labor in the field of geology that one can relate only the chief events of his sojourn. Before attempting an account of these experiences, however, I should like to indicate briefly his itinerary in Texas.

Roemer left New Orleans for Texas on the twentieth of November, 1845, and arrived in Galveston on the twenty-second. He spent seven weeks in Galveston and vicinity, wandering all over the island collecting land- and sea-plants and animals, and making shipments of these to his friends of the Academy of Sciences at Berlin. In Galveston, then a town of some five thousand people, he met, among others, William Kennedy, the British Consul, and Dr. Ashbel Smith, who some months previously had returned from his diplomatic service for the Republic of Texas at the British and French courts. While at Galveston, Roemer also made a visit to one of the ships of the Texan navy. It may be remarked parenthetically that he spoke rather scornfully of the navy in the account of his travels published after he returned to Germany.

Those weeks at Galveston were filled with new and interesting experiences: his first "norther," on New Year's Day, which broke the mildness of a memorably mild winter; his oyster-hunt on the wreck of one of the former ships of the Texan navy, the *Invincible,* which had been run aground by the Mexicans nearly ten years before; and his observation of the incredible numbers of water-birds that covered the surface of Galveston Bay. On January 4, the news came to Texas that the American Congress had passed almost unanimously a resolution calling for the annexation of Texas. War with Mexico was imminent, and Roemer began to think of the task he had come to Texas to per-

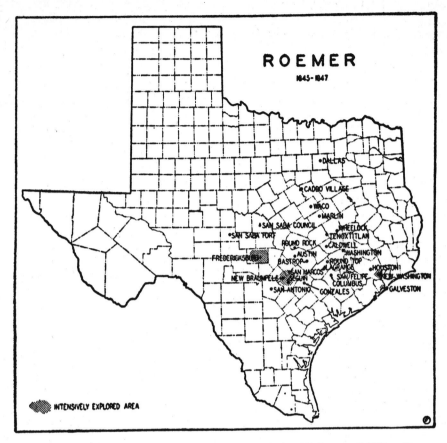

ROEMER
1845-1847

INTENSIVELY EXPLORED AREA

form—the investigation of the geology of the Fisher & Miller Grant, which the Adelsverein had begun to colonize. Because of the uncertainty of the coast route to the German colony on the Guadalupe—by way of Lavaca Bay—Roemer decided to go to Houston, and thence across country. On the twelfth of January, therefore, he set out for Houston on a steamboat, finding some distinguished fellow passengers aboard. Invited by Colonel James Morgan to stop off for a visit with him in his home at New Washington, at the head of the Bay, Roemer spent several days in that vicinity studying Pliocene fossils he found there. He was greatly impressed by the opulence of Colonel Morgan. The beautiful surface of Galveston and San Jacinto bays, here partly separated by the tract of land which has come to be called "Morgan's Point," and covered at this season of the year with endless flocks of water-fowls, filled him with delight and amazement.

On the seventeenth of January, Roemer left New Washington for Houston. He stopped five days in Houston at the old Capitol Hotel, which he graphically describes. While waiting for the departure of the freighting train with which he was to travel to the Colony, he became much interested in the stories of the Indians of West Texas told him by a frontiersman from that region; and he determined to use every opportunity to see and learn more of these people.

With Nicholas Zink and his train of merchandise wagons Roemer set out for the frontier on January 23, 1846. Because of the recent rains the roads were almost bottomless. Streams had to be headed, for in their lower reaches they were level with their banks. The first night the party stopped at Piney Point, nine miles from Houston. Nightfall of the third day found them completely exhausted in the Brazos bottom near San Felipe—the appearance of which was a grave disappointment to Roemer. Pushing on to Columbus, he noted with approval its pleasant location, its eighteen or twenty houses, all with porches, and its three stores, two taverns, and a smithy. Farther on, Gonzales, with its mean, ramshackle appearance, seemed to the naturalist the antithesis of Columbus, but he found the road from Gonzales to New Braunfels pleasant in its variety of scene and prospect. Roemer arrived at his destination after a journey of seventeen days, in which he and his companions had traveled approximately two hundred and fifty miles. Here at New Braunfels he met two of his relatives who had come to Texas to buy land, and also encountered Ferdinand Lindheimer, under circumstances which have been described in an earlier chapter.

The next thirteen weeks (February 9 to May 17, 1846) Roemer spent profitably in the vicinity of New Braunfels, making brief but important side-trips to near-by localities. Collecting-excursions with Lindheimer, visits to Flores Rancho, near Seguin, and trips about the country near New Braunfels under protection of the Adelsverein cavalry occupied his time for three full months. In fact, he remained in the vicinity of New Braunfels during most of the first year, except for a journey with Wilhelm Langenheim down the Colorado valley to Nassau Farm, near Round Top, in Fayette County (May 18 to June 7, 1846), and a month's trip with John F. Torrey, of Houston and New Braunfels, to Torrey's Trading Post on the Brazos, near present Waco (July 24 to August 28, 1846). On Monday, July 13, 1846, Roemer witnessed the first county election in newly-organized Comal County, when some of his old Hildesheimer friends were elected to office. Roemer's trip to the Trading Post was marred by an attack of malarial fever during ten days of his sojourn there, and a recurrence of this fever after his return to New Braunfels on August 28, 1846, prostrated him for some time. The dysentery, which during that summer of 1846 took toll of hundreds of lives in Texas, attacked him at the beginning of October; and in his fevered condition, he made but a slow recovery. The disease confined him to his room in New Braunfels for an entire month.

The first three months of the year 1847 were busy and most profitable ones for Roemer. He spent the last two weeks of January and the first week of February in geological study and collecting at Fredericksburg, the newly founded upper town of the Colony—work which came to rich fruition later in his book on the Cretaceous formations of Texas. From February 6 to March 7 he was with Baron von Meusebach on his famous trip of twenty-nine days to the San Saba country for a council with the Comanche Indians. On their return to Fredericksburg, the Meusebach party left Roemer at the upper settlement again. Here he remained a month, continuing his studies of the geology of the region. On Monday, April 5, he returned to New Braunfels for the last time, there to spend the three remaining weeks of his stay in packing his collections and getting them ready for shipment to Germany. He left New Braunfels for Houston on April 23, and left Galveston on May 8, 1847.

Back in Germany, Roemer found that the value of his geological investigations in Texas was cordially recognized. In June, 1848, he was made a *Privat-Dozent* in geology at the University of Bonn, a position which he held until his call in 1855 to a professorship at the University of Breslau in East Prussia. Here he remained, in spite of calls to other German universities, until his death in 1891. One of Roemer's students, the late Professor Wilhelm Dames, has described the fruitful and brilliant academic career of the geologist. "Roemer," he says, "was a master of teaching: he knew how to choose with wisdom from the mass of material just what was useful to the student as an introduction to science; and this he presented in an indescribably original and vivid way, so clearly and luminously that from merely hearing the lecture one remembered an extraordinary amount of the material under discussion. Roemer's lectures and laboratories were always crowded," Dames continues, "and many of his students were led to choose his science as their life-work. His love of teaching, his stimulating style of lecturing, his care for his students remained undiminished to the end; as an old man he taught with the same zeal, vivacity, and clarity he had shown in his youth."

Vivid glimpses of Texas in the days of annexation are frequent in the book about Texas that Roemer published after his return to Europe. Although it was based on his experiences in a land he had come to love almost as a second home, he considered it of secondary importance in comparison with his more strictly scientific writing. But to us of the present day it is intensely interesting because of the light it throws on the country, the life, and the men of early Texas. The narrative has a vivacity and at the same time an honesty and solidity that make it an invaluable source for the social history of that day in Texas. It is gratifying that this splendid book has recently been translated into English.

One of the most interesting passages in Roemer's *Texas* is the account of his visit to New Washington on upper Galveston Bay. At Galveston, as we have seen, he had made the acquaintance of Mr. Kennedy, the British Consul, and of Dr. Ashbel Smith, who had been Secretary of State of the Republic in 1845, and previously had been chargé d'affaires of Texas at the English and French courts. Roemer describes vividly the circumstances under which he met Ashbel Smith:

I am . . . indebted to Mr. Ashbel Smith, a scientifically-trained physician of long standing in Texas, for many kind advices and favors. . . . When I first visited this gentleman, I found him in a tiny, one-room house made of boards loosely thrown together. For furniture he had a bed, a small table, two broken chairs, and a chest containing books and papers. Papers in wild disorder lay strewn over the floor. Mr. Smith, a man of middle age, of a sharply-cut profile, and wearing high riding-boots, upon my entrance sat upon the book chest; on the bed lay another man, who was at once introduced as Colonel [Barnard E.] B[ee], former minister of war of the Republic of Texas. Although these surroundings were in sharp contrast with those in which European statesmen are wont to live, it was strikingly apparent to me (as I soon convinced myself) that these plain surroundings did not preclude in any wise a many-sided, thorough knowledge, and a finished urbanity of manners. During my further stay in Texas, I often found similar contrasts between the level of culture of some men and their environment; and I have often wondered how well-bred cultivated men could bear for years, with complete resignation, the simplicity and even the rawness of frontier life where they lacked even the simplest conveniences.

On the twelfth of January, 1846, Roemer left Galveston for Houston on the steamer *Spartan*. Among the passengers were Ashbel Smith, Mr. Kennedy (bound for Washington-on-the-Brazos on consular business), Colonel James Morgan, of New Washington, and the British world travelers, Mr. and Mrs. Houstoun, with whom Roemer felt already acquainted from his reading of Mrs. Houstoun's interesting work on Texas. Colonel Morgan, who like all the old "Texians," as they loved to call themselves, was the soul of hospitality, invited all of them—the Houstouns, Ashbel Smith, who was more or less of a familiar at New Washington, and Roemer—to spend a few days at his home. Few visits were ever more fully documented, for Roemer gives the sort of solid, informative account that might be expected from a German man of science, while Mrs. Houstoun's narrative is sprightly, intensely interesting from the human point of view, and not hampered too much by a minute adherence to fact. For our purposes, Mrs. Houstoun's account is of special value, for she paints several portraits of the German scientist who pokes about in the mud of Texan rivers, neglects his toilet, has a voracious appetite, is fond of cognac, and commits the crime, unpardonable to a Britisher of the middle class, of not riding well. The party arrived at New Washington in the night, but were received with cordial hospitality by Colonel Morgan's daughter-in-law, Mrs. Kosciusko Morgan, before her marriage Caroline Cox of Franklin County, Kentucky. In the days that followed the visitors had an opportunity to observe the normal routine of a Texas plantation. I quote from Mrs. Houstoun's narrative:

Our mode of life is as follows: we breakfast at nine on hot-corn bread [sic], and pork dressed in various ways; there is, moreover, good milk and eggs, tea and coffee. We dine at two, on roast pork, boiled ditto, and corn bread, and at seven o'clock in the evening we sup on the same. The food is spread before us in profusion, and, as I have before said, our welcome has been the very warmest possible. . . .

Roemer gives a good description of the upper part of Galveston Bay and the contiguous San Jacinto Bay, as well as of the establishment at New Washington:

The house of Mr. Morgan lies on the shore of the San Jacinto bay, which here has an elevation of twenty or twenty-five feet. It is an unornamented, one-storey wooden building of the architectural type common in the Southern states, surrounded by a lawn in which are scattered several red-cedar trees. . . .

On one side were the Negro quarters, on the other side the bay, and hundreds of cattle were grazing on the low peninsula now cut by the ship canal.

Countless flocks of water birds, such as I had never before seen [Roemer continues], covered the bay. In many places the surface of the water was completely blackened by the myriads of wild duck. Whole flocks of white swans, which appeared in the distance as a silver band; clumsy pelicans; geese; and various diving birds without number completed the swarm of these feathered water dwellers. . . .

The noise of their cries continued unabated throughout the night.

On the morning of January 14, guests and host rode out on the prairie, but returned before noon, for they had been invited to dinner by Mrs. Kosciusko Morgan's sister, Mrs. Sidney Sherman, who dwelt about three miles away. Near Morgan's house they passed an orange grove that he had planted some years previously, but which had been killed by a frost, and had not been replanted.

And now enters into Mrs. Houstoun's account what is intended to be the buffoon of the piece, the young German geologist, Ferdinand Roemer. She reveals in her sprightly way, more truthfully than she knew, how distrustful the British philistine of her day was of the man of science:

Among the numerous guests assembled here—for it is to all intents and purposes an 'open house'—is a young German geologist. I forget his name, but he is a Prussian by birth, and is sent out by his government to report upon the mineral resources of the tract of land chosen for the German colony. I have an idea that he is some relation of Baron Humboldt's, and it appears he enjoys considerable reputation for scientific skill and attainments. We find him gentlemanlike and well-informed, and indefatigable in his endeavors to further the cause of the particular branch of study to which he has devoted himself. He has not a tooth in his head, poor man. . . . Dr. R. is never without a cigar in his mouth (which feature is by no means of even moderate dimensions), but he is far too good-natured to mind a laugh or joke, and often makes them himself at the expense of his own personal appearance. . . . He researches amongst the mud of the Texan rivers, and his digging after geological specimens in the deep alluvial soil of the country caused great amusement to us all, and especially to the negroes, who take intense delight in watching his proceedings. . . . But the doctor, poking in the mud, is nothing to the doctor on horseback! And it is the best fun in the world to see him mounted on a little spirited half-broken mustang, with his stirrups far too short, and his breath coming thick and fast with excitement and fear. He never *quite* calls out for assistance; but at the same time, I am convinced that it is pride alone which prevents his doing so, and his face grows more and more cadaverous, as he splutters forth convulsive and guttural sounds, and prolonged ejaculations of 'Ach, a-c-h gott!' 'O o-h o-o-h' till, if I did not feel that even a geological philosopher has no excuse for being afraid, I could find it in my heart to pity his distress.

It must not be thought that Mrs. Houstoun was the sort of English snob of whom Americans in those days had such good cause to complain. She was neither unappreciative of the Texans of the rough frontier, nor unwilling to recognize urbanity and civility wherever she might find it. In a work published in 1844, entitled *Texas and the Gulf of Mexico,* she had asserted that "in this colony there exists a spirit of good will, and helpfulness, very pleasant to see. . . . If a settler happens to require the aid of his neighbor's hands, or working tools, in the performance of any manual labour, the assistance is rendered as readily as it is asked. . . . I have reason to speak gratefully of the courtesy and civility of the Texans. During our stay among them, I experienced repeated instances of good will." In Mrs. Kosciusko Morgan, Mrs. Houstoun found beauty, wit, and the finest qualities of womanliness. Mrs. Sidney Sherman she thought even more charming. And her account of the dinner at Mrs. Sherman's is not patronizing. As it gives a view of Texas in those days which is not widely familiar, I am tempted to quote from it at some length:

Our stay at New Washington (which, by the way is . . . merely four or five wooden houses, belonging to the 'lord of the manor') has been diversified by a dinner party! The lady who kindly sent us an invitation is the wife of General S. who is at present away with the army in Mexico; and she is the sister of our pretty friend, 'Mrs. Kosciusko.' The scene of the festivity was about three miles from the place, and higher up the bay. . . . I had an active Mexican pony allotted to me, while the doctor was mounted on a tall, rawboned beast, with a mouth as hard as its own bit, and a trot high and rough enough to shake even a better rider than the gentle German out of his saddle. He bore his trials, however, better than I had expected, and, happily for him, the prairie, besides being very much under water, was thickly covered with stunted trees, so that we were obliged to proceed both slowly and cautiously. At about four o'clock (the dinner hour) we arrived at our destination; it is a log house, like the one we had quitted, but it is constructed with great architectural taste, and covered (porch and all) with creeping plants. . . . But though the house was cold, the welcome was not, and we were charmed with Mrs. S. who is a most agreeable and intellectual person, full of energy and decision, and just the character to make even a prairie life an endurable, if not a happy one. She is handsome and highly accomplished, and conducts the education of her children with admirable skill; and while with her, I could not help feeling that were such women *as numerous* in America as they are *perfect,* the censure so often bestowed upon the manners and habits of American ladies might well be spared.

The dinner party in this unpeopled prairie, though totally . . . unlike any at which I had ever before been present, was most enjoyable. The *tout-ensemble* was well calculated to make an impression upon European minds, drilled by the mighty force of fashion and habit into a subserviency to the conventional rules of society, and habituated to its monotony. You must not, however, suppose that there was any want of refinement either in the conversation or the dinner itself; on the contrary, the wines were so excellent, and the 'table talk' so varied and so intelligent, that we could hardly *realize* the fact that we were in a wooden house, with nothing better than a wilderness around its rough and unpretending walls.

After a sumptuous dinner, of which, Roemer says, the *pièce de résistance* was roasted turkey-cock, they sat about the great fire talking of affairs in Europe, in America, and in Texas. Time flew fast and night came on.

It was twelve o'clock before the horses were ordered for our return [continues Mrs. Houstoun], the rain was beginning to fall, and the moon . . . had hidden her face behind the clouds. . . . We had not gone a quarter of a mile from the house, before our difficulties began in earnest, for it was only by calling aloud to each other that we could keep together, so *pitchy* was the darkness of the night. . . . And so we blundered along. . . . I thought that midnight march would never come to an end, . . . and I was beginning, in consequence, to think rather gloomily of our prospects for the night, when I was aroused by a sound near me, which bore some faint resemblance to a human voice, in supplication and entreaty. It was the Doctor, in the act of *beseeching* his refractory steed to move on; and so we listened; and presently, in guttural and most unmusical phraseology, these plaintive words were heard—'I karn nicht get on mit mine horse at arl—what can I do mit him?—he is so idle, and when I want him to go squick, he will here stay to eat.' At that moment, the moon peeped out between two driving clouds, and there was the poor foreigner, and his obstinate *monture, fixed* as it seemed till *eetarnity*. . . . This touching appeal to the compassion of his companions was not made in vain . . . and we all eventually, but not until it was three o'clock in the morning, and we were wet through [with the "heavy night-dew"] . . . reached our temporary home at New Washington. . . .

On the next day, January 15, Roemer and the Houstouns accompanied Ashbel Smith to his farm, "Evergreen Plantation," at the upper end of Galveston Bay, and spent the day with him. Roemer noted the rigorous simplicity of the appointments of the two-room house, and the rich library. "A high cupboard in the corner was filled with books, forming a small library chosen with the most careful taste," says the scientist. "Besides the Greek and Roman classics were to be found the best examples of English and French literature. Similar contrasts between a raw environment stripped to the bare essentials of life, and a refined intellectual culture, are not rare throughout the whole Western United States." Mrs. Houstoun describes in detail the domestic arrangements of the great Texan patriot:

It was late in the afternoon when we reached Mr. S[mith's] habitation, a neat batchelor's establishment, far enough from either the pleasures or the *tracasseries* of social life. A good many small wooden tenements for . . . [slaves] were dotted about, and there was some young *stock* frolicking about, in the shape both of negro children and horses; there was poultry in great plenty and variety, and the farm and farm building looked well kept and thriving. As for the house itself, there is no denying that it *was* small, neither am I prepared to say that it contained more than one room of very limited extent. . . . [At dinner] no one was, apparently, more heartily amused at the entertaining deficiency of plates and places than our host himself. With too much good taste to oppress us with apologies for the absence of luxuries, which, in that wild scene, would have been quite misplaced, he allowed us to enjoy ourselves in our own way, and we were, in consequence, quite happy. The doctor was as hungry as a hound, and devoured boiled fowls and fried eggs enough for a dozen men, at least; and though the wood fire did smoke, so that we were forced to sit with the door open, and though *one* took his place upon the bed, and another was obliged to content himself with a wooden box, I never recollect passing a more agreeable day. Our host, enlivened by some excellent French brandy, shone particularly in anecdote and repartee, and when the shades of evening began to close around the prairie home, it was with real regret that

FERDINAND ROEMER

we made our preparations for returning. . . . We mounted our horses when
the evening was far advanced, and in company with our hospitable entertainer
prepared to ride once more toward the Bay . . .

But Roemer, fearing the leaky boats in which the trip was to be made,
refused to accompany the rest of the party. Mrs. Houstoun continues:

Seeing that his fears placed him beyond the reach of persuasion, the *ex-chargé*
had nothing to do but to express a courteous hope that he would make himself
quite at home where he was, and then we wished him 'farewell.' The last
glimpse I caught of the scientific German, was the dim outline of a man seated
on a wooden bench before the door of the shanty, with his hammer and a bag
of specimens in his hand, and a considerable quantity of *Cognac* in his head.
What became of him after that we never heard. . . .

Which reminds me that one may look in vain through the *Dictionary
of National Biography* to see what became of Mrs. Houstoun.

After passing through Houston, as will be recalled, Roemer arrived
at New Braunfels about the eighth of February, 1846. There he found
the colonists building feverishly. Seguin Street, the chief street of the
town, was at the time of Roemer's arrival fairly well defined by the
houses bordering it; each house stood on a half-acre town lot which
had been assigned to the colonist by the Verein. Most of the plots
were enclosed by fences. As Roemer saw New Braunfels in 1846:

The houses were of very diverse construction, since everyone had the right
to follow his own inclination therein, and besides, the people so far had had
no experience as to what type of construction was most suitable to the climate.
As a result, some of the houses were of logs, some were of studding frame-
work filled in with brick, some were frame, and some were huts with walls
made of cedar posts driven vertically into the ground like the posts of a stockade,
with a tent-canvas or a couple of ox-hides for a roof, in lieu of shingles.
Most of the houses followed the American style of a roofed-in porch, which
in this warm climate is almost indispensable. The porch keeps the direct rays
of the hot sun from the interior of the house, in addition to furnishing an airy,
cool room for the performance of many household tasks. Many of the houses
lacked the fireplaces to be found in the homes of the American settlers, although
a fireplace is so necessary during the cold northers in winter. Since most of
the houses were built in summer, the need for heating seemed remote. Too,
the building of a suitable fireplace required a dexterity that most of the German
settlers did not possess.
At the time of my arrival in New Braunfels, there might have been from
eighty to one hundred of such houses and huts of various sizes. . . . In most
of the houses, although they were so small, were packed several families. The
interior of such a house, where, among still unpacked chests, men, women,
and children were cooped up, often looked like the steerage of an immigrant
ship.

As I entered the principal street a small house attracted my attention, upon which three business shingles hung, as follows: "Apothecary," "Dr. K.," and "Bakery.". . . . At first I thought that the baker was a boarder with the physician-owner of the house, but from my companion I learned that Dr. K[oester] actually united the professions of apothecary, baker, and physician in his own person. . . . The evangelical church of the place also stands on the principal street, a sizable frame building with window openings but no windows, built at the cost of the Verein.

Roemer is enthusiastic in his praise of Ervendberg, although he thinks of him as pastor rather than as scientist:

Close to the church stands a tiny house, the dwelling assigned to the evangelical minister, the Pastor Ervendberg, who exercised his spiritual office not in the ease of most of his German colleagues, but on a rather penurious living paid him up to this time by the Verein. On Sundays he preached, and on weekdays taught school and cultivated in the sweat of his face his cornfield and his garden.

Baron von Meusebach (or John O. Meusebach, as he preferred to call himself among the Texans), the Commissioner-General of the Colony in succession to Prince Solms, had been called to New Orleans on business and was not in New Braunfels to welcome Roemer upon his arrival. When he returned a week later, he invited Roemer to accept accommodations of the Verein. The scientist was accordingly housed in the *Sophienburg,* or Government Building, during his stay in the town.

Almost immediately Roemer met Lindheimer, for whom he came to feel the highest regard. The acquaintance, he says, "was very pleasant and valuable to me during the entire time that I spent" in New Braunfels, and he adds that he still looks back "with especial pleasure" to his work with Lindheimer.

The neighborhood of New Braunfels offered a rich collecting ground for the naturalist. Particularly attractive was the ford of the Guadalupe, a locality of surpassing beauty in Roemer's day, where he made rich collections of fossils, most of them new species. The slight falls of the Guadalupe at the entrance of Comal Creek Roemer considered the finest water with the most beautiful foliage he had seen either in Europe or America. In the vicinity of the town he observed for the first time the scissors-tailed flycatcher, and on the road to San Antonio, the road runner, while hosts of whippoorwills, bluebirds, mockingbirds, cardinals, and cowbirds gladdened his heart. In the Comal he found the fierce-biting soft-shell turtle, *Trionyx ferox,* eighteen inches long, and giant freshwater prawns as long as lobsters. Along the Guadalupe above New Braunfels, on the road to Fredericksburg, Roemer noted giant cypresses six feet thick, and in other rivers of the Colony grant—the Llano, Pedernales, and San Saba, as well as in other places on the Guadalupe—cypress trees as thick as ten feet at the base. At the so-called "Falls of the Guadalupe" (the "Waco Camp," six miles above New Braunfels) the cypresses formed a close formation in the rapidly flowing water of the river channel.

To facilitate his exploring trips, Roemer bought a mule, which, much to his amusement, was forthwith dubbed by his friends "the scientific mule." Thus equipped, he began to make more extended journeys, frequently in Lindheimer's company. But Roemer can tell the tale better than I:

For my collecting trips, which I was now obliged to begin with all possible energy, I purchased a mule that turned out to be a very useful and faithful servant, and accompanied me on all my wanderings in Texas. He patiently allowed himself to be packed with all sorts of objects related to natural history; and on some occasions when I came home of an evening from a trip, he offered a grotesque appearance, carrying, besides me, leather saddle-bags full of stones, a bundle of plants, and perhaps also a young alligator hanging from the pommel of the saddle.

Soon I was receiving aid in collecting natural-history objects from the entire population of New Braunfels, especially the youngsters, since the more striking animal forms, unknown in the homeland, aroused their attention almost as much as they did mine. Almost every day they brought me birds, snakes, lizards, turtles, fishes, and so on; and by small remunerations I was able to stimulate them to renewed efforts in my behalf.

In the first few days, I obtained a four-foot example of . . . the garfish, . . . a predatory fish abundant in the Guadalupe and the Comal, which I have often seen remaining motionless in the clear waters of these rivers, apparently awaiting its prey. The first specimen that I opened had a foot-long fish in its stomach. . . . Most of the specimens of this species were captured by harpooning with an iron spear. The scales are so hard on this fish that one can open its body only by inserting the knife between the borders of contiguous scales. . . .

On the eighteenth of March . . . an eleven-foot alligator shot in Comal Creek, about six miles from New Braunfels, was brought to me. In the place where it was shot, where the creek widens to form a pond about thirty paces long, there were shot during the summer eight other fairly large or smaller ones.

Roemer was immensely curious about everything in the new and strange land of Texas; and he eagerly embraced opportunities to accompany the Indian trader, John F. Torrey, to his Trading House on the Upper Brazos, and to go with Meusebach, *"El Sol Colorado,"* when he went up to the San Saba country in 1847 for a council with the Indians.

The name of John F. Torrey was one to conjure with among the Indians of Texas in early days. He was one of seven brothers born in Connecticut, all of whom at one time or another made their homes in Texas, and all of whom engaged in the Indian trade, under the firm name of Torrey Brothers. John F. Torrey had been born in Ashford, Connecticut, in 1817; with another Connecticut man, George Barnard, one year his junior, he came to Texas in 1838. Other brothers of John F. Torrey came, and finally, in 1858, the father, John Torrey. John F. Torrey, the son, established himself in the Indian trade at Houston in 1838 or 1839, with his old friend George Barnard as clerk. At some uncertain date, probably in the spring of 1844, the Torrey Brothers established a trading post on Tehuacana Creek, eight miles southeast of present Waco in McLennan County. It was at that time fully twenty-five miles over the border in the Indian country. The Connecticut Yankee Barnard, who was placed in charge of the post, became very popular with the Indians. When, in 1849 or thereabouts, the Indians were moved westward, Barnard moved the post and established it on the Upper Brazos near Comanche Peak in Hood County, about four miles from the present town of Granbury. Both George Barnard and John F. Torrey were trusted by the Indians, and several Indian treaties with the whites were signed by John F. Torrey as witness. Roemer felt assured of his safety in traveling into the Indian country with such a guide.

The two left New Braunfels on the twenty-fourth of July, 1846; camped the first night by the San Marcos springs, where Colonel Edward Burleson was strenuously attempting to build up a settlement; and, striking the old *Camino Real* at Bastrop, followed it to Caldwell. Here they passed the night of July 28 at the home of a stalwart Methodist, John W. Porter, of whom Roemer records that "he said a very long grace, and then read a chapter in the Bible," before the famishing travelers could fall to. It was good to be able to sleep indoors, though the weather was unbearably hot and moist; for the night before they had slept in the open on the Yegua, where the mosquitoes, augmented in number by the very wet weather that characterized July of that year, made sleep an impossibility. The next day they reached the Brazos and crossed it somewhere near old Tenoxtitlan, and on the thirteenth reached Wheelock's Settlement (present Wheelock, in Robertson County). On the last day of July they set out from Wheelock's for the Trading House, and spent the night near present Marlin in Falls County, which then had the euphonious name of Bucksnort. On Sunday, August 2, they reached the trading post. As Roemer relates:

After a short ride of a few miles on the following morning, turning around a corner of the forest, we suddenly saw the trading post before us. It lies on a hill covered with oaks, above the broad, forested flood plain of Tehuacana Creek, and about two miles from the Brazos. The establishment consists of six or seven structures made entirely of rough, unhewn logs, as is the fashion

162

of the country. These houses lack the palisades common to the forts of the fur companies of the Upper Missouri, as well as every other sort of protective fence. The safety of the trading post against Indian attack is based on its usefulness, even necessity, to the Indians.

The largest of these log cabins contains the hides and furs brought in by the Indians—buffalo rugs and skins of the common American deer (*Cervus virginianus* L.) form by far the chief part. The buffalo skins are brought by the Indians: part of them entirely raw, part of them tanned on the inside, and then usually more or less decoratively painted. The value of these depends on size, the evenness of the hair, and the quality of the decoration. . . . Another log house contained the stores of Indian goods for barter. The most important are the following: woolen coverlets; coarse woolen cloth (so-called *strouding*), especially dyed scarlet-red and blue, from which they make the characteristic breech-clout; printed calico for shirts; and thick brass wire for armlets and anklets, glass beads, powder, lead, tobacco, etc.

The other log houses contain the dwellings of the various persons staying at the trading post. There were present an agent [George Barnard] appointed by Torrey Brothers to carry on trade with the Indians, and a gunsmith and armorer placed there by the Government to care for the Indians' weapons. There was also an old trapper whom gout and rheumatism had unfitted for the life of a hunter. He had taken up his abode here a short time before, in the unconquered wilderness, to be as near as possible to the scenes of his earlier joys and deeds and as far as possible from hated civilization. He would tell with rapture to anyone who would listen tales of lonely hunting for beaver in the Rocky Mountains, and other incomparable sketches of a trapper's life. . . . There was also an Indian agent appointed by the Government who was well acquainted with the languages and customs of the different Indian tribes. . . .

The method of life followed at this extreme frontier of civilization was in keeping with the wildness and primitiveness of the surroundings. Dried buffalo flesh, smoked buffalo tongues (which are generally considered delicacies in the civilized portion of the United States), bacon, honey, and bread were the most appetizing foods. A pile of buffalo hides made an excellent bed for the night.

The second day after our arrival, a small band of Indians came for the purpose of trading. It was a picturesque, very attractive drama for European eyes—the caravan-like, long-drawn-out train coming up over the hill to the trading post. According to the Indian custom, they rode in single file; the men first, dressed in their best, and appearing grave and dignified, followed by the gay squaws, almost every one with a papoose on her back, and one before her in the saddle. The squaws rode like the men and looked after the pack horses, which were loaded with hides intended for exchange, and miscellaneous household equipment. A halt was called in the neighborhood of the post, and the squaws began at once to cut tree branches for building the tents.

Afterward the skins for sale were brought into the store, weighed, and their value determined. Goods to a corresponding amount were chosen by the Indians. Ordinarily such a visit to the trading house occupies several days and has the same happy significance to the Indians as the annual fairs in the German cities have for our German country people.

For a week Roemer stayed at the trading post while his companion, Mr. Torrey, set out for the tiny village of Dallas on the Trinity, to be gone about eight days. Since this route was largely over prairie, Roemer chose to accept the invitation of the gunsmith at the trading post, Cockswell, to accompany him on a visit to the Caddo village at the mouth of Nolands River, about sixty miles up the Brazos in the northwest part of present Hill County. In their saddlebags they took provisions for a sojourn of several days in the wilderness—coffee, salt, and biscuit; and, armed with rifles, set out on their journey. As Cockswell was known to practically all of the Indians of that region, he and Roemer apprehended little danger. It took two days' traveling to reach the Caddo village. On the second day they came upon several herds of three to four hundred buffalo each, grazing over the plain. The travelers were now near their destination.

About sunset, after a ride of some thirty miles [Roemer continues], from the top of a hill we saw lying before us the end of our journey, the Caddo village. No more suitable and entrancing place could have been chosen by the red sons of the wilderness for their settlement. The village lay within a small level plain about two miles long, which is bordered on one side by the marginal forest of the Brazos and on all other sides by the steep hills. Right across this plain flows a handsome little brook over a smooth bed of limestone. Along the bank stood several ancient live-oaks. On both sides of the brook the huts of the Indians were scattered in picturesque disorder over the plain, each with its own field of maize. Between the hills on which we stood and the village itself about one thousand head of horses were grazing on the plain. Several naked Indian boys with long hair ran yelling back and forth among them. We descended to the village. We were everywhere greeted in a friendly fashion by the inhabitants at the various huts which we passed; for the Indians all knew my companion. Although I should have liked to study the domestic economy of the Indian by direct observation, we declined the repeated invitations to sleep in one of the huts. We shrank from too close contact with the tormenting little insect which inhabits every Indian dwelling, and preferred to spread our blankets under a live-oak on the bank of the creek. Before we lay down to sleep, we received a visit from several Indian women, who brought us watermelons as a present, and received glass beads from us in return.

Next day Roemer was able to inspect the village more closely.

The dwelling of each family [he reported] consists of several huts of diverse form. One of these is always larger than the others, about fifteen feet high, cone-shaped, and closed except for a narrow opening at the ground. As it is thatched with long grass, at a distance it looks like a haystack. It is the general abode during wet and cold weather. Near this principal building stand one or more open huts, consisting of a grass-covered weather-roof supported by four uprights, under which, and at a distance of about two feet from the ground, is a horizontal lattice-work platform woven from brush. On this platform the men and women squat during the warm hours of the day. . . . Finally, there is a third sort of hut which serves for storing of supplies, and which is nothing but an oven-like, grass-covered cage supported on four high posts. . . .

164

Notwithstanding the early hour, we found all of the denizens of the first hut we entered, from the oldest to the youngest, engaged in eating under-ripe watermelons. In all the other huts we found the same condition. It actually appears that at this time of the year [August 11] watermelons comprise almost the sole food of the Indians, and in incredible amounts. Everywhere we found the Indians in the happiest humor, and as my companion assured me, these sons of nature always live among themselves in the best relations; quarreling and dissension are almost unknown.

Roemer and Cockswell spent the day—Tuesday—in inspecting the Caddo village, and started the next morning on their return to the trading post. Roemer suffered an attack of fever on Wednesday morning, and it continued throughout the day-and-a-half trip. On their arrival he was utterly exhausted, and for ten days lay in a semi-delirium. All medicaments available at the post failed to break the fever. On the tenth day, Mr. Torrey, who in the meantime had returned from his visit to Dallas, declared that he was compelled by business to leave the next morning for New Braunfels. Accordingly, although Roemer was so weak he had to be lifted into the saddle, he set out at daybreak with Torrey. The fresh morning air soon revived him, and with every succeeding hour his strength increased. That day they reached the falls of the Brazos in Falls County, not far from present Marlin, and crossing the river, passed the night there. The second night they spent with Mr. Benjamin Bryant, a slave-holding farmer on the Little River. The third night was spent in the open on the San Gabriel. The next morning, Thursday, the twenty-seventh, they had breakfast with a Yankee farmer who had been living for ten years in the country along Brushy Creek, near present Round Rock. This farmer declared in tones of unbearable exasperation that he was going to leave his present farm and move higher up the river. "The country is getting too crowded, I can not live here any longer! The nearest fellow lives only ten miles from here!" he explained to Torrey. The travelers ate dinner at the town of Austin and reached home the next day. Roemer had been gone five weeks. "The trip just ended has convinced me," he wrote, "that no region in the eastern part of the land can compare in . . . beauty and natural advantages with the location of the German settlements on the beautiful Comal."

During the interval between his return from Torrey's Trading Post on August 28, 1846, and the middle of January, 1847, Roemer was half-incapacitated at New Braunfels. A recurrence of malarial fever, followed in early October by an attack of dysentery, laid the foundation for a long period of illness from which he did not recover before the third of November. On that day he was able to take a ride down the Guadalupe, where he found a band of Delaware Indians who had been there for some time engaged in hunting.

As the reader will recall, things had not gone well in the Colony during the summer of 1846. At the upper settlement, Fredericksburg, one-fifth of the population had died of fever and dysentery. There had been 321 deaths at Carlshafen, and 400 at New Braunfels. Then, too, the Indians were threatening. In the fall of that year, a German adventurer, the director of the upper settlement, nine parts coward, had made an unauthorized expedition into the grant to the north of Fredericksburg. He had not dared to cross the Llano River, but had succeeded in arousing the suspicion and resentment of the Indians. Returning home, he had reported to Meusebach that across the Llano were many thousands of hostile Comanches.

That fearless leader laid plans for an expedition into the Indian country to conclude a treaty of peace; and on January 14, 1847, a mounted company set out from New Braunfels for Fredericksburg and the Indian country. Six days later, Roemer himself set out for Fredericksburg, arriving there on the twenty-fourth of January. For twelve days he remained in the vicinity of the town, searching the ravines and gullies of that virgin field for Cretaceous fossils, of which there was an abundance.

On February 5, Major R. S. Neighbors, United States Agent for Indian Affairs at Austin, came with a message from Governor J. Pinckney Henderson of Texas begging Meusebach to call off his proposed mission to the Indians; or, if he would not do that, at least to accept the good offices of Major Neighbors and an accompanying half-civilized Delaware chief and interpreter, Jim Shaw, in the visit to the Comanches. Roemer, glad of an opportunity to see more of the Indians under favorable circumstances, attached himself to Major Neighbors, and together they set out to overtake Meusebach and his train. On February 10, Neighbors and his company came upon Meusebach's expedition encamped with the Indians at a pleasant place in a bend of the San Saba. Meusebach had been met several miles from the San Saba valley by a deputation of Comanches, who had asked the nature of his mission. His courageous and open disarmament of his company, by the discharging of their rifles, had won the regard and friendly hearing of the Indians, and things had proceeded well upon the way to settlement when Neighbors and his companions arrived.

Roemer gives a charming picture of the camp on the San Saba: the Germans and Indians meeting in friendly groups; the white captive who could not be persuaded to leave the Indian life and go back to his brother in Austin; the handsome twelve-year-old son of a former chief, who had been captured in the Council House Fight at San Antonio, and during his sojourn with the whites had learned English; and the camp of the Indians on the other side of the clear, swift-running San Saba. In the evening the Germans sat about their campfires with their Indian acquaintances, and while the Germans sang their songs of home and fatherland, the Indians showed their friendliness by singing some of their own (to European ears) monotonous and unmelodious music.

Regarding the chief purposes of the mission—the making of a treaty of peace with the Indians, and arrangements for the purchase of land from them—Roemer wrote:

Early this morning [February 11, 1847] occurred the council with the Indian chiefs. We seated ourselves in a circle on skins that were spread in Meusebach's tent, and Jim Shaw, our Delaware guide . . . was the interpreter. First, before business was opened, came the passing of the pipe of peace twice around the circle, from which everyone took two or three puffs. The speeches on both sides were carried on in short, separate sentences, each of which was immediately translated by the interpreter. Baron von Meusebach first said to the chiefs that 'he had come with his people upon the white path' (that is, the path of peace) 'in order to see their land and to greet them as friends. They would, on their part, be received by his people in a friendly way when they came down to the towns below. They wanted now to go up the river to see the Old Spanish Fort on the San Saba. When he returned, he wished for a council with the great chiefs, Santa Anna, Buffalo Hump, and Old Owl, in order to open up to them more fully what his purpose was.'

One of the chiefs responded to this with great dignity as follows: 'The hearts of his people had been disturbed when they had seen the many strange people, who came unannounced, and whose purposes they had not known; now, since they knew that they had come as friends, and what they wished, all would be well.'

Thereupon a number of presents were laid down before the most renowned chiefs, who distributed them among the other chiefs and the braves. The chiefs received red and blue woolen blankets, thick brass wire for making bracelets, calico for shirts, and tobacco. To the braves were given span-wide strips of red and blue cloth for the characteristic Indian breech-clouts, and some tobacco.

Meusebach's party then journeyed to the Old Fort on the San Saba, and returned on the last day of February to the Comanche camp.

At noon, on the first of March [Roemer continues], the council agreed upon with the chiefs took place. A great circle of buffalo skins was laid out on the ground in front of our tent, and on this, on one side, the chiefs and the most renowned warriors seated themselves with von Meusebach, our interpreter, Jim Shaw, Major Neighbors, and several others of our company. The three chiefs, who stood at the head of the Comanche bands roaming the frontiers of inhabited Texas, sat there, very grave and dignified. In appearance they were very diverse.

Old Owl, the political chief, was a little old man who appeared very undistinguished in his dirty cotton jacket and had a crafty, diplomatic countenance. Quite different from him was the war-chief, Santa Anna, a powerfully built man with a benevolent and lively expression of countenance. Finally, the third chief, Buffalo Hump, furnished a picture of the true, unadulterated North American Indian. Unlike the majority of his tribe, he scorned European dress. With his upper body naked, a buffalo skin about his hips, yellow brass rings on his arms, a string of beads about his neck, and his long, lank, black hair hanging down, he sat there with the apathetic expression (as it seems to a European) of the North American savage. He drew especial attention to himself because in previous years he had distinguished himself for daring and bravery in many engagements with the Texans.

As soon as the council began, the wives and children of the braves, who previously had besieged us closely, retired to a respectful distance, and formed a bright decoration during the entire conference. In the middle of the circle lay a pile of tobacco and a pipe. One of the Indians took the latter, filled it with tobacco, lighted it, took two puffs, and passed it around the circle. Twice the pipe of peace made the rounds, in complete silence; then von Meusebach made through the interpreter the following propositions: 'The Comanches should permit the Germans to form a settlement on the Llano, and they should let all of the land lying northward be surveyed—especially that on the San Saba. In consideration of this, the Comanches should receive, at a council to be held in Fredericksburg two months hence, gifts to the value of one thousand Spanish dollars; and they should be treated as friends as often as they visited the German settlements.'

After this speech the chiefs for a time counseled softly together, and then Old Owl replied that they would have to let the proposals lie over and declare themselves concerning them early next morning. . . . Toward noon next day the second meeting with the chiefs took place. Matters proceeded in the same manner as described above. After several colloquies back and forth, such as are natural with the mistrustful, wary mind of the Indian, the propositions laid down by von Meusebach the day before were accepted. The council ended with mutual embraces, in which the Comanches sought to show the degree of their friendship by the heartiness of their hugs, and with a meal of venison and rice which von Meusebach had had prepared for the Indians.

Sunday, March 7, saw the party back again in Fredericksburg after an absence of twenty-nine days. Although Roemer's companions soon set out on the return to New Braunfels, he remained at Fredericksburg for nearly a month making a further study of the Cretaceous rocks of that region and putting together his notes on the San Saba expedition. There were many records of mammals from the San Saba country. Prairie dogs, Roemer reported, occurred in immense "towns" in that region, but only rarely in the other parts of Texas that he visited; beaver were not rare on the Llano and the San Saba; and javelinas, which occurred in small herds in the woods at the margin of the Comal and Guadalupe at New Braunfels, were especially abundant on the San Saba. Roemer had also been fortunate in his geological studies, and at several places on the San Saba had found exposures of Cambrian limestone, with characteristic trilobite remains. Altogether it had been a most profitable journey to "that little-known, almost mythical wonderland, with which every Texas settler at that time associated the idea of inexhaustible fertility and loveliness, as well as a wealth of noble metals."

Roemer returned to New Braunfels on Monday, the fifth of April. He had many things yet to do before his departure from Texas. There were the collections, very numerous and rich in scientific objects of great value, that must be packed for shipment across the sea. It was not before the twenty-third of the month that this packing was completed, and the numerous boxes forwarded. On that day Roemer made his farewells to New Braunfels. He had seen it take shape: indeed, it had almost grown from a village into a town during his months in Texas.

Down Seguin went the stage, over the ford of the Guadalupe, past houses of friends he was now leaving behind. There were the falls of the Guadalupe, where on warm evenings he had collected Cretaceous fossils, notably his new echinoderms and *Nautilus,* at the same time that he enjoyed the coolness of the river. All these familiar objects and places he passed now for the last time. The party reached Seguin at sunset, and spent the night there. The second night found them at Gonzales, the town looking as wretched as ever. About noon on Sunday they reached Lagrange.

The Texas prairies were a blaze of color. Among the flowers that Roemer records as having been collected on the return journey were the bluebonnet, which covered the hills with color; the pink milkwort, *Polygala incarnata;* different species of the beard-tongue, *Pentstemon;* evening primroses; and a morning-glory, *Convolvulus affinis.*

The arrangements for travel were very poor. Hotel accommodations in the days of the Republic had not improved much beyond the stage that Bishop Waugh reported when he described the "hotel" on the Houston Prairie in 1841:

Figure to yourself . . . a habitation, situated in a prairie, twelve miles distant from the nearest house on the road, either in front or in rear—inhabited by two famillies [*sic*],—built of small logs, some but little thicker than one's arm—in the form of a small pen at either end, with an open center—earthen floors— with two sheds formed of the rudest materials, and after the rudest model— exposed at tops, and ends, to the wind and rain—with something resembling a bed in each of the chambers, where the inmates were about as much exposed to the view of one another, and of the weather, as they would have been in the absence of the house itself; and you will be able to form a tolerably correct idea of this hotel of the prairie. The only thing which indicated civilization was a large pier looking glass, which strangely contrasted with the wall of the bed-chamber which it so extensively covered.

At Lagrange, the coach in which Roemer was traveling made connection with the stage from Austin, with an increase in passengers. Roemer gives a Chaucerian description of all his fellow-travelers: the garrulous elderly Catholic priest on his way to St. Louis; the German woman whose Americanization was no less than terrific; the well-to-do Irish merchant from Austin who was taking his son to school at New Orleans; the cultured young advocate returning to his home in Galveston after pleading a case before the Supreme Court in Austin; a young druggist, formerly a bartender at New Braunfels, who was going to set up shop as a physician at Washington-on-the-Brazos; and others. But this passage must be read to be enjoyed. I include an abbreviated account of the rest of the journey to Houston:

We reached [Washington] in the afternoon [April 25, 1847],—among those places called towns in Texas, the most miserable and wretched that I had ever seen. Washington was for some time the seat of government of the Republic of Texas, and hence a number of rather large houses were built here. Several manufacturing establishments were located here, so that the population amounted to about a thousand. Subsequently, the seat of government was removed to Austin, and this sealed the doom of Washington. . . . I saw several large houses standing empty, with shattered window panes, shingles missing, and planks torn loose and hanging down; and those houses still occupied seemed to enjoy no greater care for their preservation. . . . Not far from Washington we crossed the Brazos in a ferry, and then entered the broad, forested Brazos bottom. The road here was bottomless, and we proceeded but slowly. Moreover, a *Texas* thunderstorm, long threatening, now burst upon us. Since the stage was completely uncovered, I sought to protect myself as much as possible with my cloak and a buffalo robe, but that helped me only a little, for the attentive merchant from Austin held over his lady a great umbrella in such a manner that the water fell in cascades upon unlucky me. All remonstrances, even calling attention to my fever-ridden condition, having proved unavailing (since it was a question of "protecting a lady from the rain"), I resigned myself with Christian fortitude to the inevitable. In this situation, the demand of the driver that all the male passengers alight and walk until we came to better roads, since the mud was too deep to permit the passing of a loaded coach, had no terror for me. We waded a half-hour through mud a foot deep before the coachman declared that the road was getting better, and told us to get in again. In the meantime, it had become quite dark. Nevertheless, our coachman attempted to make up the time lost in the Brazos bottom by driving his horses as fast as they would go. The result was that as we passed over a little boggy creek, the wheels on one side went off the corduroy crossing into the mud, and everything came to a standstill. The stage now had to be completely unloaded, and since the jaded horses could not pull it out of the mud, we had to get help from a plantation several miles distant. After a long time the owner of the plantation came with half a dozen Negroes, who easily righted us. Late in the night we reached the station at which we were to stop. It was a large, stately manor, where the contractor of the whole Texas stage-coach system lived. By his eagerness to help and his friendliness he tried to make us forget the difficulties we had encountered, and assured us that good covered post-coaches for all the routes had already been ordered from the northern states. This bit of news was joyful to me—at least in the interest of those who should ride in the future. A good night's rest, for which I most longed, was unfortunately not to be thought of here. . . . The difficulties of the journey, however, were over, for next morning, after a good breakfast, we climbed into an excellent red "Troy coach," . . . and in it journeyed without difficulty the fifty remaining miles to Houston, over the monotonous, treeless Houston Prairie, whose level surface was unbroken by the slightest elevation. We arrived late in the evening. After I had driven here and there for more than a year on the extreme frontier of civilization, the town, with its spacious hotel, its large, brightly-lighted, decorated barrooms and separate billiard rooms, seemed very grand and glittering.

On April 28 Roemer reached Galveston after a twelve-hour passage, and here remained for a week, studying the great droves of fiddler-crabs that scuttled over the muddy beaches; gathering starfishes and mollusks (of which he found several new species); observing the birds, still present in great numbers; and hunting raccoons, which he called, German that he was, "washing-bears." He also visited the beautiful sandbeach on the seaward side, which even then bade fair to become a renowned bathing beach.

But the end was at hand, and Roemer must take leave of Texas:

On May 7 [1847], the long-expected steamer *Yacht* appeared, and on the eighth I took passage on it for New Orleans. When the strong tremor of the ship indicated that we had crossed the harbor-bar, and when, soon thereafter, the land of the narrow island [of Galveston] appeared only as a low-lying streak, I felt that it was time to say farewell to Texas. During my stay of more than a year I had grown to love the beautiful land of meadows, to which belongs a great future. It moved me to sorrow that I must say farewell to the land forever. To me there still remain rich and pleasant memories; and from afar I shall always follow with lively interest the further development of the country. May its broad, green prairies become the habitation of a great and happy people!

Science had been born anew in Texas.

Charles Wright 9

IT is early autumn in Connecticut. Over the countryside hangs a soft blue haze; goldenrod and blazing-star bloom in the sandy roadside places, and in the moist meadows, asters and gentians. Down the dusty road from Hartford to New Haven the stage and mail-coach makes its way, drawn by sweating, panting horses. There are plenty of passengers, for this is a Monday, and in Connecticut of the eighteen-thirties one waits until the Sabbath is past before setting out on a journey. Hence the well-loaded coach, the full boot, the horses steaming.

Today, as always on Mondays, the coach is late. Early evening draws on, dusk and candlelight. The stage finally pulls up at the Yale green in New Haven, graced with its noble elms and two churches worthy of the genius of a Christopher Wren. Bearded lads of twenty with rough homespun clothes and light baggage descend, clearly boys who are coming down to Yale to take the entrance examinations. Tomorrow—Tuesday, September 13, 1831—these examinations are to be held in the gallery of the old chapel. Among the examiners will be the gracious, handsome, venerable Silliman; pungent-witted and sharp-tongued Kingsley; Olmsted the physicist, who is destined to be the first American astronomer to observe Halley's comet; F. A. P. Barnard, later to be connected with Columbia College; Henry Durant, who will become in after years president of the University of California; Horace Bushnell; and William A. Larned.

Two lads from the up-country are of particular interest. On first sight they appear of about the same age, say twenty. Good friends, apparently, well-worn to each other's moods and needs. One is tall and fair, with a graceful and debonair manner, the other short, sturdy, with awkward body, and wit a little thick. Stubbornness, earnestness, wistfulness are written large in his face. His name is Charles Wright, and he comes from Wethersfield. He looks up to

172

his companion, Samuel Galpin, from the same village, with an air of dependence that obliterates the year of difference in their ages. Perhaps he resents a little Galpin's easiness. They have prepared for college together in the Wethersfield Grammar School under a Yalensian, Sherman Finch, of the class of 1828. Now they have come to New Haven for the essay of their lives. Great things hang upon the issue of tomorrow.

At this time Yale is in her one-hundred-and-thirtieth year of training for leadership. Her five hundred men are drawn from the length and breadth of the Union. Old Yale men occupy places of trust and influence in Church and State. In New England, where the only aristocracy is that of intellect, young men like Wright and Galpin zealously seek to win the accolade of learning, some of them coming from homes of poverty that are barely able to spare the scant two hundred dollars for a year's expenses at Yale. Hopefully, humbly they gather at the school on the day before Commencement, eager to gain a place on her rolls.

That Tuesday morning was an experience for the ninety-odd boys who came up for examination. Professor Silliman, teacher of chemistry and geology, affectionately known to two generations of Yale men not as the father of American chemistry but as "Uncle Ben," read all the candidates' letters of recommendation, and put the men at ease. Entrance requirements were simple in those days, being confined largely to Latin, mathematics, grammar, some geography, and occasionally Greek. When the examinations were over, the newly-accepted matriculates strolled over the campus, dotted with six buildings, among which Old South Middle College, or Connecticut Hall, held the attention, as it still does.

In the evening two great events, long remembered, took place: the first, an address by the venerable Chancellor James Kent of New York, who delivered a Phi Beta Kappa address devoted to the ancient glories of the college. Still later in the same evening the new students attended a meeting of the alumni, at which the first campaign for an endowment of $100,000 was launched. And so to bed, for the greater glories of Commencement Day still lay before them.

At daybreak they were wakened by the ringing of all the church bells. Soon people came pouring into the town from all quarters, for Commencement Day was the event of the year, with orations and addresses galore. The class of 1831 already gave promise of great things: it included such men as Noah Porter, who was to be forty-six years at Yale, first as professor and later as president; Lyman H. Atwater, a future professor at Princeton; and Trusten Polk, to be "before-the-war" Governor of Missouri. These three were among the leaders of the class elected to membership in Phi Beta Kappa, and wore the green ribbon which was proper on such occasions.

At the end of the Commencement ceremonies came the conferring of the degrees, with President Jeremiah Day standing gownless in a long dress coat with white collar and stock, his head surmounted by a very tall, tilelike hat of beaver. With studied grace he tipped his hat to each candidate, as for each he pronounced the words of the Latin formula: "... *omnia jura et privilegia.*" In the heart of every neophyte was born the determination also to become a son of Yale. To Charles Wright the impulse must have come with redoubled force. Many members of his family and many of his relatives—the Butlers, Demings, Goodriches, Standishes, Welleses, Curtises, and Bucks of Wethersfield and vicinity—had taken degrees at Yale. Two of Charles Wright's relatives, Elizur Wright, father and son, had also been elected to Phi Beta Kappa. It would be no wild flight of the imagination to see the new matriculate, stirred by the greatness of the day and by his family tradition, making a great resolve that the green ribbon should be his in another four years. Yet it would have been characteristic of Charles Wright if the burning resolution had been accompanied by a sudden cold doubt as he asked himself whether he was worthy to carry on in the name of his family.

Commencement over, Wright and Galpin, like the other new matriculates, returned to their homes, to assemble again six weeks later for the opening of the school year. Their careers had begun.

Fifty years after the events just described, Thomas Thatcher, a grave Yale professor then grown old, wrote to two distinguished American professors of botany for information to be used in a history of the class of 1835. "What can you tell me of the work that Charles Wright has done in his chosen field?" was the burden of the letters. Professor Asa Gray of Harvard University, the dean and peerless leader of American botanists, wrote in reply:

You cannot over-estimate the services which Charles Wright has rendered to Botany. He has been not only a capital and indefatigable explorer and collector, but also an acute observer. I have myself profited not a little by his observations and critical remarks. . . . Mr. Wright's name is frequent and imperishable in the record of Science. He will always be known as having done very much to develop the Botany of Texas, New Mexico, and Arizona, then of Japan and other parts of N. E. Asia, and also of Cuba and San Domingo. Very few have done so much in such various quarters of the world; and hardly any collectors have been more helpful to the botanists of this generation.

Professor Daniel C. Eaton, botanist of Yale, wrote:

As a collector of plants from the Arctic regions to the Torrid . . . and as an acute and diligent observer of plants in their native regions, he stands almost

without an equal; Sir Joseph Hooker being the only equal I can think of. . . .
He has laid the botanical world under great and lasting obligations.

And the famous German-American botanist, George Engelmann of
St. Louis, in the course of his description of *Opuntia wrightii,* a new
species of cactus discovered by Wright, says that now it "bears a name
which . . . is forever inseparably connected with the botany of our
Southern Boundary."

An investigation of the botanical literature of the Southwest will
show important papers based on collections made by Wright during
the years 1844-1852—papers by Engelmann and others, and especially
those by Professor Asa Gray, in his *Plantæ Wrightianæ,* published in
two thick quarto volumes by the Smithsonian Institution in its *Contributions to Knowledge.* Wright discovered many hundreds of new
species of plants not only in the Southwest, but also, as botanist with
the Ringgold Expedition, in many other parts of the world; and
eminent botanists in many lands sought to honor him by giving new
species of plants his name. It would be impossible to trace the development of our knowledge of the natural history of the Southwestern
frontier without giving an important place to this man.

Wright came into Texas in 1837, just after the state had won its
independence; he lived here through the period of the Republic,
through annexation, and through the Mexican War; he worked
on the Boundary Survey Commission of the United States, both as
botanist and as surveyor; he was a professor in the first institution
of higher learning established in Texas, the short-lived Rutersville
College. On any one of these scores Wright's life would be of significance. Yet though he lived in all of these movements, he was not
driven by them. He came into eastern Texas when it was a turbulent
section, dominated by a group of horse-thieves and lawless land-speculators, and still retained his hold on himself. He consorted with
a friend and fellow-botanist who was ruined by wine, women, and
politics. Yet he was aloof from common temptation. His life seems
to have been swayed by very simple and yet strange impulses: a love
of nature, an eagerness to discover new things, an impatience of
physical idleness, an overmastering love of travel. These were the
factors that contributed to his superlative attainments as a botanical
collector. And yet the biographer who attempts to unravel Wright's
nature, to find the sources of his inspiration, is baffled. One cannot
say whence it came; only his works are open to the world.

Charles Wright belonged to a family that had played a large role
in the history of Connecticut, especially of Wethersfield. Numerous
members of the family, at every advancement of the frontier, had

gone out of Connecticut to help in the settlement and organization of embryo states. In fact, Connecticut seems to have been the point of dispersal of the family. In Wethersfield especially the Wrights have been numerous ever since the early days of the Republic. Thus in the census of 1790, eleven Wrights, heads of families, are enrolled from Wethersfield township in Hartford County alone. Thomas Wright, the immigrant ancestor from whom Charles Wright was descended, was a member of the Massachusetts Court of Assistants before the colonial government was established at Boston. He removed to Wethersfield in 1639, and in the course of his life held several civil offices. His great-grandson Nathaniel Wright (1722-1796) was the grandfather of Charles Wright.

The old Wright homestead on Jordan Lane in Wethersfield was the birthplace of the botanist. He was the son of mature age. His father, James Wright, a carpenter and joiner, had married late in life Mary, daughter of Elizur and Abigail (Deming) Goodrich. James Wright was then forty-eight; his wife was ten years his junior. To this couple were born four children, two boys and two girls. Charles, second of the children, was born October 29, 1811. His brother John, of whom he was inordinately fond, was two years his senior; Abigail, the baby of the family, was five years his junior; while Mary Ann was three years younger. We see portrayed here the history of many a family in the intellectual aristocracy of New England: earnest, pious, contained, they built, upon a hard soil in an intemperate climate—despite constant warfare with the Indians— a tradition of government and a sobriety of civilization that were important elements in the founding of America. From such stock, with such traditions, was the botanist sprung.

For most college-bred men, their campus days are a focus of sentiment which grows more and more intense as the college years themselves recede into the past. It was not so with Charles Wright. When he was a student at Yale he was a shy, diffident lad who could be drawn out only by confidences. Among his classmates, he liked best —after Galpin—Butler, Gager, and Thatcher, but they were most amiable men, beloved of all. Although every freshman at Yale was supposed to join one of the three literary societies devoted to composition and declamation, Wright avoided such exercises. One does not wonder that a self-conscious boy with Wright's physical handicap— a moderate strabismus—was, in the circumstances, somewhat retiring: many years later Wright's classmate Gardiner could still recall the "merciless barbarians" who acted as critics of the literary exercises. In after life, Wright recalled instead of literary activities his long rambles in the vicinity of New Haven on Wednesday and Saturday afternoons—solitary wanderings during which he did his first botanical collecting. From whom he learned his botany is unknown; Gray could not tell, after many years of acquaintance with Wright. It is possible, but not certain, that James Dwight Dana, the famous geologist, who was an upper-classman during Wright's first years at Yale, was his inspiration. Wright was the kind of boy likely to develop a silent, pitiable hero-worship of an older student.

Yale College in Wright's day, while slender in resources, possessed an intellectual evangelism that is rare at the present time. As Gilman narrates in his biography of Dana:

> The college was then a very small institution, where everything was managed upon a simple and economical plan; but it represented the best traditions of New England, and gave its pupils a thorough training in Latin and Greek, and in mathematics, with an introduction to natural philosophy and astronomy, as well as chemistry, mineralogy and geology. [President Jeremiah] Day, [Professor Benjamin] Silliman, and [Professor J. L.] Kingsley were the lights of the institution. The library was small, and could not have been very stimulating to a student of science. There was, however, an excellent cabinet of minerals . . . [which] had been brought to New Haven twenty years before, at the instance of Silliman, and was bought by the college, through his instrumentality, in 1825.

Simple and rigorous living went with high thinking. Morning prayers were held in the chapel at five in the summer and six in the autumn and winter. Then followed the three regular recitations before breakfast, of Greek, Latin, and mathematics. Until 1842 students were required to take their meals in the college commons. Evening prayers were held at five. Until 1850, the Christmas season was included in "term time," which extended into the first, or even the second, week of January. The course of study offered few electives, and these only in the junior and senior years. The curriculum, with its preponderant emphasis on the classics, had little appeal for a mind with a bent for the methods and facts of science.

Wright's career as a student of Yale began on Wednesday, October 26, 1831, with his attendance on evening prayers in the college chapel. The next day at eleven, together with the other members of his class, he went again to the chapel to recite the preface of Livy and get his chapel and class assignments. Under Professor Kingsley (whom Timothy Dwight dubbed the "American Addison" and President Woolsey thought possessed an incomparable Latin style) Wright studied the *Ars Poetica* of Horace and Tacitus' *Agricola* and *De Germania*. His Greek he began under Theodore D. Woolsey and completed with Henry Durant, then a tutor at Yale.

It was a wonderful group of classmates that Wright had. Among them were John Brocklesby, in later life a distinguished mathematician and professor in Trinity College in Hartford; Samuel Ware Fisher, subsequently president of Hamilton College (1858-67); Alexander Smith Johnson, who became a famous New York jurist; and Thomas A. Thatcher, later professor of Latin at Yale (1842-86). It is interesting to note that fellow collegians during Wright's period of residence included, in addition to James Dwight Dana, such men as Josiah Clark, later of Smith College; George Edward Day, the Hebraist; three leading professors-to-be at Western Reserve University, Emerson, St. John, and Seymour; Alphonso Taft, later Minister to Russia, and father of President Taft; and the future Chief Justice Morrison R. Waite. Truly a seminary of learning! Mere converse with such spirits was a liberal education. No wonder that when Wright came, almost immediately after graduation, to the raw frontier of the Southwest, he was acutely aware of the dearth of intellectual companionship.

Timothy Dwight, in his *Memories of Yale Life and Men,* has given a compact picture of the Yale of his day—1845—and has left an account of freshman teaching. Conditions had not greatly changed in the ten years since Wright's graduation. Dwight recounts that:

An instructor's desk . . . was in one of the corners of each of the rooms, and the seats for the students were oak boards, painted white, extending along the walls which furnished the only back against which one could lean. The center of each room was vacant, except in certain cases, where three or four chairs, or one or two extra benches, were found necessary because the numbers were so large that all could not otherwise be provided for. In these rooms we began to translate Livy, and the *Odyssey* of Homer, and to form the acquaintance ot Day's *Algebra.* We translated the passages assigned us. We answered, according to our ability, the mathematical or other questions that were put to us by the instructors. It was useful work. It had its bearing on the future. But it was not very stimulating or calculated greatly to awaken enthusiasm. . . . It was no weak, second-rate, half-useless education, that was offered us.

Thus may one see the pedagogical method used with Charles Wright, before "educational experts, teaching more and more about less and less" had revolutionized American education. It was this hard, crusty diet, "not very stimulating or calculated greatly to awaken enthusiasm," that took these men and in disproportionate numbers molded them for leadership.

The first vacation in Wright's freshman year fell in mid-winter; and, like many another Yale student poor in pocket but rich in purpose, he walked the fifty miles home to Wethersfield through the snow. During the last week of June, cholera broke out at Yale. It was a part of the great cholera epidemic which swept the United

States, Texas, and Mexico in the years 1832-33, and which Thomas Drummond was to encounter in Velasco a year later. The students, terrified, returned to their homes, and classes were suspended at the college.

Wright's sophomore year was uneventful. He studied rhetoric and oratory under Professor Chauncey A. Goodrich (son-in-law of Noah Webster, and a relative of Wright's), but no amount of forcible inspiration on Goodrich's part could make an orator of this pupil. The one bright spot of the year was the Phi Beta Kappa oration by Edward Everett on Class Day, August 21, 1833. On that occasion, after the introduction by Roger M. Sherman, a puff of wind blew Everett's manuscript out of his hand as he arose to speak. Rising to the occasion, without notes he "launched forth upon a tide of oratory which held the rapt attention of the audience for nearly two hours."

In his junior year Wright took Greek under Woolsey and natural philosophy and astronomy under Olmsted. He was fond of mathematics, surveying, and astronomy, although he neglected geology and mineralogy for botany. His interest in astronomy was greatly stimulated only a few weeks after he enrolled with Olmsted by the wonderfully brilliant meteoric shower of November 13, 1833, which burst upon his view as he was going to morning chapel, at five o'clock. "The heavens are falling! the heavens are falling!" cried the students. Strange how that phenomenon threw Olmsted into ecstasies and the Millerites into tantrums.

At last the round of college work came to the final year, during which Wright studied metaphysics, ethics, and logic under President Day; political economy under Daggett; chemistry and geology under Silliman; religion under Kingsley and Fitch; and still more rhetoric under Goodrich. The long road seemed in retrospect but a short one; privation, dogged determination, self-denial, faithfulness had their reward. Charles Wright stood very straight before Jeremiah Day on August 19, 1835, and on his coat lapel was pinned a long green ribbon.

Some weeks before Wright's graduation, he had been called into the president's room. In the light of Day's character, one can partially reconstruct the scene. Slowly, deliberately, patiently, as though he were opening a matter of great diplomatic consequences, this great man informed Wright: "I hold in my hand a communication addressed to me by a considerable planter at Natchez, in our extreme southwest border state of Mississippi." Day went on: "He desires that I should recommend to him a young gentleman of scholarly attainments and character, of my confidence, to serve in the station of tutor for his children. The compensation is adequate; the situation a very respectable one. Many of our young Yale graduates find it agreeable to accept such a station. Mr. Thomas Thatcher of your class goes to a similar office in Georgia, and it would afford me great pleasure if you could enable me to address to this gentleman my recommendation of you for this situation." Wright was glad to accept the place, and in due course of time was informed that his services were desired. He left Wethersfield in October, 1835, only a few weeks after his graduation, and taking the Mississippi River route, duly arrived in Natchez.

President Day, kindly, gentle, benign, hardly knew into what a situation he had projected his "young gentleman of scholarly attainments and character." "Respectable," indeed! At the time of Charles Wright's coming to Natchez, it had the most unenviable reputation of all the frontier towns of the Southwest. Dr. Anson Jones, in one of his memorandum books, has the following entry concerning Natchez under the date of August 1, 1838: "This place is so notoriously infamous, that I had fancied it much larger, not expecting a spot so small could have held vice and profligacy enough to make it so distinguished. It must have been very much condensed." Further testimony to the reputation of Natchez for vice and outlawry may be found in other writings. Thus Robert Alexander, who in August, 1837, came to Texas to be a Methodist missionary with Dr. Martin Ruter and Littleton Fowler, found the Natchez station, to which he had been appointed in 1836, one of the most difficult situations in the whole Southwest.

As Wright entered into his work in this unsavory environment, he found some comfort in the fact that his classmate Pettengill was near at hand as tutor to the children of a sugar planter of Louisiana. For two years Wright remained on the plantation near Natchez. In 1836, he persuaded his fellow-villager and classmate Galpin to come to Natchez to teach in a select-school there. When the panic of 1837 came, in the financial crash that wrecked so many enterprises in Europe and America, Wright's employer failed in business, and Wright consequently lost his position.

At this time the road to Texas was open. Texas was an independent republic; lands were cheap; "On to Texas!" was in the air, as many emigrants ruined in the financial disasters of the panic set out for the new country to retrieve the losses sustained in the old. Thus, in the spring of 1837, Charles Wright came to Texas. How he came and where he went is told by Professor Thatcher, the historian of Wright's class:

His life in Texas began in 1837, when he went thither from the vicinity of Natchez, "botanizing by the way." . . . For the first few years his headquarters were not far from the western boundary of Louisiana [at Zavalla], on the Neches River, from which position he made excursions—chiefly as a surveyor, at first, and subordinately as a botanist—in various directions up and down the river, and eastward to the Sabine [in present Angelina, Jasper, Tyler, and Newton counties]. He also spent some time in teaching.

Whether or not he realized it at the time, Wright was destined to make Texas his home for the next fifteen years—if indeed, during his productive years as a botanist, Wright can be said to have had a home. It was a fruitful period for the advancement of knowledge of the botany of the Southwest. Lindheimer, it will be recalled, was just then beginning to collect plants in the region of Houston and San Felipe. South of San Antonio and as far as Laredo and Mata-moros, Jean Louis Berlandier had made, in 1828-34, his extensive collections for DeCandolle. Only a few years later Lindheimer would make with Roemer a collection of plants from the banks of the Guada-lupe in Comal County that would show the world the richness of the Texan flora. Five years before Wright's arrival, Thomas Drummond had gathered seven hundred and fifty species of plants for Hooker in the Austin Colony. But all of this had been done in central and "southwestern" Texas. No collecting of note, besides Dr. M. C. Leavenworth's slight efforts, had been done in eastern Texas. Hence Asa Gray, busily engaged in various magisterial works on American botany, received with something like delight a letter from Wright in eastern Texas in 1844. It will be better to let Gray recount the early experiences of Wright in the Neches country, especially since he quotes from a manuscript autobiography of Wright apparently now lost. Gray says:

[Wright made] his headquarters for two or three years [that is, until about 1840, when he went to Town Bluff, a now-deserted village in Tyler County] at a place called Zavalla, on the Neches [in present Jasper County]; he oc-cupied himself with land surveying, explored the surrounding country, "learned to dress deerskins after the manner of the Indians, and to make moccasins and leggins," "became a pretty fair deer hunter," and inured himself to the various hardships of a frontier life at that period. When the business of surveying fell off he took again to teaching; and in the year 1844, he opened a botanical cor-respondence with the present writer, sending an interesting collection of the plants of Eastern Texas to Cambridge.

The correspondence thus begun was to have consequences of the most far-reaching importance for both Wright and Gray. Wright's first letter, now lost, was sent to Gray sometime in the spring of 1844; Gray's letter of reply, also lost, was dated June 21 of that year. All the letters that passed subsequently between them are carefully preserved in the Gray Herbarium of Harvard University, and from them we are able to reconstruct all of Charles Wright's botanical travels in Texas. Dr. E. O. Wooton made a careful collation of Wright's field notes of Texas collections preserved in the Gray Herbarium, which has aided greatly in the interpretation of his trips and collections.

Two sorts of observers have written of the frontier. There have been such perfect examples of the snob as, say, Mrs. Trollope from across the water, or our own Timothy Dwight, once president of Yale. On the other hand, there have been those like the historian Turner, who have looked beneath the lawlessness of pioneer life (which in the nature of things must be only temporary) to the final effects of the concourse on the frontier of active, restless, daring minds hungering for freedom. In his *Travels* President Dwight gives a classic picture of the frontier of Vermont in the first decade of the nineteenth century, a picture strangely reminiscent of the descriptions of Texas current in the 'forties. Without doubt Dwight's picture is correct in two dimensions, but it is fundamentally false in view of the fact that it neglects the third dimension, the whence and whither of the situation. For Mr. Dwight never learned that history is a dynamic and not a static thing. The passage is as follows:

These men [the Vermont frontiersmen] cannot live in regular society. They are too idle, too talkative, too passionate, too prodigal, and too shiftless to acquire either property or character. They are impatient of the restraints of law, religion, and morality; grumble about the taxes, by which rulers, ministers, and school-masters, are supported; and complain incessantly as well as bitterly, of the extortions of mechanics, farmers, merchants, and physicians, to whom they are always indebted. At the same time they are usually possessed, in their own view, of uncommon wisdom; understand medical science, politics, and religion, better than those, who have studied them through life; and although they manage their own concerns worse than other men, feel perfectly satisfied, that they could manage those of the nation far better than the agents, to whom they are committed by the public. After displaying their own talents and worth; after exposing the injustice of the community in neglecting to invest persons of such merit with public offices; in many an eloquent harangue, uttered by many a kitchen fire, in every blacksmith's shop, and in every corner of the streets; and finding all their efforts vain, they become at length discouraged; and under the pressure of poverty, the fear of a gaol, and the consciousness of public contempt, leave their native places, and betake themselves to the wilderness.

On the other hand, as Turner points out, a certain disorder and confusion is to be expected in the coming together of large numbers of nonconformists (for most frontiersmen are pre-eminently recusant in temperament); and out of the intellectual tumult of the frontier,

182

often accompanied by widespread emotional upsets of a religious nature, came many intellectual traits of value in the American character. The frontier, particularly frontier Texas, where so many diverse racial stocks merged on a large scale—English, German, French, Czech, Hungarian, Irish, Spanish, and Mexican—served as a zone for a free admixture of ideas and bloods that has significance and promise for the future. I quote from Turner's *The Frontier in American History*:

> I have refrained from dwelling on the lawless characteristics of the frontier, because they are sufficiently well known. The gambler and desperado, the regulators of the Carolinas and the vigilantes of California, are types of that line of scum that the waves of advancing civilization bore before them, and of the growth of spontaneous organs of authority where legal authority was absent. . . . The humor, bravery, and rude strength, as well as the vices of the frontier in its worst aspect, have left traces on American character, language, and literature, not soon to be effaced. . . . From the conditions of frontier life came intellectual traits of profound importance. . . . To the frontier the American intellect owes its striking characteristics. That coarseness and strength combined with acuteness and inquisitiveness; that practical, inventive turn of mind, quick to find expedients; that masterful grasp of material things, lacking in the artistic but powerful to effect great ends; that restless, nervous energy, that dominant individualism, working for good and evil, and withal that buoyancy and exuberance which comes with freedom—these are the traits of the frontier.

The same contrasting viewpoints that appear in discussions of the American frontier in general are evident in the many descriptions of early settlers in Texas, ranging from the highly laudatory account of Austin's Three Hundred by Thomas J. Pilgrim to the violently denunciatory screed of Francis C. Sheridan in the *British Diplomatic Correspondence*. Probably Charles Elliott, of all the British diplomatic agents, saw the Texans most clearly when he spoke of them as rough and wild, but possessing a constancy and courage that was admirable; scheming, enterprising, and invariably much better informed than the English immigrants. In sharp contrast with Joseph T. Crawford, who saw Texas as affording perfect security of persons and property, Sheridan reported unalloyed iniquity. I cannot refrain from quoting, for the sake of those Texans who never saw Texas through foreign eyes, the account that Sheridan, a colonial secretary under Governor MacGregor of the Windward Islands, wrote to the acting private secretary to the Governor. The letter is dated July 12, 1840:

> The population [of Texas] which may be estimated at 150,000 Souls are chiefly Americans, a few Germans, and some English and Irish.—These are principally Bankrupts, Swindlers and Felons from the United States occasionally

diversified with an Oasis of respectability which only renders the Desert of Villainy around more conspicuous by contrast. . . . Murder and every other Crime is of great frequency in Texas and the perpetrators escape with the greatest impunity. Many murders were committed in the Island of Galveston and in the Country during my stay on the Coast, and I could never learn that one offender was brought to justice. It is considered unsafe to walk through the Streets of the principal Towns without being armed.

The Sabine River country, which was at the borderline of Texas and the United States, was a region of extreme lawlessness. Morrell, surely no prejudiced observer, in his *Flowers and Fruits from the Wilderness* states that the Sabine River country was the refuge of thieves, robbers, counterfeiters, and murderers. From this region, he says, counterfeit Texas Land Office certificates were emitted by a band "composed of men of intelligence, and who were sworn enemies to morality and religion." The plots of the counterfeiters were uncovered in 1842, but the courts were afraid to execute justice, with the result that after a period of dreadful anarchy and confusion, an outraged people were led to adopt methods of elemental justice (or sometimes injustice) by forming bands of "regulators" and "moderators."

During his first years in Texas, Wright was thus living in a region where life and property were never secure. Indian troubles brought on by Lamar's bombastic and extravagant reign contributed further to the hardships faced by the inhabitants of East Texas. Altogether, it was quite too much for a quiet, studious-minded man. There was but one bright spot in Wright's situation: his friendship for a physician, Dr. John A. Veatch, with whom he shared a love of botany. In later years, when Veatch organized a company during the Mexican War to defend Eagle Pass on the Rio Grande, he found it easy to persuade Wright to join his venture.

In the summer of 1844 Wright made a business journey to Columbus, on the Colorado River, where a distant relative lived. On this occasion he determined to remove to the Colorado, and did so about the middle of April of the following year. Shortly afterward he learned that a vacancy existed at a little college located at Rutersville, near Lagrange, in Fayette County.

Years afterward, Asa Gray, diverted by Charles Wright's facetious account of days of small things, stigmatized Rutersville as a "so-called college"—perhaps a natural remark from the direction of Cambridge. But in its environment, the College represented an intellectual adventure that was anything but contemptible. It was one of the innumerable ghostly throng of colleges that with the advancement of the frontier everywhere sprang up, flourished, dwindled, and died. Usually they were the working out in stone or wood of some great man's ideal. This is not the place for a recital of the heroic work of the early Methodist missionary Martin Ruter, who came out to Texas at the age of fifty-three from the presidency of Allegheny College in Pennsylvania, and in his short year and a half of activity before he claimed the crown of martyrdom traveled the length and breadth of early Texas, organizing churches, establishing a ministry, and preaching the need and duty of a college. As the result of his preaching, after his early death in 1838 his followers founded a college in the newly-surveyed town of Rutersville, and called to the presidency the Reverend Chauncey Richardson, a former student of old Wesleyan University, in Middletown, Connecticut. A charter was sought and obtained in February, 1840. For some years the institution was prosperous, in spite of the border warfare of 1842, when the Mexican general, Adrian Woll, marched on San Antonio and captured it. But Indian warfare was a constant menace to the institution. Only five years before the time of Wright's coming to Rutersville College, the Indians had made attacks within hailing distance of the school itself. An incident described in Wooten's *History of Texas,* which Wilbarger says occurred in the spring or summer of 1840, will throw some light on the character of the country and the obstacles facing those heroic souls who, in a land but half-wrested from the Indians, sought to carry the benefits of higher education into the wilderness:

It often became the duty of the boys at school to mount their ponies and accompany their elders in pursuit of bands of Indians. A notable instance occurred at Rutersville soon after the opening of the school. Two young boys in the neighborhood while hunting horses were attacked by Indians, and one of them, Henry Earthman, was killed; his brother Fields escaped and brought the news to the school.
The excited boys joined in the search for the body, which lay a mile away in a dreadfully mutilated state. The scalp had been taken, the hands cut off and thrown into the grass, and the heart, with ligaments unsevered, laid on one side of the body; it was found to have a bullet in the center, and was, no doubt, exposed in a spirit of bravado to show how unerring was the aim of the red man. Nearly all the boys in the school, ranging from fourteen to sixteen, joined in the pursuit of the Indians, which lasted about six weeks. In fact, one of them still living [Mordell S. Munson] says they did little but hunt Indians while at school at Rutersville prior to 1842.

I have quoted this passage at some length so that the reader may understand into what sort of place Wright was going when, in the spring of 1845, he accepted "the assistant-principalship of the male department" of Rutersville College. The College, whatever its shortcomings, must be viewed as a courageous attempt to overcome the limitations of the frontier. It was the first institution of higher learning to open in Texas—and although its life was short, it accomplished under frontier conditions a task that I doubt Harvard or Yale would have attempted. It never was large: in the fifteen years of its existence probably not more than fifteen hundred pupils, nearly all of sub-collegiate grade, attended it. But it was a noble dream whose fruition was commensurate with the possibilities of time and place.

The first announcement of Wright's appointment to a position on the faculty of the College appeared in the Lagrange *Intelligencer* of May 19, 1845, and was followed by a similar notice in the *National Register,* of Washington, Texas, under date of June 26. Thus slowly did news travel the seventy intervening miles. Wright's work at the college began with the twelfth session, on July 21. It was an absorbing task: he had little time left to pursue his botanical work, after teaching—as he said—"everything from abecedarianism to the highest branches." During Wright's connection with Rutersville College his correspondence with Gray almost ceased. There could have been little comfort in comparing Rutersville with Cambridge. But other interests claimed Wright's attention, such as addresses on temperance before the Fayette County Temperance Society, teaching elocution to the students of the college, and (ironically enough) serving as president of the college literary society. When the Methodist Conference met in 1845, H. S. Thrall, the principal of the preparatory department of the College, was assigned to a circuit, and Wright was promoted to the principalship with the opening of the thirteenth session, on January 19, 1846. He was completely in charge of the department that spring while President Richardson traveled in Texas securing funds and attended the first General Conference of the Southern church at Petersburg, Virginia, in May, 1846. Overloaded with work, Wright sought in vain for an additional teacher in his department to lighten his burden.

The last contemporary newspaper reference to Wright's work at Rutersville is to be found in the *Intelligencer* of July 14, 1846, in a scurrilous initialed note which stated that the college would be closed at the end of the thirteenth term, and intimated that the life of the institution had been sacrificed to Richardson's egotism because he discharged men of character and ability whom he considered "disruptive influences." However that may be, Wright's correspondence indicates that his attitude toward the President was not negative, but neutral. After the end of the school session, Wright continued in Rutersville for another year (until late October or early November, 1847) acting as a tutor in private families.

Wright's work at Rutersville represents some of the first science field-work done in the schools of Texas. The Lagrange *Intelligencer*

186

stated, in the issue in which Wright's appointment was announced, that "Young men who may desire to study surveying, geology, or botany, will have the opportunity of accompanying one of the tutors on short excursions, for the purpose of learning these sciences *practically* as well as theoretically." The departments of mathematics and science in the College used such familiar old books as the Davies texts in higher mathematics; Norton's Astronomy; Turner's Chemistry; and Comstock's works on Geology, Mineralogy, and Botany. Most of the students, of course, were in the preparatory department, where they studied Anthon for Greek, Andrews & Stoddard for Latin, Cooper's Virgil, and so on.

From November, 1847, to July of the following year, Wright taught in Austin, devoting all his spare time to botanizing. About the middle of July he set out from San Antonio for Eagle Pass to join his friend Veatch, whose company was posted there guarding the Mexican frontier. During July and August of 1848, while holding a commissary position in Captain Veatch's company, Wright botanized on both sides of the Rio Grande, and returned to San Antonio about the middle of September.

Here he found a letter from Gray inviting him to come north to Cambridge for the winter as a curator, to assist in sorting out his own rich collections which had been accumulating at the Gray Herbarium since 1845. With great alacrity he accepted the invitation and left for the north. Arriving at Wethersfield the third week in November, he shortly afterward went over to Cambridge, and spent the winter and spring partly there and partly at Wethersfield. During the winter of 1848-49, while Wright was with Gray, the United States War Department was making preparations for a survey of the boundary between the United States and Mexico. Gray early conceived an ardent desire to have Wright accompany this expedition as botanist, and wrote Engelmann concerning his plan. He was successful in gaining permission from the Secretary of War for Wright to accompany the expedition, but could not get a guarantee that transportation or rations would be furnished—a failure that was later to cause Wright much exasperation and trouble. By the end of February Gray and Wright had practically completed their part of the arrangements. On February 26 Gray wrote to his old teacher, Professor John Torrey:

Having determined on an expedition for Wright, you may be sure I was not going to be altogether disappointed. Accordingly I have got one all arranged (Lowell and Green subscribing handsomely) . . . and thus far everything has wonderfully conspired to favor it. Wright has left me this morning to go to his mother's in Connecticut (Wethersfield); there to make his portfolios and presses; comes on to New York soon; takes first vessel for Galveston (I expect a letter from Hastings telling when it sails), and to reach Austin and Fredericksburg in time to accompany the troops that are to be sent up, by a new road, across the country to El Paso, in New Mexico. Look on the map (Wislizenus) and you will see the region we mean him to explore this summer; the hot valley of the Rio del Norte [Rio Grande], early in the season, the mountains east, and especially those west in summer. He will probably stay two years, and get to Taos and Spanish Peaks this year or next. We shall have government recommendations to protection, and letters to an officer (commanding) who, through [Professor Joseph] Henry, has already made overtures to collect himself or aid in the matter.

Wright left New York for Texas about the first of April, 1849, and arrived in Galveston the twenty-fourth of that month. On reaching Galveston he learned that the military train which he was to accompany would leave San Antonio the first of June. He therefore proceeded from Galveston to Houston, and from Houston west across

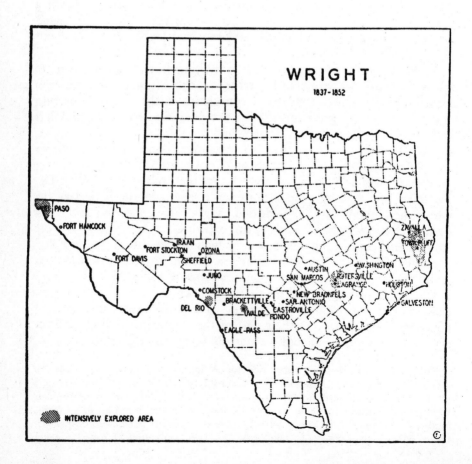

WRIGHT

1837-1852

INTENSIVELY EXPLORED AREA

the Brazos bottoms of present Waller and Austin counties to Rutersville, which he reached on May 12. The interval before the departure
of the train he spent as follows: during the ten days from May 15 to
May 25 he followed the Colorado from Lagrange to Austin; May 27
and 28 he spent in the neighborhood of San Marcos and on the road
to New Braunfels; on the twenty-ninth he was at New Braunfels and
on the Guadalupe, and he arrived in San Antonio on the thirtieth
of May. He had timed his arrival well, for the baggage train which
he was to accompany left San Antonio the next day.

Wright's account of the trip from Galveston up to Austin, contained
in a letter to Gray, is highly valuable. Those matters that are of general interest I have here excerpted from the mass of botanical data:

Austin   May 26th/49
My Dear Doctor
Let me report progress You know the date of my departure from New York
and probably that of my arrival in Galveston [April 28] I took the first boat
for Houston Unable to transport my baggage by stage I put it on a road waggon,
(unfortunately) overloaded . . . with a weak team By a blunder of the driver
he started on the wrong road and one as bad as roads ever get to be The
result was that he was obliged to hire himself hauled out of the mud into the
right road and on that we had divers unloadings and reloadings to perform on
our way I footed it through mud and water and had a fair chance to botanize
for aquatics or amphibia.
    I stopped a few days with my friends at Rutersville and then got here some
days before the waggon
    On my way up and here I have collected some 250 species probably which
will furnish some 2000 specimens some few rather bad—injured by rain and
most of which we had a plenty. They are mostly old and known plants but
will do for exchanges.
    I have been here a week and have now ascertained that on monday next or
soon thereafter a waggon will start for San Antonio and the quartermaster . . .
has promised me transportation I have written to Gen Harney which I hope
will secure me transportation if not subsistence to El Paso I intend to procure
one to Major Henry which will secure me his favor and assistance.
    The train will leave San Antonio on the 1st prox and Mr. Chapman says
will be three months on the route—200 m per month ample leisure to botanize
by the way. . . .
    I may have to lay in provisions at San Antonio to El Paso and join some of
the messes of privates unless some of the officers should take a liking to me as
I hope they will and it may diminish my expense These have been rather greater
than I expected My trip to New York and back to Wethersfield early in March,
Hotel bill for several days about the 1st Ap. my passage money not 25 dols but
27 1/2 Hospital money at Galveston, wharfage, storage, drayage, tavern expenses,
passage and freight to Houston, & a repetition of like little charges these with
my expense up the country though I have tried to be economical have considerably reduced my funds Still I think I will have enough for the present campaign & if you will have arrangements made to supply me for the next I think
I will be able to do something handsome for yourself and other friends.

You need not hope to hear from me again before I arrive at El Paso unless something important should occur

Affectionately
Yours
Charles Wright

Poor Wright! He was to learn that few army officers of the pioneer period had any overmastering love for those men of science—many of them naturalists and geologists of maturity, and even of international reputation—who went out with expeditions such as this one. Even when the investigator was recommended by the Secretary of War, by Professor Joseph Henry, Secretary of the Smithsonian Institution, or by the Secretary of State himself, still it was optional with the commanding officer whether he should furnish rations and transportation. The following letter, written to Gray on that Thursday at San Antonio while the baggage train was making ready to start, will show some of the uncertainties of the trip:

San Antonio   May 31st/49

My Dear Doctor

I have just put my baggage on one of the Army waggons with that of my good friend Dr. Baker whom I fortunately met here and to whom I am much indebted

I had a letter to Gen Harney from Mr. Miller Secretary of State explaning my pursuts [sic] and wishes The Gen. gave me but little encouragement and at the solicitation of Dr. Baker *allowed* me to put my baggage on the waggon without the *least assurance* of subsistence and I have been obliged to muster up all the Yankee confidence natural to me (which *is* and always *was* but *little*) with what the Dr had to spare assisted too by Mr. Shelton to bear me out in undertaking   I shall start after the train this evening and I shall try to get something to eat out of somebody. Now can not you get a special order from the *head* of the Commissary Department to furnish me with support and transportation. The officers all plead that they have no authority to grant these favors and if they grant them to one for a certain purpose—as to me for botanizing—how can they refuse them to others for other purposes? I have no assurance that my collections will be transported back from El Paso though I have no doubt that they can be more easily brought back than I can be conveyed there as the waggons will return empty. The officers all express a desire to serve me but at the same time say they have no authority without assuming responsibility which they are unwilling to do . . . I am rejoiced that I am in time late as it is, to go with the train and you will doubtless share my joy at the favorable prospect before me   It is supposed we will be three months on the route (—travelling slowly—) of only about 500 miles . . . There is still some cholera here and the weather is getting very hot and I shall have to be very prudent to avoid sickness I must start this evening and walk 15 miles to overtake my waggon—not a very pleasant evening to walk either in prospect or in execution . . .

My kind regards to Mrs. Gray
Yours sincerely
Chas Wright

The whole of the trip to El Paso, a distance of 673 miles, Wright made on foot, for transportation of his trunk and drying paper only was furnished by the Government. Following the southern trail that later became the route of the Southern Pacific railroad, the party arrived in El Paso on September 12, 1849, after a journey lasting 104 days. During part of this time Wright boarded with one of the messes of the transportation train, and endured many privations and hardships. The return, which began on October 12 with thirty-five wagons, took forty-two days, so that Wright reached San Antonio on November 23. The route followed led through the Hueco and Guadalupe Mountains, down Delaware Creek to the Pecos, and down the valley of the Pecos by the so-called Upper or Fredericksburg Road.

Wright had early besought Gray to furnish him with a horse and covered cart such as Lindheimer had, for collecting plants; but Gray pointed out the fact that Thomas Drummond during his fruitful explorations in Texas had traveled on foot. The difficulties of such collecting impressed themselves on Wright in the first few days of the trip, when the military company was retarded in its movements by rains that were disastrous to plant collections. The official record of the weather of the trip for the first few days, published in the War Department's report, shows the following:

June 1—Day exceedingly unfavorable; the rain fell in torrents, which added to those that had fallen a few days previous, made the roads extremely bad. The command, however, moved on, and encamped for the night on the Leon Creek. *June 2*—A violent thunder storm arose early in the morning, and the command remained in camp. *June 3*—Moved to San Lucas Springs; and before the tents were pitched, again the rain began to fall. The prairies were now inundated, and the roads impassable.

In the face of this weather, under difficulties and disappointments which it is hard for us now to appreciate, Wright in his despair wrote to Gray a letter unburdening his heart. I reproduce it in its entirety so that the reader may realize the sort of obstacles a naturalist-collector like Wright had to meet: cold, rain, burning heat, maddening flies, bitter saline water, short rations, and, above all, the sense of abandonment. It was easy for Wright, in his loneliness and despair, to blame Gray for all the discomfort and hardship of his position. Fortunately Gray could understand and forgive such complaints in view of Wright's work for science. Wright's letter follows:

My Dear Dr   Quihi June 2nd/49
I wrote you so recently that if I were not full I would keep silence But steam is so high that if I do not blow off fearful consequences may follow.
Yesterday morning [June 1, on the banks of the Medina] we had a violent

norther cold and accompanied with rain after which and when ready to start my baggage, paper &c was distributed about into three or four waggons It was so packed that it was not much injured This morning about daylight we had another more severe accompanied with hail My collections were nearly all wet and I have had no time to dry them so they will be much damaged My paper is nearly all wet I should not wonder if we have another storm tonight

Now these are misfortunes attendant on my dependent situation and I can not prevent them The officers care nothing about my affairs and the waggoners have a little curiosity to gratify by looking on while I change my plants and care no more about it or rather would be pleased if they were sunk in the river and their load would be lightened

You will recollect I suppose a suggestion made to you that I should be equipped with a waggon and horse from which you dissented instancing the labors of other botanists who had made large collections. But I venture to say that Drummond did not attempt to save 12-15 specimens of each species or if he did he had an art which I do not possess

The outfit which I proposed seemed to you perhaps large but I am sincerely of the opinion that the entire cost of the outfit might have been *clear* saved *the present year* I would rather have a horse and carriage and ten dollars in my pocket than have five hundred as I am so far as it facilitates my operations I have money in my pocket but it does me no good I can buy nothing with it I sit uninvited and see others eating and it is a severe trial to my feelings to *thrust* myself among them The men have their rations and often none to spare and how am I to get along to El Paso I know not If I had consulted my own feelings alone I should have stopped at San Antonio and turned back But you and Mr Lowell had expectations which would not have been realized and I felt reluctant to disappoint you You wrote to me [Jan. 17, 1848] of working like a dog I know how you live—then call your situation dog-paradise and mine hog- and ass-paradise combined and you *may* realize my situation—sleep all night if you can in the rain and walk 12-15 miles next day in the mud and then overhall [*sic*] a huge package of soaked plants and dry them by the heat of the clouds

I have been now three or four days in such a state of uncertainty about the possibility of going on that I have no enjoyment and today I have not saved a specimen—have merely collected some seeds as I walked along the way As for studying the plants I have not attempted it so long that I have almost forgotten I have been vexed enough to cry or swear when thinking that I have the pleasing prospect of being dependent for six months on a parcel of men who call me a fool and wish me at the bottom of the sea

There is a man who is bound for California in our company—provided with a carriage and mules provisions and cooking utensils—independent as a wood sawyer and dependent on others only for safety against enemies If I had such a one my expenses would be very trifling I could collect twice as many specimens of twice as many species and twice as well preserved I could attend to them at any time I pleased in wet or dry weather and have the assurance that the rain at least could be prevented from coming to them I could also take them to Houston or other seaport and put them on shipboard myself and then I would know they would depend for their forwarding on no careless agent

I am fully resolved that this season will close my botanical travels on horseback or on foot if I can not operate to better advantage I'll give it up and turn my attention to something else

I can now only *hope* that when Capt. French arrives in camp by [*sic*] situation will be improved by an appointment or in some other way . . . You now know my sentment [*sic*] on the mode of botanizing in *this* country & if you wish to continue it on *my* plan I am ready to do all I can . . .

Affectionately yours
Charles Wright

In spite of Wright's discouragement, the results of the expedition, when they were analyzed, proved to be very rich, numbering some fourteen hundred species, besides many cacti and packages of seeds of wild plants—all of which, with the exception of the cacti, went to Gray. After sending off the collections, Wright spent some months (from January to November, 1850) with Colonel Claiborne Kyle at San Marcos, acting as tutor; and in his free time hunted deer, made buckskin, and gathered extensive collections of mosses and lichens for Sullivant and Tuckerman. From December, 1850, until the summer of 1851 he conducted a small school at New Braunfels, and here, as has been related, struck up a warm friendship with Ferdinand Lindheimer. During this time Wright was preparing for participation in further explorations in the West, and in the spring of 1851 he joined the Graham Survey of the boundary. Of the experiences of this trip, Gray says:

He joined the party under Col. Graham, one of the commissioners for surveying and determining the United States and Mexican boundary from the Rio Grande to the Pacific, accepting the position partly as a botanist, partly as one of the surveyors [after about the first of November, 1851], which assured a comfortable maintainance [*sic*] and the wished-for opportunity for botanical exploration in an untouched field. Attached only to Col. Graham's party, he returned with him without reaching farther westward than about the middle of what is now the territory of Arizona, and in the summer [probably in August] of 1852 he returned with the extensive collections to San Antonio, and thence to St. Louis, to deliver his Cactaceæ to Dr. Engelmann, and with the remainder to Cambridge. These collections were the basis of the second part of the *Plantæ Wrightianæ* and . . . in part of the *Botany of the Mexican Boundary Survey,* published in 1859. . . . No name is more largely commemorated in the Botany of Texas, New Mexico, and Arizona than that of Charles Wright. . . . Surely no botanist ever earned such scientific remembrance by entire devotion, acute observation, severe exertion, and perseverance under hardship and privation.

Thus Wright bade farewell to the Southwest, after fifteen fruitful years in Texas, eight of which he had devoted unreservedly to the advancement of knowledge of its flora. With his departure our detailed account of his life ends.

Wright hastened to Wethersfield and Cambridge, and after a winter in Cambridge with Gray, made ready in the spring of 1853 to accompany Ringgold's North Pacific Exploring Expedition as botanist.

193

He sailed on the steamer *John Hancock,* from Norfolk, on June 11. The itinerary led to the island of Madeira, the Cape Verde Islands, and the Cape of Good Hope, where Wright made very extensive plant collections—nearly eight hundred species; to Sydney in Australia; to Hongkong, and northward along the coasts of Japan; to Kamchatka and the Bering Straits; and finally to the coast of California. He arrived at San Francisco in October, 1855, and in February, 1856, secured permission to detach himself from the expedition and to return home by way of Nicaragua (where he spent some weeks on an island in Nicaragua Lake) and Greytown. After a summer in Cambridge and in Wethersfield with his mother, he began in November of 1856 his eleven years' botanical exploration of Cuba. His work in that region was of the highest value.

In 1868 Wright acted as Director of the Herbarium at Cambridge, during Gray's absence in Europe; and in 1871 he made a short, and not very successful, collecting trip to Santo Domingo. With this trip his active botanical career may be said to have ended. Returning to Wethersfield, he devoted himself to gardening and farming, and, for a time, to work at Cambridge during the winter and spring months. For six months during the winter of 1875-6 he acted as librarian of the Bussey Institution of Harvard University.

The last ten years of his life Wright spent largely at Wethersfield, in the house where he was born. As he wrote to the historian of his class at Yale, Thomas Thatcher, he worked on the farm and in the garden, "with now and then a day devoted to botany." In winter, "besides reading and keeping warm," he did "whatever is needful to be done at this time of year—which with us, is not much. Once or twice a year I make a visit of a few days at Cambridge." With his invalid brother John and his two sisters, all unmarried, he faced old age serenely. During these final years, when occasion offered, Wright collected plants so assiduously in the vicinity of Wethersfield that it is extremely difficult for more recent botanists to find any species not previously reported by him. But meanwhile an organic disease of the heart, dating back to his Cuban days, began to sap his strength and warn him of approaching death. Life went suddenly, on the eleventh of August, 1885, when he was doing the evening work of caring for the animals on the little farm. As he did not return at the expected time, search was begun; they found his body lying as if in repose.

It was a fitting death for one who had lived Wright's life. As a young man he had left the peace of quiet Wethersfield and had gone out to the rugged frontier, where an unfriendly environment and constant danger from the Indians were part of the day's expectations.

194

Then had come the exploring trips—in the Southwest, in South Africa, Japan, Cuba, Central America—with their privations, hardships, and loneliness, and also their inspiration. At last, worn with his labors, he had come to the quiet village of his birth, to his ancestral home; and there gently and quietly he paid his score. The explorer rested at last.

In any analysis of Wright's character, as man and botanist, certain traits stand out predominantly: simplicity and directness of mind; bluntness of speech; an oversensitiveness to what others might say or think of him that was almost pathological; a faithfulness to his purposes which drove him doggedly on to their accomplishment. Gray, in his obituary notice, says that Wright was a "person of low stature and well-knit frame, hardy rather than strong, scrupulously temperate, a man of simple ways, always modest and unpretending, but direct and downright in expression, most amiable, trusty and religious." A perusal of the thirty-seven letters Wright sent to Gray from Texas, and the innumerable letters later sent from the cruise around the world and from Cuba—as well as of Gray's letters to Wright, still preserved at the Gray Herbarium—fortifies this estimate. Asa Gray had indeed, as he loved to say, a *fidus Achates* in Charles Wright. No two men ever worked more devotedly to advance one another's interests. They were almost of the same age—Gray was eleven months older—and they early seem to have taken each other as equals. Wright's love and admiration did not prevent him in those lonely days in East Texas—when he could write that he had "lost ten years in the backwoods"—from taking Gray sharply to task when some real or fancied neglect on Gray's part wounded him. Nor did he mince words: "I think hard of it that you have not written for so long a time," Wright says in his forthright way, when he has not received a letter from Gray in many months. "Surely you can speak after almost a year's silence." Again and again in his letters Wright appeals to Gray to write him often concerning the progress of botany, forgetful of the many hours his friend spent daily in the building up of the Harvard Herbarium, in the establishment of the Botanical Garden, in the preparation for his lectures at Harvard College, and in writing the *Manual of North American Botany,* the *Illustrated Genera,* and other works, as well as articles in the journals. One can understand the reason for the appeals and for the resentment. Wright, with the physical defect of vision that marred his attractiveness, felt his loneliness keenly; and that loneliness, together with a little jealousy of Gray, broke out in resentment at the least show of neglect or condescension. So it was that not only Gray, but others, often found Wright a somewhat prickly associate.

In writing to Sir William J. Hooker, Gray once said of Wright: "He has now some good friends in Cuba, and deserves them, for he is one of the most hearty, single-minded, and disinterested persons I ever knew, as well as an admirable collector; but being rather rough in exterior, he does not like to come into contact with official people, unless properly accredited." Gray must often have been troubled at Wright's outbursts of feeling. "You may well complain that I neglect you but . . . I have been, am so—busy is not the word for it," Gray says in one letter. "I can't think of any to express it. I suppose that I have now lying by me more than fifty unanswered letters, though I keep answering the most pressing as fast nearly as they come in." "Do not growl at me if you can help it," he writes in another. One reads with emotion Gray's letter to Wright in answer to several in which he has been taken rather strongly to task for his neglect of the collector. It throws much light on the conditions under which lived America's foremost botanist and its leading botanical collector:

Cambridge, Massachusetts Jan 9 [1848]

Dear Friend

That I ought to have replied to your letter of the 19th Nov.—to say nothing of that of Sept. 21 & June 18. there is no doubt. The latter I have carried in my pocket a good while, hoping to catch a moment somewhere and sometime to write to you. .˙. . But I have not had an hours [sic] leisure not demanded by letters of immediate pressing consequence, or in which I was not too tired to write.

There are many correspondents whom I neglected almost as much as I have you. I have worked like a dog, but my work laid out to be finished last July is not done yet.

But from about the time of your last letter a providential dispensation has prevented me from doing what I would, namely the sickness, by typhoid fever of a beloved brother (a Junior in college here) who required every leisure moment from the time he became seriously sick up to the 9th Inst—a week ago—when it pleased the Sovereign Disposer of events, to whom I bow, to remove him to a better world—and I am but recently returned from the mournful journey to convey to the paternal home (in Western New York), his mortal remains. This has somewhat interrupted the printing of the last sheets of my Manual of N. Botany,—which, with all my efforts at condensation—has extended to almost 800 pages!! (12mo) including the Introduction. It will be difficult to get the vol. within covers. A year's hard labor is bestowed upon it. I hope it will be useful & supply a desideratum. As a consolation for my honest faithfulness in making it tolerably thorough—and so much larger than I expected it would prove, it is now clear that I shall get nothing or next to it for my year's labor,—that, at the price to which it must be kept to get it into our schools &c. there is so little to be made by it that I cannot induce a publisher to pay the heavy bills, except upon terms which swallow up the proceeds—or at the very least I may get $200 if it all sells—a year or two hence.

Meanwhile I have paid the expenses principally incurred on the 1st vol of Illustrated Genera—which I cant [sic] print and finish till the Manual is out,

—have run heavily into debt—in respect to these works, which were merely a labor of love for the good of the science & an honorable ambition—and how I am going to get through I cannot well see. I am also responsible for heavy bills for my late brother. I should despond greatly if I were not of cheerful temperament. To crown all, I expect to marry in the spring; but then my wife will aid me in my heavy correspondence; so you may get letters oftener.

I wish I could write to you as you wish, all about Botany &c—I wish I could aid you as I desire, but I fear it is impossible. I must have rest and less anxiety. Two more years like the last would probably destroy me. If I had an assistant or two, to take details off my hands I might stand it: as it is, I cannot. Carey spent 3 months with me last season, and was to study and ticket your Texan coll. in my hands—take a set for his trouble, and Mr. Lowell & Mr. S. T. Carey would take what they needed and pay for them, so that I could pay your book-bill at Fowle's. The utmost Carey found time to do was to throw the coll. into orders —*There they still lie,* in the corner! There perhaps they had best, now, till the coll. of the past season reaches me when I will try to study them alltogether [*sic*] along with Lindheimer's collections—a set of which still wait for me to study them. Will you wonder that I am a little disheartened, when, in spite of every effort, I made so little progress.—And in 6 weeks, I begin to lecture in college again,—and in April the garden will require more time than I could give it. Such are merely some of the things on my hands, some of my cares! Still I am interested in you, and in your collections, & will do what I can. . . . [Here follows extended technical discussion of botanical matters.]

Forgive my long neglect: accept my apologies. I'll see if I can do any better hereafter, when I have a wife to write letters for me.

Yours sincerely
A. Gray.

Wright's diffidence toward strangers manifested itself in his hypersensitiveness to criticism, real or fancied. "Whenever Capt. French gets in an ill humor he begins to grumble about the weakness of his teams and the transportation of botanists' tricks," Wright wails, while on his El Paso journey. "I don't feel quite at home here as I did on board the Steamer [*John Hancock*]," he writes from the flagship *Vincennes* of the Ringgold Expedition. "Here the majority of the mess have a most sovereign contempt for science and no esteem for its devotees." He seems to have been always on the alert for praise or blame. "I don't eat the bread of idleness and have frequently heard the remark as I passed a company of men at play or sitting in conversation 'that is a mighty industrious man,' " he writes in one of his letters, with evident satisfaction. Yet through his correspondence runs a sense of inferiority, which now and again rises to the surface. It is to Gray's great honor that he discovered this devoted, loyal friend, and by his encouragement and patience enabled Wright to do outstanding work for the advancement of American botany. Wright realized this, and the friendship begun in 1844 remained unmarred to the end.

In the early days, Texas was a testing place of character. The prevailing conditions—instability, formless public opinion, and lawlessness—compassed the ruin of many men who came out to the frontier. Others, however, were of such stuff that every hardship, every difficulty but seemed to strengthen and purify them. Lindheimer and Wright, though markedly different in many respects, were alike in this: they came to Texas in its chaotic, lawless period; they lived through the period of the Republic and into its statehood in the American Union. In the end they emerged as men who had given unique service to the scientific leaders of their day and generation. With all their faults, they accomplished a task that is with difficulty calculable. With regard to Wright, it can be said in the words of Asa Gray that he accomplished "a great amount of useful and excellent work for botany in the pure and simple love of it; and his memory is held in honorable and grateful remembrance by his surviving associates."

Gideon Lincecum 10

FRONTIER teacher, Indian trader, pioneer physician, explorer, naturalist—how shall one begin to unravel the life-skein of that many-sided man, the self-taught naturalist, Gideon Lincecum? A pioneer in three states—Georgia, Mississippi, and Texas—he lived a long and active life in surroundings typical of the American frontier. He was born in 1793 on the fringe of civilization in Georgia, but drifted westward in the family's restless wanderings to escape the press of oncoming civilization. His love of adventure led him to make explorations in Texas as early as 1835, more than a year before the battle of San Jacinto; and in 1848, shortly after Texas was annexed to the United States, he came west again and settled at Long Point, Washington County. His death in 1874 coincides, roughly, with the passing of the frontier in the Texas that he knew. He lived and died a frontiersman. Remote from all that men call civilization, without formal training, impatient of restraint, yet acutely observant and splendidly self-reliant, he did yeoman service as pioneer physician and frontier naturalist.

Charles Darwin corresponded with Lincecum on occasion, as did also Agassiz and Alexander von Humboldt; Darwin, in fact, sponsored the publication of some of Lincecum's researches in the journal of the Linnæan Society of London. The Academy of Natural Sciences of Philadelphia published a paper of Lincecum's filled with data so remarkable that conventional, school-trained naturalists were skeptical of his minute and astonishing observations and unorthodox conclusions. For men of science of his day read Lincecum's communications on natural history with either approval or sharp dissent; there was no middle ground. A strong, positive personality, he dominated people through sheer native endowment. Without the school men's training in scientific method, at first he lacked their precision, but he almost entirely overcame this defect through patient observation.

199

Although at one time Lincecum's observations and work were discussed by naturalists at home and abroad, although scientists aligned themselves as allies or opponents, little was known of his personality until the appearance of his autobiography, which, although written in 1871, did not find its way into print until 1904. The circumstantial account of Lincecum's early life given here makes plain the basis and origin of his overmastering love of nature. Yet the account of his work in Texas, and of the last thirty years of his life, is altogether too brief. The student of Lincecum's career must find the record of his scientific work in his published papers, all of which appeared after 1860: the list includes at least fourteen papers on natural history, chiefly of insects, and should be supplemented by the posthumous autobiography, an essay on Choctaw traditions, and a life of the Choctaw chieftain Pushmataha—long papers which, like the autobiography, appeared in the eighth and ninth volumes of the *Publications* of the Mississippi Historical Society.

Lincecum alone, of all the naturalists whose names are here linked with the advance of natural history in early Texas, was a true son of the frontier. Of those early comers to Texas whose pioneer work laid the foundations of our present knowledge, Boll, Engelmann, Fendler, Lindheimer, Roemer, and Wislizenus were products of German university or Gymnasium; Belfrage was trained in a Swedish technical institute. Thomas Drummond obtained his training in Scottish schools, and Charles Wright was a graduate of Yale College. To Lincecum alone, with his five short months at a backwoods school in border Georgia, was denied the adventure of higher education.

We are indebted to Lincecum's autobiography for our knowledge of his family and connections. Gideon's father was Hezekiah Lincecum, an unfrocked Baptist preacher of French-English descent who had married a certain Sally Hickman. Hezekiah, true to the restless spirit of the frontier, and to his blood—for he was a son of Miriam Bowie, and close kin to the father of the Texas Bowies—led the family in successive removes from place to place in western South Carolina and Georgia, stopping only long enough, one is tempted to say, for the mother to bear her children. Gideon, their eldest, was born in Hancock County, Georgia, April 22, 1793. In the succeeding years frequent changes of scene bred in the boy an enduring love of the frontier—the hunting in the deep forests, the fishing in the rivers, the life among friendly Choctaws: predilections that manifested themselves repeatedly in later life. Descriptions of the travels of Lincecum's boyhood years crowd the pages of the autobiography, and he turns always with delight to undimmed memories of fishing, hunting, and trekking through the wilds.

200

Here we learn that on a certain journey when Gideon was ten years old, he preferred to walk, and as the wagons rolled on through the forests or over the rough roads, he would shoot at the birds with his bow and arrows. "I shall never forget the exceeding gladness that filled my boy's heart the morning we set out," he says in one place; and adds, with a mixture of enthusiasm for nature and boyish barbarity, "I ran ahead of the moving company, shooting my arrows at every bird I could see." When the boy was about eleven years old, his father had a barbed fish-spear made for him to use in the creeks and branches of Georgia, which were then filled with pike. The memory of his first day's use of the spear, and the yard-long string of fish he brought home, evoked ecstatic reminiscences in the memoirs. It is significant of the temperament of the man that after a long life, filled with a man's work in many fields and with much honor among his kind, it was the early life of nature which engaged his memories and called forth his most enthusiastic comment.

When Gideon was in his twelfth year, his father made a third attempt to go to Tennessee. "I was delighted that we were on the road," says Lincecum. "I was an expert with a bow and arrow, and could run far ahead, shooting and killing many birds in the course of the day." Later, in describing a journey from Georgia across the Alabama line to the then small village of Tuscaloosa, he says:

The journey, the way we traveled, was about 500 miles, all wilderness; full of deer and turkeys, and the streams were full of fish. We were six weeks on the road; and altogether it was, as I thought and felt, the most delightful time I ever spent in my life. My brother Garland and I "flanked it" as the wagons rolled along and killed deer, turkeys, wild pigeons; and at nights, with pine torches, we fished and killed a great many with my bow and arrows, whenever we camped on any water course. Little creeks were full of fish in that season.

This enthusiasm lasted into Lincecum's mature years. When he was a man of twenty-five, with a growing family, his father suggested they go together to the Tombigbee River country. The fresh, unspoiled spirit of the man is revealed in the following account of the trip, from the autobiography:

[My father's] descriptions of the dark, heavy forests, the wide thick cane-brakes, and the clear, running river, . . . put me into a perfect transport. . . . [We made the arrangements] and got to my father's house about dark [on the day appointed]. They were all delighted to see us, and we were in a perfect ecstasy over the prospect of a wagon trip through the wilderness. We made the preparation and set out on the 1st day of November, 1818. The weather was fine. We were twelve days *en route* and the heavens were perfectly cloudless during the entire trip. The autumnal leaves and nuts were clattering down everywhere. Shellbarks, hickory-nuts, and chestnuts strewed the ground, and grapes, muscadines, persimmons and various wild autumnal fruits were plentiful. It was delightful to observe the women and children wallowing in the dry leaves in the evening, and gathering such quantities of nuts as to require assistance to get them into camp. Then such cracking and roasting nuts and loud merry talk till bedtime. We killed plenty of deer, turkeys, ducks, wild pigeons, and had the music of great gangs of wolves around our camp every night. The entire trip was delightful beyond description.

One may pass in rapid review the chief events of Lincecum's boyhood and early manhood. When he was fourteen years old his father provided for the boy his first, last, and only schooling. Lincecum writes:

There came a man . . . and made up a school . . . a mile and a half from our home. Father entered my sister, brother, and me as day scholars at the rate of $7.00 each per annum. We three started the next day and did not miss a day until father moved to the new purchase five months later. I was fourteen years old, and it was the first schoolhouse that I had ever seen. I began in the alphabet. There were some very small boys, seven years old, who could read. . . . In accordance with the instructions of the master to come up and recite when I was ready, I managed to say a lesson every fifteen or twenty minutes during the first day. I was then spelling words of four letters. By hard study at night I was able to spell words of two syllables on the morning of the second day. . . . There was so much talk about the new spelling book—Webster's— that father got me one. The teacher soon told me to bring paper and ink to school. . . . At the end of five months I could read, the master said, "very well," could write a pretty fair hand by a copy, had progressed in arithmetic to the double root of three, and had committed Webster's spelling book entirely to memory.

In the War of 1812, Lincecum served during the years 1814-15 in Captain Varner's company (Colonel Freeman's regiment) of General Floyd's brigade of dragoons. He had two short periods of service, one before and one after his marriage to Sarah Bryant on October 25, 1814. At this time he was also reading medicine in a desultory way, apparently without preceptor or adviser. He had always been interested in medicine, however, and even at this time, when he had just reached his majority, he looked forward eagerly to a frontier practice.

His life in Georgia was further diversified by a term as teacher in a backwoods school, an experience which reveals Lincecum's knowledge of human nature and his ability to adapt himself to circumstances. His account relates that:

The country near the [Ocmulgee River, in Georgia] was densely settled. At a little gathering one day I heard some of the men say that the boys had turned out and ducked and abused . . . their schoolmaster so badly that he had

202

quit the school. Some of the men remarked that their children were so bad that they feared that they could never find a man that would be able to manage them. . . . It struck me at once that this would be a more profitable employment than hunting and fishing, and I told [the school committee] to make out their articles . . . and tell me where and when to go and I would undertake it. . . . These children had been born and raised to the age I found them among the cows and drunken cowdrivers on the outer borders of the State, and they were positively the coarsest specimens of the human family I had ever seen. I saw very distinctly that no civil or ordinary means would be applicable to their conditions.

But the school turned out to be a great success. By introducing pupil self-government, Lincecum was able to work a complete change in conditions at the school. The school directors sought to engage him permanently, but he declined.

In 1818 Lincecum went to eastern Mississippi, on the Tombigbee River, near the site of the present town of Columbus. After building a house, he crossed the river to visit the Choctaws, a friendly tribe who had the reputation of being the pre-eminent agriculturists among the southern Indians. Lincecum possessed an unusual facility in learning Indian languages, and he had the knack of making friends with the Indians. Thus he became an authority in his day on their languages and customs. We know from the autobiography that he could use the Choctaw language with ease, and Stephen Daggett states that Lincecum spoke the Chickasaw language fluently, was well acquainted with the family of the leading man and chief councilor of the Chickasaw nation, and was familiar with the Chickasaw and Choctaw customs. In 1819, the year after his removal to eastern Mississippi, Lincecum set up as an Indian trader, and for several years dealt in sugar, coffee, whiskey, and dry goods, all brought by boat from Mobile.

These events are of interest in considering a naturalist in the making, even though they do not aid directly in interpreting the man's scientific work. The same may be said of Lincecum's multifarious political activities. In 1821 the State Legislature appointed him Commissioner to organize Monroe County, Mississippi, and Chief Justice of the County, with power to appoint all other officers. He was the first postmaster at Columbus, and first Master of Lowndes Lodge, No. 171, F. & A.M. The gift of getting along with people indicated by Lincecum's selection for these offices makes it seem natural that when in 1830, at the age of thirty-seven, he became a physician, in the frontier manner of arrogating a title and hanging out a shingle, he met with immediate and assured success.

Lincecum's career as a physician is illustrative of the low estate of medicine on the frontier. In the older settlements the physician was trained under the apprentice system by a process of "reading medicine" with a practitioner for a couple of years, followed in most cases by two years' attendance on lectures at some medical school. At an earlier period in America, any physician could certify to the medical attainments of a neophyte, who, thus armed with his license to kill or cure, might set up immediately in practice for himself. Lincecum had neither preceptor nor formal training before he engaged in the practice of medicine. He says in the autobiography that in 1813-14 he was "confining himself entirely to the study of medicine," and that in 1818 he "could mix drugs and practice medicine as far as it was known in the interior of the country in those days." In 1830 he was enabled to begin regular practice under conditions of some interest:

I had, during my whole life [says Lincecum], done all my reading in medical works, and knew all that had been published on the subject; and had felt seriously inclined to set up shop and try to make a living in that way. But I had no medicine nor the means to procure it. . . . I continued to hunt and spend my time in the woods, until about the first of August, 1830, . . . my nearest neighbor . . . sent for me to tell him what to do. He was very sick, and also considerably alarmed. He had some remnants of medicine in his old medicine chest. I hunted amongst them, and finding some that suited his case, relieved him. . . . In the course of the night he remarked to me, "You know more about this disease and its antidotes than any of the doctors in this country, and I am surprised that you don't get some medicine and set up shop. . . ." Several other people encouraged me by assuring me that I should have their practice. Under these circumstances . . . I concluded to try it . . . and laid in $80 worth of drugs and furniture: . . . I was surprised at its being so much more than any doctor's shop anywhere around. . . . The neighbors all flocked in to see the grand drug store, as they styled it, and they looked upon it as a perfect wonder. . . . It was soon widespread that I had more medicine than all the doctors in the country, and that the man who understood the profession well enough to apply all the remedies in that shop was no ordinary doctor.

His practice was extensive, and to a high degree successful. That Lincecum knew little of medicine as a science emerges clearly in many places in the autobiography: in the confidence of the extract above, with its naïve acceptance of popular judgment and approval; in accounts of Lincecum's quarrels with fellow-practitioners; in his diatribes against the "allopathic physicians," and "steam doctors"; and in his final adoption of "botanical medicine" and Indian herb-medicine, which he learned from the Alikchi Chito, or "Great Indian Doctor" of the Choctaws. He made the remark in the autobiography that he "had felt the need of good medical works written by Southern Practitioners; all our medical books have been composed by Northern practitioners and their prescriptions really did not suit Southern complaints." This belief may seem a darkness like an incubus over the mind of the frontier practitioner but for his day and place he was an enlightened man, and there was really much justification for his plaint. Certainly there is no question that Lincecum was more highly regarded than most of his colleagues. Among his medical associates at Columbus were Drs. S. B. Malone and Dabney Lipscomb, both of them educated under the preceptorial system. It was not until 1835 that Dr. S. S. Franklin, a graduate of Yale with Greek and Latin and fluxions and a medical degree, came to Columbus to set a new standard of medical training.

Gideon Lincecum, it might be remarked, though he might pooh-pooh the classical training and formal studies of the colleges, nevertheless was greatly intrigued by classical history and literature, as is shown in the names of his sons, all physicians in their day: Leonidas, Leander, Laocoön, Lucullus, and Lysander. One wonders what Lincecum's reaction was to the young Yalensian Franklin, with his new knowledge of the recent advances in medical practice, culled from findings of London hospital and Parisian *Charité*.

Most of Lincecum's period of practice was spent in the town of Columbus, where he had among other friends and associates such men as James T. Harrison, later a member of the Confederate Congress, and Tilghman M. Tucker, Governor of Mississippi in 1842. Lincecum lived in Columbus until he moved to Texas in 1848, except for an interval during which he resided at Cotton Gin Port, a now-abandoned town on the Tombigbee River not far from Columbus.

Lincecum had first visited Texas in 1835. He tells how it came about as follows:

At this period, 1834, people began to talk about what a fine country Texas was said to be. They had a great meeting on the subject and made up an emigrating company which consisted of one hundred heads of families. This company included mechanics, school teachers, preachers and doctors. They bound themselves by signing an appropriate article to go all together to that country, if the exploring committee on their return should report favorably of it. The committee consisted of ten men, who were considered good judges of country, and whose veracity was reliable. . . . [He was physician of the exploring party.] . . . On the 9th of January [1835], we set out. . . . We crossed the Tombigbee River at Cotton Gin Port . . . and our progress was delayed two or three days by high water. The remainder of our journey to San Felipe in Texas was quite pleasant, no accident or mishap occurring to any of the company. From San Felipe we went over to the Colorado, which we struck five or six miles above where Columbus now stands. We turned up the Colorado and crossed it at a ferry belonging to Capt. Jesse Burnham fifteen miles below where LaGrange now stands. From there we continued up the country until we reached Bastrop. We remained several days at that place. The 4th of March came, and with it a severe norther that drifted the snow waist high against the back of our tent.

On the sixth of March the party turned southward; on the ninth they reached Jesse Burnham's ferry on the Colorado. At this point the Committee decided they had seen enough of Texas, and resolved to return to Mississippi. But Lincecum demurred. "I have seen nothing yet," he declared. "I cannot consent to return until I make myself able to make a satisfactory report . . . of this great country." He accordingly refused to accompany the other members of the party when they set out for home.

With the departure of his Mississippi friends, Lincecum experienced the first loneliness he had ever felt in his life. But there was much to do: he had come to Texas to spy out the land, and he was determined not to leave until he had arrived at a true judgment. As the narrative of his subsequent travels in Texas is full of interest, I shall quote from it at some length:

I mounted and rode up to Captain Burnham's [Lincecum continues] . . . and I very thankfully accepted his kind proposition to make his house my home. I unpacked and deposited my luggage, turned my horses out on the prairies, and I was at home. . . . I did not, however, spend much time at Burnham's, I went to Texas to explore and make myself acquainted with everything that belonged to it; and to carry out that design, most of my time was consumed in traversing her vast grassy plains. I found no difficulty in procuring on the prairies plenty of venison to subsist on, and sometimes honey. I began my excursion trips by staying out a week the first experiment. . . . [and then] remained with [Burnham] five or six days, answering his questions. But the weather fine, I journeyed coastwise, examining the mouths of the rivers from Brazos to Aransas Bay. I was gone a fortnight this time. I lived plentifully all the while. . . . When I returned from this trip Burnham was pretty smartly out with me. He said he expected me to stay with him and keep him company. Instead of that, he said I preferred lying out in the woods. He never saw such a man. No one else had ever done so in Texas. "You must not try that again," said he. "It is the time of the year for them to come down, and the prairies are already full of Comanches. . . . You are a strange man . . . and you will get killed sure."

After remaining at Burnham's ten days, Lincecum set out across country on a route that led him near the sources of the Navidad and the Lavaca rivers. He reached the San Marcos and followed it to its junction with the Guadalupe. Proceeding southward from this point, he arrived at the Nueces, where he turned northward and came almost to the future site of Fredericksburg. He struck the Colorado at Bastrop, where he remained only one day, and three days later was back at Burnham's, on the fifty-fifth day since he had set out. Lincecum set out on another trip of exploration east of the Colorado. Reaching San Felipe the evening of the second day out, he visited Gail Borden, who had been ill for some time. Apparently on this occasion Lincecum prescribed for Borden's illness, for he says, "After attending to Gale Borden's case, I . . . left San Felipe . . . the fourth day after my arrival," heading east: it was the beginning of the long journey back to Mississippi. He had no path, but averaged about twenty-five miles a day. At the Trinity he made a raft for his belongings, and swam his horses over. Continuing eastward, he reached the Sabine at Hickman's Ferry, seven miles below Gaines' Ferry. When he finally got back to Columbus (on August 5, 1835) he had been gone seven months, lacking four days.

During Lincecum's trip to the Guadalupe country he was captured by the Comanches and taken to their camp, where he won the respect of the Indians by claiming to be a great medicine man with a medicine whose odor would destroy life (ammonia), and another (peppermint) whose taste or odor would restore life to the dead. After a few days his captors allowed him to leave camp, supposedly to secure

LINCECUM
1835-1874

GAINES' FERRY

•FREDERICKSBURG
LONG POINT
BRENHAM
BASTROP
BURNHAM'S FERRY
LAGRANGE
COLUMBUS SAN FELIPE
GONZALES

INTENSIVELY EXPLORED AREA

an important medicinal plant growing near. Lincecum took advantage of the opportunity to make his escape.

I rode slowly away until I got out of sight [he says] and then, changing my course, rode rapidly all that night, all the next day and night, and until 12 o'clock the day following. I did not stop two minutes at a time during the whole route. I was greatly fatigued and my horse became so hungry that he would bite off the limbs of bushes as thick as my finger.

When he was in San Felipe just before setting out on his journey back to Mississippi, Lincecum enlisted in Captain Moseley Baker's company of volunteers that was being organized to meet the invading Mexicans under Cos; but because of the strong protests of other members of the company—old friends who had known Lincecum in Georgia and Mississippi, and who were aware of his wife and children at home—his name was taken off the list. The removal of his name grieved Lincecum deeply.

Captain Baker assured me [he says] that as I had joined the first company of volunteers that had been raised in defence of the colony, and being fully competent to fill the office, there would be no opposition to my being surgeon-general to the forces that would occupy Texas west of the Brazos; that he was going to the convention, and that he intended to exert all his influence to obtain the appointment for me. He had no doubt of success.

When his name was erased from the rolls, Lincecum reluctantly decided to leave San Felipe. "It was a sad night for me," he says in speaking of his departure. "I felt that it would be better to remain." He came from fighting stock, and his regret was entirely genuine.

After his return to Mississippi in 1835, Lincecum remained there until March 30, 1848, when once again, this time with his family, he set out for Texas to make a new home on another frontier. He was fifty-five years old. Settling on a league of land near Long Point, Washington County, which he had selected in 1835, he became a resident of Texas just after it had been made a state of the Union. Here he lived for almost twenty years, a picturesque character even in that day of violently individual personalities, enjoying his violin and his studies in natural history.

In some ways Lincecum was a trial to his neighbors, especially to the elect. He was in religious opinion rather free: he bequeathed his family Bible to a designated son because the son was "the most superstitious of all." Mr. Soule Kirkpatrick of Cotton Gin Port, an old gentleman of high character who was a devout Methodist, always characterized Lincecum as "that old infidel, Gid Lincecum." Lincecum's grandson, Dr. Addison L. Lincecum of El Campo, Texas, has recorded an interesting comment on the old naturalist's habits during his residence at Long Point:

About thirty-five years ago [says Dr. Addison Lincecum], I was camped in the river bottom in Washington county, and an old fellow came to camp for a visit. I was lying on my blanket watching a bird attempt to carry material up into a tree for nest-building purposes, and commented on its persistence. The old fellow remarked, "We uster have an old fool here who would spend a week watching that bird." Later he told me that he referred to Dr. Gid Lincecum, and when I told him that the doctor was my grandfather, he terminated his visit.

Lincecum's wife died late in 1866 or early in 1867. After her death, Lincecum—now past seventy—made an extensive collecting trip in Central Texas. Later in 1867, resentful of the heavy hand of Reconstruction that was being laid on the state, Lincecum decided to leave the country, as did other friends and neighbors. He went to Mexico, and in 1868 was living near Tuxpan, on the coast south of Tampico in the State of Vera Cruz. John Henry Brown of Dallas visited Lincecum there, and later wrote an account of the visit which was published in the Dallas *Daily Herald* for December 12, 1874.

In Mexico [runs Brown's narrative, in part], he stated to Hon. John H. Brown, that for fifty-eight years, at daylight, on each Christmas morning, he had stood in the door, barefooted, in his night-close [*sic*], and played the Scottish air of Killy Kranky, and that on forty-eight of these occasions he had used the violin then in his possession, made to order for him in Paris, in 1820, whereupon he played the piece in his own hospitable home, opposite the city of Tuxpan. He was then seventy-five, and on his birthnight, a few nights before, he had been fire-hunting, killed a dear [*sic*] and carried it home on his shoulders, a distance of two or three miles.

Dr. Addison Lincecum reports yet another incident related to his grandfather's stay in Mexico:

Gideon Lincecum was . . . a very excellent violinist, and at his death his violin was at his request buried with him. In 1917 I was in Tuxpan, Mexico, studying the Anopheline family of Mosquitoes; and while there I became acquainted with an old Indian who was mozo for Grandfather while he was [living there]. This old Indian told me that "El Doctor" spent his moonlight nights on the river playing his fiddle and communing with nature, and that he was very regular in his daily program, would rise at daybreak, play a Scotch air on his fiddle and then take a plunge in the river. When the natives found out that I was a grandson of him, I became also a native and was treated most courteously and with some degree of reverence.

Lincecum's great gusto and energy in his advanced age, so evident in glimpses like these, were his by inheritance. His father, he says in the autobiography, was a large, powerful man, six feet tall, weighing in the prime of life two hundred pounds. Gideon seems to have resembled his father physically. He was of the same height and weight—a commanding figure. When he left Mississippi for Texas, at the age of fifty-five, he already possessed a patriarchal beard of snowy whiteness, as a crayon portrait of him now hanging in the lodge-room of a Masonic lodge in Columbus shows. He had a florid complexion, and an oil portrait which was still to be seen at Hempstead in 1929 shows his eyes to have been a rather clear, light blue.

Just how and when Lincecum began the systematic study of botany and zoölogy is not known. He had studied Indian herb-medicine with the Alikchi Chito in the early 'thirties in Mississippi, and according to the autobiography, he began to study systematic botany in 1833-34, when he was about forty years old. The first mention of his collections appears in the account of his trip to Texas in 1835, when he gathered a good pack-horse load of specimens which he brought back to Mississippi. After he settled in Texas in 1848, Lincecum undertook many studies concerning the natural history of the state, and made for individuals and institutions extensive collections of Texan animals and plants. His unpublished diary contains frequent references to letters sent to and received from such correspondents as Professor Joseph Leidy, Edward D. Cope, Elias Durand, H. C. Wood, and Ezra Townsend Cresson. In 1860 Lincecum sent to Charles Darwin a large collection of Texan ants and other *Hymenoptera,* together with notes on their habits—receiving in reply what he described as "one of the most polite letters I ever received." One passage of his diary, of date July 16, 1867, dealing incidentally with some of his correspondents of the Academy of Natural Sciences of Philadelphia, will perhaps throw as much light on Lincecum as on the men whom he appraises. "I consider Leidy the busiest and most liberal minded man in the Academy of Natural Sciences," said Lincecum. "Cope is a religious fanatic. Durand is a religious pretender. Wood is a light-gutted puritan, and Cresson is a Gentleman. " Lincecum made some important collections of ants and other *Hymenoptera* for Cresson and Professor A. S. Packard; he also collected *Coleoptera* for Samuel Lewis and Henry Ulke, *Lepidoptera* for George William Peck, and botanical specimens for Elias D. Durand. He seems to have become acquainted early with Durand, with whom Lincecum jointly published in the *Proceedings* of the Academy of Natural Sciences for 1861 a paper entitled, "On a Collection of Plants from Texas." In that same year Lincecum presented a collection of more than a thousand plants to the Academy; and he sent to Durand another collection of more than a thousand specimens, which Durand in 1868 turned over to the Herbarium of the *Jardin des Plantes* in Paris, with his own collection of ten thousand specimens of North American plants.

I have not been able to find evidence that Lincecum corresponded with Dr. Asa Gray of Harvard or Dr. George Engelmann of St. Louis, chief mentors and counselors of Texas botanists of that day. His chief dependence seems to have been placed on Durand, and on S. B. Buckley (a weak reed, it would appear), who, true to form, named a familiar species of *Helianthus* by the new genus-name *Linsecomia*—the classification being incorrect and the nomenclature never accepted.

When Lincecum decided to leave Texas in 1867, he sent to the Smithsonian Institution the collections which he had made early in 1867 on his trip through eighteen counties of Central Texas. "Fourteen different accessions were received from Dr. Lincecum, the first being in 1867 and the last in 1874," says Dr. A. Wetmore, now Secretary of the Smithsonian Institution. "The material consisted of mammals, fossils, shells, birds, insects, alcoholic specimens, and one Negro skull, and we have letters from Dr. Lincecum transmitting the majority of them." Some of the letters were worked over in 1874 for publication, and printed in the eighth volume of the *American Naturalist*. A great collection of Texan butterflies—numbering, according to Lincecum, two thousand specimens—was sent to George William Peck of New York.

The variety of interests indicated by these collections is impressive. All fields of natural history intrigued Lincecum: mussel-shells, fossils, plants, birds—all were grist to his mill. His sincere love of nature appears everywhere in his diary, and in the articles that he wrote, particularly on the behavior of the tarantula, the tarantula-killer, the gossamer-spider, and the scorpion of Texas. Such was the variety of his enthusiasms, sometimes, that he reminds one of old Gilbert White of Selborne. But of course Lincecum's great work on Texan natural history, for which he was once well known, was on the Agricultural or Red Ant.

The country in the neighborhood of Long Point showed a great abundance of colonies of the harvesting or Agricultural Ant. Every Texas boy knows the familiar mounds, frequent enough in woodland, cotton-patch, or grassland. At intervals Lincecum observed the habits of this most interesting creature. In 1859 he called the attention of S. B. Buckley to the ant and its behavior, and in 1860 Buckley published one of the first notices of the occurrence of harvesting ants in North America. Lincecum then laid before Charles Darwin his observations on the ant, and Darwin communicated them to the Linnæan Society of London, in a note read in April, 1861. Certain of Lincecum's conclusions (such as that the ants plant a certain kind of grass on their mounds, for use as food) together with his unfortunate tendency to personify their behavior, led Forel to say, in his *Les Fourmis de la Suisse*: "These observations, although reported by Charles Darwin, inspire little confidence in me."

Dr. H. C. McCook, whose excellent work on *The Agricultural Ant of Texas* is familiar to all entomologists, himself a notable student of ant behavior, relates in his book how Lincecum's observations were received at the Philadelphia Academy of Natural Sciences. After the appearance of the Linnæan Society paper, Lincecum in 1866 published another on the same subject in the *Proceedings* of the Academy. McCook, referring to Forel's criticism, says:

The doubt which is thus raised is a fair index of the state of mind which I found to exist among the older members of the Philadelphia Academy, who had more or less knowledge of the author, and the origin of the paper above referred to. While it was believed that there was some basis of fact in the communications made they were thought to contain much that was fanciful, and, indeed, a shadow of doubt rested upon the whole. . . . The original manuscripts of this paper, as well as [others] . . . were in the hands of . . . the American Entomological Society. Mr. Cresson kindly placed these manuscripts in my hands. They were carefully read, and the reason for the suspicion with which they had been viewed was everywhere quite manifest. The venerable writer had many peculiar notions about society, religion, and the genus homo generally, which he could not refrain from thrusting—in the most untimely manner and objectionable words—into the midst of his notes. These idiosyncrasies, together with some peculiarities of spelling, grammar, and rhetoric more original than regular, had evidently raised in the minds of officers and members of the Academy a question, not as to the integrity of the author, but as to his accuracy as an observer. . . . The unpublished papers in my hands have been freely used in the preparation of this work, and have contributed some valuable facts.

Yet, on the whole, the result of McCook's work in the field was a general corroboration of Lincecum's observations, with some correction of erroneous interpretations. As McCook says,

The observations of Dr. Lincecum were, in many important points, confirmed during that visit, and thus a strong degree of authenticity given to other *facts* recorded by him which I was not so fortunate as to note.

In his chapter on "Migrations and Movements," McCook publishes from Lincecum's manuscripts an interesting record of the partial migration of a large ant-colony or "formicary," and shows that he had come independently to a knowledge of the well-known ant habit of compelling fellow colonists to join a migratory movement determined upon by one part of the community. Lincecum, says McCook in this connection,

expresses himself in the language of personification, which is usual with him. Indeed, he evidently believed the ants to have quite as high a social organization as man, and not infrequently stops in his manuscript to assert the superiority of the emmet faculties and administration of affairs over those of the "genus homo."

At page 152 of his book McCook quotes from Lincecum in illustration of this point, showing how the old physician believed the ants had political affiliations, governmental ordinances, and so forth. "They conceal the entrance of a new city until they consider themselves sufficiently strong," Lincecum says in his final paper (1874) on the agricultural ant. A "dissolute course" of life on the part of the males, according to the old doctor, resulted in their dying off in great numbers. The following extract will illustrate still further his tendency to attribute to insects intelligence of a high order:

There are many other interesting achievements performed by this sagacious race of insects. I have recently discovered a great difference in their mental operations and capacities. Individuals there are which possess great intellectual superiority to the common laboring classes, which is manifested in the fact that they assume the leadership in all their important public works and army movements. Some are much more sagacious and cautious in avoiding traps and dangerous contrivances set for them by the scarcely superior human genus. One of our Germans invented a very destructive ant trap. It is set over the entrances to their city and is so contrived, that going or coming it is sure to entrap them; but not all of them. Occasionally a well-formed fellow is observed to arrive at the top of the precipice, where he stops and gravely surveys the awful abyss below, filled with frantic and terribly distressed thousands—who have incautiously precipitated themselves into inevitable ruin—and after viewing the dreadful and disastrous condition of his fellow laborers, he seems to understand the true nature of their misfortune, and turning from the irremediable calamity, hastens down the inclined plane into the grass weeds, beyond the reach of further observations.

Naturally, such writing raised acute objection among many scientists. Yet one who studies the papers, printed and manuscript, left by Lincecum finds much ground for agreement with Elias Durand in his overpartial estimate of the old physician. It is a pity that Lincecum did not have direct contact with first-rate minds in his studies of natural history. Buckley, the State Geologist, and Richard Burleson, who also considered himself a geologist, were men who could contribute little or nothing to his scientific development. Durand, in writing to Mrs. L. L. Doran, Lincecum's daughter, had this to say:

What a pity that such genius as your good father be thus sequestered from the great stores of the scientific books and immense collections of natural curiosities of our great cities? [*sic*] It is true that his active mind finds, in the forests, constant employment in the study of nature, and such men as he are wanted to watch the most minute operations of nature; but what a great assistance would he not find in our large libraries and how many false deductions would he have to rectify in authors who have not the chance, like himself, to catch nature on the spot. I hope the labors of your father will not be lost to the present generation or its posterity.

In forming a total estimate of Lincecum's qualities as a naturalist, one must acknowledge first of all his spontaneous and sincere love of natural history, and his universal curiosity regarding natural objects. On the other hand, his knowledge in any field was fragmentary and somewhat disorganized. He took himself and his work much too seriously—primarily because of the backward condition of science in official Texas, where the State Geologist and his staff on the Geological Survey were men of very mediocre ability. The friendly correspondence of such men as Cope, Leidy, and Cresson encouraged in Lincecum the error of minimizing the differences between himself and them. His naming by Professor Henry as Weather Observer at Long Point for the Smithsonian Institution seemed to Lincecum a recognition of outstanding ability.

Yet, when all is said, and especially when one considers the conditions of Lincecum's early life and the backwoods environment which framed his whole career, his native abilities as an observer stand out more and more clearly. He was surely, in his day, if we except Dr. Shumard, the most able among the naturalists in Texas who were conspicuously in the public eye. Charles Wright and the German naturalists, of course, had strong claims to eminence; but they worked in silence, unnoted by the public.

Rough, untrained, sometimes uncouth, this brave old man held through long years to the even tenor of his way. The generation that knew him as physician and naturalist is fast passing; only here and there are those who were acquainted with him, who can appreciate the handicaps under which he worked. In the light of all that can be learned of Lincecum's career, one can only say: it is cause for wonder not that he did so little, but that he accomplished so much.

214

Julien Reverchon 11

JULIEN REVERCHON, French-American resident of Dallas and student of the botany of the Southwest, was born at Diemoz, near Lyons, in the fourth decade of the nineteenth century. His father, J. Maximilien Reverchon, was born at Lyons in 1810, and died at Dallas in 1878; his mother (born Florine Pete) was the daughter of a distinguished Lyonnais advocate. Julien's grandfather, Jacques Reverchon (1746-1829), had been a Jacobin member of the National Convention (1792-95), as well as of the Council of Five Hundred and of the Council of Elders; he was the citizen-representative from Saône-et-Loire, Rhône-et-Ain, whose reports on the rapacity of the Maratists at Lyons Taine quoted in *Les Origines de la France Contemporaine.* Yellowing papers bearing the signatures of Buonaparte (while he was General-in-Chief of the Army in Italy), Robespierre, Carnot, and the Duc de Kellerman, ablest of Napoleon's cavalry generals, are still in the possession of the family, reminders of the days of Valmy, Marengo, Austerlitz, Tormes—and Waterloo. One priceless document, an order directed to the Representative Reverchon by the Committee of Public Safety of the National Convention, is signed by Barère, Carnot, Prieur, Collot d'Herbois, Billand-Varenne, Saint-Just, Couthon, Robespierre, and Lindet—a bloody crew. Fortunately for him, Jacques Reverchon was an ardent lover of the Revolution, and throughout the struggle was able to retain the confidence of its successive leaders.

His intense love of liberty was manifest in his son Maximilien and in his grandson Julien, the subject of the present chapter. It is interesting to note, however, that while the great preoccupation of Jacques Reverchon was with political emancipation, the son and grandson were interested rather in socio-economic and intellectual liberty.

In 1829 Jacques Reverchon died at Lyons, leaving his nineteen-year-old son to observe and participate in the upheavals that during the next two decades were to bring about the exile of the recalled Bourbon, Charles X, the reign of Louis Philippe, the Revolution of 1848, and the establishment of the Second Empire as the result of Louis Napoleon's coup d'état in 1851. Thus Maximilien and Julien Reverchon, father and son, witnessed the apparent failure of all the aims of the French Revolution in the midst of the most dramatic social, economic, and political changes within the French nation. This fact is important in understanding the attitudes and actions of the two men.

I have said that Julien Reverchon was born in the fourth decade of the nineteenth century. The year was probably 1837, although most of the authorities, including Dr. E. G. Eberle in his excellent biographical sketch of Reverchon published in the Dallas *Morning News* (December 31, 1905), fix the time three years earlier. The date is given as August 3, 1837, in a short biographical sketch published during Reverchon's lifetime in the thirteenth volume of Sargent's *Silva of North America.* And Dr. J. H. Barnhart, formerly bibliographer of the New York Botanical Garden, suggests it is highly probable that Julien Reverchon was born in 1837, since his next older brother, Elisée Reverchon, was almost certainly born in 1835. I believe Barnhart is correct.

Lyons, in the early years of Julien's life, was still a beautiful old city almost untouched by modern industrialism. The position of Lyons as an intellectual center dates at least from the fifth century, when it was the capital of Burgundy; and some of its beautiful old churches date back to the sixth century. Much of the beauty of the city has been destroyed in the last hundred years: at present, a great smoky manufacturing center, it might be called the Pittsburgh of France. In Julien's childhood, however, it still retained its ancient charm, and in addition was important as the seat of intellectual and social movements of virility and promise. Fourier, the great French social philosopher, and his successor in the Fourieristic movement, Victor Considerant, were residents of Lyons, and thus the city became the center of a great movement for social reform. Fourier himself died at Lyons two months after Julien's birth. Thereafter Considerant, the gifted young *Jurassien,* with the aid of his versatile and talented mother-in-law, Mme Clarice Vigoureux, assumed the leadership in the Fourieristic movement. As everyone knows, Fourierism came to its finest flowering in the United States, and at La Réunion, near Dallas, reached its end as a movement not only in America, but throughout the world.

216

Fourierism greatly occupied the mind of Maximilien Reverchon. As a child Julien heard many a discussion on the subject of the new social panacea which Fourierists believed could cure the ills of a society making the transition from the older order of things to the factory system. When Julien was nine years old, his father, then owner of a fine, highly developed farm near Lyons, went to Algeria to found a colony on the plan of Fourier. The colony was unsuccessful, and his farm had to be sacrificed. In 1848 Maximilien took part in the February revolution which caused the downfall of Louis Philippe; when the party of Napoleon III inaugurated the Second Empire in 1851, he left France in despair. Considerant had also left the country and was in Belgium making plans to establish a Fourieristic colony in America.

America was at that time the Promised Land for social-reform movements, especially for communistic or associational projects. At the beginning of the nineteenth century the Industrial Revolution in Europe had brought in its train economic and social disorders of the greatest magnitude. With the rise of the factory system, the disparity between the possessing and the working classes had become more evident year by year. Social philosophers, aware of the glaring contrasts that had developed, were bending earnest efforts to an amelioration of social and economic conditions, and were offering drastic solutions, some utopian, some realistic, for the insistent problems which confronted Europe. That most early efforts of this sort should have been idealistic and visionary was only natural, for social philosophers of the day were still under the spell of the enchanting lucubrations of the French Encyclopedists. Realism in social thinking came slowly, near the middle of the century; and only after a number of experiments on the plan of miniature social systems or communities had been made in an unsuccessful effort to do away with the hard fact of human inequality.

Saint-Simon, pupil of D'Alembert, stung into action by the moral and physical suffering of the poor, established the school of thought which after his death resulted in the Community in the Rue Monsigny. Robert Owen progressed from his philanthropism at New Lanark in Scotland to the egalitarian communism that flowered at New Harmony on the Wabash. Étienne Cabet, a native of Dijon, founded the Icarian movement that achieved a precarious and stormy existence in Texas, Illinois, Missouri, and Iowa. But the utopian social philosopher whose theories were destined to have the greatest influence in America, both in the number of communities founded and in the character of the men who took leadership of them, was Charles Fourier.

Maximilien Reverchon became greatly interested in the movement to establish a Fourieristic colony in Texas. Considerant, returning to Belgium after a visit to America in 1852-53, had organized *La Compagnie Franco-Texienne* to back the formation of a "phalanx" of Swiss, Belgian, and French emigrants who planned to go out to Texas, the Land of Promise. Maximilien decided to join this group, but his wife was unsympathetic. After the Algerian fiasco her interest in communistic projects had markedly cooled; refusing to go with her husband, she remained in France with the two elder sons and a daughter. But Maximilien, accompanied by his son Julien—then a lad of nineteen—set out for America to join Considerant's colony at La Réunion. The boy was never to see his mother and brothers again, although his sister later came to America. Julien's mother seems to have been a woman of talent, and she must have been sympathetic with her son, for she had taught him at home and encouraged his interest in the wild plants growing around Lyons—an interest not confined to Julien, but shared by his two older brothers, Paul and Elisée. Julien and Elisée seem to have acquired an especially thorough knowledge of botany. When Julien came to America he is said to have left a collection of more than two thousand species of plants with Elisée, who continued his botanical studies and later did excellent botanical exploration in France, Spain, Greece, Turkey, and northern Africa. Paul Reverchon became a physician in France.

Julien Reverchon and his father arrived at La Réunion in the month of December, 1856. The first colonists had reached the site eighteen months before, so that the Reverchons found on their arrival a group of cultivated French, Swiss, and Belgian musicians, artists, and artisans, including Considerant himself and the gracious, charming, and highly accomplished Mme Vigoureux; Allyre Bureau, formerly musical director of the Odéon in Paris; Émile Remond, a geologist; and Cantagrel, an engineer. Culture and skill were common among the colonists: at the subsequent dissolution of La Réunion in 1858, all Texas was laid under obligation, both culturally and industrially, to the colonists who migrated into different parts of the state. Most of the educated immigrants could speak English, and all were well received by the citizens of Dallas, then a village of four hundred inhabitants. It was in the intellectual atmosphere of this Fourieristic colony that Julien Reverchon spent the impressionable years of his early manhood.

The experience of the forty-odd other Fourieristic colonies established in the United States was destined to be repeated at La Réunion. As was the case at Brook Farm, at the North American Phalanx in Monmouth County, New Jersey, and elsewhere, Fourier's plan of life, with its stress on order in nature rather than justice (which is emphasized in practically all other types of utopian social systems), appealed primarily to visionary persons, impatient of realistic thinking in social matters. At La Réunion, where in the beginning at least everything depended on farming, there were only two practical farmers among some three hundred and fifty colonists. In 1858 the colony began to disintegrate rapidly, and before the end of the year the venture had definitely failed. With the breaking up of the community, many of the colonists left the vicinity of Dallas, but a few remained to make valuable contributions to the intellectual life of what was then a frontier village. Maximilien Reverchon, foreseeing the doom of the venture, had secured a small farm near Dallas, and had established the home which he occupied until his death in 1879.

Here, in the lean years which elapsed between 1858, when the colony was abandoned, and 1864, when he married, Julien Reverchon lived a lonely, absorbed life, a young man intensely interested in plants and animals. Lacking the social graces of the cultivated Frenchman, he compensated for a sense of inferiority by an intense devotion to the study of nature. He was a tall, gangling youth, not gifted in conversation, who drew the amused comment of the members of his own group. It was a distinct surprise when Marie Henry, daughter of Paul Henry, a colonist, and granddaughter of Captain Deshogues, a soldier of the Old Guard at Waterloo—an attractive French girl who could have chosen the most polished man of her circle—married this timid, awkward boy. But Julien Reverchon did not appear to be deeply affected by his marriage. In the course of time his interest in nature gradually took the place of almost all others; and the death twenty years later of his two sons led him to concentrate his full devotion upon his scientific activities.

One who knew Reverchon as a fellow-colonist and citizen in those early years has recorded that he was a man of simple, unassuming demeanor; taciturn though not sullen; of brief yet cheerful speech; not social, but polite. His most striking features were his observant, roving eyes, and a brow that projected prominently, like Darwin's. Upon the members of the colony he made an ineradicable impression: after the lapse of many years they still remember his tall form as he wandered over the hillsides with his botanical collecting case or his insect-net. There is an element of pathos in the picture of Reverchon in his early years: the gangling boy denied the love of a mother devoted to him, because of his father's senseless devotion to social panaceas and will-o'-the-wisps; the fine, sensitive nature wrapped up in a clodhopper body; and the hard frontier conditions repressing a child of the beautiful and cultured city of southern France. Julien

219

Reverchon's marriage gave him the hope of heirs—little more, for it could hardly be called a happy one. And then after a time that last hope fled, and he faced a childless old age.

Yet, for all Reverchon's retiring nature and self-contained way of life, on the dairy-farm west of Dallas from which he gained a meager livelihood, he can hardly have remained wholly untouched by the surge and bustle of the frontier community. He saw the village of Dallas grow from a collection of straggling streets and scanty houses in 1856 to a town of almost five thousand inhabitants in 1870, six years after his marriage. He saw it after the coming of the railroads in the early 'seventies boom to a town of more than ten thousand inhabitants in 1880, and finally, in 1900, attain a population of some forty thousand. He saw Dallas change from a community of immigrants who had brought with them the stable traditions of the Old South, to a heterogeneous, chaotic, unassimilated population to which

every state in the Union and every country of Europe had made its contribution. He lived to see the little frontier town become the bustling commercial distributing center for eighteen counties, so busy that (it is said) a special police force was necessary in 1875 to prevent congestion of wagons in the streets. He saw the fruition of early cultural movements in that raw community: the Dallas Library, founded in 1871; the Dallas College, in 1873; and the formation of a literary and scientific coterie in which Major John Henry Brown, the historian, and Jacob Boll were leading lights. He saw the building of Field's Theater, where, sandwiched in between "variety theaters" (which in later days drew the editorial fire of Captain Rust's *The Southern Mercury*), were presented such diverse attractions as Bishop Alexander C. Garrett's lecture on Darwin's *Descent of Man* (October 25, 1875), and Victoria Woodhull's appearance in March of 1876, when, after an hour-and-a-half lecture on some subject too scandalous to be mentioned in the newspapers—probably woman suffrage— she was led off the stage by her sister, Tennessee Claflin, before a completely mystified audience.

There may have been much truth in the statement of the Dallas *Herald* in 1876 that Dallas had as much culture as any city of its size in the Southwest, and that the great majority of the people who settled there had stood well in their home communities, having come to Texas in most instances to improve fortunes shattered by the Civil War. But many characteristics of Dallas in the 'seventies must be explained by the chaotic state of a somewhat primitive society almost overwhelmed by the rush of a heterogeneous population to the frontier. Bishop Garrett, Eliza Calvert Hall (Mrs. Obenchain), Brown, Boll, and Reverchon were almost anomalous representatives of orderly and civilized society amid this flux of humanity.

The years of Reverchon's life immediately after his marriage were almost barren of scientific results. As Dr. Eberle said in his obituary notice of Reverchon, the "needed attention to his farm and business interests [curtailed the time] which he wished to devote to [science], but as he became more comfortable he was enabled to enlarge his [botanical] collection with more satisfaction, and also entered into correspondence with the foremost botanists of the country, notably Asa Gray, Sereno Watson, Engelmann, and Trelease." It seems a pity, to one looking back over the past, that Reverchon did not "wrest the stars from their concurrences" as did his friend Jacob Boll, or perhaps Gustaf Belfrage. Here before him lay north-central Texas, botanically almost virgin country. To the west and northwest lay territory wholly unexplored. In fact, Lindheimer's rich collections of plants from the New Braunfels region and Wright's admirable work represented almost the only scientific investigations which had been carried on in the interior of the state. But it was not until the arrival of Jacob Boll in the village of Dallas in 1869, to make his abundant collections for the Harvard Museum, that Reverchon was stimulated to a renewed devotion to his early botanical interests. He began once more to build up a herbarium of local botanical specimens, and continued the work through the years with such effectiveness that at his death his collection, comprising, it is said, about twenty thousand specimens of more than two thousand six hundred species of the Texas flora, was the best collection of the plants of the state in existence.

After Boll returned from Switzerland and from Cambridge, in 1874, and decided to make his home in Dallas, Reverchon became a fast friend of the Swiss naturalist. Edward Drinker Cope of Philadelphia was indebted to Reverchon for his meeting with Boll in 1877, when he employed Boll as fossil-collector from the Texas Permian. I quote in substance Reverchon's account of the transaction, related from memory in 1902, some three years before his death, to his heir, Dr. R. M. Freeman:

Professor Cope had seen my name in connection with some scientific collections of plants, and while he was in Texas in 1877, came up from Houston to offer me a job as collector for him. I was not a geologist, but a botanist, so refused the offer, and suggested Jacob Boll. As I recall it, he offered me $300 monthly, and expenses; also a wagon and team. I presume he made the same offer to Boll. Boll accepted. After Boll's death, he again wrote me regarding some one to take the vacant place, and I suggested Old Man Cummins. Cummins took the place and held it for three years.

In the archives of the Gray Herbarium at Cambridge are to be found letters written by Reverchon to Asa Gray, Sereno Watson, and the Reverend Thomas Morong—all botanists actively working on the flora of the Southwest. The first letter of Reverchon to Gray that has been preserved is dated October 28, 1877; and there are simple, cordial, earnest, even zealous letters on personal and botanical subjects up to the time of Gray's death in 1888. In these letters we see how the old flame of interest and the desire to work again in botanical fields was consuming Reverchon. But he was, perforce, first horticulturist and dairyman, and then botanist, so that extended trips for botanical collecting were hardly possible for him. Nevertheless, Reverchon seized some opportunities. In 1877 he discovered about a dozen new species of plants in Dallas County alone; and during the first two weeks in August of that year, stimulated by a visit from Gray, he made a flying trip to Brown County, collecting on the way in some eleven counties south and west of Dallas. In 1879 Reverchon collected most of the spring and summer near Dallas, and in September and October of that year he and Boll accompanied a group of land-locators and agents into Baylor County and other parts of Northwest Texas, Boll collecting fossils and Reverchon seeking for plants. It was here, in September, "on a sand island of the Brazos River near Seymour, Baylor County," that Reverchon found the plant (one of the Spurge family) from which Asa Gray named the genus *Reverchonia,* thus immortalizing the collector. Gray wrote: "With great satisfaction I dedicate [this genus] to M. Jules Reverchon of Dallas, Texas, . . . a valuable correspondent, an acute and sedulous botanist." Gray also honored Reverchon with a *Campanula.*

In May of 1880 Reverchon collected plants at Fort Worth. Two years later he made a month-long trip to West Texas, going as far as Fort Concho, in present Tom Green County. He then turned back to the Colorado River, and explored in Mitchell, Nolan, and Scurry counties. It was while he was away from home on this trip that his two sons fell ill of typhoid fever and died.

Reverchon made his last extended trip in 1885, traveling in a wagon, accompanied by his wife, into Southwest Texas. Here he explored a very interesting country—the whole basin of the Llano River, and most of the Edwards Plateau region at the headwaters of the Guadalupe, Medina, Cibolo, Hondo, Seco, and Sabinal rivers. Reverchon and his wife left Dallas in May and, retarded by almost constant rains, reached Uvalde the last of June. His most successful collecting was done in the valley of the Llano and in Sabinal Canyon—"a paradise for the botanist," as he found it.

Other phases of Reverchon's scientific activity included membership in the Torrey Botanical Club, and the writing of papers contributed to the *Bulletin* of the club and to such other botanical and horticultural journals as the *Botanical Gazette, Garden and Forest,* and the *American Botanist.* In the last decade of his life he was Professor of Botany in the Baylor University College of Medicine and Pharmacy at Dallas.

Reverchon died at Dallas, December 30, 1905, and was buried in the old French cemetery near the site of La Réunion. His collection of plants was secured by the Missouri Botanical Garden at St. Louis, where it is still preserved.

Reverchon's work as a botanical collector evoked grateful response and appreciation from other botanists besides Asa Gray. Thus Vasey, a specialist in grasses, named a species of each of the three botanical genera *Aristida, Diplachne,* and *Panicum* in his honor. Wright named a species of sedge for Reverchon; Sargent, the tree-specialist, author of the famous *North American Silva,* named a fine, showy red-thorn *Cratægus reverchonii;* and Sereno Watson named two wild beans of the genera *Psoralea* and *Vicia* after Reverchon. Such honors as these I mention as concrete evidence of the esteem in which Reverchon was held by competent botanists. The printed dedications of new species by these men are explicit on this point. Thus Sargent in dedicating *Cratægus reverchonii* says: "I am glad to associate with this plant, which is one of the most distinct species of the *crus-galli* group, the name of the accomplished botanist and indefatigable collector, M. Julien Reverchon, who first made it known."

In surveying the life of Reverchon one is impressed by his great dependence upon his environment. At the time when he came to America with his father, the congenial surroundings of his childhood and his precocious interest in botany might have led any observer to expect great things from the young Frenchman. In a society given over to intellectual interests, where science and art spoke from out centuries of culture, Reverchon might easily have become famous as a scientist. But he was not of the stuff that buckles and bows an environment to suit the inward will. At La Réunion, the rigors of life on the frontier almost overwhelmed his early desire to work in botany; like Vesalius at the Spanish court, though perhaps for a different reason, he well-nigh forgot the early gleams which had beckoned him toward a scientific career. But at last, just as the duodecimo of Fallopius came to reawaken forgetting Vesalius, Jacob Boll brought a new stimulus to Reverchon. Reverchon rose to repossess the past "and see what usury age can take from time." During the last three decades of his life it was granted him to make some amends for his early turning aside from the chosen path and his partial surrender to the frontier way of life.

Reverchon's career is symbolic. Texas has been a vortex into which have flowed thought-currents from every part of Europe. But too often the force of the currents has been spent without result, as men became exhausted in the struggle which all newcomers had to make in order to maintain themselves in a new and unsubdued environment. La Réunion itself went to pieces because the strength of the colonists was unequal to this conflict. But the exceptions to the rule are all the more remarkable. Thrice fortunate are they of whom it could be said, as it could be said of Boll and Lindheimer and Wright, and perhaps of Belfrage: "What they will, *they will.*"

Gustaf Wilhelm Belfrage 12

THE reader who has followed the story of science in frontier Texas through the earlier chapters of this narrative will have realized, as I have been forced to conclude many times in tracing the careers of early-day scientists, that frontier Texas escapes the easy adjectives sometimes used to describe it. The simple picture of farmers and cattlemen fighting Mexicans and Indians becomes less simple as our knowledge of the intellectual history of the region is gradually increased. Nearly every one of the men who figure in this study represents another complexity in the tradition of the state, a variation, great or small, in the elements that have gone into the making of present-day Texas. German liberal and French Utopist, Genevese and Scot, the frontier naturalists are a striking company. Yet perhaps the most exotic figure of all is Gustaf W. Belfrage, the Swedish nobleman who spent the last fifteen years of his life collecting insects in Texas.

It is a vivid experience to read the inventory of his estate which was filed with the probate court of Bosque County in 1883. This meager list of the few articles belonging to the scientist whose collections even then were scattered from Washington to St. Petersburg is almost indecent in its revelation of stark poverty. The following schedule, taken from the records of the court, includes every article of clothing or household furniture which the appraisers found in Belfrage's house:

1 Gallon Can)	15
2 wash basins) . . . value at	15
2 coffee pots and 2 frying pans	25
2 shoe brushes, 5c 1 can of Cyanili of Potassim	10
1 clock	1.00
1 looking glass	25
1 bed quilt	75
1 sheet and piece of ducking	25

1 pr of gloves	40
1 light summer coat	45
1 Jeanes coat	25
1 Linen coat	25
1 pr of pants	25
1 table cloth (oil)	25
1 Razor	40
7 shirt collars and 2 boxes blackening	40
1 Flannell Undershirt	35
2 handkerchiefs 2 scarfs	25
1 woolen scarf	30
1 pr of old slippers 1 old straw hat	25
1 sofa	5.00
1 straw mattress and cotton pillar	35
1 Work table	15
1 stove and drum	5.00
4 cane bottomed chairs	3.00
2 cotton towels	05
1 frying pan	25

But in the house were also these:

Library. The collection of Books comprised 194 bound and unbound, volumes a pamphlets, nearly all of which were works & treatises on subjects, relating to Zoology. It being a greed that not the probable scientific value of the different articles of property belonging to the Estate but the price that may be obtainable at home should be assumed as basis for the appraisement the [collection?] was valued at $35.00

Collection of Insects. The insect collection was found to contain, probable errors & ommissions, except[ed] . . . a total of pinned insects in good order, or but slightly damaged. Thirty six thousand Eight hundred and eighty one (36881) specimens, Besides those pinned there are also Coleoptera in papers, saw dust and in alcohol, some Lepidoptra in papers and pinned on the stretch board, and several boxes containing insects more or less damaged. . . . the value of the whole collection was fixed at $368.00

1 Box of empty bottles	25
1 Students Kerosine lamp	1.00
1 valise of manuscript no value	
1 bottle of ink 1 bottle of perfume	40
1 dozen Faber lead pencils	20
1 box and lot of empty bottles	50

And, last of all,

1 homebuilding (no lot or land)	50.00

The total value of the estate, including the insect collections and books, was set at $491.40.

The biographer of Gustaf Belfrage must somehow find a principle of unity that will enable him to bring into focus such diverse elements of the man's story as are suggested by the ancestral vaults of his titled ancestors in the *Riddarholms kyrka* at Stockholm; the thousands of insects, mounted with the most intelligent care, which are preserved by many museums in the United States and Europe; and, in the Norwegian cemetery near Norse, Texas, an unmarked grave. From materials as varied as these must be pieced together an account of this scientist whose life belongs, after all, to the history of Texas, and thus to the history of the American frontier.

An idea of Belfrage's contribution to American zoölogy can be gained from Professor Calvert's life of Ezra Townsend Cresson, published in 1929 in the *Transactions* of the American Entomological Society. Cresson's notable study, *Hymenoptera Texana*, which appeared in 1872, says Professor Calvert, was based in large part on the "splendid collection of insects by Mr. G. W. Belfrage, made in Bosque Co., the fine collection in the Museum of Comparative Zoölogy at Cambridge, Mass., made by Mr. J. Boll in Dallas Co., and a small collection of Mr. L. Heiligbrodt, made in Travis and Bastrop Counties." Cresson's monograph listed more than six hundred species of hymenopterous insects, distributed among nineteen families, and described nearly three hundred species new to science. It was a monumental work. And of the new species described, 243 were based on specimens gathered by Belfrage: surely an amazing yield for one small county!

Yet the antecedents and the life of this extraordinary man were long almost completely shrouded in obscurity. It was known that early in the year 1867 he began to sell insects, *entomostraca,* and mollusks collected near Waco, Texas; that the *Naturhistoriska Riksmuseum* at Stockholm, the British Museum, the Museum of Comparative Zoölogy at Cambridge, the Peabody Academy of Science at Salem, the Boston Society of Natural History, and the museums in Brussels and St. Petersburg all possess valuable collections of Texan insects acquired from Belfrage during the period 1868-73; and that the United States National Museum has the very fine Belfrage Collection purchased after Belfrage's death. Most zoölogists knew Belfrage's name through his advertisements printed in British, German, and American journals between 1869 and 1881, and through frequent references to him, always brief, in the publications of entomologists in many lands. His name, further, is preserved for all time in the scientific designations of a score and more of species, chiefly insects.

But whence he came was unknown until recently; indeed the man himself was almost forgotten save by the few curious minds who may have encountered the brief obituary note published in the *American Naturalist* in 1883, the year following Belfrage's death. The details of Belfrage's life were unknown even to those best informed regarding the history of American entomology; and Dr. Sjöstedt, director of the entomological section of the *Naturhistoriska Riksmuseum* in Stockholm, told me that none of the many members of the Belfrage family in Sweden from whom he had sought details could give him any information concerning the naturalist.

Even the Scandinavian settlers in central Texas among whom Belfrage lived from 1868 to 1882 knew almost nothing about him. In the course of my investigations, during which I interviewed practically every old settler, Norwegian or Swedish, who conceivably might be a source of information, I continually encountered the element of mystery. "He was descended from Swedish royalty," said one. "He was a Swedish Baron," said another. "His father was a General in the Swedish army," said a third. " 'Why did he come to America?' I do not know. Mr. Belfrage was a courteous gentleman who treated everyone with respect. He minded strictly his own business"—with a covert glance at the questioner—"and I believe never made anyone his confidant. He had his faults—grave faults—but you must not mention them, and blemish his noble character." Words to this effect time after time from grave old men, who treated me with simple old-world courtesy. Who was this "G. W. Belfrage" who could so impress a simple country people that fifty years after his death they would resent even a suggestion of criticism of their hero by an outsider?

Gustaf Wilhelm Belfrage was born in Stockholm, Sweden, April 12, 1834, and died on Meridian Creek, near the hamlet of Norse, in Bosque County, Texas, December 7, 1882. He was derived from an ancient Scotch-Swedish family, being the tenth in line of direct descent from William Belfrage of Pennington and Tulliochie, Lord High Admiral of Scotland, and sixth in line from Hans Befritz Belfrage. The latter, who was the son of *Magister* Henry Belfrage and his wife, Janette Balram (daughter of James, Baron of Balram, and Elizabeth Stuart), came with his mother to Sweden in 1624 as a twelve-year-old boy. It has been suggested that the migration of Janette Balram may have been due to religious persecution. After he had reached manhood, Hans Belfrage established a home at Vänersborg on the southern shore of Lake Vänern, in the province of Västergötland. He was evidently an ambitious man, holding the most responsible positions in his town, and acquiring several farms (or "estates") in the vicinity. From the eldest son of Hans Belfrage, Hendrick Johan Belfrage, who became a lieutenant-colonel of artillery, is traced the descent of Gustaf W. Belfrage.

The Belfrage clan in Sweden has been to a great extent a military family, though many members have been eminent in business and banking. In the Scottish line, the purely intellectual note is more striking. Among the eminent members of it are the Reverend Dr. Henry Belfrage (1774-1835), noted divine and leader of the Secession Kirk of Scotland; his sister Joanna Belfrage Picken, Scottish-Canadian poet; Andrew Belfrage, Scottish-Canadian artist and poet; a prominent living London physician; two British-American actors and playwrights; and a family of British engineers. Several members of the Swedish branch of the family have migrated to America. The Swedish branch is the more numerous.

Perhaps the most eminent of the whole Swedish line was Gustaf Belfrage's grandfather, Major-General Johan Lennart Belfrage. He was possessed of most unusual ability in managing his properties and investing funds, and came to own more than a score of farms in Skaraborgs-län, a province of Västergötland. A humane man of great simplicity of life, noted for his kindness to his tenants and his generosity to the Church, the Major-General lived a frugal, contained life. In 1795 he married the Baroness Hedwig Charlotta von Köhler, daughter of Baron Axel Johan von Köhler, vice-president of the High Court of Justice in Götaland. Shortly thereafter, he and his bride went to live at *Malma säteri* (Malma manor) in Skaraborgs-län. Here the Major-General lived for perhaps twenty-five years, and here died in 1820 at the age of sixty-six. At that time his son Axel Åke, Gustaf's father, was twenty-four years old, a newly appointed lieutenant in the Svea Lifeguard.

Afzelius, the Swedish historian and mythologist, best known as a collector of Swedish folk songs, has left in his memoirs a description of the Major-General and of Gustaf's father, whom he describes as "a beautiful light-haired boy in shirt-sleeves, lying on the floor, playing with his tin soldiers"; the Major-General, he says, was a "large-built, stately man, with a countenance that begot confidence in the beholder." As I write, a photograph of the Major-General's portrait by Sparrgren lies before me. Surely a misrepresenting picture! Here we behold a tall figure in uniform, with a long Nordic face dominated by cold blue eyes; a patrician nose, a small, positive mouth, and a firm chin—the whole countenance filled with a stern pride. But in actuality the man was all benevolence, kindness, justice. An autobiography written in 1814 contains the following passage, whose accuracy is corroborated by contemporary testimony: "My estates shall bear true witness that with the blessing of God frugality and industry bring human support and happiness. Twenty-seven of my cultivated and built-up little farms are now settled by well-to-do and industrious tenants." This was Gustaf's paternal grandfather.

After the death of the Major-General, the property began to be dissipated. Gustaf's father, Axel Åke Belfrage, the General's oldest child, lacked completely his father's competence in money matters. Axel seems, however, to have had a successful career in the army and at court. He attained a captaincy, and in 1830 was made Chamberlain in the palace at Stockholm. On December 30 of the same year Axel married the Baroness Margareta Sophia Leijonhufvud, daughter of Baron Axel Gabriel Leijonhufvud and his wife, Maria Fredrika von Spangen. The Leijonhufvud family, one of the most noble of Sweden, dates back to the fourteenth century. It has given many patriots, men and women, to Swedish history. Gustavus I, liberator of his country and founder of the Swedish royal line of Vasa, married a woman of the family as his second wife. One branch of the family who have translated the old Swedish name into the German equivalent "Löwenhaupt" hold the dignity of counts or earls. So distinguished is the family that its members are honored by burial in the *Riddarholms kyrka* in Stockholm, the Westminster Abbey of Sweden.

The wedding of the Chamberlain Belfrage and the Baroness Leijonhufvud took place in the fashionable *Klara kyrka* in Stockholm, with Pastor Franzén, the eminent Swedish poet, officiating. Of this union came two sons: Axel Leonard, born in 1832, and the subject of this biography, Gustaf Wilhelm, born two years later.

The marriage which began auspiciously in the union of two distinguished lines of Swedish nobility ended disastrously; in 1849 Gustaf's mother, the Baroness Leijonhufvud, secured a legal separation from the Chamberlain. Apparently no one knows the real reason for the separation. Dr. Sixten Belfrage, as well as Jenny Belfrage in her *Bidrag till Släkten Belfrages Historia,* states that "the causes of the marital separation are unknown, but it may have been due to Axel Åke's inability to handle funds." If Gustaf Wilhelm shall later be called a spendthrift and a wastrel, it will be well to recall his father's character and Gustaf's early experiences.

Axel Åke Belfrage advanced to the rank of brevet-major in 1840, and later (1844) quitted the army. He returned to Mariestad on Lake Väner, near his birthplace, where he died in 1885 at the venerable age of eighty-nine.

Gustaf's father, while he lacked the progressiveness of the Major-General, nevertheless was actively interested in agriculture, as is evidenced by his election to membership in the Academy of Agriculture in Stockholm. Of his two sons, the elder, Axel Leonard, lived a life similar to his father's, except that he had no country estates to attend, for these had long since been sold by order of a bankruptcy court. He was an officer in a regiment in Stockholm and served as aide-de-camp to the Grand Duke of Ostergötland, later King Oscar II. Gustaf's brother survived his father but a short time, dying on December 31, 1885. He had succeeded to the title of *caput familiae* of the Belfrage clan in Sweden on the death of his father the preceding April. Since both of the Chamberlain's sons died without issue, this branch of the family became extinct.

So much for the background and general family history. But what of Gustaf Wilhelm, the naturalist? The family genealogy dismisses him with the simple note: "Entomologist. Resided the last years of his life in Cli[f]ton in Texas, U. S. A., whence he sent home to the Academy of Science in Sweden large collections of insects. Died Dec. 7, 1882, in Cli[f]ton."

The first bits of information regarding Gustaf Belfrage's early life which I was able to procure were furnished me through the kindness of Dr. Sixten Belfrage. I translate part of a letter from him, with a few supplementary notes:

Unfortunately, very little is known about G. W. B. In January, 1854 [at the age of twenty], he became a student in the *Skogsinstitut* [the high school of forestry] in Stockholm, where are trained chiefs of the various districts of the Crown Forests. For some unknown reason G. W. B. was never graduated. The exact time of his departure from the *Skogsinstitut* is not known. . . . [In the *Adelskalendar* for 1857, G. W. B. is recorded as a "steward of the forest" at Stjärnsund; in 1863 and 1865, he is recorded as "living in America."] . . . In these accounts, the interesting fact is that G. W. B. was steward on the Stjärnsund property in Närke. This property was at the time the private property of the Royal House, and the fact that G. W. B. had this post was undoubtedly due to his father's position as Chamberlain, or the influence of his mother's family. It is possible to believe that the reason that B. left the *Skogsinstitut* was that this position, which was undoubtedly just as good as being a royal forester in the employ of the government, presented itself to him. But it may also be that they procured this position for B. because he did not have a degree that would give him a right to a government position. It seems that he did not stay very long at Stjärnsund. The fact that the *Kalendar* of 1860 gives him merely the title "steward of the forest" points to the fact that at that time he had no position . . . [Belfrage's] journey to America must have taken place at the earliest in 1860, at the latest in 1862 [since the statements in the calendars are based on the data of the preceding year]. . . . Perhaps the most correct supposition is the year 1861 or 1862.

Such was the best information that Professor Sixten Belfrage's careful search elicited. Within the past few years, however, through the efforts of Professor Dr. Yngve Sjöstedt, who caused the archives of the *Naturhistoriska Riksmuseum* and of the Academy of Sciences in Stockholm to be searched, more information has been brought to light concerning Belfrage's departure from Sweden and his movements in America. In addition, the United States National Museum, the Museum of Comparative Zoölogy at Cambridge, and the Boston Society of Natural History possess data concerning some of the obscure points of Belfrage's life.

Belfrage actually left Sweden for America late in 1859 or early in 1860; during his last few months in Sweden he had been living in retirement at Köping, a small town west of Stockholm at the head of Lake Mälar. He was about twenty-six years old. The real reasons for his leaving the homeland are still not clear; it is certain only that "in some way he made it impossible for himself to remain in Sweden." Men who knew Belfrage in Texas years later have told me that he was disinherited, and that he came to America after an unfortunate marriage. Belfrage undoubtedly made these statements to one or two intimate companions, but we must remember that he was always fond of mystifying his acquaintances regarding his past. Dr. Sixten Belfrage says:

That he was married is not known: [it is] not improbable, but it seems unreasonable to suppose that such an event would not have been reported by his brother to the Calendar of the Nobility. Perhaps it was a mésalliance that [his family] sought to conceal; or perhaps it was not a legitimate marriage.

Wrangel and Bergstrom, in their genealogy of Swedish nobles, and Anrep state that Gustaf died unmarried.

In a letter written March 18, 1859, to the great Swedish entomologist, Professor C. J. Boheman, Belfrage speaks of his prospective departure as final: "I am going to leave my country forever," he says, "and depart for the land of the Yankees." His letters to Professor Boheman and to Dr. Carl Stål, members of the staff of the *Naturhistoriska Riksmuseum,* reveal that for some time he had contemplated leaving Sweden, and that he looked to his family for an annual allowance.

Some additional light is thrown on Belfrage's life before he came to America by other letters, which suggest that before 1857 he had been on terms of almost filial intimacy with Professor Boheman. It is possible that Belfrage had met Boheman through his father, who may have known Boheman in the army. Also, certain passages in the very intimate letters from G. W. Belfrage to Carl Stål raise the question whether the two had not at some time studied together at Uppsala. Unfortunately, we do not have any of the letters that Belfrage received from Swedish correspondents, for at his death these were burned.

Belfrage's first letter from America, written from New York in response to a letter several months old from Boheman, is dated August 8, 1861. From this document it appears that Belfrage has been in

America for some time; that he has already sent a collection of insects to Boheman; and that he is "suffering from that common disease called a lack of money." The war excitement is raging in America, and his pecuniary embarrassment offers Belfrage the hard alternatives of selling his insect collections at a great sacrifice, enlisting in the Federal army, or starving. A few other letters written late in 1861 give fleeting glimpses of mental and physical distress. Belfrage's want was so great that on one occasion he was without food or shelter for two days and nights, and was obliged to sell valuable collections of insects at a ruinously low figure.

After a year's silence Belfrage emerges again in the correspondence, this time in Chicago. Here he remained until the end of 1866, with occasional collecting trips along Lake Michigan and Lake Superior, and to the Swedish colony at Altona, Knox County, Illinois. One letter written in 1864 and one in 1865 reveal Belfrage's two most pressing needs: insect needles in quantity for use in mounting his collections, and money, always money.

During 1866 Belfrage entered into correspondence with all of the leading American entomologists: Cresson, Ulke, Packard, Uhler, Henshaw, Hagen, Scudder, and the rest. They encouraged him to carry out a long-cherished plan to go to Texas on an insect-collecting trip. Late in 1866, accordingly, armed with letters from the American Consul at Stockholm and the Swedish Academy of Science stating that he was a Swedish subject collecting for the Academy, Belfrage set out. "If I go South without such letters," he wrote to Boheman, "you will understand what kind of brotherly love I can expect from the Southerners after having lived among the 'damned Yankees!' " He arrived in Houston from New Orleans on January 4, 1867, penniless, or nearly so; but soon he was able to secure an income from sales of insects, particularly to American and British students, who paid much better than Continental entomologists.

Among the tales about himself that Belfrage liked to circulate are some picturesque anecdotes concerning his life just preceding his arrival in Texas. He loved to recount to his companions how he had hoboed through the state of South Carolina during the War, and then had arrived in Waco, penniless, where he was befriended by a Swedish merchant, Samuel J. Forsgard. To others he told how he got a thousand dollars in Waco by enlisting as a substitute in the Confederate army just before the end of the War. These amusing tales are without foundation. Belfrage, as we have seen, was in Chicago until 1866, and came to Texas with definite commissions to collect insects.

He had long wished to explore and collect in West Texas and New

Mexico; the plan recurs like a fixed idea in his correspondence. More than once during his residence in Houston in 1867 and the first half of 1868, he expresses the hope that he may be able to procure a mule and wagon and travel into West Texas so that he may "collect a hundred thousand insects per annum"; but no opportunity for making this expedition offered itself. In April of 1867 he made a fruitless exploring and collecting trip to Quintana, at the mouth of the Brazos River. The only other event of importance during Belfrage's stay in Houston was a fire in his lodgings in February of 1868 which destroyed all his books and many of his early collections.

From the very first of his residence in Texas Belfrage entered into correspondence with numerous entomologists in Europe and America, and soon established himself as a most gifted and skilful collector. His correspondence with Cresson dates at least from March of 1867; and in the years 1868-71 he sold large collections of insects to the

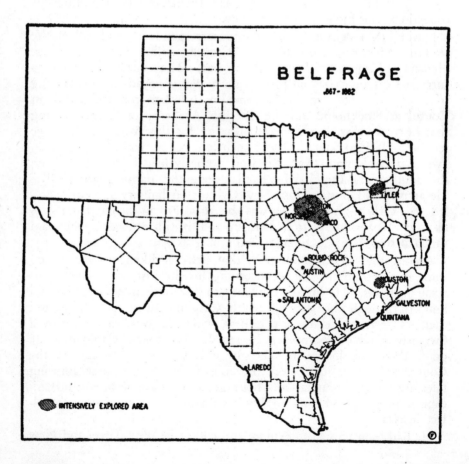

BELFRAGE
1867-1882

INTENSIVELY EXPLORED AREA

234

Swedish Academy of Science at Stockholm, which are recorded in various volumes of the transactions of the Academy. He sold to Dr. H. A. Hagen a collection of insects from Waco (including Neuroptera, Orthoptera, Hymenoptera, and Hemiptera), which Hagen later presented to the Museum of Comparative Zoölogy of Harvard College; and in 1869 Belfrage exchanged a large collection of Texan insects with the Boston Society of Natural History, through Scudder and Packard. He also sent to the Peabody Academy of Science at Salem abundant specimens of certain entomostraca, *Thysanura* and *Ixodes* from Texas, and as early as 1872 had gained among the scientists of that institution an enviable reputation as a "careful and observing collector of insects." Packard, in the introduction to his work "Geometrid Moths of the United States," acknowledges his indebtedness to "large collections in the Museum of the Peabody Academy of Science . . . containing many types of new species from Bosque County, Texas, collected by G. W. Belfrage, and from Dallas, Texas, through Mr. Boll. I have also had the privilege of examining the types of a few Texas species [collected by Boll?] contained in the Museum of Comparative Zoölogy. I have also received the larvæ and notes on a few species from Mr. Belfrage." The Texas collection in the *Naturhistoriska Riksmuseum* at Stockholm, says Professor Dr. Sjöstedt, "is quite a comprehensive one, and specimens are abundantly scattered throughout the insect orders of the Museum."

Belfrage's mother had died early in the year 1867, leaving him from her estate the interest on a fund of about ten thousand dollars—say an income of between $300 and $400 a year—which was sent to Belfrage annually through his uncle, General Baron A. G. Leijonhufvud. By this time the other members of Belfrage's immediate family had completely cut him off, and doubtless his older brother had not served exactly in the role of peacemaker. An observer inclined to conjecture might draw certain inferences from the situation, seeing the older son following closely in his father's footsteps and doubtless overawing the younger, who responded by a defense reaction of the revolt type. No doubt in his father's and elder brother's estimation, Gustaf was a ne'er-do-well; yet he appears to have retained the confidence of his mother.

The added income from her estate led Belfrage to carry out his plan of moving to the hamlet of Norse, in Bosque County, in the summer of 1868. During the late autumn of that year he collected insects in the pine woods of East Texas, and in April, 1869, he made a month-long trip to the Mexican border, probably at Laredo. During the following year he went on an expedition into West Texas that lasted two months. After each of these trips he was for a long time afflicted with malarial fever. It is evident from these facts that Belfrage collected in several parts of Texas, not merely in Bosque and McLennan counties, as Cresson and others have thought.

As far as I can discover, the great trip to New Mexico Belfrage had planned never materialized. In 1869 he had announced his intention of making the trip in the *Canadian Entomologist,* saying:

At the request of several gentlemen in this country and Europe, I intend to make an extensive eight or nine months' Entomological collecting tour in Western Texas and Southern New Mexico, if sufficient means can be raised. . . . I shall be obliged by receiving early information from all desiring to subscribe, stating at the same time their wishes. . . . If anything should happen during the tour to prevent my fulfilling my engagements, or if anyone dislikes his share, the money will be refunded.

But Belfrage's advertisements as late as 1877 indicate that this plan had not been carried out.

Although Belfrage had taken up his residence near Norse in 1868, until 1875 he received his mail through the Forsgards at Waco. After that his mail address was "Clifton," nine miles from Norse. From 1870 to 1879 Belfrage lived with Mr. Carl Questad, an old Scandinavian farmer whose house stood on a beautiful hill near Norse overlooking Meridian Creek. In this locality of rare beauty the naturalist made many of his magnificent collections. When I visited the place in the spring of 1930, Dr. O. M. Olson pointed out two great live oak trees, saying: "Belfrage set his light-traps under those trees to catch night-flying insects nearly sixty years ago. He used lights to attract insects, and most of his work was done at night. We got magnificent beetles and moths in this way: I remember how delighted Belfrage was with the first pair of glowworms [*Lampyrid* beetle larvae] that I found for him: in his generous, carefree way he gave me five dollars for the pair. Then he would sell them for a tenth of that amount!"

In 1879 Belfrage built himself a small hut on Meridian Creek on the Chris Pederson farm, about three miles from the Questad place. Here he lived alone for the few remaining years of his life, and here he was found dead, on the morning of December 7, 1882.

Belfrage was a prodigious collector: as early as 1869 he advertised an exchange-collection of 25,000 Texan insects. He had already won the cordial approval of naturalists as "an active and zealous collector," and his mounting of specimens attracted especial commendation. He sold insects continually and extensively throughout the thirteen subsequent years, both to amateurs and to serious students. Yet at the time of his death his collections comprised 36,881 pinned specimens in good order, in addition to beetles in paper, sawdust, and alcohol, and butterflies in papers!

An editorial obituary notice in the *American Naturalist,* written, presumably, by Professor A. S. Packard, who had long been a correspondent of Belfrage, contains a striking tribute to Belfrage's work as a collector. It is interesting to find Belfrage's name once more coupled with that of Jacob Boll:

If the insect fauna of Texas is, at the present time [1883], better known than that of most of the Western States of this continent, it is largely due to the skill and industry of Mr. Belfrage and the late Mr. Jacob Boll, who were the foremost among the few really careful and conscientious collectors in the country. The number of new and interesting species discovered by Mr. Belfrage is really astonishing, considering that they were collected in a very limited area of the state, and several of his discoveries were named after him by our most prominent entomologists. The care and neatness he exhibited in preserving and preparing his specimens, as well as the honesty with which he filled the orders of his numerous correspondents, deservedly procured him a reputation as a collector which extended far beyond the limits of this country.

As far as I can learn, Belfrage published no entomological papers. In a letter to Cresson, dated July 26, 1873, Belfrage stated that he was working at a paper on the insects of Bosque County, but it was never published. Belfrage's letters to Stål give rise to the conjecture that this was the "valise of manuscript" listed by the appraisers of Belfrage's estate as being "of no value." It was burned, along with his letters.

Apparently no portrait of Belfrage is extant, either in Europe or in America. Dr. Knut Belfrage of Lidköping, Sweden, possesses a great collection of family portraits, but none of the entomologist. In the absence of portraits, one must depend on accounts of his appearance and personal characteristics furnished by contemporaries of Belfrage still living. Mr. H. C. Bradstreet, postal clerk at Clifton during the naturalist's sojourn there, said (1930) that he was "a very tall man, spare, face tolerably full, with a moustache; of jovial disposition and expression; an active man . . . very highly educated." Mr. Frank Kell, president of the Wichita Falls & Southern Railway, said of him:

As a boy I well remember G. W. B., and knew of the work which he was carrying on in that section. He was not communicative to anyone, and being only a small boy, I had no opportunity of learning anything whatever of his antecedents or individualities further than [that] he was generally recognized as a cultured man and one with pronounced eccentricities.

Dr. O. M. Olson, Belfrage's personal physician and younger companion in collecting, said of his personal appearance:

He was very tall, spare, broad-faced, moustached, weight 160 pounds, with a jovial expression, and an agreeable, companionable disposition; in industry he was active and indefatigable. The townspeople at Clifton thought very well of him.

Mr. J. N. Colwick, president of the Bosque County Historical Society, records impressions of Belfrage that he gained as a boy of twelve years:

> He looked to me to be one of the tallest men I had ever seen (probably six feet three inches). He had deep blue eyes, and was a very slender man, features pleasant, and so was his disposition. . . . He was a truthful, reliable man: "his word was as good as his bond." . . . He was not of a social disposition, but spoke pleasantly to those speaking to him.

Even in Belfrage's later years, when his love of strong drink had seriously impaired his health, he still was a charming, cultivated companion. The inventory of his estate shows his poverty toward the end of his life; there is evidence of a struggle against overwhelming personal temptation, yet in it all he retained some of the refinement of his youth and early manhood. Belfrage's intemperate habits, which dated back to his student days in Stockholm, grew upon him during his sojourn in Texas. General and excessive drinking was then much more common than it has been in later years. Whiskey was distilled in Bosque County, and sold for a dollar a gallon. As Belfrage grew older, in his solitude, the bottle mastered him. Again and again he fought to regain possession of himself, with repeated failure. His credit became impaired; often, in the absence of money, when the mania was upon him, he is said to have drained his specimen-jars of their alcohol. When a remittance came for specimens sent to scientists in England, Italy, France, or Russia, the money went quickly. A former drinking companion relates that a purse of gold rubles from Radochkoffsky was spent in a single night. Belfrage's death was due, officially, to "heart failure"—one wonders if it really did not result from acute alcoholism.

Belfrage's friends—and mine—led me to an unmarked grave* in a corner of a country churchyard, now part of a larger burial ground for the Norwegian church. As I looked over the newer plot, with its garish and ostentatious monuments, I recalled Madame de Staël's indictment of Florence at the church of Santa Croce—that resting place of some of the most illustrious dead of Europe: Rossini, Boccaccio, Machiavelli, Aretino, Michelangelo, Galileo. *"Nous prions pour nos*

---

*On April 20, 1940, the Texas Entomological Society dedicated a monument to Belfrage in the Norse cemetery, near the spot where he is buried, with appropriate ceremonies.

morts," said a priest. *"Oui, vous avez raison. . . . C'est la seule pro-priété glorieuse qui vous reste."*

And to me this unmarked plot is more sacred than the flag-draped *Riddarholms kyrka* of far-off Stockholm, or the ancestral vaults of the Leijonhufvuds.

*   *   *

And now this series of essays on Naturalists of the Frontier in early Texas must have an end, even though the presentation of men and movements has been partial and inadequate as a mirroring of the interaction between the naturalist and frontier ways of life. The eleven men whose lives have been sketched at length are but a hand-ful compared with the scores of workers, some of humble and slender gifts, others of outstanding ability and accomplishments, who during the frontier period contributed to our cultural and scientific advance.

But whether mediocre or brilliant, famous or obscure, they came and worked, and passed, these Naturalists of the Frontier, across the stage of history—some of them men of brain and heart and honor, others men of whom we cannot speak with admiration. They are not all to be gauged by the same standards: their environments, diverse and not always favorable, helped to make them all. But they were one in their devotion to the advancement of our common knowledge. Their love for nature carried them through the difficulties and hard-ships of the frontier days; and much can be forgiven them, for they have loved much.

Notes on Scientists of the First Frontier 13

I

IN 1850 the third annual meeting of the American Association for the Advancement of Science was held in Charleston. This recognition of the rank of the Carolina city among American scientific centers (the first meeting of the Association had been held in Philadelphia and the second in Boston) followed more than a hundred years of artistic and scholarly activity there. Early in the eighteenth century it had become widely known as a city of wealth and culture; its society was considered brilliant and metropolitan. It took its styles from London or Paris, whither wealthy Charlestonians sent their sons to complete their formal education. In the eighteenth century young men from Charleston usually attended one of the two English universities for liberal training, or the Scottish universities for professional work in medicine, law, or theology. Charleston became famous as the demesne of the Gadsdens, Laurens, Pinckneys, and Rutledges; and in the nineteenth century was enriched by associations with Calhoun, James L. Pettigru, and Hayne.

Cultural institutions had their beginnings in Charleston in the colonial period. The Charleston Library Society was founded in the middle of the eighteenth century, and though the library was almost completely destroyed by fire during the Revolutionary War, in 1808 it had reached ample proportions again and was supplied with substantial books. In 1773 an abortive museum society was formed, the ancestor of the present fine museum of Charleston. The College of Charleston held its first commencement in 1794.

At the beginning of the last century Charleston had some twenty thousand inhabitants. British travelers in the United States spoke in high praise of the city: the comforts of its hotels, the pleasures of its society, and the warm, frank courtesy of its citizens. Tasistro, an Irish actor playing in Charleston in 1840, found there many "men of superior minds and highly cultivated intellects" who frequented Hart's Circulating Library in King Street, where were to be obtained "scientific tracts of all sorts and sizes" along with other substantial intellectual pabulum. Mesick summarizes thus the opinions of English travelers:

> Charleston seems to have been the most agreeable and the most admired of the Southern towns. It was declared to be the only place in the Southern states which realized the English idea of a city. C. A. Murray in 1835 [said] it was nearly as well known to the civilized world as Bristol or Liverpool. The best society there was considered much superior to anything else of the kind found in America, and was much like that of England in its Episcopal religion, its people of English birth, and its regard for established institutions.

In the late eighteenth century, several scientific men of wide reputation practiced medicine in Charleston. Three of them, all Scots, were outstanding. John Lining (1708-1760), who died in Charleston after thirty years' practice of medicine, was interested experimentally in electricity, and published in the *Philosophical Transactions* of the Royal Society of London accounts of experiments supplementary to those of Franklin. Dr. Lionel Chalmers (1715?-1777) practiced medicine in Carolina for more than forty years, and also died in Charleston. Perhaps the greatest of the three was Alexander Garden (1730?-1791), a graduate in medicine at Aberdeen and Edinburgh. For many years in addition to his medical practice he indulged botanical interests, and in 1772 was elected a Fellow of the Royal Society. André Michaux and François André Michaux, father and son, also had a horticultural garden at Charleston in the last decade of the century, though this contributed little to the development of science in that section.

In the first half of the nineteenth century, Charleston had a goodly number of scientific men who may be divided, roughly, into three generations. There was the older generation, composed of Governor John Drayton, Dr. J. L. E. W. Shecut, Stephen Elliott, and James McBride, whose productive scientific activities extended approximately through the first two decades of the century. This group was followed in the period 1821-1840 by one in which Joel R. Poinsett, the Reverend Dr. John Bachman, and Dr. Samuel Henry Dickson were leading workers. The third generation (after 1841) included Robert Wilson Gibbes, the Ravenels (Edmund, Henry William, and St. Julien), and Dr. John Edwards Holbrook, the famous herpetologist. It was the scientists of this generation who presented papers at the Charleston meeting of the American Association in 1850.

In the development of a creative scientific atmosphere in Charleston, several institutions were influential. First among these in order of their establishment may be mentioned the Literary and Philosophical Society of Charleston, founded in 1813 by Dr. Shecut and several others. This institution lasted only a few years, but in that period was able to enlist the active co-operation and fellowship, and the services as curator of the collections, of that truly distinguished ornithologist, Felix L'Herminier, a former student of DeBlainville in Paris who had come as a refugee from the French West Indies during the Napoleonic wars. L'Herminier, whose own collections formed the basis of the society's natural-history exhibits, was curator of the cabinet during the years 1815-1817.

In 1824 the Medical Society of South Carolina established a medical school in Charleston; on the faculty were Drs. S. H. Dickson and J. E. Holbrook, who later distinguished themselves as naturalists. In 1832 the Medical College of the State of South Carolina was organized, and immediately called to its faculty a number of eminent physicians and teachers, among them Dickson and Holbrook of the old Medical College of Charleston. In 1853 the Elliott Society of Natural History, so named in honor of the banker-naturalist Stephen Elliott, who had died twenty years before, was organized under the presidency of Dr. John Bachman, collaborator (as we have seen) with John James Audubon. Bachman had as fellow officers Gibbes, Dickson, the Ravenels, and others.

II

Charleston, during this period, was of course not a frontier town; I have discussed scientific activities there mainly as a background for an account of the inland centers where naturalists worked under conditions more typical of the frontier. In South Carolina outside of Charleston scientific work was almost entirely confined to the College of South Carolina, established at Columbia in 1801, largely through the efforts of Governor John Drayton. It is the distinction of this college, which opened for students in 1805, to have had on its faculty in the pioneer days two thorough scholars and substantial men of science: Dr. Thomas Cooper (Professor of Chemistry, 1819; President, 1820-1834) and Lardner Vanuxem, who occupied at South Carolina College the first professorship of geology in the United States (1819-1826). Regarding President Cooper, who in philosophy was a materialist and in religion a freethinker, and against whom a certain religious group in South Carolina waged bitter sectarian warfare, history records a verdict singularly in accord with that pronounced on him by John Adams: that he was "a learned, ingenious, scientific and talented madcap." The versatility of his talents, the extent of his knowledge, and his conversational powers made him pre-eminent in the South.

An Oxonian of good family and fortune, he had associated himself with the Girondists in the French Revolution; leaving France after their downfall, he became professor of chemistry in Dickinson College, and later in the University of Pennsylvania. He was a warm friend of the chemist Priestley, then living in retirement in Pennsylvania. In 1816 he was a candidate for the presidency of Transylvania University, but was not considered by the board of trustees. In the light of history, this was fortunate. His zest for violent controversy and his outspoken irreligion would have made impossible that development of Transylvania which took place under the beneficent rule of Horace Holley.

It is the glory of old South Carolina College at Columbia, that Dr. Cooper, in almost his first official act as president, had established a geological professorship, and called Vanuxem to fill it. In America, only Yale and South Carolina College gave courses in geology in 1821.

III

Few men of science worked in Georgia and Alabama during the pioneer period. In 1758, Henry Ellis, F.R.S. (nephew of the great pioneer marine zoölogist, John Ellis, whom Linnæus called a "bright star of natural history" and "the main support of natural history in England"), was governor of the colony. Henry Ellis was a good zoölogist for his day, as appears in some of his works on the exploration of Hudson's Bay. In 1758 he published in the *Philosophical Transactions* of the Royal Society an essay on "The Heat of the Weather in Georgia." During the last decades of the eighteenth century John Abbot, "an accomplished collector and artist" (born about 1760, and still living in London in 1840), made during several years a collection of insects for sale in Europe. In 1797 the English botanist, Sir James Edward Smith (founder of the Linnæan Society of London) published from Abbot's notes and drawings a work in two volumes folio with 104 colored plates, entitled *The Natural History of the Rarer Lepidopterous Insects of Georgia.*

For many years Dr. Lewis LeConte (1782-1838) of Georgia was one of the most prominent naturalists of the frontier South. He was a member of a family that, North and South, was to give many gifted men to science. Dr. LeConte came from the North (he had been born in New Jersey) to the management of the family estates near Woodmanston, Liberty County, Georgia, shortly after completing his medical training with Dr. David Hosack, the most prominent physician of New York City. When he came South, Dr. LeConte gave up the practice of his profession; but on his Liberty County plantation he established a botanical garden (especially rich in plants from the Cape of Good Hope) and a chemical laboratory. He was, as an observer of nature, equally gifted with his better-known brother, Major John Eatton LeConte, U.S.A. He published, however, very little over his own signature, being quite willing that his observations should be given scientific currency by others. His zoölogical and other manuscripts were destroyed at the burning of Columbia near the close of the Civil War. His two sons, John LeConte (1818-91) and Joseph LeConte (1823-1901), both born on the Liberty County plantation, studied and later taught at the University of Georgia, and in 1869 both became connected as professors with the University of California.

In Alabama, in 1838, the future English naturalist, Philip Henry Gosse, F.R.S., was for nine months a backwoods schoolteacher on the Alabama River in Dallas County. He returned to England in 1839, and twenty years later published his *Letters from Alabama, chiefly relating to Natural History*. This is a valuable social as well as scientific study of backwoods Alabama. To the naturalist, the work is of very substantial interest, because of the many interesting observations, especially of the insects, made in that frontier region.

But these scattered facts do not indicate any concerted effort at scientific advance in these two states; and they seemed to be little touched by developments elsewhere.

IV

In North Carolina, the only naturalist-worker of the first two decades of the last century was the Moravian botanist Louis D. von Schweinitz. He was born in Pennsylvania in 1780, and died in 1834. About 1812 he became associated with the administration of the Southern Province of the Moravian church in America at its center in Salem, North Carolina; and it was while he was at Salem that he made his fundamental studies and valuable additions to our knowledge of the fungi of the American flora. Altogether, von Schweinitz described for the first time in the literature of science more than fourteen hundred new species of plants, among them about twelve hundred species of fungi. Two valuable works on the botany of North Carolina from his pen were published in the years 1818 and 1821. Besides von Schweinitz, I know of no other man of science who worked in the Old North State before 1817, except Dr. Hugh Williamson (1735-1819); but as Williamson's particular interests were mathematics and astronomy, his work falls without the purview of this chapter.

The University of North Carolina was founded in 1789, in a time of small and precarious beginnings, and went into operation six years later. The next year there came to the university as professor of mathematics a young Princetonian, Joseph Caldwell, who in 1804 was made president of the university. He held this office from 1804 to 1812, and again from 1817 to 1835. To Caldwell's exertions, as perhaps to those of no other man in the history of the institution, the university owes its existence; for in a critical period he saved it from dissolution. Caldwell was in person small and delicate, with an expansive forehead, bushy eyebrows, regular features, and a keen glance; he displayed strong powers of reason, great determination of character, and invincible firmness and self-possession. Professor Denison Olmsted of Yale commented upon Caldwell's sound judgment, his capacity for self-denial, his generosity, his courage, and his perseverance.

Although during Caldwell's administration, and for many years after, the university had no direct support from the state of North Carolina, "still it flourished and was progressive and vigorous." The first state geological survey in America was organized by members of its faculty in 1823; and the first college astronomical observatory was built there in 1827.

In 1817 Dr. Caldwell called to professorships in the young university two graduates of Yale—Denison Olmsted and Elisha Mitchell, both of the class of 1813—who were to have a marked influence on the scientific development of North Carolina. Olmsted was professor of mineralogy in the University of North Carolina for eight years (1817-25); he left the institution to accept a professorship of mathematics and natural philosophy at Yale. Mitchell had charge of mathematics and natural philosophy at the University of North Carolina during this period; when Olmsted accepted the call to Yale, Mitchell was transferred to the chair of mineralogy, and occupied it to the end of his life. During the years when they worked together Olmsted and Mitchell published, largely in the *American Journal of Science & Arts* ("Silliman's Journal"), a series of papers on the geology and mineralogy of North Carolina. At Olmsted's repeated solicitation a state geological survey was authorized by the legislature, and Olmsted was appointed State Geologist. Mitchell succeeded Olmsted as State Geologist in 1825, and published two reports of progress in 1826 and 1827. In the latter year President Caldwell personally advanced the money for the construction of an astronomical observatory for the use of Mitchell and his colleague in mathematics. The money advanced was repaid to Caldwell by legislative act a few years before his death in 1835.

One is disappointed in the results of Mitchell's many years of work at North Carolina. Surely, with his native gifts and sound training, he should have accomplished more in the untilled field of the South. But in an institution where a professor was obliged to hold himself in readiness night and day to police student pranks and to detect and frustrate night escapades, productive research may have been difficult. Another probable cause of his relative barrenness was the fact that he spread his interests too widely. At the University of North Carolina he "read so extensively in many directions as to acquire the reputation of universal knowledge." Had he but confined himself to his special field, he might have become one of America's greatest men of science.

Among the professors of the University during Olmsted's and Mitchell's days may be mentioned another Yalensian, Ethan Allen Andrews, who was professor of ancient languages from 1822 to 1828; and Nicholas M. Hentz, the entomologist, who was later to become a specialist in American spiders. Hentz held the professorship of modern languages and belles-lettres from 1826-1830. Before and during his sojourn at the University of North Carolina he published several excellent papers on scientific subjects, chiefly on insects and spiders. Hentz was a member at an early date of the American Philosophical Society, the Academy of Natural Sciences of Philadelphia, and the Boston Society of Natural History. Almost twenty years after his death, his monograph on the American spiders, a very important one, was published by the last-named society.

V

During the first quarter of the last century, two towns of the old Southwest frontier contended for the intellectual hegemony of the West: Lexington in Kentucky, and Nashville in Tennessee. They had been founded at about the same time—Lexington in 1779 and Nashville in 1780—and each saw developed within itself an institution of learning that bade fair to rival in promise, as far as the cultivation of the sciences was concerned, even the University of North Carolina under Caldwell's administration. It can truthfully be said that during the regime of President Holley Transylvania University at Lexington came nearer to being a university in the true sense of the term than any other institution of its time in America. While a similar statement cannot be made of the old University of Nashville, nevertheless under the brilliant leadership of Dr. Philip Lindsley it was an ornament to the West, and a true seat of learning.

Lexington early became the center of a prosperous planter-population in the fertile plains of north-central Kentucky. Early English travelers speak of its gay appearance, its comfortable-looking villas, its great number of handsome family coaches, and other signs of wealth. It possessed a very good library, founded about the year 1795, which had grown to several thousand volumes in 1837. As Rusk says, in his excellent history of the literature of the Middle American Frontier:

246

Of such literary activity as the frontier could boast, the towns were the centers; but of these there were fewer than a score, which attained a population of more than five thousand by 1840, and there were only a few of smaller size which were notable for cultural influence. To Lexington, permanently settled in 1779, the acknowledged supremacy belonged until the second or third decade of the nineteenth century, when it passed to Cincinnati. In Lexington the first newspaper of the West was established (1787); and to this town somewhat later Transylvania University, by far the most influential college of the pioneer country, drew a number of distinguished scholars and a student body representing several states and territories. Many travellers record the town's early fame: it was the Athens of the West, where literature was a common topic of conversation; its streets and buildings had a charm not to be found in most of the Atlantic coast cities; its wealth was equalled by that of few towns of its size in any part of the world. Such, at any rate, was the all but unanimous opinion of travellers from about 1810 to 1840, of this first metropolis of the backwoods, which had less than seven thousand inhabitants at the later date.

In considering the cultural influences of early Lexington, it may be well to speak of the group of artists who lived there during the first decades of the nineteenth century. A number of portrait-painters, whom we may pass over, had lived in Lexington from almost the beginning of the settlement. In the period under discussion, artists from Cincinnati, Pittsburgh, and other towns of the North and East made their homes in Lexington during the winters, painting portraits of wealthy Kentucky planters and statesmen. This group of artists included John Wesley Jarvis, Waldo, and Matthew Harris Jouett. They had all been associated with the early development of art in Cincinnati; and all of them were excellent colorists. Jouett "painted portraits of such remarkable truth, beauty of colour, and refinement, at the same time naturalness of composition" that his work set the standard of taste in the West. Another local painter deserving passing mention is Joseph H. Bush. Joel Tanner Hart, Kentucky's native sculptor, worked for some time as a stonecutter in a Lexington monument-yard. It was here that he was found by Shobal Vail Clevinger, the Cincinnati sculptor, who was engaged at the time on a bust of Henry Clay. Clevinger encouraged Hart to attempt a bust of Cassius M. Clay, and thus started him upon a pathway of achievement that led him ultimately to Florence.

Transylvania University was the oldest seat of higher learning west of the Allegheny Mountains. Although it was founded in 1798 by the union of two Kentucky academies, its work had not reached collegiate level before it entered upon the era of President Horace Holley's administration (1818-1827). Probably no other university ever witnessed so rapid an increase in material and intellectual prosperity as did Transylvania during the nine years of Holley's presidency; within four years after he took office the university had become one of the most famous institutions of America. European savants knew of Lexington as "the seat of Transylvania University," chiefly through the writings of such professors as the naturalist Constantine Samuel Rafinesque, and the advanced and progressive physicians and teachers of medicine, Dr. Daniel Drake and Dr. Charles Caldwell, whose publications in their respective fields found a wide distribution.

Holley, who was elected president of Transylvania in 1817, was not the first choice of the trustees of the university. In 1813 they had offered the presidency to the liberal and progressive Dr. Eliphalet Nott, president of Union College, but he had declined the election. They then had selected as acting president a harsh, overbearing divine, the Reverend James Blythe (later president of Hanover College), who served in that capacity until Holley assumed office five years later. Meanwhile the trustees had endeavored to secure as president Dr. Philip Lindsley, then vice-president of Princeton, but he had also declined.

Horace Holley was a native of Connecticut. He had graduated from Yale in 1803, had studied law and then theology, and in 1805 had been ordained to the ministry. Ten years in the pastorate of the Unitarian church in Boston had developed his latent qualities of leadership; he accepted the presidency of Transylvania University because of the opportunities it offered for intellectual leadership in the West. Personable, scholarly, "of ordinary size, perfect in symmetry, with a handsome, smiling face, bright eyes, a remarkably sweet, musical, well-modulated voice, and clear articulation," he promised to be the leader who could mold a university to his ideal. But almost from the first sectarian bitterness sought to overthrow him and destroy his wide influence; and what ecclesiastical machination had in vain attempted with respect to Dr. Thomas Cooper and the South Carolina College, it achieved at Transylvania. Personal jealousy rationalized into theological distrust, and fanned into a religious bigotry seldom paralleled in educational history, resulted in the resignation of President Holley in 1827. To be sure, his departure killed the university, but the opposition to Holley was of the rule-or-ruin sort.

The nine years that Holley spent at Lexington as president of Transylvania made up the Golden Age of the university. As Rusk has summarized it:

Transylvania, though it became nominally a university in 1798-1799, remained in fact, an excellent grammar school until 1818, when Horace Holley . . . came to Kentucky resolved to make Transylvania known as the center of higher education in the West. Within half a dozen years this ambition had been achieved, for in 1824 the faculty of fifteen members contained such eminent men as Charles Caldwell and Daniel Drake, the leaders of the medical profession in the West; James Blythe, later president of Hanover College; Robert Hamilton Bishop, first president of Miami University; Mann Butler, the second historian of Kentucky; and Constantine Rafinesque, the celebrated scientist and cosmopolite. These men were not only eminent teachers but the editors of magazines, and authors of scores of books and pamphlets which formed no small part of such Western pioneer literature as was of solid value. The student body of over four hundred was drawn from fifteen separate states, more than a third of them from outside Kentucky. When Holley resigned, in 1827, the University, now embracing schools of medicine and of law together with the older departments of liberal studies, had graduated between six and seven hundred students. And though the sectarian and professional quarrels which helped force Holley's withdrawal were renewed from time to time until the ruin of the old Transylvania was accomplished, the institution continued throughout the pioneer period to exercise a remarkable influence; perhaps the majority of Kentuckians of note during these years were at one time or other connected in some way with Transylvania.

Among those professors at Transylvania who reflected credit on the university during the Holley regime were Drake, Caldwell, and Rafinesque. Drake came to Transylvania first in 1817, for a year's stay. In the medical school he was the predecessor of Rafinesque in the teaching of materia medica. Later Drake returned to Transylvania, and from 1825 to 1827 was dean of the medical school. As Rafinesque knew him in 1825, Drake was in but his thirty-eighth year; yet his "industry, [intellectual] honesty, temperance, accurate observation, and ambition" had already marked him as one of the greatest men of science of the Mississippi Valley. Drake had been born in great poverty in New Jersey; at the age of three he had been brought by his parents to Kentucky. From 1800 to 1804 he had studied medicine as an apprentice with Dr. William Goforth, the pioneer physician of Cincinnati, and after ten years of practice, largely in Cincinnati, Drake had taken the M.D. degree at the University of Pennsylvania. Possessed of a mind avid for all facts relevant to a given problem, and great ability to draw correct inferences from the facts, he was an unusual figure in medicine on the frontier. Garrison in his *History of Medicine* speaks of his combative nature which fought for the possession of no less than the rigorous truth. Drake's love of fact he probably inherited or learned from his Quaker mother, Elizabeth Shotwell. Garrison describes Drake as "of a tall, commanding figure, simple and dignified in manner. As a lecturer, he had a splendid voice, and was possessed of fiery eloquence, causing him at times to sway to and fro like a tree in a storm. He was gentle, fond of children, hating coarseness, and had a genuine poetic side. . . ."

Drake published chiefly in the field of medicine; only a few works on natural history proper came from his pen. In 1815, in his book *A Picture of Cincinnati* (a work of some two hundred pages), he describes carefully the Indian antiquities, such as mounds, in the neighborhood of Cincinnati. In 1817 he published an account of the geology of the valley of the Ohio in the *Transactions* of the American Philosophical Society, of which he was a member. His *Inaugural Discourse on Medical Education* delivered at the Ohio Medical College, Cincinnati, in 1820, was of great value, and was expanded twelve years later into his *Practical Essays on Medical Education and the Medical Profession in the United States.* In 1827 Drake established the *Western Medical & Physical Journal.* In this journal appeared other papers of interest to the naturalist, such as his "Notices of the Principal Mineral Springs of Kentucky." In 1832 there appeared from his pen two treatises on the Asiatic cholera, which visited Cincinnati that summer on its way to the Southwest. But it is impossible to sketch adequately this frontiersman of science. His watchful eye, his penetrating mind, his catholic interest embraced all elements of his environment. As will appear later, he was to be an intellectual force in Cincinnati, both in the founding of the Western Museum, which he fathered, and in the formation of a literary and scientific coterie on the plan of the "Wistar parties" which he had attended when he was a student of medicine in Philadelphia.

In 1818 Dr. Charles Caldwell followed Dr. Daniel Drake as professor of materia medica at Transylvania (although Rafinesque also seems to have done some such teaching), and for eighteen years he was associated with the medical school in Lexington until in 1837 he became one of a group who founded a medical institute in Louisville. Caldwell was a North Carolinian who, after serving a medical apprenticeship in his home state, in 1796 had got his M.D. degree at the University of Pennsylvania, where from 1810 to 1814 he had been professor of natural history. Caldwell wrote copiously in his field—his bibliography includes some two hundred titles. He was a teacher of great influence in the field of medical education. Of general interest to men of science are his *Medical and Physical Memoirs* (1826/7) and his *Essays on Malaria and Temperament,* which were published in 1831. His *Discourse on the Genius and Character of the Rev. Horace Holley, LL.D.,* published in Boston the year after Holley's death, is of perennial interest to the student of American higher education.

Perhaps the most conspicuous naturalist in America during the years 1816-1835 was Constantine Samuel Rafinesque (1783-1840). He was in the truest sense a cosmopolite. He had been born in a suburb of Constantinople, of a French father and German mother of Greek birth, and had been reared in Marseilles, in Livorno, and in other Italian cities. He came to America for the first time in 1802, but returned to Europe in 1805. After ten years spent in Sicily, he returned to the United States at the end of 1815. Rafinesque's biography has been written at length and competently, by Call and by Fitzpatrick; and has been discussed in briefer essays by such eminent naturalists as Copeland, David Starr Jordan, William H. Dall, and others. Therefore no account of his life is needed here, although because of its sympathetic understanding I subjoin the interpretation of Rafinesque given by G. Brown Goode in one of his delightful historical essays read before the Biological Society of Washington. Erroneous statements by Goode are elided in the quotation:

The most remarkable naturalist of those days was Rafinesque . . . Nearly fifty years ago [Goode wrote in 1887] this man died, friendless and impoverished, in Philadelphia. His last words were these: "Time renders justice to all at last." Perhaps the day has not yet come when full justice can be done to the memory of Constantine Rafinesque, but his name seems yearly to grow more prominent in the history of American zoölogy. He was in many respects the most gifted man who ever stood in our ranks. When in his prime he far surpassed his American contemporaries in versatility and comprehensiveness of grasp. He lived a century too soon. His spirit was that of the present period. In the latter years of his life, soured by disappointments, he seemed to become unsettled in mind, but as I read the story of his life his eccentricities seem to me the outcome of a boundless enthusiasm for the study of nature . . . . The most satisfactory gauge of his abilities is perhaps his masterly "Survey of the Progress and Actual State of the Natural Sciences in the United States of America," printed in 1817. His own sorrowful estimate of the outcome of his mournful career is very touching: "I have often been discouraged, but have never despaired long. I have lived to serve mankind, but have often met with ungrateful returns. I have tried to enlarge the limits of knowledge, but have often met with jealous rivals instead of friends. With a greater fortune I might have imitated Humboldt or Linnæus."

But brief notice is required of Rafinesque's sojourn at Lexington. He was persuaded to come there by John Clifford, a wealthy Englishman resident of the town who indulged scientific interests. On a business trip to Philadelphia, Clifford met Rafinesque and, extraordinarily enough, promised him a professorship at Transylvania University. Rafinesque came to visit the West, and stayed until almost the end of the Holley regime. His extraordinary genius, his encyclopedic knowledge, and his mind thinking thoughts forty years ahead of his time won respect for Rafinesque's scholarship; but his habit of parading his professional connections brought him into ridicule. On the title-pages of his many pamphlets he would set forth with a pompous pedantry, common enough in his day, the list of the scientific and learned societies of which he was a member, so that the real name of the author "bore the proportion to his scientific title, as a paper kite to the length of its tail." Thomas Peirce, of Cincinnati, pasquinaded him as "Professor Muscleshellorum," in his satirical *The Odes of Horace in Cincinnati* (1822). Sorry wit, of course, but fortunate for Peirce, who thereby gained a certain immortality. *He lampooned Rafinesque.*

Holley seems to have appreciated Rafinesque, and to have cultivated the "little, dark, foreign-looking professor," who brought him verses that he had composed in Latin, French, Italian, and English, for his comment and approval. It was while Rafinesque was associated with Transylvania that he published those works that have contributed most to his reputation: his *Ichthyologia Ohiensis* (1820), a descriptive work on the fishes of the Ohio River; his *Monographie des Coquilles bivalves de la Rivière Ohio* (1820), a famous work on the fresh-water mussels of the Ohio River, which Peirce must have seen or heard about; and his monograph on the roses of North America, published in French at Brussels in 1820.

Rafinesque left Transylvania under unhappy circumstances in June, 1825. The next fifteen years were tragic ones for him, and for American science. Obscure they are in many details, for Rafinesque was no longer regularly associated with any college or university. Mental trouble came upon him; his tendency to see differences and to describe new species became a monomania. He died, obscure, friendless, and alone, in a garret in Philadelphia. But the fame of his genius as shown in his early work, especially that done at Transylvania, has steadily brightened to the present day. Almost a hundred years from the date of his final departure from Transylvania, his dust was brought back with ceremony to be reinterred on the campus of the university his pioneer work had helped make famous.

Dr. Samuel Brown during most of Rafinesque's term at Transylvania was professor of the theory and practice of medicine in the medical school. He was a highly intelligent and progressive man of science; a Virginian who after graduating from Dickinson College had taken his degree in medicine at the University of Aberdeen. Dr. Brown had resided in Lexington from 1797 to 1806, and with his brother and Henry Clay, in 1799, attempted unsuccessfully to have slavery excluded by the Constitution from Kentucky. Later he practiced medicine in Natchez, and in Huntsville, Alabama. He died in 1830 in Lexington, at the age of sixty-one.

Rafinesque's successor at Transylvania was the excellent botanist, Dr. Charles W. Short. He became professor of materia medica and medical botany in the University in the autumn of 1825, and remained there thirteen years. In 1838, when Caldwell, Yandell, Cooke, and Drake founded the medical department of the present University of

Louisville, he went with them. He developed into an excellent botanist, and during the years 1828-1837 published a series of valuable botanical papers in the *Transylvania Journal of Medicine and the Associated Sciences*. His "Sketch of the Progress of Botany in Western America" appeared in 1836.

Outside university connections, another pioneer Kentucky man of science must be mentioned, Dr. Ephraim McDowell (1771-1830), a native of Virginia who had studied medicine and surgery with the grand old anatomist and surgeon John Bell of the University of Edinburgh. Dr. McDowell practiced medicine in Danville, Kentucky, for thirty-five years. It was at this outpost of civilization that he performed, in 1809, the first known ovariotomy; he later developed remarkable skill in performing this operation, as well as lithotomy. His deserved fame as a great and enterprising surgeon has been well noted by medical historians, and need not be further referred to here.

VI

In 1819 Louisville, Kentucky, was already a town of considerable size, with 670 dwellings (principally of brick), three banks, three bookstores, a music store, and a goodly quota of other mercantile houses. And although it still was distinctly a raw frontier town as compared with the cities of the Atlantic seaboard, yet there were many evidences of a developing culture. John James Audubon, for instance, after his financial disaster, thought there was enough interest in art in Louisville in 1819 to justify his advertising in the Louisville paper as a drawing-master and portrait-painter.

It is interesting to note the presence in Louisville at this time of George Keats, the brother of the poet; and his wife, Georgiana. George Keats had come to the frontier town in 1818, had entered business, and had had a part in Audubon's business disasters. Some of John Keats's letters to his brother George betray the irritation and distrust felt by the Keatses toward Audubon and his wife. In a letter of reply to Georgiana Keats's complaint of the rawness of the frontier society, and the social affectations of the Kentucky women, John Keats very sensibly held the mirror up to English society, and showed that the American frontier exaggerated only slightly the affectations of politeness and fashion of the English bourgeoisie. In her complaint, of course, Georgiana seems merely to have reflected current British censure of America; for life at Louisville at that date, as well as later, offered many of the amenities of Atlantic cities. Captain Basil Hall was delighted with the "incomparably fine trees"; the very pleasant houses—"numerous gay villas" as he says; the hospitable people; and the excellent hotel accommodations—"the best ordered, upon the whole, that we met with in America." Even Mrs. Trollope in the same year liked the scenery and the trees! In 1830, when the population of Louisville had grown to ten thousand, Stuart spoke approvingly of the place, although he deprecated the lack of religion and the looseness of morals characteristic of frontier river towns.

During the third decade of the century a number of cultivated persons made their homes in Louisville, such as the great Unitarian preachers James Freeman Clarke, Ephraim Peabody, W. H. Channing, and James H. Perkins. Clarke was editor of the *Western Messenger* in Louisville from 1833 until 1840, when he returned to Boston.

The Medical Institute of Louisville, which later became the medical department of the present University of Louisville, was founded in 1837. The original faculty was composed of the former Transylvania professors, Drs. Drake, Short, and Caldwell, John Esten Cooke, and L. P. Yandell. Yandell was a Tennessean who in 1830 had been a cordial friend and fellow student of fossil life with Dr. Gerard Troost, an eminent naturalist whom Lindsley had brought to the University of Nashville in 1828. These men established together a medical school which for a time surpassed that of Transylvania, though shortly afterward medical leadership in the West passed to Cincinnati in the Medical College of Ohio.

VII

Cincinnati, or as it was known earlier, "Fort Washington," was first settled at the end of 1788, and in 1801, when it had a population of perhaps eight or nine hundred, was made the capital of the Northwest Territory. In 1810 its population had increased to twenty-five hundred. It quickly became one of the principal towns of the Old West. Fearon, in 1817, found it a very interesting place of eight to ten thousand inhabitants, seven churches, "a large and fine" schoolhouse with a school on the Lancastrian plan, and some very handsome houses. Three years later John Woods, an English traveler, speaks of it as a "noble looking town, by far the best I have seen in the western country," with twelve thousand people, a number of large factories and mills, and well-stocked stores. In 1835 the Hon. Charles Augustus Murray, following Mrs. Trollope in Cincinnati by a few years, speaks in a tone widely different from hers of the independence and enterprise shown by its citizens. Its thirty churches, its college, and other public institutions come in for praise and discriminating comment in Murray's account. Among other things, he pays his court in no uncertain terms to Mrs. Trollope:

When I think of the short period that has elapsed since the red Indian, the bear, the elk, and the buffalo roamed through these hills; since the river . . .

254

flowed in silence through the massive and impenetrable forest; and turn from that fancied picture to the one now before my eyes, . . . I am filled with astonishment and admiration at the energy and industry of man, . . . and I do pity, from the bottom of my heart, the man (and, above all others, the Englishman) who can see nothing in such a scene but food for unjust comparisons, sneers, raillery, and ridicule.

Thus much for Mrs. Trollope, and her *Domestic Manners of the Americans!* It will be recalled that she wrote her book of caustic strictures from what she saw (or did not see) during a residence of two years in Cincinnati, in the course of which she was engaged in an unsuccessful mercantile venture that was widely known to the unregenerate as "Trollope's Folly," and to the urbane as the "Trollopean Bazaar."

The germ of many cultural and intellectual movements lay in the Cincinnati of pioneer days. About 1815, the Western Museum was founded by Robert Best, M.D., who seems to have been a capable collector. In 1818, the Western Museum Society sent out prospectuses and letters signed by Daniel Drake, Dr. Elijah Slack, president of the Cincinnati College and previously vice-president of Princeton (one has reason greatly to fear that he is the discoverer to Mrs. Trollope of Shakespeare's obscenity), and three amateur students of natural history, who engaged in business pursuits in Cincinnati. The principal aim of the Western Museum Society was to form a collection of objects of natural history and Indian antiquities of the Western country. Dr. Robert Best served as curator for a time; Audubon was a taxidermist and preparator; and Hiram Powers was a wax-modeler in the Museum. Rapid prosperity followed on the foundation of the Society and Museum—a typical frontier reaction of quick response —and its funds were in excess of four thousand dollars in 1820. The Society became extinct, however, in the early 'thirties, and the collections finally passed into the hands of the organization later known as the Cincinnati Society of Natural History. During the years 1826 to about 1835 the collections of the Society were under the charge of Mr. J. Dorfeuille, a Lyonnaise amateur naturalist who followed the trade of type-founder in Cincinnati. Murray, in 1839, found the Museum in a deplorable condition:

The museum contains little worthy of notice; moreover, its contents, mean as they are, are miserably deficient in order and arrangement. I was surprised and disappointed, as I had heard much of the valuable collection to be seen in this establishment. There are a few fossil mammoth bones of extraordinary size, and also a number of skulls found in some of the ancient mounds, differing materially in form from those of the modern race of Indians.

Mrs. Trollope acknowledges that during her sojourn in Cincinnati she found three persons who in culture and intellect were apparently her equals. These were good old Nicholas Longworth, the viticulturist, who got a poem from Longfellow by the expedient of presenting Longfellow with a cask of the blood of the vine from his extensive vineyards at Cincinnati. He was a piquant and rare character, full of whimsies and eccentricities; a man of Scotch meanness and Scotch generosity, who left a fortune estimated at between ten and fifteen million dollars. There was also Timothy Flint, who during the years 1831-1833 was editor of the *Western Review* at Cincinnati. He was a Congregational clergyman from New England, a graduate of Harvard, who after coming west still kept up his study of analytical chemistry and other branches of natural science. The third friend made by Mrs. Trollope was the artist Chester Harding. Could Mrs. Trollope but have explored the culture of the Cincinnati of her day, she would have found as fellow-residents Hiram Powers, the sculptor, and Martin Baum, a lover of all progress, who was actively instrumental in founding the first public library in 1802, the Western Museum in 1817, the Literary Society in 1817, and the first Agricultural Society in 1818. She would have found Albert von Steiner, who made some of the drawings for Wilson's celebrated work on ornithology; Matthias Schwab, who established here what was perhaps the first organ factory in the United States; Dr. Friedrich Reese, later Roman Catholic Bishop of Detroit; Dr. Wilhelm Nast, formerly of Tübingen, founder of German Methodism in America; and Frederick Eckstein and Gottfried Schadow, early teachers of Hiram Powers.

The early life of Hiram Powers is strikingly characteristic of the frontier of America. He came to Ohio with his family as a fourteen-year-old boy. On the death of his father, he removed to Cincinnati, where, after a short miscellaneous and profitless attempt to find himself, he discovered his métier. A German sculptor (was it Eckstein?) taught him clay-modeling, and his major interest in life was found. He took charge of the waxwork department of the Western Museum during the seven years preceding his removal to the national capital in 1835. While in Washington he modeled a number of busts of well-known men. In 1838 he finished his piece, "Eve Tempted," pronounced by Thorwaldsen to be a masterpiece; and five years later that piece by which, perhaps, he is best known—"The Greek Slave." He died in Florence in 1873.

About 1833 Dr. Daniel Drake instituted at his home in Cincinnati a series of "Social and Literary Reunions." At these parties gathered as regular attendants such cultivated persons as General Edward King, Judge James Hall (then editor of the *Western Monthly Magazine*),

Professor Calvin E. Stowe, Dr. Lyman Beecher and his daughter Harriet, Mrs. Caroline Lee Hentz and Professor Hentz (whom we earlier noted at the University of North Carolina), and Dr. Drake. The cultivated group in Cincinnati grew in numbers, boasting the accession of such men as Ephraim Perkins, William Henry Channing, David Guion the stonecutter, and his protégé, the sculptor Shobal Vail Clevinger. The sculptors Clevinger, Eckstein, and Powers had studios in Cincinnati in the late 'thirties, and were in constant contact and sympathy.

The years 1835 and 1837 saw the debut into the scientific world at Cincinnati of three excellent naturalists: John G. Anthony, J. L. Riddell, and Dr. Jared P. Kirtland. In his leisure from business affairs, Anthony published at later dates excellent papers on the mollusca in the *Proceedings* of the Academy of Natural Sciences of Philadelphia, the *Annals* of the Lyceum of Natural History of New York (now the New York Academy of Science), and the *Proceedings* of the Boston Society of Natural History (of all of which organizations he was a member), as well as in Silliman's Journal. While his publications all belong to a later date than that set as the close of the frontier period, nevertheless it was in 1835 that he began the extensive studies and correspondence on the biology of the mollusca which were the basis of his later scientific reputation.

Riddell, a former student of Amos Eaton at Rensselaer School who was graduated in medicine from the Medical College at Cincinnati in 1835, published valuable papers on the geology and botany of Ohio. It is of interest to Texans to learn that in April and May, 1839, he made a trip to Texas, and published his observations on the geology of the Trinity country, Texas, in Silliman's Journal of that year.

The third and greatest of this trio of naturalists of the frontier period in Cincinnati was Dr. Jared P. Kirtland. He lived in Cincinnati during the period from about 1837 to 1842. He came from Connecticut, with an M.D. degree gained at Yale in 1815. He arrived at Poland (now Belpré), Ohio, in 1823, and practiced medicine there for several years before he came to Cincinnati. Later he removed to Cleveland, where he became one of the founders of the Cleveland Medical College and of the Cleveland Academy of Science. He published in many fields of zoölogy; during the years 1834-1840 his most valuable contributions dealt with the habits and the sexual characteristics of the fresh-water mussels; with birds; and with the fishes of the Ohio River.

VIII

Brief mention should be made of certain other naturalists of the Northwest Territory. In 1826, Duke Bernhard of Saxe-Weimar-

Eisenach made in his American travels a detour from Cincinnati to Circleville, a town on the Scioto River twenty-six miles south of Columbus, to visit Caleb Atwater. He found Atwater, as he said in his *Reisen,* "a great antiquarian, [living] more in the antiquities of [the moundbuilders of] Ohio than in the present world." Atwater was one of the most interesting pioneers of the Northwest Territory. He was a large, heavily molded man with dark eyes and complexion and a Roman nose. Morose and eccentric, utterly careless of earning money, he was forced to engage in a constant battle against penury. A Massachusetts man with an Amherst degree (1804), he came to Circleville, Ohio (so named because the town was built on a great circular fortification left by the moundbuilders), and engaged in the practice of law. But his primary interest was the study of archeological and educational problems, and the promotion of conservation and internal improvements. He published a number of mediocre papers on geological and meteorological subjects in the period 1818-1826; but his best pioneer work was his extensive paper on the moundbuilders and their remains in Ohio, published in the first volume of *Archaeologia Americana* (1820); his book on Ohio (1827); and his extensive work, *The Writings of Caleb Atwater,* extending to over four hundred pages, which appeared at Columbus in 1833. Atwater's advocacy of state-wide education and internal improvements was notably endorsed in the election of 1824. He died in 1867 in the village where he had lived for fifty-two years, a neglected, disappointed, and unhappy man, forgotten by his generation.

At Marietta on the Muskingum, one of the earliest settlements in the Ohio country, lived Dr. S. P. Hildreth, physician-naturalist and historian, who practiced medicine there and engaged in scientific and historical research for more than fifty years. Marietta, which had been founded in 1788, was a shipbuilding center; even seagoing vessels were built in its yards. In the first decade of the nineteenth century, ships from this strange seaport eighteen hundred miles from the sea sailed as far away as Russia. Marietta was the home of Dr. Hildreth from 1808 to 1863. His papers on scientific subjects, published in Silliman's Journal over a long period of years beginning with 1825, show an acute and perceptive mind; but his work of most enduring value is his historical studies of the pioneers of the Old Northwest Territory. Hildreth was a Harvard man; he had taken his M.D. diploma from the Medical Society of Massachusetts in 1805, and had come to Poland (Belpré), Ohio, to practice in 1806, seventeen years before Kirtland. After two years in Poland he came to Marietta at a time when Washington County had only 5800 inhabitants (a density of population slightly less than that of Washington County, Texas, in 1850). He lived to see the establishment, in 1830-32, of Marietta College, and the development of the town into a true center of culture in Ohio.

Another frontier naturalist was Increase Allen Lapham, who during the years 1828-1837 published several papers in Silliman's Journal on the geology of Ohio. In 1836 he settled in Milwaukee, and during the pioneer period in Wisconsin published some useful papers on botanical and zoölogical subjects. Probably his best known work is his *Antiquities of Wisconsin,* which was published by the Smithsonian Institution in 1855.

IX

Nashville, charmingly situated in a bend of the Cumberland River in middle Tennessee, was founded during the last two decades of the eighteenth century. As Tennessee was settled and became a state (its population increased from 35,000 in 1790 to 105,000 in 1800, and to 262,000 in 1810), Nashville grew in population and importance. Cumberland College was founded in 1806, on the foundation of Davidson Academy (1785); the Nashville Bank was founded in 1807; and in 1826 Cumberland College became the University of Nashville.

Two years before this date, Dr. Philip Lindsley had come into the presidency of Cumberland College, which was then moribund, as the successor of James Priestley, LL.D., who had been president of this institution almost since it was chartered. Lindsley ranks with the best college presidents of his day. Like President Joseph Caldwell of the University of North Carolina, he was a graduate of Princeton, although a half-generation later than Caldwell. At the age of twenty-seven he had been made professor of languages at Princeton. He was of a fine, intelligent, and commanding countenance, and had a dignified air. He was, according to his Princeton associates, an ardent scholar, with a taste for the niceties of grammar and style. His classical attainments were accurate and thorough: indeed, said some of his compeers, perfect accuracy, even to the minutest details, was one of the peculiar characteristics of his scholarship. In 1817, on the removal of Elijah Slack to Cincinnati, he was made vice-president of Princeton; and in the same year, at the age of thirty-one, he was offered the presidency of Transylvania University and twice declined; Horace Holley, it will be remembered, was finally elected. In 1822 Lindsley was elected acting president of Princeton; and next year he was simultaneously elected president of Princeton, of Ohio University at Athens, and of Cumberland College. All three elections he declined. In 1824 he was again elected to the presidency of Cumberland College, was persuaded to visit Nashville, and finally accepted the position. Among

259

the factors inducing Lindsley to accept the presidency of this little frontier college was undoubtedly a recognition of the immense possibilities of the prospective university in the Old Southwest, together with the example of Holley's unparalleled success in the place which he himself had declined seven years before.

Lindsley worked heroically at Nashville. His Presbyterian orthodoxy saved his institution from the bigoted inquisition and denunciation of such theologians as had ultimately undermined Holley's work at Transylvania, and had seriously crippled the work at South Carolina College. But at the end of twenty-six years of devoted work —years in which steadfastly he had declined proffered advancements, saying "This one thing I do!"—his work at Nashville came to an end. In 1850 the University closed for lack of funds. In a baccalaureate sermon delivered at the university two years before the end came, Lindsley presented his *apologia*. Better than anything else that might be said, it shows under what conditions Lindsley came to the Southwestern frontier and the limitations under which he worked:

> When this college was revived and reorganized at the close of 1824 [Lindsley arrived in December, and found thirty students in attendance], there were no similar institutions in actual operation within two hundred miles of Nashville. There were none in Alabama, Mississippi, Louisiana, Arkansas, Middle or West Tennessee. There are now some thirty or more within that distance, and nine within fifty miles of our city. These all claim to be our superiors and to be equal at least to Old Harvard or Yale. Of course we cannot expect much "custom", or to command a large range of what is miscalled patronage. I have a list now before me of twenty colleges or universities in Tennessee alone. Several of these belong exclusively to individuals, and are bought and sold in open market like any other species of private property. They are invested with the usual corporate powers, and may confer all university degrees at pleasure. This is probably a new thing under the sun; but Solomon's geography did not extend to America.

Competent educational leadership and an opportunity to do intellectual pioneering invariably attract to university faculties scholars of integrity and worth. This was true at the University of Nashville when Lindsley was president. Possessed of much more restricted resources than Holley had at Transylvania, Lindsley nevertheless attracted to himself men of competence and promise.

Among the first men to come to Nashville under Lindsley was the young chemist George Thomas Bowen, a graduate of Yale, who had come to Cumberland College in 1825 as professor of chemistry. Bowen had so devoted himself to chemical and physical studies under Silliman during his undergraduate days at Yale that in his senior year (he took his degree in 1822) he had published two papers on mineral analysis in Silliman's Journal. His career at Nashville was very promising, but was cut short by his untimely death in the fall of 1828. He was a member of the American Geological Society and of the Academy of Natural Sciences of Philadelphia. The work of Bowen in the University was assumed at his death by his new colleague, Dr. Gerard Troost, who, the preceding spring, had been made professor of geology and mineralogy. Troost was an amiable and delightful character. He was a Hollander who, after studying medicine, natural history, and pharmacy in the Universities of Leyden and Amsterdam, had become a pupil of the great French mineralogist, the Abbé Haüy, in Paris; and had familiar personal acquaintance with Baron von Humboldt, the geologist Werner at Freiburg in Saxony, and Goldfuss at Bonn. It was he who translated Humboldt's *Ansichten der Natur* into Dutch.

In 1810, Troost had come to America and settled at Philadelphia. Two years later he assisted in the founding of the Philadelphia Academy of Natural Sciences, and was its first president, retaining the office until 1817. From 1825 to 1827 he was a member of Owen's community at New Harmony, Indiana. Through his friendship with Lindsley and Bowen (Bowen had met Troost in Philadelphia while Bowen was a medical student there after his graduation from Yale), Troost was induced to remove to Nashville in 1827. His geological and mineralogical collections, almost the finest private collections in the United States, his magnificent collection of the birds of Java (containing four hundred species), and his excellent library were brought from Philadelphia, and Troost settled in Nashville for the rest of his life. He died in Nashville in 1850, the year of the closing of the University.

Among his few colleagues at the University of Nashville were James Hamilton, A.M., a graduate of Princeton, who was intermittently professor of mathematics from 1827 to 1849; Nathaniel Cross, professor of ancient languages (1838-1850); President Lindsley; and Hamilton's successor in the chair of mathematics, Alexander P. Stewart, who after the Civil War became Chancellor of the University of Mississippi.

Troost was one of the most unusual naturalists of the frontier. He held memberships in the Museum of Natural History of Paris (to which he had been elected in 1810), the Geological Society of France, the Academy of Science and Letters at The Hague, the American Philosophical Society, the Academy of Natural Sciences of Philadelphia, and others. Professor L. C. Glenn, for many years professor of geology in Vanderbilt University, in his carefully written critical biography of Troost has given a charming picture of the naturalist:

Dr. Troost soon began to make geological expeditions over the state of Tennessee, and in an address delivered before the legislature on October 19, 1831, we find him already well informed regarding many of the state's natural history resources. . . . Physically, Dr. Troost was short and thickset with a distinctly German . . . physiognomy. . . . His manners were kindly and courteous and marked by unassuming simplicity. In his travels over the state [as State Geologist, which position he held from 1831 to 1850] he readily won the friendship and regard of all classes of people. . . . In his speech he retained enough of his Dutch accent to render his foreign birth apparent. . . . Dr. Troost was a scholar as well as a savant and philosopher. He was well acquainted with classic and general literature and was a master of several languages, ancient and modern, and perhaps there were but few works in Dutch, German, French, or English on any branch of natural science that he had not read or examined. Numerous references in his writings show that he kept up with the times and purchased the scientific works of his day in which he was interested as fast as they appeared. His library [now irretrievably lost] is described as large and judiciously selected and abounding not only in the standard works on science in the several languages above [mentioned] but also in valuable engravings, prints, and lithographs. . . . His interest in natural history which had already led him to the possession in 1828 of over 400 species of mounted birds from the island of Java alone, increased in his later life, and in his excursions over the state he collected natural history specimens as eagerly as geological ones. He became particularly interested in reptilian life, and snakes especially became a hobby with him. . . . Featherstonhaugh tells of Dr. Troost's travelling on top of a stage coach with two large rattlesnakes in a basket when, the cover coming unfastened, their peering heads caused a precipitate scattering of driver and passengers on top and within. Not in the least disturbed, Troost removed his coat, tied it over the basket and sought to quiet the fears of his fellow passengers by the advice, "Gendlemen, only don't let dese poor dings pite you unt dey won't hoort you." . . . Though a hard student he was not a recluse, but was a polished man of the world. He had travelled and seen much in the old world and had lived among the *savants* of Paris and mingled on easy and equal terms with the most polished circles of the city. He had been long familiar with the tone and atmosphere of fashionable society and never lost his fondness for the endearments of social life.

Troost's bibliography includes forty-five printed papers. His manuscript monograph on the Fossil Crinoids of Tennessee was to have been published posthumously by the Smithsonian Institution in the early 'fifties; but in an unlucky day it was submitted by Professor Joseph Henry, Secretary of the Smithsonian, to Professor James Hall of Albany, for revision before publication. Hall, as the world knows, suppressed and pirated it.

Troost's private museum which he had brought to Nashville was sold, part of it abroad some years before his death, and part, chiefly the geological portion, many years after his death. It was purchased in 1874 by the public library of Louisville for $20,500, which was considered about one-third of its proper value. It seems incredible that a collection of such richness could have been amassed by a teacher in a frontier college whose salary never exceeded a thousand dollars a year.

Troost deserves a place beside Rafinesque among the naturalists of the frontier. He lacked the coruscating genius and the multifaceted type of mind of Rafinesque; but he had staying power and enduring patience. In the end, he accomplished a great amount of good and useful work for the advancement of science; and his influence made itself felt in many widespread parts of the country in the persons of students whom he had taught, now themselves become teachers. Among his younger colleagues in the colleges of Tennessee and the frontier West he was genuinely helpful. To some of them, for instance to Dr. L. P. Yandell, later of Transylvania University and the Louisville Medical Institute, and to Professor James M. Safford (1822-1907), who from 1848 to 1873 was professor of the sciences in Cumberland University, Lebanon, Tennessee, he gave constant aid and inspiration. One of Troost's students at the University of Nashville, Richard B. Burleson, later came to Texas and as professor at Baylor University and as assistant on the Geological Survey of Texas under Buckley, contributed in a modest way to the development of the teaching of science in the early colleges of Texas.

Thus when the frontier period had passed, and in 1850 the American Association for the Advancement of Science held its meeting in Charleston, the Old South had had as investigators in the field of natural history a considerable number of gifted and vigorous workers. The South, however, had become preoccupied with the States' Rights movement, to which old Dr. Thomas Cooper of South Carolina College had already lent his aid in the 'twenties. From this time educational movements in the South dwindled; the last substantial man of science to come into the section before the Civil War was the geologist Alexander Winchell, who from 1850-53 was principal of various struggling academies in Alabama. With his departure to accept a professorship in the University of Michigan, in January, 1854, scientific investigations in the Old South by students of other sections may be said to have come to an end; and the Civil War, following shortly thereafter, wrote *Finis* to a chapter which in the frontier period had begun gloriously.

Appendix A

PRINCIPAL SOURCES OF THE FOREGOING CHAPTERS

Acknowledgments: In the course of researches extending over twenty years, I have incurred on every hand obligations so numerous as to make a detailed and specific acknowledgment out of the question. I desire here, however, to make record of my special obligation to the following persons for the loan of books and manuscript material, or for suggestions, information, and criticism: Miss Stella Drumm, Librarian of the Missouri Historical Society; Miss Nell C. Horner, Librarian of the Missouri Botanical Garden; Miss Ruth D. Sanderson, Librarian of the Gray Herbarium at Cambridge; Dr. John Hendley Barnhart, Bibliographer of the New York Botanical Garden; Dr. E. W. Gudger, Associate Curator, Department of Ichthyology, the American Museum of Natural History; Professor Jesse M. Greenman, Curator of the Herbarium of the Missouri Botanical Garden; Professor B. L. Robinson, late Curator of the Gray Herbarium; Professor L. L. Woodruff, of Yale University, and Mr. Andrew Keogh, Librarian of the University; and Mr. Alfred C. Potter, Librarian of Harvard University. Mrs. Austin H. Clark, Acting Librarian of the United States National Museum, has also helped me generously during my visits to the library under her charge. I am also under deep obligation to Professor James Franklin Jameson, head of the Division of Manuscripts of the Library of Congress. Mrs. Mattie Austin Hatcher and Miss Winnie Allen, Archivists of the University of Texas library, and Mr. E. W. Winkler, Bibliographer of the library, have given me unstinted aid, and I am under a very great obligation to them. This book first came into the mind of Professor John H. McGinnis of Southern Methodist University; and he has shown the greatest solicitude for my researches, and has given constant encouragement. My wife, Mrs. Bessie Teeple Geiser, has given unfailing help and most valuable criticism; and I have been glad to avail myself of her excellent knowledge of American history, and training in methods of historical research. Finally, I owe to Professor Henry Nash Smith, now of the University of Minnesota, a debt of thanks that can be known in its full extent only by writers who have worked with an editor of wide and deep scholarship, and critical ability of a high order.

My colleague, Professor Edwin J. Foscue, has generously helped by the preparation of the maps that accompany the text; and Professor George Bond has helped greatly in critical reading of the manuscript and the proofs.

CHAPTER I. THE NATURALIST ON THE FRONTIER

No student attempting to comprehend phenomena of the Frontier can avoid making serious study of the two classics in this field, Frederick J. Turner's *The Frontier in American History,* 1920, and Frederick L. Paxson's *History of the American Frontier, 1763-1893,* 1924. I have also, in the course of this chapter,

264

derived much help from an acute and penetrating essay by Professor Henry Nash Smith, entitled, "What Is the Frontier?" printed in the *Southwest Review,* XXI, 97-103, 1935.

CHAPTER II. JACOB BOLL

Obituary Notices: Galveston *Daily News,* Oct. 10, 21, 1880; Dallas *Daily Herald,* Oct. 1, 19, 1880; *American Naturalist,* XIV, 609-10, 1880.

Biography, critical estimates, documented: S. W. Geiser, (a) *Southwest Review,* XIV, 184-98, 1929; (b) Dallas *Morning News,* Oct. 21, 1928, portrait and facsimiles; (c) Dallas *Morning News,* Sept. 30, 1930; (d) *American Midland Naturalist,* XI, 435-52, portrait, 1929; (e) *Dictionary of American Biography;* (f) *Der Schweizer,* Nov. 30, 1929. Heinrich Frey, *Mittheilungen der schweizerischen entomologischen Gesellschaft,* VI, 47-51, 1880; August Siemering, *Der Deutsche Pionier,* XII, 399-400, 1880; *Appleton's Cyclopædia of American Biography.*

Descriptions and critical estimates of the work of Boll: R. T. Hill, Bulletin 45 of the U. S. Geological Survey, 1887; E. D. Cope, Bulletin 17 of the U. S. National Museum; S. W. Geiser, Dallas *Morning News,* July 25, 1929, Sept. 30, 1930; Heinrich Frey, *loc. cit.*

Other sources: Jacob Boll's Field Notes in Cope Collection, library of the American Museum of Natural History; letters from Jacob Boll in the library of the Museum of Comparative Zoölogy, Cambridge; letters to Boll, in possession of Miss Edith Beilharz and Mrs. Morgan M. Mayfield, Dallas; *Manuscript Proceedings* of the Boston Society of Natural History, March 23, Oct. 26, 1870; Apr. 21, Oct. 25, and Nov. 22, 1871; Jan. 3 and Feb. 28, 1872; *Manuscript Proceedings* of the Cambridge Entomological Society, Nov. 10, 1876 and Nov. 12, 1880; *Annual Reports* of the Trustees of the Museum of Comparative Zoölogy, 1870, 1871, 1872, and 1874.

Publications of Jacob Boll: Verzeichniss der Phanerogamen- und Kryptogamen-Flora von Bremgarten, dem untern Freiamt, Hallwilersee, Limmathal, und den angrenzenden Theilen des Kantons Zürich. Aarau, Druck und Verlag von J. J. Christen, viii + 127 pp., 1869; (with H. Frey) "Nordamerikanische Tineen," *Stettiner entomologischer Zeitung,* XXXIV, 201-24, 1873; (with H. Frey) "Einige Tineen aus Texas," *ibid.,* XXXVII, 209-28, 1876; "Ueber die Befruchtung der nordamerikanischen Yucca-Arten," *ibid.* XXXVII, 401-04, 1876; (with H. Frey) "Tineen aus Texas," *ibid.* XXXIX, 249-79, 1878; "Texas in its geognostic and agricultural Aspect," *American Naturalist,* XIII, 375-84, 1879; "Geological Examinations in Texas," *ibid.,* XIV, 684-86, 1880.

CHAPTER III. JEAN LOUIS BERLANDIER

Biography, critical, documented: S. W. Geiser, *Southwest Review,* XVIII, 431-49, 1933.

Other materials: Berlandier & Chovell, *Diario de Viage de la Comisión de Límites . . . ,* 1850; Sanchez, *Southwestern Historical Quarterly,* XXIX, 249-88, 1926; Berlandier, Chovell, and Terán Manuscripts in the Berlandier Collections of the Library of Congress, the library of the U. S. National Museum, the Yale University library, the library of the Gray Herbarium of Harvard University, and the library of the University of Texas; Baird-Couch letters in the library of the Smithsonian Institution; and a transcript of a Couch-Baird letter in the library of the Gray Herbarium. Materials descriptive of the political situation in Texas at the time of the expedition, and of the weather conditions encountered, are to be found in "J. C. Clopper's Journal" (*Quarterly* of the Texas Historical Association, XIII, 44-80, 1909), in some letters in the *Bexar Archives* of the time (especially that of Tomás M. Duke to Ramón Músquiz, June 27, 1828), and a number of letters of S. F. Austin, Ramón Músquiz, and Terán, printed in the *Austin Papers*, the letters dating from January to September, 1828. Censure of Berlandier is to be found in *Mémoires et Souvenirs de Auguste-Pyrame De-Candolle*, 1862, pp. 336-38.

CHAPTER IV. THOMAS DRUMMOND

Biography, critical, documented: S. W. Geiser, *Southwest Review*, XV, 478-512, portrait, 1930; Perley Spaulding, *Popular Science Monthly*, LXXIV, 48-50, portrait, 1909; *Dictionary of National Biography.*

Other materials: W. J. Hooker, *Companion to the Botanical Magazine*, I, 39-46, 1835 (original letters of Drummond to Hooker are preserved in the library of the Royal Botanical Gardens at Kew); Thomas Drummond, *Botanical Miscellany*, I, 178-219, 1830; John Franklin, *Narrative of a Second Expedition to the Shores of the Polar Sea . . .* , 1828, preface, also pp. 308-13; John Richardson, *Fauna Boreali Americana*, 1829-36, containing valuable notes on Drummond at the following places: I, xiv, xvi-xviii, 27-28; II, xv; III, xiv-xv; Edward R. Preble, *North American Fauna*, No. 27, pp. 58-61, 1908; Britten & Boulger, *Biographical Index of British and Irish Botanists*, 1893.

CHAPTER V. AUDUBON IN TEXAS

A completely documented account, here followed without documentation, appeared in S. W. Geiser, *Southwest Review*, XVI, 109-35, 1930.

CHAPTER VI. LOUIS CACHAND ERVENDBERG

Biography: S. W. Geiser, *Southwest Review*, XXII, 241-84, 1937; H. Seele, *Neu-Braunfelser Zeitung*, Jan. 12, 1888 (obituary of Mrs. Ervendberg).

Other materials: Church Books of the First Protestant Church of New Braunfels; Viktor Bracht, *Texas im Jahre 1848*, 1849; F. Roemer, *Texas . . .* , 1849, p. 120; *Comite-Bericht des Vereins zum Schutze deutscher Auswanderer in Texas*, 1850; Sarah S. McKellar, San Antonio *Express*, Sept. 8, 1935 (Sect. D, pp. 1, 3); R. L. Biesele, *The History of the German Settlements in Texas, 1831-1861*, 1930, pp. 126, 217-18; Johannes Mgebroff, *Geschichte der Ersten Deutschen Evangelisch-lutherischen Synode in Texas*, 1902, pp. 8, 122-23; G. G. Benjamin, *German American Annals*, VII, 49-51, 1909; M. Tiling, *History of the German Element in Texas from 1820-1850*, 1913, pp. 56-57; Friedrich Wilhelm von Wrede, *Lebensbilder . . .* , 1844, pp. 183-84, 253-54; Adams, *British Diplomatic Correspondence concerning the Republic of Texas*, 1918, p. 356; Ludolph F. Lafrentz, *Jahrbuch der Neu-Braunfelser Zeitung, 1926*, pp. 23-24; Gammel's *Laws of Texas*, II (pp. 948-50 for charter of the Hermann's University; p. 1384, for Act amending the Charter); Prince Carl von Solms, *Berichte* to the management of the Adelsverein, reprinted in *Jahrbuch der Neu-Braunfelser Zeitung, 1916, passim* (especially the Sixth and Tenth reports). The narrative of Bernhard Monken (1902), reprinted in the *Jahrbuch . . .* for 1924, pp. 23ff; A. H. Sörgel, *Neueste Nachrichten aus Texas*, reprinted in A. B. Faust, *The German Element in the United States*, 1909, I, 497-8; H. Seele, *Die Cypresse . . .* , 1936, pp. 55, 59, 103-4, 120-21, 137 (for materials on the summer of 1846 at New Braunfels, and the conditions at the *Waisenfarm*); F. L. Olmsted, *A Journey Through Texas,* 1857, (pp. 143-46 for a sympathetic account of social conditions in New Braunfels in 1854—the account of Ervendberg is found at pages 169-72); *Neu-Braunfelser Zeitung,* Oct. 5, 1855 (for date of Ervendberg's departure from New Braunfels). Asa Gray, in *Proceedings* of the American Academy of Arts & Sciences, v, 174-90, 1862, gives an account of Ervendberg's plant collections at Wartenberg.

Manuscript materials: Besides Church Records, and extensive German and Mexican correspondence, the following should be mentioned: Ervendberg-Gray correspondence in the Gray Herbarium; letters of Gustav W. Eisenlohr to Jakob Friedrich Eisenlohr, in possession of Eduard G. Eisenlohr of Dallas; records in office of Clerk of Courts of Colorado County, Texas, for real-estate holdings of Ervendberg at Blumenthal; records of Clerk of the District Court of Comal County, Texas, regarding the *Waisenfarm* and other matters related to Ervendberg's departure from Texas.

CHAPTER VII. FERDINAND JAKOB LINDHEIMER

Biography: S. W. Geiser, *Southwest Review,* xv, 245-66, portrait, documented, 1930; *Dictionary of American Biography;* J. W. Blankenship, Eighteenth Annual Report of the Missouri Botanical Garden, 1907, pp. 127-41, portrait; *Allgemeine Deutsche Biographie,* xviii, 697-98, 1883. Other sources of biographical character are F. J. Lindheimer's *Aufsätze und Abhandlungen,* 1879; F. Roemer, *Texas* ! . . , 1849, pp. 143 ff.; George Engelmann and Asa Gray, *Proceedings* of the Boston Society of Natural History, v, 210-64, 1845. See also Rosa Kleberg in *Quarterly* of the Texas Historical Association, ii, 170-73, 1898. August Siemering has a brief biography of Lindheimer in *Der Deutsche Pionier,* xi, 380-82, 1880, with a number of factual errors.

Manuscript materials: Lindheimer-Engelmann letters in the library of the Missouri Botanical Garden; Engelmann-Gray letters and two Lindheimer-Gray letters in the library of the Gray Herbarium. There are also some letters to J. W. Blankenship from M. E. Lindheimer and other Lindheimer descendants in the library of the Missouri Botanical Garden.

CHAPTER VIII. FERDINAND ROEMER

Biography, critical, documented: S. W. Geiser, *Southwest Review,* xvii, 421-60, portrait, 1932; F. W. Simonds, *American Geologist,* xxix, 131-40, portrait, 1902; Wilhelm Dames, *Neues Jahrbuch für Mineralogie, Geologie und Palaeontologie,* Jahrgang 1892, i, 1-32, *Anhang;* Roemer, *Texas* . . . , 1849, *passim.*

Other materials: John K. Strecker, *Baylor Bulletin,* xxxi, No. 3, *passim,* and Dr. John W. Lockhart, in the Galveston *Daily News,* April 30, 1893, have excellent accounts of the Tehuacana Trading House of Torrey & Barnard at the time of Roemer's visit; Mrs. M. H. Houstoun, *Texas and the Gulf of Mexico, or Yachting in the New World,* 1844; *Hesperos, or Travels in the West,* 1850, ii, 114-29; F. Roemer, *Die Kreidebildungen von Texas, und ihre organischen Einschlüsse,* 1852.

CHAPTER IX. CHARLES WRIGHT

Biography, critical, documented: S. W. Geiser, *Southwest Review,* xv, 343-78, 1930; *Field & Laboratory,* iv, 41-48, 1935; *Dictionary of American Biography;*

Thomas Thatcher, *Biographical and Historical Record of the Class of 1835 in Yale College* . . . , 1881, pp. 174-80; Asa Gray in *American Journal of Science, Third Series,* xxxi, 12-17, 1886; E. O. Wooton, *Bulletin* of the Torrey Botanical Club, xxxiii, 561-66, 1906; *Yale Obituary Record, 1880-90;* John R. Bartlett, *Personal Narrative of Explorations and Incidents* . . . , ii, 548-9, 1854; *Senate Executive Document* No. 64, 31st Congress, 1st Session, pp. 40-54, 1850.

Manuscript materials: Documents in the Alumni Office of Yale University; the Gray-Wright and Wright-Gray correspondence in the library of the Gray Herbarium; Wright-Engelmann correspondence in the library of the Missouri Botanical Garden. In the archives of the General Land Office of Texas are four letters written (1841) when Wright was County Surveyor of (old) Menard County (the letters are Nos. 1590, 1630, 1654, 1672).

CHAPTER X. GIDEON LINCECUM

Biography: S. W. Geiser, *Southwest Review,* xv, 93-111, portrait, documented, 1929; "Autobiography" of Gideon Lincecum, in *Publications* of the Mississippi Historical Society, viii, 443-519, 1904; obituary in Dallas *Daily Herald,* Dec. 12, 1874; *Dictionary of American Biography.*

Manuscript materials: Journals, letters, and other materials in the archives of the University of Texas library; letters from Lincecum in the library of the Smithsonian Institution.

Publications of Gideon Lincecum: (with Elias Durand) *Proceedings* of the Academy of Natural Sciences of Philadelphia, xiii, 98 ff.; *Journal* of the Linnæan Society of London (Zoölogy), vi, 29-31, 1862; *Proceedings* of the Academy of Natural Sciences of Philadelphia, xviii, 323-31, 1866; three papers in Vol. 1 of the *American Naturalist* (pp. 137 ff., 409 ff., 203 ff.), 1867; *Practical Entomologist,* i, 110, 1866; *Texas Almanac,* 1867, p. 195; *Proceedings* of the Academy of Natural Sciences of Philadelphia, xix, 24, 1867; *American Naturalist,* vii, 483-4, 1873; four papers in Vol. viii of the same journal, at pages 513, 564, and 593, 1874; "Autobiography," as above; "Choctaw Traditions about their Settlement in Mississippi, and the Origin of their Mounds," *Publications* of the Mississippi Historical Society, viii, 521-42, 1904; "Life of Apushimataha," *ibid.,* ix, 415-85, 1906. Lincecum also published a number of short papers in various issues of the *Texas Almanac,* 1857-74, as well as newspaper articles, usually signed, "Gid."

CHAPTER XI. JULIEN REVERCHON

Biography: S. W. Geiser, *Southwest Review,* xiv, 331-42, 1929; Dallas *Morning News,* Dec. 31, 1905; Nov. 23, 1919; March 26, 1922; June 15, 1924; May 8, 1927; March 19, 1933; C. S. Sargent, *Silva of North America,* xiii, 175-6, 1902.

Manuscript materials: Letters of Reverchon to Asa Gray, Thomas Morong, Sereno Watson, C. S. Sargent, and Lester F. Ward in the Gray Herbarium library; Reverchon-Engelmann correspondence in the library of the Missouri Botanical Garden.

Publications of Julien Reverchon: Botanical Gazette, xi, 56-59, 211-16, 1886; *Garden & Forest,* v, 615, 1892; *ibid.,* vi, 503, 524, 1893.

The genus *Reverchonia* is described by Asa Gray in *Proceedings* of the American Academy of Arts & Sciences, New Series, viii, 107, 1881.

Chapter XII. Gustaf Wilhelm Belfrage

Biography: S. W. Geiser, (a) *Southwest Review,* xiv, 381-98, 1929; (b) Dallas *Morning News,* Feb. 23, 1930, photographs; (c) *Entomological News,* xliv, 127-32, 1933; (d) *Field & Laboratory,* i, 47-50, 1933.

Other materials: Jenny Belfrage, *Bidrag till Släkten Belfrages Historia,* 1916; Cresson, "Hymenoptera Texana," *Transactions* of the American Entomological Society, iv, 153 ff., 1872; *American Naturalist,* xvii, 424, 1883. Advertisements inserted by Belfrage occur in volumes of *Entomologische Nachrichten, Bulletin* of the American Entomological Society, *North American Entomologist, Canadian Entomologist.*

Manuscript materials: Belfrage-Boheman letters (forty in number) and Belfrage-Stål letters in the archives of the Swedish Academy of Sciences, Stockholm (these were transcribed under supervision of Professor Dr. Yngve Sjöstedt, to whom I am under greatest obligations); letters by Belfrage to Baron von Osten Sacken, Philip R. Uhler, the Boston Society of Natural History, Samuel Henshaw, Alpheus Hyatt, Dr. H. Hagen, and Rowland Hayward, in the libraries of the Boston Society of Natural History and the Museum of Comparative Zoölogy at Cambridge; personal letters from Docent Dr. Sixten Belfrage, University of Lund, Sweden, and Captain Lennart Belfrage, *caput familiae* of the Belfrage clan in Sweden; personal letters from numerous old friends and acquaintances of Belfrage in Bosque County, Texas; probate records of Bosque County, Texas; letters of E. T. Cresson to Belfrage, published in Calvert's life of Cresson (*Transactions* of the American Entomological Society, lii, *Supplement,* xix-xxiii, 1928).

A great number of species of arthropods were named in honor of Belfrage, by Cresson (eleven in the "Hymenoptera Texana" alone), Zeller, Chambers, Fish, Grote, Morrison, Scudder, Stretch, J. B. Smith, Harvey, and Packard.

Chapter XIII. Notes on Scientists of the First Frontier

The present account, without the complete documentation of the original, follows S. W. Geiser, *Southwest Review,* xviii, 50-86, 1932.

Appendix B

A PARTIAL LIST OF NATURALISTS AND COLLECTORS
IN TEXAS, 1820-1880

Note.—The following list includes naturalists and collectors known to have worked in Texas in the period indicated. It is, of course, not complete. Dates of birth and death are given where this information is available; the omission of dates indicates a lack of definite information. Bibliographical references are included within parentheses. Where no reference is given, the reader is to understand that the facts presented are derived from miscellaneous sources—unpublished letters, manuscripts, etc.—which the author has consulted, but which are not readily accessible. The *Dictionary of American Biography* is referred to as *DAB; Appleton's Cyclopædia of American Biography* is referred to as *ACAB*.

ABERT, Lieutenant James William (1820-97).—This earnest student of ornithology, a member of the corps of Topographic Engineers, United States Army, traversed Panhandle Texas in 1846, and published his results in *Senate Executive Documents,* Vol. IV, No. 23, 30th Congress, 1st Session, 1848. (*ACAB*)

ADAMS, W. H.—Geologist and engineer; investigated deposits of coal in Mexico and Texas in the Eagle Pass region, and published his results in *Transactions* of the American Institute of Mining Engineers, X, 270-73, 1882.

ASHBURNER, Charles Albert (1854-89).—In the spring of 1879, Ashburner, then a member of the state Geological Survey of Pennsylvania, made an investigation of the "Brazos Coal Field" along the Clear Fork of the Brazos, in the northern part of Stephens County and the southern part of Young County. (*Transactions* of the American Institute of Mining Engineers, IX, 495-506, 1880; *ACAB, DAB*)

AUDUBON, John James (1780-1851).—The great ornithologist came to Texas in the spring of 1837, exploring Galveston Bay and Buffalo Bayou as far as Houston. He was accompanied by his son and Edward Harris. (Chapter V of the present work; *Southwest Review,* XVI, 108-35, 1930)

AUDUBON, John Woodhouse (1812-62).—Besides making the trip to Texas in 1837 with his father, J. W. Audubon collected mammals, etc., extensively in Texas during several months of 1845-46, and returned to Texas in March of 1849 for a brief trip through the Rio Grande valley at Brownsville en route to California.

BARTLETT, John Russell (1805-86).—This famous antiquarian and bibliographer, then much interested in ethnology, was in 1850 appointed Commissioner for the United States to run the boundary line between the United States and Mexico. He continued in this position until February, 1853. (*ACAB, DAB*)

BEHR, Ottomar von (1810-56).—A member of a noble family of lower Saxony dating from the twelfth century, von Behr came to Texas about 1846, later settling at Sisterdale. He was a kinsman of the distinguished California entomologist and physician, Dr. Hans Hermann Behr (1818-1904), and worked in meteorology and natural history. (*Bios*, v, 148-50, 1934)

BELFRAGE, Gustaf Wilhelm (1834-82).—The Swedish entomologist came to Texas in 1867 and worked chiefly in McLennan, Bosque, and (perhaps) Williamson counties. E. T. Cresson's *Hymenoptera Texana* (1872) was based largely on his collections of Hymenoptera. (Chapter xii of the present work; *Southwest Review*, xiv, 381-98, 1929; *Entomological News*, xliv, 127-32, 1933; *Field & Laboratory*, i, 47-50, 1933)

BENTON, Lieutenant James Gilchrist (1820-81).—Benton was an ordnance expert with the United States Army stationed at San Antonio, 1849-52. In 1854 he sent collections of fossils to the Smithsonian Institution. (*ACAB*)

BERLANDIER, Jean Louis (1805-51).—The Swiss naturalist came to Mexico in 1826 and explored for plants and animals in Texas, 1828-34. (Chapter iii of the present work; *Southwest Review*, xviii, 431-59, 1933)

BIGELOW, Artemas (1818-1901).—Collected plants in Texas during the summer of 1839. (*Alumni Record* of Wesleyan University, Connecticut, 1883, p. 19)

BIGELOW, Dr. John Milton (1804-78).—In 1850-53 Bigelow was Botanist of the U. S. and Mexican Boundary Survey under Bartlett; in the autumn of 1853 he accompanied Captain Whipple on the Pacific Railroad Survey along the Thirty-fifth Parallel, thus collecting along the Canadian River in Northwest Texas. His valuable papers appeared in the fourth volume of the Pacific Railroad Reports.

BLAKE, William Phipps (1828-1910).—Geologist on one of the Pacific Railroad Surveys (Williamson's). He was charged with preparing for publication Marcou's specimens and notes on the geology of the Whipple Survey. Later he made studies on the Big Wichita and Brazos rivers, and subsequently became professor of geology in the University of California. (*DAB; Who's Who in America; American Men of Science*)

BOLL, Jacob (1828-80).—Swiss naturalist and entomologist, whose collections in all fields of natural history in Texas are of the greatest importance. He came to Texas in 1869. (Chapter ii of the present work; *Southwest Review*, xiv, 184-98, 1929; *American Midland Naturalist*, viii, 435-52, 1929)

BOLLAERT, William.—This accomplished British antiquarian, ethnologist, and geographer (a Fellow of the Royal Geographical Society) resided and traveled in Texas from 1840-44. His journals, notes, personal narrative of residence and travel in Texas (1274 MS. pages), together with thirty-eight sketches, are in the Ayer Collection of the Newberry Library, Chicago.

BRACHT, Viktor.—After coming to Texas in the German immigration of 1844-47, Bracht was very observant of the fauna and flora of Texas, and in his book, *Texas im Jahre 1848*, 1849, gives an independent account of the natural history of the region.

BUCKLEY, Samuel Botsford (1809-83).—Buckley came to Texas in 1859. He was twice State Geologist of Texas, and also published on the botany of Texas and on North American ants. His work was uneven in quality, and frequently of little value. (*Southwest Review*, xvi, 133-4, 1930)

BUNSEN, Dr. Gustav (?1805-36).—Gustav Bunsen, brother of the well-known German-American educator, Georg Bunsen, came to Texas in 1836 from Belleville, and was killed (with most of Grant's men) on the Agua Dulce, about 26 miles west of San Patricio, March 2, 1836. He was well trained in the sciences.

BURLESON, Richard Byrd (1822-79).—Burleson came to Texas in 1855; he was Professor of Natural Sciences at Baylor University, 1857-61, and at Waco University, 1861-79. He had studied science with Gerard Troost at the University of Nashville. In 1874 he joined Buckley's second Texas Geological Survey, and contributed to Buckley's *Report* of 1876.

BUTCHER, H. B.—Collected birds in the vicinity of Laredo, 1866-67; sent collections of birds to the Smithsonian Institution (1866, 1867); published a paper on the birds of Laredo in the *Proceedings* of the Academy of Natural Sciences of Philadelphia, xx, 148-50, 1868.

CARTER, B. F.—Collected mollusca casually in Texas and sent some specimens to the Smithsonian Institution (1859).

CHURCHILL, General Sylvester (1783-1862).—Father-in-law of Spencer F. Baird. He accompanied General John Ellis Wool to Mexico *via* the "Wool Road"; in October, 1846, he collected fishes for Baird at the crossing of the Rio Grande.

CLARK, John Henry (b. 1830?).—Naturalist, surveyor; a native of Anne Arundel County, Maryland, and a former student of Spencer F. Baird at Dickinson College. Clark served as Zoölogist and Assistant Computer under Colonel J. D. Graham with the U. S. and Mexican Boundary Survey, 1850-55; during a part of this period Charles Wright was Botanist with the expedition. With Arthur Schott, Clark made very fine zoölogical collections; those of the vertebrates contained perhaps a hundred new species. (Dall, *Spencer Fullerton Baird*, 1915, *passim;* Bulletin 194, U. S. Geological Survey, 1902, pp. 14 ff.)

CONSTANT, Louis.—A Berliner who collected protista in Texas for Professor Christian Gottfried Ehrenberg. About 1844-46, he was successively at Cat Spring, Austin County, and at Indianola; and he lived in Austin County as late as 1861. (*Monatsberichte der Königlichen Preussischen Akademie der Wissenschaften*, Berlin, 1849, p. 87)

COUCH, Lieutenant Darius Nash (1822-97).—In 1853-54, Couch made an expedition into northern Mexico and southern Texas; he brought back to the Smithsonian Institution the fine Berlandier collections and manuscripts; subsequently he was for a time on duty at the Smithsonian Institution. (*ACAB; DAB;* Dall, *Spencer Fullerton Baird*, 1915, *passim*)

CRAWFORD, Dr. Samuel Wylie (1829-92).—An army surgeon attached for a time to Fort Clark (present Brackettville). He sent to the Smithsonian Institution (1853-57), for use in the Pacific Railroad Reports, large collections of vertebrates from the vicinity of Fort Clark and Las Moras Springs. He lived in Texas from 1851-60.

CRESSON, Ezra Townsend (1838-1926).—During the year 1859, this entomologist, later to attain eminence in his field, lived at New Braunfels, Comal County, and made collections of insects and other natural-history objects. (*Transactions* of the American Entomological Society, LII, ix [supplement], 1928)

272

DEAN, G. W.—In 1853 Dean collected, at Galveston, reptiles for the Smithsonian Institution.

DIFFENDERFER, Dr. W. L.—As surgeon and naturalist with Captain Pope's Expedition (1854) Diffenderfer collected plants, birds, and small mammals. Torrey and Gray published on his plant collections in Volume II of the Pacific Railroad Reports.

DOUGLAS, David (1798-1834).—Audubon and Bachman (in *Quadrupeds* . . . , I, 290, 1856) suggest, mistakenly, that Douglas collected for Professor William J. Hooker. Drummond was the first collector sent by Hooker to Texas.

DRESSER, H. E.—Dresser collected birds in Texas about 1865 and in *Ibis* (1865, pp. 312-30, 466-95; and 1866, pp. 23-46) published an extended paper on the birds of southern Texas.

DRUMMOND, Thomas (?1790-1835).—The Scottish botanical collector did distinguished botanical and zoölogical collecting in Texas in 1833-34, chiefly in the old Austin Colony and on Galveston Island. (Chapter IV of the present work; *Popular Science Monthly,* LXXIV, 48-9, 1909; *Southwest Review,* XV, 478-512, 1930)

DURHAM, George T.—Durham, who at that time was a resident of Austin, published valuable articles on "Game in Texas" in the *Texas Almanac* for 1868 and 1869.

EMORY, William Hemsley (1811-87).—After the Mexican War, Emory was assigned to duty as Chief Astronomer for running the boundary between California and Mexico (1851); in 1854 he was appointed Commissioner and Astronomer for running the boundary under the Gadsden Treaty. He collected mammals along the Rio Grande for the Smithsonian Institution (1853).

ERNST, Friedrich (d. 1858).—Ernst came to Texas in 1831 and founded Industry, Austin County. A former head gardener of the Grand Duke of Oldenburg, he was the first able botanist and horticulturist in the colony of Texas. (*Bios,* V, 142, 1934)

ERVENDBERG, Louis Cachand (1809-63).—From 1849 to 1855, Ervendberg was actively interested in scientific, experimental agriculture at "New Wied," near New Braunfels, Comal County. He collected plants for Asa Gray at New Braunfels, and (after 1855) near Tantoyuca, Vera Cruz, Mexico. (*Bios,* V, 144, 1934; Chapter VI of the present work)

FALCONER, Thomas (1805-82).—Falconer was a member of the Santa Fe Expedition of 1841-42, and published an account of the expedition in London in 1844. He had good scientific training, was of some note as a traveler, and in 1844 published a second book, on the discovery of the Mississippi River, and the boundaries—western, northwestern, and southwestern—of the United States.

FEATHERSTONHAUGH, George W. (1780-1866).—A brilliant British geologist (F.R.S., F.G.S.), Featherstonhaugh made a brief stop on Texan soil near Texarkana, in December, 1834. (Merrill, *The First Hundred Years of American Geology,* 1924, 136-38; Featherstonhaugh, *Excursion Through the Slave States,* 1844, II, 148-94)

FENDLER, Augustus (1813-83).—Fendler came to Houston in 1839, and lived there in obscurity for a year. Later he became a most distinguished botanical collector for Asa Gray. (*Popular Science Monthly,* LXXIII, 240-43, 1908)

FLEWELLING, R. T.—In the *Texas Almanac* for 1870, 99-103, is a paper by this student on the Cotton Caterpillar.

FOARD, Dr. Andrew Jackson (d. 1867).—As army surgeon at Fort Davis, Foard sent mammals from that locality to the Smithsonian Institution (1858). He also sent large collections of Texas vertebrates for Volume IX of the Pacific Railroad Reports.

FORCKE, August (1814-1903).—Forcke, who had had German university training in the sciences, came to Texas in 1846 with Prince Solms's colony, as official apothecary at New Braunfels. (*Bios,* v, 145, 1934; Brown, *Indian Wars and Pioneers of Texas,* 189—, pp. 694-95)

FORSHEY, Caleb Goldsmith (1812-81).—Engineer, naturalist. He collected mollusks, etc., for naturalists in Philadelphia and for the Smithsonian Institution, and published (1853-79) a series of papers, chiefly on the geology and hydrography of Louisiana, on the physics of the Mississippi River, and on the geology of the Mississippi Delta. He came to Texas about 1855 as engineer. Later he became Superintendent of the Texas Military Institute (Galveston and Rutersville). A valuable paper on phenology in Fayette County for 1858-60 was published in the *Texas Almanac* for 1861. (*ACAB*)

FRIEDRICH, Otto (1800-80).—Lepidopterist and naturalist, living in the hills close to present Gruene, near New Braunfels. He came to Texas for the second time in 1850. (*Southwest Review,* XVII, 444-45, 1932)

FROEBEL, Dr. Julius (1805-93).—A noted German revolutionary, mineralogist, physiographer, and economist, nephew of the famous Professor Froebel. He came to Texas about 1853 and collected materials in Texas for the Smithsonian Institution. (See his *Aus Amerika: Erfahrungen, Reisen, und Studien,* 2 vols., 1857-58)

FURMAN, John H.—Furman published a paper, "The Geology of the Copper Region of Northern Texas and the Indian Territory," in the *Transactions* of the New York Academy of Sciences, I, 15-20, 1882.

GANTT, Dr. W. H.—Sent samples of infusorial earth, and birds' eggs and nests, from Union Hill, Washington County (three miles north of present Burton), to the Smithsonian Institution (1857-59).

GIRAUD, Jacob Post (1811-70).—Giraud published in 1841 a folio paper of 16 leaves (8 plates) entitled, "A Description of Sixteen New Species of North American Birds . . . collected in Texas in 1838." I have not seen this, but from the fact that but three of Giraud's "species" have subsequently been collected in Texan territory, I surmise that Giraud himself did not collect them. The types of these "species" were presented to the Smithsonian Institution in 1867.

GLENN, John W.—State Geologist of Texas (1873-74); made no scientific publications. (Hill, Bulletin 45, U. S. Geological Survey, 1887)

GRAHAM, Colonel James Duncan (1799-1865).—Topographical engineer, naturalist. He came into Panhandle Texas in 1820 with Major Stephen H. Long's Expedition; he was Principal Astronomer and Head of the Scientific Corps of the U. S. and Mexican Boundary Survey, 1850-54. (*ACAB, DAB*)

HALDEMAN, Lieutenant Horace (d. 1883).—While in service at Fort Martin Scott (Fredericksburg) and Fort Gates (present Gatesville) in the late 'forties and early 'fifties, Haldeman sent numerous insects and other natural-history objects to S. S. Haldeman (see below). Three new species of Hymenoptera, one new species of Hemiptera, and two new species of Coleoptera, all collected at Fort Gates, were described by S. S. Haldeman in Stanbury's report on the Great Salt Lake Region (1853).

HALDEMAN, Samuel Stehman (1812-80).—My friend, Mr. F. F. Bibby, of the Texas Agricultural Experiment Station, believes that the elder Haldeman collected insects in Liberty and Hardin counties. Of this I am not at present certain; but in a letter to Spencer F. Baird (Dec. 3, 1847), Haldeman suggests that he is contemplating a collecting trip to the Southwest during the summer of 1848.

HALL, Elihu (1822-82).—One of the organizers of the Illinois Natural History Society at Bloomington (1858), and in 1862 plant collector in the mountains of Colorado with Dr. C. C. Parry and J. P. Harbour. In 1872 Hall collected 861 species of plants in East Texas, which Asa Gray distributed to subscribers. (*Botanical Gazette,* IX, 59-62, 1884)

HANCOCK, John (1824-93).—Hancock settled in Texas in 1847, became Attorney-General, and later established a military telegraph along the frontier of Texas. He was interested in mineralogy, and presented to the U. S. National Museum (1880) a collection of minerals from Texas and Arizona.

HARRIS, Edward (1799-1863).—Came to Texas with the Audubons in 1837. He collected principally birds and birds' eggs. (*Cassinia,* VI, 1-5, 1902; *Southwest Review,* XVI, 108-35, 1930)

HAYES, Dr. S.—An army surgeon (?). Hayes collected in the neighborhood of Fort Belknap bird-skins, mammals, and various other specimens for the Smithsonian Institution (1859).

HEATON, L. D.—Collected Texas reptiles for the Smithsonian Institution (1870).

HEERMANN, Dr. Adolphus L. (1818-65).—In 1853, Heermann collected birds in Texas as he was traversing the state to join Far-Western expeditions connected with the Pacific Railroad Surveys (*Cassinia,* XI, 1-6, 1907). He died in San Antonio.

HEILIGBRODT, Ludolph (1847-1911).—While he was working as clerk in a store at Serbin, Texas, Heiligbrodt came across the published works of Hermann Burmeister. These stimulated him to collect insects; he later became (for forty years) first janitor, then teacher in the schools of Bastrop, Texas. Cresson's *Hymenoptera Texana* (1872) used his collections.

HERBST, Carl Friedrich.—Long a resident of Brenham, he became interested in silk-raising in the closing days of the Republic; in 1878 he planted some thousands of Japanese and Italian mulberries to serve as food for silkworms. He was active in urging silkworm cultivation in this state. (*Schütze's Jahrbuch für Texas, 1883,* 1882, pp. 110-11)

HERFF, Dr. Ferdinand Ludwig Johann Arnold von (1820-1912).—He studied at Bonn, Berlin, and Giessen. At Berlin he sat under Johannes Müller; at Giessen studied with Professor Justus von Liebig. He took his M.D. at Giessen (1842) and came to Texas in 1847 with the Darmstädter Kolonie (Bettina, near present Castell). During his days at Bonn, Herff had become interested in botany, and early in his Texas career he planned to explore botanically the Rocky Mountains and California, with Duke Paul of Württemburg; this project was never carried through. He practiced medicine in San Antonio, 1849-1908, and became the most distinguished surgeon in the Southwest.

HIELSCHER, Theodor.—Published in *Schütze's Jahrbuch für Texas, 1883, 1882*, pp. 63-73, highly interesting observations on coal at Eagle Pass, and a notice of finding vertebrate fossil remains in the same locality. His work was done in the 'seventies.

HUFF, William.—About 1835-45, Huff collected large numbers of Pleistocene mammals in the vicinity of San Felipe, Austin County. (*Southwest Review*, xvi, 132, 1930)

ISAAC, J. C.—From Ilges' Ranch, Wyoming. He worked as fossil collector for Edward Drinker Cope in the Bad Lands of South Dakota (1876); in the winter and spring of 1877-8, Isaac and Jacob Boll collected together for Cope in the Wichita country of Northwest Texas. (Osborn, *Cope: Master Naturalist*, 1931, *passim;* Sternberg, *Life of a Fossil Hunter*, 1909, *passim*)

JAMES, Dr. Edwin (1797-1861).—As surgeon with Long's Second Expedition (1820), James collected plants and fossils along the Canadian River in the Texas Panhandle. (*Popular Science Monthly*, lxxv, 497-8, 1908)

JENNEY, Walter Proctor.—Worked (1874) on the geology of western Texas near the Thirty-second Parallel. Between 1874 and 1889, he published five geological papers.

JEWETT, Colonel Ezekiel [B.?] (1791-1877).—Sent Texas reptiles to the Smithsonian Institution (1857). (*American Naturalist*, xi, 505, 1877; *American Journal of Science*, Third Series, xiv, 80, 1877)

KALTEYER, Friedrich (1817-84).—The elder Kalteyer studied at Mainz and Giessen, at the latter place with the famous chemist Justus von Liebig, then just beginning to turn his attention to animal and plant chemistry. Kalteyer came to Texas in 1846; for a time he practiced medicine at Boerne; he lived at San Antonio as apothecary for many years. He was an intimate friend of Dr. Ferdinand Herff.

KALTEYER, George H. (1849-97).—In 1872, Kalteyer sent teeth of a Cretaceous shark, *Ptychodus*, from Texas to the Smithsonian Institution; in 1873-4 he made chemical analyses for the Texas Geological Survey under John W. Glenn; in 1885, upon the incorporation of the Museum of Natural History at San Pedro Springs, San Antonio, he was elected vice-president and director.

KELLOGG, Dr. Albert (1813-87).—Professor W. L. Jepson (*DAB, s.v.* "Albert Kellogg") states that Kellogg came to Texas with the elder Audubon. This would have been in 1837. My evidence, to me conclusive, seems to show that neither in 1837, in 1845-6, nor in 1849 (all the possible dates) did Kellogg accompany any of the Audubons to Texas. The statement, based by Jepson on Edward L. Greene's published sketch of Kellogg, seems thus to be in error.

KELLOGG, F.—A resident of Wheelock, Robertson County. In the early 'sixties Kellogg sent birds' eggs and Tertiary shells to the Smithsonian Institution.

KENNEDY, William (1799-1871).—A widely-educated, acute-minded Britisher, in the consular service in Texas (1839; 1841-47). His *Texas* (2 vols., with total of 984 pages, London, 1841) is a classic, of great scientific value. (Hill, Bulletin 45, U. S. Geological Survey, 1887, p. 13)

KENNERLY, Dr. Caleb Burwell Rowan (1830-61).—From 1854 to 1857, Kennerly collected all sorts of materials for the U. S. and Mexican Boundary

Survey. He was a former student of Spencer F. Baird at Dickinson College. (Dall, *Spencer Fullerton Baird,* 1915, *passim*)

KERR, Washington Caruthers (1827-85).—Kerr, in later life a noted geologist in North Carolina, was graduated from the University of North Carolina in 1850, came to Texas in that year, and during 1851-52, held a professorship in Marshall University, at Marshall. He left this place in 1852 for Cambridge, Massachusetts, to accept a position as computer in the office of the *Nautical Almanac. (ACAB, DAB)*

KIMBALL, James Putnam (1836-1913).—Kimball was a prominent consulting geologist of New York City who published notes on the geology of western Texas and Chihuahua. (*American Journal of Science,* Second Series, xlviii, 378-88, 1869)

KING, Dr. William Shakespeare (d. 1895).—As an army surgeon in Texas, King sent mammals to the Smithsonian Institution (in 1859 and earlier), and these were used in working up the reports in Volumes viii-x of the Pacific Railroad Reports.

KIRBY-SMITH, Captain Edmund (1834-93).—On the Texas military frontier (1852-58), Kirby-Smith collected plants for the U. S. and Mexican Boundary Survey while in command of its military escort (1852-55).

KLAPPENBACH, Georg.—A former Burgomaster of Anklam, near Stettin, Klappenbach lived at New Braunfels, 1846+. He was an amateur geologist and paleontologist, with a remarkable collection of fossils. (*Bios,* v, 144, 1934)

KÜCHLER, J.—A scientifically-trained German of Gillespie County who published, about 1859, a paper on climatic fluctuations in that region, from 1725 to 1858. Küchler based his conclusions on the characteristics shown by the growth-rings of aged post-oak trees which he compared. His data are reprinted in the *Texas Almanac* for 1861, 137-38.

LANGENHEIM, Wilhelm.—An amateur geologist and collector, also of New Braunfels. He came to Texas in 1830 and participated in the Revolution. Later he went back to Germany and did not return to Texas until 1846. (Roemer, *Texas,* 1849, pp. 196 ff.)

LEAVENWORTH, Dr. Melines Conkling (1796-1862).—Collected plants for a short time in East Texas in 1835. (*American Journal of Science,* Second Series, xxxv, 306, 1863)

LECLERC, Dr. Louis Joseph Frédéric (b. 1810).—A French physician born in Tours, a graduate of the Faculty in Paris, and later connected with the medical school and hospital at Tours, Leclerc first described the famous San Felipe deposits of Pleistocene mammals, which he saw in the summer of 1838. He published his "Texas et sa Révolution" in the *Revue des deux Mondes* in 1840, and later in the year had it reprinted in book form.

LINCECUM, Dr. Gideon (1793-1874).—A naturalist resident in Long Point, Washington County, 1848-74. His most noted observations were made on the Agricultural Ant. (Chapter x of the present work; *Southwest Review,* xv, 93-111, 1930)

LINDHEIMER, Ferdinand Jakob (1801-79).—Lindheimer came to Texas in 1836, and in 1843-52 collected plants for Asa Gray. (Chapter vii of the present work; *Southwest Review,* xv, 245-66, 1930)

LONG, Major Stephen Harriman (1784-1864).—Long was leader of the expedition through Panhandle Texas in 1820 with which Dr. Edwin James was

Naturalist. (*DAB; National Cyclopædia of American Biography*, xi, 365, 1909)

McCLELLAN, Captain George Brinton (1826-85).—Collected alcoholic material for Baird and Girard, while connected with Marcy's Exploration of the Red River (1852). (Dall, *Spencer Fullerton Baird*, 1915, pp. 282-83)

McCOOK, Rev. Henry Christopher (1837-1911).—In 1876 McCook studied the Agricultural Ant near Barton's Spring, Austin; his book based on this study, *The Natural History of the Agricultural Ant of Texas*, was published in 1879.

McELDERRY, Dr. Henry (d. 1898).—Served as Surgeon in the late 'sixties with the troops on the Upper Brazos (Double Mountain Fork), and sent fossils to the Smithsonian Institution (1870).

MARCOU, Jules (1824-98).—The world-famous geologist did extremely careful work on the geology of the Whipple Survey in Panhandle Texas (1852-3). Through a misunderstanding with Jefferson Davis, then Secretary of War, he was deprived of his notes and specimens; and another scientist was assigned to write his report. American prestige in Europe suffered seriously as a result of this episode.

MARCY, Captain Randolph Barnes (1812-87).—Reported briefly on mammals collected during his Red River exploration (1852), in the printed account of the expedition (1854, pp. 300-01; see also Dall, *Spencer Fullerton Baird*, 1915, p. 283). He also made an exploration (1854) of the sources of the Big Wichita and Brazos rivers (report published 1856).

MARNOCH, Gabriel William.—Came to Texas probably in the late 'sixties, settling on Helotes Creek, northwest of San Antonio. He was natural-history collector for E. D. Cope (1877). (Cope, Bulletin 17, U. S. National Museum, 1880, *passim*; Osborn, *Cope: Master Naturalist*, 1931, pp. 235-40)

MARSHALL, Lieutenant Louis Henry (d. 1891).—An officer of the Third Infantry, Marshall collected fishes, reptiles, and insects on Pope's Expedition through Northwest Texas (1854). (Pacific Railroad Reports, Vol. ii)

MENGER, Dr. Rudolph (1851-1921).—Native of San Antonio, Menger studied at Leipzig (1869-1874), and took his degree of M.D. there. He was an indefatigable naturalist. (*Schütze's Jahrbuch für Texas, 1883*, 1882, pp. 83-90; Menger, *Texas Nature Observations and Reminiscences*, 1913, *passim*)

MERRILL, Dr. James Cushing (1858-1902).—Merrill served for twenty years as surgeon at Western and Southwestern army posts; he sent birds, insects, mammals, and fishes from Texas to the U. S. National Museum, and published "Notes on the Ornithology of Southern Texas" (*Proceedings* of the U. S. National Museum, i, 118-73, 1878).

MEUSEBACH, Baron Ottfried Hans von (1812-97).—Meusebach came to German Texas in 1845 as Commissioner-General of the Adelsverein colony. Excellently trained in the sciences, he actively explored the mineral resources of the Fisher & Miller Grant, and facilitated the explorations of Roemer, Lindheimer, and others. (*Southwest Review*, xv, 256, 1930; *Bios*, v, 144-45, 1934)

MICHLER, Lieutenant Nathaniel (1827-81).—Michler, a topographic engineer of the United States Army, was well trained in the sciences and collected natural-history specimens on several explorations made in Texas for the War Department. (*ACAB, DAB*)

MITCHELL, Joseph Daniel (1848-1922).—Mitchell, one of our first native Texan naturalists, was a gifted amateur student of Texas mollusks, insects, and reptiles. He served as collaborator with the U. S. Bureau of Entomology, and published an extended memoir on the snakes of Texas in an early volume of the *Proceedings* of the Texas Academy of Science. Mitchell lived at Victoria, and his activity commenced about 1876 or 1878.

MÖLLHAUSEN, Heinrich Balduin (1825-1905).—In 1853-54, Möllhausen was topographer and artist with Whipple's Survey along the Thirty-fifth Parallel; the birds collected by Möllhausen and Dr. C. B. R. Kennerly on this survey were described by Spencer F. Baird in the Pacific Railroad Reports, Vols. III and IV.

'MONTEIL, Nicolas Antoine (1771-1833).'—In *Appleton's Cyclopædia of American Biography,* 1888, IV, 365, 'Monteil' is reported as having worked at the Champ d'Asile in 1817. My own investigations, together with those of Dr. John Hendley Barnhart twenty years ago, compel me to say that this is one of many 'scientific' hoaxes found in that *Cyclopædia.* 'Monteil' is entirely fictitious. (*Field & Laboratory,* III, 11-12, 1934)

MONTGOMERY, Edmund Duncan (1835-1911).—A distinguished British-American biologist and philosopher, who lived at Hempstead, Texas, 1872-1911. (*Southwest Review,* XVI, 200-35, 1931; *DAB*)

MOORE, Dr. Francis, Jr. (d. 1864).—After serving as a surgeon in the Texan Army in 1836, Moore became editor of the Houston *Telegraph and Texas Register* (1837-57), and in 1860 was State Geologist of Texas. He was author of *Map and Description of Texas* (143 pp., 18mo., Philadelphia, 1840; 2nd ed., 1844) and of newspaper articles on Texas natural history.

MOORE, John W.—A native of Connecticut, Moore was alcalde of Harrisburg for some years preceding 1836. He was an army-contractor during the Texan War of Independence. The elder Audubon tells of his collecting plants for him, when Audubon came to Texas in 1837. (R. Buchanan, *Life and Adventures of Audubon the Naturalist,* 1864, chap. lvi; *Southwest Review,* XVI, 122, 1930)

MOSS, Theodore F.—Appointed Geologist of Bartlett's Advance Party with the U. S. and Mexican Boundary Survey. I have been unable to find more information concerning Moss; Darton lists no publications by him, and Dr. R. T. Hill does not mention him in his historical account of geological work done in Texas (1887).

MUNSON, Thomas Volney (1843-1913).—Munson came to Denison, Texas, in 1876, and there did all of the horticultural investigation on the grape that made him famous. (*DAB, s.v.* "T. V. Munson")

NEHRLING, Henry (1853-1929).—Nehrling studied the birds of Texas at Houston and at Fedor (Lee County), 1879-82, and published his observations in his *Die Nordamerikanische Vogelwelt* (1891).

OLMSTED, Frederick Law (1822-1903).—Olmsted, later to become famous as a horticulturist and landscape architect, toured Texas on horseback in 1854-55, and in 1857 published his well-known *A Journey Through Texas.*

PARKER, William B.—In the autumn of 1854, Parker accompanied Captain Marcy through North Texas to the sources of the Big Wichita and the Brazos; a popular book (xii + 242 pp.) on his travels was published in Philadelphia in 1856.

PARRY, Dr. Charles Christopher (1823-90).—In 1850-53, Botanist and Geologist on the U. S. and Mexican Boundary Survey under Major W. H. Emory. (*Proceedings* of the Davenport Academy of Sciences, vi, 35-52, 1893)

PEASE, Captain Walter B. (d. 1882).—Sent Lepidoptera from Texas to the Smithsonian Institution (1866).

PITCHER, Dr. Zina (1797-1852).—Collected fossils and plants in Texas along the Red River, opposite Fort Towson (1833). The fossils were sent to Dr. S. G. Morton of Philadelphia, who described them in his synopsis of Cretaceous fossils of the United States (1834). Later Pitcher was instrumental in founding the Medical School of the University of Michigan.

PLUMMER, Captain Joseph Bennett (1820-62).—Collected birds, reptiles, and fossils in Texas for the Smithsonian Institution (1859).

POSELGER, Dr. Heinrich.—Possibly, though not certainly, the son of the celebrated mathematician of Berlin, Friedrich Theodor Poselger (1771-1838). In the period 1850-56, Heinrich Poselger collected plants for the U. S. and Mexican Boundary Survey on the lower Rio Grande; he also collected near Corpus Christi. He sent his cacti to Dr. David Dietrich, custodian of the herbarium at Jena. Poselger describes some varieties of cacti which Engelmann recognizes in his "Cacti of the U. S. and Mexican Boundary Survey," 1859.

RAVENEL, Henry William (1814-87).—In 1869, Ravenel was sent to Texas by the United States Government to investigate a disease of cattle prevalent here. At this time he collected fungi extensively in East Texas, and M. C. Cooke, I believe, published on Ravenel's collections in 1878. Ravenel also collected in East Texas for the Smithsonian Institution mollusks and alcoholic material (1869).

REINHARDT, Louis (1833-190—).—As a boy of fifteen, Reinhardt was sent out from the Technical School at Darmstadt with the Darmstädter Kolonie to botanize in Texas. (*Quarterly* of the Texas Historical Association, iii, 33-40, 1899)

REMER, Dr. Wilhelm (?1802-?1860).—A member of a famous Breslau family of scientists, Remer came to Texas in the German immigration of 1845. (*Bios*, v, 150-51, 1934)

REMOND, Émile (1840-1906).—A member of Victor Considerant's Fourieristic colony, "Réunion," near Dallas. He was a geologist, with particular interest in clays and cement-materials. He collected numerous Cretaceous and Pleistocene invertebrate and vertebrate fossils: his collection was long exhibited at the State Fair of Texas.

REVERCHON, Julien (1837-1905).—Came to Dallas from Lyons, France, in 1856; also a colonist of Réunion. He explored for plants extensively in North and Northwest Texas, and (in the late 'seventies) along the old army road from Fort Belknap to Fort Inge. (Chapter xi of the present work; *Southwest Review*, xiv, 331-42, 1929)

RIDDELL, John Leonard (1807-65).—Student under Amos Eaton at the Rensselaer School, Troy, N. Y.; Professor of Chemistry in the Medical College of Louisiana (1836-65); inventor of the binocular microscope. Riddell investigated the geology and botany of the Trinity country of Texas in April-May, 1839. (*American Journal of Science*, xxxvii, 211-17, 1839)

RIDDELL, William Pitt (1828-72).—Brother of J. L. Riddell. In 1858-60 he was Chemist and Assistant Geologist of the Texas Geological Surveys under Shumard and Moore.

ROEMER, Karl Ferdinand (1818-91).—In 1845-47, this great German geologist spent eighteen months in Texas; later he published two books and six papers on his findings. (Chapter VIII of the present work; *Southwest Review*, XVII, 421-60, 1932)

ROESSLER, Anton R.—Young, ambitious, and well-trained (possibly in Vienna), an excellent cartographer, Roessler published a number of geological contributions (1868-76); but his best work was done on the mapping of Texas. (Hill, Bulletin 45, U. S. Geological Survey, 1887)

SCHLOTTMANN, Dr. Adolphus (d. ?1873).—A native of Hamburg with a medical education gained in Germany. He came to Texas in 1853, and was physician and apothecary at Round Top, Fayette County, 1853-73. He collected insects and sent a collection to the Smithsonian Institution from Fayette County (1872).

SCHOTT, Arthur (1814-75).—In 1853-55, Schott was First Assistant Surveyor under Major Emory on the U. S. and Mexican Boundary Survey. He collected many Orthoptera and Coleoptera later described by Dr. J. L. LeConte. He also surveyed the Rio Grande from Eagle Pass to the mouth of the Pecos; he was artist of the Boundary Survey, and made the many topographic sketches and colored ethnological plates included in the reports of the Survey. He published six geological papers dealing with the Rio Grande country (1855-66). With John H. Clark he made splendid collections of animals for the Survey, and collections of fossils and minerals in the Rio Grande valley.

SENNETT, GEORGE B. (1840-1900).—During the years 1877-78, Sennett made two trips of some two months each to collect birds along the lower Rio Grande in Texas; he made a third, longer trip in 1882. He published his results in the *Bulletin* of the U. S. Geological Survey of the Territories, Vol. IV, No. 1, pp. 1-66, 1878; Vol. V, No. 3, pp. 371-440, 1879.

SHARP, Dr. Redfield.—An army surgeon stationed at San Antonio; he sent specimens of insects and reptiles in alcohol from San Antonio to the Smithsonian Institution (1866).

SHINN, James (1807-96).—A famous Quaker horticulturist, who went from (?Houston) Texas to California in 1855. He became one of the most expert and influential horticulturists in California. (Bailey, *Cyclopedia of Horticulture, s.v.* "Horticulturists")

SHUMARD, Dr. Benjamin Franklin (1820-69).—The elder Shumard was State Geologist of Texas (1858-60). He published twenty-one geological papers (1852-73), and his collection of reptiles and fishes was sent to the Smithsonian Institution (1873).

SHUMARD, Dr. George Getz (1825-67).—Brother of B. F. Shumard, G. G. Shumard served as geologist and naturalist on various expeditions in the Red River region of northern Texas, 1852-60; he was also Assistant State Geologist on the Texas Survey under his brother, 1858-60. He published five papers on Texas geology, most of them between 1852 and 1856.

SIEMERING, August.—Between 1849 and 1855, Siemering made extensive collections of plants of the upper Guadalupe, near Sisterdale. A highly intelligent man with German university training in the sciences (although his major interest was classical philology), he later became editor of the *San Antonio Zeitung*. (*Bios*, V, 147, 1934)

SMITH, William P.—An English zoölogical collector, sent to Texas in 1841 by Edward Smith Stanley, 13th Earl of Derby, to collect specimens for his museum and menagerie at Knowlsley near Liverpool. Smith corresponded also with Audubon and Bachman. (*Quadrupeds* . . . , I, 238, 1856)

STOLLEY, George.—In DeCordova's *Texas Immigrant Traveler's Guide,* 1856, 49-58, Stolley gives observations of much interest on the zoölogy and geology of the Fort Belknap and Double Mountain region of northwest Texas.

STRAUCH, Adolph (1822-83).—Horticulturist and landscape architect. Strauch came to Galveston in 1851 from London, after a period of training at Kew. Later he removed to Cincinnati. (Bailey, *Cyclopedia of Horticulture, s.v.* "Horticulturists")

SWEITZER, Jacob Bowman (d. 1888).—Collected fishes at Fort Brown, and sent specimens to the Smithsonian Institution (1880).

SWIFT, Dr. Ebenezer (1819-85).—Swift was in charge of Fort Chadbourne, *ca.* 1853-56, and sent a large collection of vertebrates from that locality to the Smithsonian Institution. (Pacific Railroad Reports, Vol. IX)

TAYLOR, Nathaniel Alston (1836-1913).—Taylor was of a distinguished North Carolina family, a graduate of the University of Pennsylvania. He came to Texas in 1859, and published geological articles of interest in Birke's *Almanac* (1880, 1881) and in several Texas newspapers. With H. F. McDaniel he published (1878) *The Coming Empire* (recently reprinted under his own name, as "Two Thousand Miles on Horseback"), a book containing valuable geological data. (Hill, Bulletin 45, U. S. Geological Survey, 1887)

THOMAS, Major George Henry (1816-70).—During his sojourn in Texas (1855-60), Thomas sent skins of mammals and alcoholic specimens from Fort Mason to the Smithsonian Institution.

THURBER, Dr. George (1821-90).—Botanist under John R. Bartlett on the U. S. and Mexican Boundary Survey, 1850-53.

TRÉCUL, Dr. Auguste Adolphe Lucien.—In 1849 Trécul visited Texas on his scientific mission to North America to study and collect farinaceous-rooted plants used for food by the Indians. Wright met him at Castroville in November. His unpublished reports are in the archives of the Museum of Natural History in Paris.

TUERPE, ALBERT.—Tuerpe was actively interested in the geology of Texas; he discovered coal on the banks of the Rio Grande at Eagle Pass in the middle 'seventies (Hielscher, *loc. cit.*), and in 1880 sent specimens of the "mud eel," *Siren lacertina,* to the Smithsonian Institution.

VAN VLIET, Captain Stewart (1815-1901).—During the years 1848-57, Van Vliet, stationed part of the time at Brownsville, collected fishes, reptiles, and mammals at Brownsville and Brazos Santiago for the Smithsonian Institution and the naturalists of the Boundary Survey. (Dall, *Spencer Fullerton Baird,* 1915, pp. 244, 284)

VEATCH, Dr. John Allen.—A native of Kentucky who came to Texas about 1836. Veatch was an amateur botanist and surveyor in Vehlein's Grant (*ca.* 1837-45). He was also an explorer in Lower California, and his plants were described by Albert Kellogg. (*Proceedings* of the California Academy of Sciences, II, 15-37, 1859; *American Journal of Science,* Second Series, XXVI, 288-95, 1858; *Hesperian, or Western Monthly Magazine,* III, 529-34, 1860)

WALKER, Dr. E. M. (d. 1868).—Walker, at that time registered from York-town, Texas, took his M.D. degree from the University of Louisiana (present Tulane University) in 1854. On January 9, 1854, a paper by him on the Agricultural Ant of Texas was read before the New Orleans Academy of Sciences. Walker returned to Yorktown to practice, and was elected a corresponding member of the New Orleans Academy of Sciences. (*Proceedings of the New Orleans Academy of Sciences,* I, 47-48, 1854)

WEBB, Dr. Thomas Hopkins (1801-66).—Made important zoölogical collections, especially of fishes, reptiles, and insects, while connected with the U. S. and Mexican Boundary Survey (1850-53).

WIEDEMANN, Dr. Eduard (?1800-44).—Wiedemann, an Esthonian naturalist, was assistant surgeon in the Texan Army in the early 'forties and collected for museums in St. Petersburg (?1838-44). (*Bios,* v, 143-44, 1934)

WISLIZENUS, Adolphus (1810-89).—Collected plants in the vicinity of El Paso in the late summer of 1846. He published a book on his travels from St. Louis to Chihuahua via Santa Fe and El Paso (1848).

WOOD, Ensign Moses Lindley, U.S.N. (b. 1854).—Retired with rank of Commodore, U.S.N., 1909. He sent reptiles in alcohol from Texas to the U. S. National Museum (1880).

WOODHOUSE, Dr. Samuel Washington (1821-1903).—In 1850 Woodhouse was a member of Sitgreave's Survey through Panhandle Texas; he published on birds and mammals; no new species are in his Texas collections. Torrey described his plants. (*Cassinia,* VIII, 1-5, 1904)

WREDE, Captain Friedrich Wilhelm von (d. 1845).—Wrede collected for German naturalists intermittently in eastern and central Texas from 1839 to 1845. He was not a naturalist in the technical sense, but had Gymnasium training in the sciences. (*Bios.* v, 142, 1934)

WRIGHT, Charles (1811-85).—Wright came to Texas in 1837, and collected plants for Asa Gray, 1844-52. (Chapter IX of the present work; *Southwest Review,* xv, 343-78, 1930; *Field & Laboratory,* IV, 23-32, 1935)

WÜRDEMANN, Gustavus Wilhelm (1817-59).—While connected with the U. S. Coast Survey, Würdemann collected and sent to the Smithsonian Institution (1853-4) reptiles, fishes, and invertebrates from Brazos Santiago, Texas (among them, ten new species of marine fishes) and fishes, reptiles, and invertebrates in alcohol from Aransas Bay, together with skins of birds and mammals. In 1853 he was in charge of five parties making hourly tide observations on the Texas coast from the entrance of Matagorda Bay to the mouth of Rio Grande.

WÜRTTEMBERG, Duke Paul Wilhelm of (1797-1860).—Visited the German settlements in Texas (April and May, 1855) while on his third journey to the Americas. Duke Paul, who possessed an excellent scientific training, was instrumental in bringing to the United States on this journey such authentic men of science as Heinrich Balduin Möllhausen and the Hungarian, János Xantús de Csiktapolcza [or Vesey] (1825-94), whose magnificent natural-history collections sent to the Smithsonian Institution while he was connected with the Coast Survey are still the wonder of museum administrators. (*Bios,* v, 147, 1934)

YOAKUM, Dr. Franklin L.—Yoakum was early in life a country physician. He perhaps entered the ministry of the Cumberland Presbyterian Church in

Texas, and became president of Larissa College (in present Rusk County) in the late 'fifties. His administration was a time of great prosperity for the college; the institution had an admirable astronomical telescope, and some microscopes and other equipment for biological and geological studies. Yoakum was meteorological observer at Larissa College for the Smithsonian Institution during the years 1858-60. (F. Eby, *The Development of Education in Texas*, 1925, 138)

YOUNG, Mrs. Maude Jeannie (1826-82).—A teacher of botany in Houston (*ca.* 1865+), Mrs. Young published her *Familiar Lessons in Botany, with Flora of Texas*, in 1873. She also wrote a number of graceful essays and verses. (Texas Technological College *Bulletin*, vii, 28-53, 1931)

Appendix C

INCOMPLETE LIST OF THE AUTHOR'S PUBLICATIONS ON
THE HISTORY OF SCIENCE IN EARLY TEXAS

The present list of my publications on Science in Early Texas is printed in order to furnish to Texas historians a nearly complete list, readily accessible, of papers and notes in this field. The scattering of my publications in a number of serials makes this seem desirable.

(1) Prof. Jacob Boll won fame as a naturalist, while making his home in Dallas from 1869-80. Dallas *Morning News,* Oct. 21, 1928, *portrait, facsimiles.*

(2) Naturalists of the Frontier: I. Jacob Boll. *Southwest Review, 14,* 184-98, 1929.

(3) Naturalists of the Frontier: II. Julien Reverchon. *Ibid., 14,* 331-42, 1929.

(4) Naturalists of the Frontier: III. Gustaf Wilhelm Belfrage. *Ibid., 14,* 381-98, 1929.

(5) Jacob Boll (1828-80). *Dictionary of American Biography,* 2, 419-20, 1929.

(6) Naturalists of the Frontier: IV. Gideon Lincecum. *Southwest Review, 15,* 93-111, *portrait,* 1929.

(7) Famous Swiss Americans: Jacob Boll, Naturalist. *Der Schweizer,* v. 45, Nov. 30, 1929.

(8) Professor Jacob Boll and the natural history of the Southwest. *American Midland Naturalist, 11,* 435-52, *portrait,* 1929.

(9) Naturalists of the Frontier: V. Ferdinand Jakob Lindheimer. *Southwest Review, 15,* 245-66, *portrait,* 1930.

(10) Naturalists of the Frontier: VI. Charles Wright. *Ibid., 15,* 343-78, *portrait,* 1930.

(11) Naturalists of the Frontier: VII. Thomas Drummond. *Ibid., 15,* 478-512, *portrait,* 1930.

(12) Naturalists of the Frontier: VIII. Audubon in Texas. *Ibid., 16,* 109-35, *map,* 1930.

(13) Pioneer scientist lies in unnamed grave . . . [G. W. Belfrage.] Dallas *Morning News,* Feb. 23, 1930, *photographs.*

(14) Naturalists of the Frontier: IX. Ferdinand von Roemer and his travels in Texas. *Southwest Review, 17,* 421-60, *portrait,* 1932.

(15) Naturalists of the Frontier: X. Notes on scientists of the first frontier. *Ibid., 18,* 50-86, 1932.

(16) On the type localities of certain Texas Phyllopoda. *Field & Laboratory,* *1,* 47-50, 1933. [Deals with G. W. Belfrage.]

(17) G. W. Belfrage's [Texas] insect localities. *Entomological News, 44,* 127-32, 1933.

(18) Naturalists of the Frontier: XI. In defense of Jean Louis Berlandier. *Southwest Review, 18,* 431-49, 1933.

(19) Gideon Lincecum (1793-1874.) *Dictionary of American Biography, 11,* 241-42, 1933.

(20) Ferdinand Jacob Lindheimer (1801-79). *Ibid., 11,* 273-74, 1933.

(21) Notes on Texas Crustacea. *Field & Laboratory, 2,* 29-31, 59-60, 1933-4. [Jacob Boll.]

(22) That first Texas botanist. *Ibid., 3,* 11-12, 1934. ["Nicolas Antoine Monteil," fictitious botanist.]

(23) Herbert Spencer Jennings, apostle of the scientific spirit. *Bios, 5,* 2-18, *portraits, illustrations,* 1934.

(24) Charles Theodore Mohr (1824-1901). *Dictionary of American Biography, 13,* 77-78, 1934.

(25) Edmund Duncan Montgomery (1835-1911). *Ibid., 13,* 95-96, 1934.

(26) Thomas Volney Munson (1843-1913). *Ibid., 13,* 335-36, 1934.

(27) Elisabet Ney (1833-1907). *Ibid., 13,* 478-79, 1934.

(28) Some frontier naturalists. *Bios, 5,* 141-52, 1934. [Ferdinand Jakob Lindheimer (1801-79), Otto Friedrich (1800-80), F. W. von Wrede (d. 1845), Eduard Wiedemann (?1800-44), Louis Cachand Ervendberg (1809-63), Georg Klappenbach (d. 1868), Baron Ottfried Hans von Meusebach (1812-97), Ferdinand Roemer (1818-91.), August Forcke (1814-1903), August Siemering (1830-83), Prince Paul of Wuerttemberg (1797-1860), and Dr. Wilhelm Remer.]

(29) Charles Wright's 1849 botanical collecting-trip from San Antonio to El Paso; with type-localities for new species. *Field & Laboratory, 4,* 23-32, 1935.

(30) Charles Wright (1811-85). *Dictionary of American Biography, 20,* 545-46, 1936.

(31) A century of scientific exploration in Texas. Part I: 1820-1880. *Field & Laboratory, 4,* 41-55, 1936.

(32) Naturalists of the Frontier: XII. Louis Cachand Ervendberg. *Southwest Review, 22,* 241-84, 1937.

(33) *Naturalists of the Frontier.* University Press in Dallas, Southern Methodist University, 1937. 341 pp.

(34) A century of scientific exploration in Texas, Part Ib: 1820-1880. *Field & Laboratory, 7,* 29-52, 1939.

(35) *Scientific Study and Exploration in Early Texas.* Southern Methodist University, Dallas, 1939. [Items 31 and 34, with inner and outer titles, prefatory note, and index, issued in 200 copies.]

(36) Dr. Benno Matthes: an early Texas herpetologist. *Field & Laboratory, 9,* 37-44, *portrait,* 1941.

(37) [Philander Priestley in Texas, 1831.] *Southwestern Historical Quarterly, 44,* 501-02, 1941.

286

(38) [Photography in early Texas.] *Ibid., 45,* 188-91, 1941.

(39) [Travels of James Chambers Ludlow (1797-1841) in Texas, 1822.] *Ibid., 45,* 195-96, 1941.

(40) [Lum Woodruff, early Texas meteorologist.] *Ibid., 45,* 284, 1942.

(41) [John Allen Veatch (1808-70), early Texan naturalist.] *Ibid., 46,* 169-73, 1942.

(42) [*with Donald Day*] D. Port Smythe's journey across early Texas [1852]. *Texas Geographic Magazine, 6,* 1-20, *map, facsimile,* 1942.

(43) [Full moons in Texas, 1805-99.] *Southwestern Historical Quarterly, 47,* 58-61, 1943.

(44) [Note on Dr. Henry Cooley (d. 1833), amateur botanist and mineralogist of early Texas.] *Quarterly Bulletin of the Cooley Family Association of America, 4,* 20-21, July, 1943.

(45) [Timothy B. Phelps, early educator in Texas.] *Southwestern Historical Quarterly, 47,* 172-73, 1943.

(46) [Major lunar eclipses in Texas, 1755-1880, an aid in chronology.] *Ibid., 47,* 180-81, 1943.

(47) [Note on Edward Fontaine (1814-84), early Texas naturalist.] *Ibid., 47,* 181-83, 1943.

(48) [William Douglas Wallach (1812-71) in Texas.] *William & Mary College Historical Magazine* (II), *23,* 532, 1943.

(49) [Col. L. M. H. Washington and Hamilton Washington in Texas.] *Southwestern Historical Quarterly, 47,* 303-04, 1944.

(50) [A. M. Gentry (1821-83), pioneer railroad-builder in Texas.] *Ibid., 47,* 308-09, 1944.

(51) Geographers of early Texas: a bibliographic note. *Texas Geographic Magazine, 7,* 37-38, 1943.

(52) Southwestern Siftings: I. William Douglas Wallach. *Southwest Review, 29,* 291-97, 1944.

(53) Dr. David Porter Smythe, an early Texan botanist. *Field & Laboratory, 12,* 10-16, *portrait,* 1944.

(54) William Douglas Wallach, pioneer Texas hydrographer. *Ibid., 12,* 27-31, *portrait,* 1944.

(55) Southwestern Siftings: II. Abram Morris Gentry. *Southwest Review, 29,* 463-69, 1944.

(56) Note on Dr. Francis Moore, Jr. (1808-64). *Southwestern Historical Quarterly, 47,* 419-25, 1944.

(57) David Gouverneur Burnet, satirist. *Ibid., 48,* 33-37, 1944.

(58) John Solomon Rarey in Texas. *Ibid., 48,* 105-07, 1944.

(59) Ghost towns and lost towns in Texas, 1840-1880. *Texas Geographic Magazine, 8,* 9-20, 1944.

(60) Benjamin Taylor Kavanaugh, and the discovery of East Texas oil. *Field & Laboratory, 12,* 46-55, *portrait,* 1944.

(61) [J. W. Lanfear, and the Coopwood camel-herd of Bastrop County, 1876-78.] *Southwestern Historical Quarterly, 48,* 107-08, 1944.

(62) Racer's Storm (1837), with notes on other Texas hurricanes in the period 1818-1886. *Field & Laboratory, 12,* 59-67, 1944.

(63) Probate inventories as a source of social history. *Southwestern Historical Quarterly, 48,* 401-02, 1945.

(64) Memorandum and inquiry regarding Robert Harris Upham [1810-?36]. *Ibid., 48,* 402-04, 1945.

(65) Masonic Lodges as time-indicators of a town's prosperity. *Ibid., 48,* 422-23, 1945.

(66) Dr. L. J. Russell, and the Pike's Peak gold rush of 1858-59. *Ibid., 48,* 573-76, 1945.

(67) Notes on some early Texas hurricanes. *Ibid., 48,* 588-89, 1945.

(68) The first Texas Academy of Science. *Field & Laboratory, 13,* 34-39, 1945.

(69) One hundred lashes for a good man. [Dr. L. J. Russell, early medical botanist in Texas.] *Southwest Review, 30,* 374-376, 1945.

(70) *Horticulture and Horticulturists in Early Texas.* viii + 100 pp. University Press in Dallas, Southern Methodist University, 1945.

(71) Early medical writings on Texas, of interest to historians. *Southwestern Historical Quarterly, 49,* 145-48, 1945.

(72) Collectors of Pleistocene vertebrates in early Texas. I. William P. Huff (1811-86). *Field & Laboratory, 13,* 53-60, *portrait,* 1945.

(73) John Wright Glenn (1836-92), early State Geologist of Texas. *Ibid., 13,* 64-69, *portrait,* 1945.

(74) George Washington Curtis and Frank Arthur Gulley: two early agricultural teachers in Texas. *Ibid., 14,* 1-13, *portraits,* 1946.

(75) Dr. Ernst Kapp, early geographer in Texas. *Ibid., 14,* 16-31, *portraits, illustrations,* 1946.

(76) Jacob Boll's collecting in the Texas Permian: a note and a correction. *Ibid., 14,* 102-04, 1946.

(77) Notes on some workers in Texas entomology. *Southwestern Historical Quarterly, 49,* 593-98, 1946.

(78) Notes on temperature depressions in early Texas. *Ibid, 50,* 120-22, 1946.

(79) Chronology of Dr. Ernst Kapp (1808-1896). *Ibid., 50,* 297-300, 1946.

(80) Notes on some workers in Texas entomology, 1839-1880. *Field & Laboratory, 15,* 35-41, 1947.

(81) Greenleaf Cilley Nealley (1846-1896), Texan botanist. *Ibid., 15,* 41-46, *portrait,* 1947.

(82) [*with Bessie T. Geiser*] A Brief Short-Title List of Published Works on the History of Science. (*Southern Methodist University Studies, No. 1,* 1947, 35 pp.)

Index of Names

DESIGNED by Merle Armitage
PORTRAIT by Li Browne
PRINTED by Progress-Bulletin